FEMINISM IN ACTION

M. PATRICIA CONNELLY
PAT ARMSTRONG

EDITORS

CANADIAN SCHOLARS' PRESS   TORONTO   1992

Feminism in Action: Studies in Political Economy

First published in 1992 by
Canadian Scholars' Press
402-180 Bloor St. W.
Toronto, ON M5S 2V6

Canadian Cataloguing in Publication Data

Main entry under title:

Feminism in Action

Includes bibliographical references.
ISBN 1-55130-012-5

1. Feminism - Canada. 2. Women in the labour movement -
Canada. 3. Women - Canada - Social Conditions. I. Connelly,
Patricia, 1939- . II. Armstrong, Pat, 1945- .

HQ1453.F45   1992   305.4'0971   C92-095614-9

Printed in Canada

FEMINISM IN ACTION: STUDIES IN POLITICAL ECONOMY

CONTRIBUTORS

Sedef Arat-Koc teaches Women's Studies and Sociology at Trent University in Peterborough.

Pat Armstrong teaches in the Sociology Department at York University in Toronto.

Hugh Armstrong is an Associate Dean at Centennial College in Toronto.

Linda Briskin teaches in the Social Science Division at York University in Toronto.

M. Patricia Connelly teaches in the Sociology Department of Saint Mary's University in Halifax.

Ruth A. Frager teaches History and Women's Studies at McMaster University in Hamilton.

Jane Jenson teaches in the Political Science Department at Carleton University, Ottawa.

Carla Lipsig-Mummé teaches Labour Studies and is Director of the Centre for Research on Work and Society at York University in Toronto.

Martha MacDonald teaches in the Economics Department at St. Mary's University in Halifax.

Heather Jon Maroney teaches in the Institute of Women's Studies and the Department of Sociology at Carleton University, Ottawa.

Dorothy E. Smith teaches in the Department of Sociology in Education at the Ontario Institute for Studies in Education in Toronto.

Madeline Parent is a feminist and trade unionist living in Montreal, and is the Quebec representative on the National Action Committee on the Status of Women (NAC).

Susan Prentice teaches Sociology at Trent University in Peterborough.

Gillian Walker is the Director of the School of Social Work at Carleton University in Ottawa.

Rosemary Warskett teaches at the Labour College of Canada, and is a doctoral candidate at Carleton University in Ottawa.

All the articles in this volume were first published in *Studies in Political Economy*. For further information on this journal, write SPE at P.O. Box 4729, Station E, Ottawa, Canada, K1S 5H9.

INTRODUCTION

This book is about feminist praxis and about the theoretical assumptions that are reflected in women's struggles to improve their conditions. In the early stages of postwar feminism, there was a tendency to think of women as passive victims of their bodies, of their ideas, of men or of capitalism. Increasingly, however, feminists have been recovering the history of women's collective and individual efforts to transform their lives and have been re-examining the strategies of the modern women's movement. In the process, feminists have become more aware of the contradictory nature of their struggles and of the different consequences for women in different classes, in different racial and ethnic groups and in different regions of the country and of the world.

In our view, class has to be reconceptualized through race and gender within regional, national, and international contexts. The static categorizing of class that has been used in so much of class analysis does not capture the experience of gender, race, ethnicity or class. Class is dynamic and relational and it is a fundamental basis of change. While gender, race, ethnic and national identities are never absent, they interact with class in various ways with one being more salient than another at different points in time. The problem for socialist feminism is to develop a theoretical account of these different types of oppression and the relations between them, with a view to ending them all. To end the subordination of women, we need theory, research and action. Theory guides our research and action, and research and action provide the basis for our theorizing.

Research then, can be much more than an uncovering of evidence indicating women's active participation in collective action or a documenting of women's current successes and failures. Research can be a central component of praxis, providing a guide to and a reflection on action. Research can make more transparent why, under what conditions, with whom, for what purposes and with what consequences individual women join with others to struggle for change. Indeed, by definition, feminist research is about making change. It is about understanding women's oppression and creating an alternative vision of the future. Our vision of the future in turn helps to define our strategies for research, action and change.

Articles in this book illustrate this process and these concerns. Some articles challenge existing theories and concepts and suggest new approaches to theory and research rooted in women's experiences. Others mainly focus on action and its relationship to theory. All of the articles are concerned with understanding the way in which women experience the intersection of class, gender, race, ethnicity, regionality, nationality and the way in which women have acted or potentially could act to make their own history. They reveal the complex and often contradictory processes that provide the basis for action, raising clues for a more systematic understanding of how gender, class, race, ethnicity, and ideology intersect within a specific region or nation. For some, the variety of experiences described in these pages will reinforce the argument that a comprehensive theory is neither possible nor desirable. For us, it indicates the need to start with different questions and to reconstruct our notions of class. There is a common thread to these articles. They all point to the need for an analysis that looks at the historically and regionally specific conditions in and out of the households that encourage people to join together around particular issues and on the basis of different shared relations at different times.

What is clear is that the political economy sets the stage for class, gender and race relations. Class, however, cannot be understood simply in terms of production relations or gender relations. While classes are always to some extent divided by gender, whether or not women will unite with men will depend on the issue as well as on the current conditions, on the time and the place. Whether or not race and ethnic relations assume dominance also depends on the issue, on the conditions, on the time and place. The central questions are concerned, then, with the various configurations of gender, class and race which form the basis for action under specific regional or national political, economic and cultural conditions. The articles collected here address these questions.

In her article, Dorothy Smith argues that contemporary political economy accepts the standpoint of the 'relations of ruling' and as a result its agenda is set by the 'main business' of a capitalist economy. The standpoint of the 'relations of ruling' objectifies society, social relations and people's experiences. In accepting this standpoint, political economy participates in this objectification. Political economists, in their analysis of class, create categories without any subjects and without any historical trajectory. Marx and Engels, on the other hand, located subjects in a moment of history and in the process of class struggle. Although political economy recognizes class as gendered, much of women's lives become invisible from the standpoint of the relations of ruling, where the point of production is treated as the exclusive site of class and class struggle. Just as women are marginal to the 'main business' so are they marginal to the concerns of political economy analysis. The task as Smith sees it is to shift to standpoints where women's experience becomes visible and where their experience is not objectified; that is, standpoints outside the 'relations of ruling'. She argues that we need a political economy that analyzes how our lives are caught up in the historical, political and economic process; one that recognizes the multiple sites of experiences in contemporary capitalism, and one that does not objectify these experiences. In this kind of analysis, the concept of class becomes essential as a method of analyzing the organization of relations in which women's lives and struggles are embedded.

Martha MacDonald and Patricia Connelly also argue that class must be understood in a historical context, one that includes gender and household dynamics. They ask—How do we go beyond a class analysis of women to a gendered class analysis? How do we move from the theoretical recognition that a gendered class analysis is necessary, to conducting research that will help us better understand our potential for political struggle? With these questions in mind, they analyze data from their research in six fishing communities in Nova Scotia. Most contemporary Marxist analyzes classify genderless individuals into class positions at one point in time and then consider the likelihood of class consciousness and struggle for those in particular positions. MacDonald and Connelly, however, examine the work histories of specific women and men, showing the complexity of their class position over the life cycle. They examine family household work patterns and argue that people in the fishing communities experience class not just as individuals but as members of household units containing unequal gender relations. Households develop strategies for labour allocation and workplace struggle based on combined household class positions and unequal gender relations inside and outside the home. MacDonald and Connelly then apply this approach in case studies of two communities, showing how women and men experienced the political and economic changes in the fishing industry. They conclude that using a gendered class analysis, one that applies a dynamic concept of class which includes gender relations and the household, makes better sense than does the traditional class analysis, of the class identification and political struggles within the communities.

For Madeleine Parent, class, gender, ethnicity and race were constantly intertwined concerns and her early experiences ensured her lifelong commitment to struggle for equality in these areas. Prevented from attending the all male undergraduate programs at the French universities controlled by the

Catholic Church, Parent attended the English and male dominated McGill University, where she fought for scholarships for poor women as well as for poor male students. As part of the French minority and a declared francophone, prejudice became part of her experiences on the McGill campus. From university she joined the union movement, where she put great effort into involving women, identifying problems specific to women and making women's contributions to the unions visible. In discussing her years of union activity, Parent describes unions that provided support for women and unions that did not; historical periods that encouraged the involvement of women and times that did not; state intervention that restricted possibilities for women and state policies that created the conditions for women's active involvement in both paid employment and struggle; men who accepted women as similar workers and men who did not. Although she is firmly convinced women should not develop separate unions, she is equally convinced that all unions need women's committees that bring women together to share their problems and unite them in their demands. In discussing her activities in the women's movement, Parent describes the tensions involved in representing a broad spectrum of women; working class as well as professional women; visible minorities as well as anglophone and francophone white women; differently abled as well as able women; rural as well as urban women; women in all regions and nations. Parent argues that the women's movement and the union movement must work as democratic organizations in social solidarity with other democratic organizations to recognize and defend the particular concerns of women and of racial, ethnic minorities. Parent emphasizes the importance of both alliances and flexibility in strategies for working towards equality.

Ruth Frager's research suggests that, while Madeleine Parent was becoming an active feminist in Montreal during the 1930s, conditions in the Toronto garment industry prevented Jewish women from organizing around their specific concerns, in spite of their inferior wages and jobs. A relatively small and geographically isolated group of Jewish garment workers faced anti-semitism, a monolithic Anglo-Saxon majority and unstable employment. This combination of factors encouraged them to unite as Jews and as workers. At the same time, the segregation of women's work and women's domestic responsibilities, women's limited access to the means of learning English, and an ideology that stressed the importance of the family and the legitimacy of male dominance discouraged women from uniting around women's issues. While francophones like Parent were organizing on the basis of ethnicity and gender, separate Jewish communities were deemed essential to union operations and separate women's committees were denounced as divisive for the class struggle.

Moreover, according to Frager, the women's movement of the time offered little support to the women employed in the garment industries. Frager's
research suggests that specific historical conditions may encourage the dominance of ethnicity and class over gender as the basis for action. It also suggests
that separate organizations based on relations other than those of class may
be effective in achieving certain ends. However, her research implies as well
that such strategies which do not take women's specific concerns into account
have contradictory results for women.

The next two articles also examine women's position in unions and the
need for alliances. Drawing on her more recent experience in the union movement, Rosemary Warskett analyzes the failure of the union campaigns to organize bank workers who are predominantly women earning low wages and
receiving few benefits. She argues that the explanation lies not in women's
passive attitudes or low commitment to the workplace, as some would argue,
but in an examination of the historical role of the state in moulding and channelling the labour movement's opposition to capital via the Canadian labour
relations system. Using the certification drives of the Service, Office and Retail
Workers Union of Canada (SORWUC) and other unions, she shows how the
process of certification produced divisions among workers, limited the unions
ability to mobilize on a wider basis and created lengthy delays harmful to the
unionization drive. When pro-labour victories were eventually achieved against
the anti-union strategies of the banks, the Canadian Labour Relations Board
had little power to undo the harm which such strategies had inflicted on the
unions in the interim. Warskett shows that the certification process, while providing some protection to unions, did little to strengthen the power of the
women bank workers collectively. She argues that the union movement must
take a critical stance towards the liberal ideology of neutrality which envisions
the state as a neutral arbitrator between two equally powerful interest groups -
labour and capital. The union movement must recognize that any gains
embodied in labour relations law have been made over time and through class
struggle. It must recognize that the institution of law is based on the contours
of class struggle. She concludes that the experience of the bank workers
points to a strategy that de-emphasizes a reliance on decisions made by the
labour boards and emphasizes opening up the organized labour movement to
the concerns of the marginalized—women, indigenous Canadians, immigrants
and youth—in order to build the collective power of workers.

Carla Lipsig-Mummé takes up many of the points made in the previous
articles as she explores the role of women's committees in the labour movement and their relationship to other social movements, especially the women's

movement in Quebec. She examines these issues in her study of the 1983 Montreal strike by the predominantly female members of the International Ladies Garment Workers Union's (ILGWU). This strike, the first industry-wide strike in forty-three years, began as a rebellion against the homework which was contributing to the deunionization of the industry. It soon became a revolt against the union leadership who chose to ignore members' concerns in favour of colluding with employers in the name of saving the industry. Lipsig-Mummé discusses the historical development of the ILGWU indicating the important differences between the United States and Canada. She shows that, for at least two generations in both countries, it has been an undemocratic, highly bureaucratic organization based on different configurations of ethnic, racial and gender inequality. In Montreal in 1980, a feminist opposition developed within the union in the form of a multi-ethnic Action Committee for Garment Workers. This committee contributed to the strike by educating and mobilizing the membership and exposing the collaboration between union officials and employers. Significantly, however, the Committee members refused to take a much needed leadership role once the strike was in full swing. Their refusal was based on their view that taking responsibility and power would undermine their credibility and eventually lead to co-optation and possibly corruption. This strategy allowed the old leadership to regain control and the strike was lost. Lipsig-Mummé concludes, as does Parent, that women's committees are essential to challenge the traditional union elite, and linkages to wider social movements are essential to combat institutional union racism and sexism. She adds an important lesson learned from her research: feminists must be prepared to take authority within, and responsibility for, the new unionism struggling to be born. Feminists must learn to humanize power, to feminize it and to redefine it collectively.

In the next article, Sedef Arat-Koc takes up the issue of foreign domestic workers, clearly illustrating the complex ways in which race, ethnicity and class intersect with gender. An increasing number of women with young children have entered the labour force, but most men have not increased their parenting and housework responsibilities, employers have not provided accommodation for the family responsibilities of working people and the state has not moved towards providing universally accessible and affordable childcare. As a result, Arat-Koc states, Canadians are experiencing a *crisis in the domestic sphere*. To solve this crisis, the state has devised a scheme to attract immigrant women who would provide domestic and childcare services on a temporary or guestworker basis. This solution puts Canadian and foreign women in an employer-employee relationship. Rather than solving the crisis in the domestic sphere, it emphasizes class, racial, ethnic and citizenship differences at the expense of gender unity. Arat-Koc argues that feminists must support domestic workers in their struggle for equal treatment with other workers. She goes on to draw out the implications of the state's solution to the domestic crisis for feminist theory and practice. She shows that, in addition to creating divisions among women, the live-in domestic solution maintains the low status and low value attributed to housework and childcare at the same time as it reinforces the definition of this work as women's work. It also discourages the struggle for socialized services and more flexible work arrangements in the interest of both male and female workers. Arat-Koc points out that feminism still lacks a clear vision of positive alternatives to privatized and gendered home life. Without such a vision, an overall strategy for change is not possible and women remain vulnerable to state schemes such as this that add class and racial dimensions to women's inequality.

Susan Prentice examines another way women and the state have attempted to solve childcare problems. She recounts women's collective response to the attempts to close the daycare centres that had been opened during the Second World War. Issue-oriented and uniting a broad range of women, the various actions organized to retain these services were coordinated by the Communist Party and supported by their members in a variety of municipal government positions. These efforts were effective in the immediate postwar years but the ideology of the cold war, combined with state strategies designed to undermine daycares through technical regulations and structural means, eventually served to counteract these victories. Like Parent, Prentice's approach suggests that different alliances can be effective under different circumstances and that strategies focused on what are defined as women's issues can be an important basis for change. Her research indicates the complex nature of state policies, demonstrating that appeals to the state can be useful. However, the research shows as well, that these gains are under constant threat as the state strives to maintain both the ideological and material conditions for creating profit. It also suggests that struggles on women's issues can be undermined by those based predominantly on class.

Jane Jenson takes up and expands upon similar themes in her article on "Babies and the State". Using her concept of the universe of political discourse and the specific examples of Britain and France, she argues for a focus on "the material, political and ideological parameters of discourse" in particular social formations at particular periods in time. She, too, maintains that the capitalist state has participated in constructing and maintaining women's subordinate position, in large measure because such states need, for both their labour force and their military force, the babies only women produce. Although these shared concerns made "the social construction of maternity... a likely area of state activity," state strategies varied with specific national situations. These policies reflected not only the conditions of capitalist production and the balance of political forces but also the strategies pursued by political actors such as women's groups. For Jenson, it is not sufficient to focus on objective conditions or to search for the basis of difference. "It is also necessary to examine the meaning given to these relations by the social forces engaged in political struggle. Only by examining the universe of political discourse within which meaning is constructed can we understand the ways that employment and sexual differences were given political meaning..." Only with a detailed analysis of the specific conjunctures "will the space for resistance to the state become visible."

Heather Jon Maroney also examines a discourse constructed to maintain women as producers of babies, in this case in order to maintain national identity in Quebec. She examines the historical and contemporary relationship between the terms nation, birth and women, showing that, into the 1960s, clerical nationalist discourse gave women a central place as "fertile, obedient and loving daughters of the church, wives of men and mothers of children." Women were mothers of the nation, but men in positions of power in the church and the state ran that nation. By the 1970s, however, the state was promoting development, science was replacing faith as the nation modernized, and language was becoming the focus for maintaining the nation. In this context, the Quebec women's movement was able to expose and attack the ideological underpinnings of the clerical nationalist discourse and provide a positive program for reproductive self-determination and for reformed maternity and childcare. However, by the 1980s, the birth rate had fallen drastically and the state conceived the need for a new strategy to ensure national survival. This new strategy took the form of a demographic pro-natalist discourse, based on the state authority of politicians and the scientific authority of demographers. Together they developed pro-natalist policies designed to encourage women to bear children. The demographic discourse took the family rather than women as the focus of its concern, thus laying the basis for the exclusion of women as legitimate participants in the policy debate. Although feminists continued to struggle their voices were seldom heard and they were effectively marginalized. Maroney's analysis raises two important issues for feminist strategy and theory: "How to respond to the appropriation of militant feminist demands and discourse in the interests of other political agendas" and "How to analyze (and advance) the contradictory politics of feminism, childbirth, ethnicity and nation."

Although Linda Briskin addresses the general question of feminist strategies for change, her argument also has particular relevance for women's relationships with the state. Starting from what she calls the "standpoint of strategic practice," she uses the concepts of mainstreaming and disengagement to
analyze the effectiveness of feminist practice in Canada. Instead of beginning
with a distinction among the various currents in feminism, Briskin examines
how the different forms of feminist practice interact within the common context of the Canadian political economy. While Briskin argues that both mainstreaming and disengagement "are necessary to the feminist vision," she con-
tends that the goal is to maintain "an effective tension between the two,"
avoiding the tendency to depend on either strategy. Unlike the radical feminists who tend towards disengagement and the liberal feminists who are much
more sympathetic to mainstreaming, socialist feminists have combined strategies, sometimes favouring one, sometimes the other. Although this approach
has its own contradictions, Briskin's analysis suggests that Canadian socialist
feminist practice has been more effective than that of either the British or the
Americans in making gains for women, precisely because it has varied the
strategy depending on the time, place, issue and membership and because it
has tried to accommodate difference.

The effectiveness of feminist practice in specific Canadian cases is the
question taken up in the two final articles in this collection. Like Briskin, Pat
Armstrong and Hugh Armstrong place the notions of tension and contradiction at the center of their analysis. Through an examination of Pay Equity legislation in Ontario, they argue that "the state is indeed a contested terrain; one
in which there is no 'level playing field' but one in which women can win
some significant, if contradictory, victories." These contradictions constitute
both the limits of, and the possibilities for, change through state legislation.
Armstrong and Armstrong stress the importance of theory to strategy and
argue that the effect of legislative action is restricted not only by the nature of
the state but also by the theoretical understanding of those demanding action.
The consequences of legislation are not pre-determined and will depend, to a
large extent, on how women understand and use the legislation to transform
both it and the conditions of women's work. The authors caution that, even
though the legislation may represent a victory for the large group of women
who formed the Equal Pay Coalition, it can serve to further divide women
from each other and can serve to entrench new management methods of control. Those least likely to benefit from the legislation are the immigrant and visible minority women who are concentrated in small workplaces and in non-

unionized shops. However, all women may benefit if "common sense" can be transformed by struggles over legislation that make women's pay demands legitimate and that challenge the notion of a free market based on equity and choice. Finally, they argue that the organization of a pay equity coalition outside of specific union structures is just one indication of the need for a "radical rethinking of how women can achieve collective change in ways that reflect a new labour process and a new female worker."

Like Jenson, Gillian Walker makes the notion of discourse pivotal to her analysis, and like Maroney, she also explores the contradictory outcomes of feminist efforts to bring about change. Walker uses the particular example of feminist strategies around wife battering to examine the interaction between the state and the women's movement. In analyzing what she terms the four stages in strategies around wife battering, Walker shows how "the analysis of women's oppression became secondary to the strategy of invoking women's rights as individuals under the law. The emphasis on individual rights in the criminal justice system specifically obscured the different experiences and location in the social structure of black, minority, native, immigrant and white working class women and men." Moreover, the construction of the category "battered wife" allowed the battered wife to be treated as a specific instance of "family violence" or as a part of the theoretical framework which separates features of peoples' lives into pieces which can be managed and administered. When the issue became defined as an instance of women's victimization by male violence, it could be readily integrated into the criminal justice system and again severed from its context within social structures. While such strategies, Walker argues, did make gender power relations visible and did alter professional discourse, they also channeled action into social services or legal redress. "Neither of these mobilize women unless they are put in a feminist context; nor do they address the totality of women's lives." Feminists must examine the actual relations, and "the discursive forms substituted for them." The task then is to relocate these relations within the broader structures of the "relations of domination and control" which are the relations of ruling, as Dorothy Smith points out in the first article of this collection.

The analyzes presented by the various authors in this book have implications for our theoretical understanding of the basis for action. They imply that no single strategy, and no strategy that assumes the constant dominance of class, gender or race in all situations, will be effective. Instead, we need a theoretical framework that comprehends class, gender, and race; one that provides us with tools to help us figure out which will be the salient force or forces under specific historical conditions and in specific situations. The articles in this volume provide tantalizing clues as to how this can be accomplished.

CHAPTER 1

FEMINIST REFLECTIONS ON POLITICAL ECONOMY

DOROTHY E. SMITH

BEGINNING IN OUR LIVES

These reflections on feminism and political economy originate in my experience as activist and academic in the women's movement. They arise from my efforts to translate into a political and scholarly practice the discoveries of the power relations organizing the personal and domestic as feminists have experienced and analyzed them. These reflections bear the traces of those extended conflicts, challenges and debates that feminists have brought to Marxism and political economy. Indeed they are intended to bring to bear upon these last some of what I have learned in these practices and debates as part of an attempt to develop a feminist politics of epistemology.

Rethinking how we work as social scientists began for me with a problem which came into view in relation to political practice. A group of feminists, most, but not all, of us socialists, got together in Vancouver some years ago to found a women's research centre. We thought we would reverse the normal flow of information and inquiry that transfers knowledge about people to the institutions which produce knowledge for the ruling of society, namely, to universities and academic discourses. We thought of a women's research centre as a means of producing knowledge for women, making the stored-up knowledge and skills of academe serve the people who are usually their objects. We set up a research centre outside the university and, in constant difficulty with funding, we went to work.

My experience of that work was concurrent with another kind of discovery. I had been teaching women's studies at the University of British Columbia and was becoming more and more sharply aware of the full implications of our (women's) exclusion from the making of the social forms of consciousness (the knowledge and culture) of our kind of society. What had seemed at first merely a problem of absence, to be remedied by including women as topics in appropriate sites, has come to be seen as a deeper and virtually total gender warping of culture and intellectual life. It became clear that remedies must be much more radical; that there were problems about the relationship of social science to those who became its objects; about conceptual and theoretical practices that incorporated one-sided assumptions based on one class, race and gender standpoint; about the exclusion of the standpoint of experience from social scientific versions of the world.

The emphasis on women's experience as a primary site and source of knowing originates in this dilemma. The political logic of consciousness raising extended into the realms of culture and intellectual life. The very grounds of knowledge were being called into question. As it has for many other feminists in the social sciences, this issue, the grounds of objectified knowledge of society and social relations, has remained for me a major preoccupation.

Working with the Women's Research Centre posed such issues in a different way. We saw them at first, I think, as problems arising from the fact that we wrote and talked in a specialized language, mystifying the ordinary events of people's lives and the power relations organizing them. But they were not, I came to see, merely problems of the unhappy and often clumsy abstractions in which social scientific discourse thinks. The problems would not be solved by finding ways of making social scientific discourse ordinarily understandable. There was something else. The whole method of thinking, how social science addressed the world, created a very peculiar relationship between women and their experience. Rather than beginning in their own actual situations and with their own good knowledge of the practicalities and organization of their everyday and everynight worlds, social scientific methods of writing its texts created a standpoint from which the reader reflected on her life as if she stood outside it; taking up the relevancies and focus built into the conceptual structures of the discourse. She became an object to herself. Popularization made no difference; the conceptual structures were recursively present. As a practical problem, texts written in social science wouldn't do the kind of job to which we were committed, which was to expand women's knowledge of what was going on *from where they were* in real, as contrasted with textual, life.

This then became a major object of my interest. I thought I would rewrite sociological methods of thinking and writing its texts and constructing its knowledge to make a feminist method; I thought we would have more than a sociology in which women had a place, a sociology in which women had become, however belatedly, the objects of sociological interest. I thought we would want a sociology that would create an account or accounts, analysis or analyses, of how societies were put together so that the worlds of our every-day/everynight experience happened as they did. Then we would have a knowledge from *our standpoint*, making claims to comprehend a scope of history and society equally with those that have been made by men. We would be capable of analyses and of developing knowledge relevant to women's struggles. It would be a knowledge and an analytic capacity written to be read or heard from the standpoint of women — a standpoint which is *outside* the textually mediated conversations of the relations of ruling (embodied in established social science), and situated in the particularities of the local everyday and everynight worlds of our immediate experience.

THE RELATIONS AND APPARATUSES OF RULING[1]

I am emphasizing the experiential grounds of this thinking, because they are ordinarily excluded as merely "subjective." Of course, they have been central to the modes of organization and politics of the women's movement and I have also come to see them as central to the feminist challenge to academic discourse, at least in the social sciences. Within the social sciences, identifying practices of organizing the relevancies of a given discourse to exclude the knowledge arising in experience, maintaining the sharp division between the authoritative knowledge of the expert and the experiential knowledge of the layperson, and institutionalizing the dependence of the latter on the former is standard practice. For of course, an experiential knowledge isn't recognized as knowledge on the terrain of professional, scientific and other academic discourses. I distinctly remember the way in which I learned the peculiar practices of a sociology, which purported to speak of the same world as the one in which I lived, and yet required me to exclude from classroom or term paper any reference to a knowledge which I had acquired on bases other than through the authorized texts of discourse. This was an observation that had a later relevance as I slowly discovered methods of doing a social science to which such conventions did not apply. Indeed, on the contrary.

As I began to see the objectified methods of thinking and writing texts characteristic of the social sciences, I also began to see them as integral to that great complex of relations and apparatuses of ruling at work in contemporary society at a level abstracted from the everyday, everynight particularities of our local worlds. In this context, the social sciences appeared as a systematically constructed consciousness of society which creates a synthetic standpoint, locating the reading subject outside the actual time and place in which she reads, and in a conceptual space isomorphic with that of the abstracted, extra-local relations of ruling contemporary capitalist societies.[2] A number of observations fell into place: Why was it that sociology (at least when I was in graduate school in the United States) was a required course in *community colleges*? Why was it that when people thought about themselves sociologically, they seemed to disintegrate into a multiplicity of selves each located in a role, or in the contemporary version, a multiplicity of subjects, each located in a different discourse? Why was it that the ordinary observations of experience were not admissible to thought as part of a discourse purporting to analyze and explain the same world as that which we inhabited? Why was it that politically active graduate students had such an alarming tendency to want to study the movements in which they were active? Why was it that the social sciences wanted to *explain* people's behaviour (to whom?) rather than, say, explaining the behaviour of the economy, or the society, or the political process to people, as these enter into, organize and disorganize peoples' lives?

The phrase "relations and apparatuses of ruling" is used here to identify that extraordinary complex of relations and organization mediated by texts that govern, manage, administer, direct, organize, regulate, and control contemporary capitalist societies — at least those of the fully "developed" first world. Normal sociological and political economic practices divide these relations and apparatuses of ruling into a variety of spheres which are treated as quite distinct from one another, although they interact in various ways: management, state, professions, mass media, and so forth. The latter, however, are increasingly inter-coordinated, forming a far from monolithic complex, interpenetrated by the social relations of those "conversations" in texts to which Foucault has given the name "discourse."[3] This complex comes into view in a distinctive way from the standpoint of those whose primary site of knowledge of the world is the place where they're plumped down as bodies, the local historical sites where their work comes to hand rather than to mind. This complex is the contemporary development of what Marx in his time, when it was still at almost a primitive stage, described as the 'superstructure'.

The relations and apparatuses of ruling come into view from women's perspective in another distinctive way. Though these forms of organization are in principle impersonal, rational, and universal, in fact they hold a gender substructure. Earlier in this phase of the women's movement, we thought of gender issues as arising when women and men meet or when women meet with women; we had a curious blindness to the gender organization of the supposedly gender neutral.[4] We saw gender bias as an imperfection of processes that were properly gender neutral. More recently we have come to see gender as pervading all social relations.[5] The earlier accounts of patriarchy, as vested not only in the interpersonal relationships between women and men, but also in the massive organization of masculine power in the state (and in its mobilization of violence to regulate and impose its will), and in the legal, cultural, scientific and professional establishment,[6] can be seen as attending to the same organization of power which is characterized in other discursive settings as rational, impersonal, universal.

From the traditional sites of women's work and consciousness, oriented towards particular others and situated in local contexts of action, the ruling relations and apparatuses appear as abstracted systems, translating local events into the extra-local organizational forms of ruling. The emergence of bureaucracy, objective systems of management, professional discourse and analogous forms of control and organization can be traced as it occurs in multiple independent sites. The late 19th century transition from forms of capitalist enterprise identified with individual owners to the corporate forms of monopoly capital provided the basis for the development of systematic approaches to management.[7] In the early 20th century transitions from the forms of local organization vested in a local class structure to relations vested in new administrative forms of management in municipal affairs, education, public health, and so forth are initiated. The same period sees, particularly in North America, the very rapid development of professions as an institutionalized form standardizing skills, knowledge and practices in the many actual local sites of professional practice.[8] Correlatively, the organization of "higher learning" breaks free from local organization.[9] There is a progressive organization of academic discourse at national and international levels; news media evolve away from a position embedded in local interests and struggles, in which they have an active role, to an organization at the extra-local levels. This shift entails new practices of 'objectivity', essentially concerned with avoiding the identification of news stories with any one side.[10] Academic, professional, political and cultural discourses evolve as coordinators of the actual local sites in which life and work must always actually proceed. These and related developments in state administrative organization at national, provincial and municipal levels, create a new level of organization in society. Organization, execution, regulation is progressively leached out of local settings and particularized relations. They are transferred to this new level of organization in which communication, control, organization become differentiated and specialized functions, creating a layer of relations governing and coordinating local sites.

This complex of relations and apparatuses of ruling is mediated by texts, that is, by written, printed, or otherwise inscribed words and images (on television and movie screens, on the computer monitor). Those who inhabit it (as do most of us in this business, as a matter of our work, indeed almost of our being) take its textual ground for granted as a basis for what we know in an ordinary way about the world. Our knowledge, practices of thinking, theorizing, images of the world, are textually grounded and grounded in the relations of ruling. The "knowledge-power" relationship that Foucault has proposed is a metaphor for this reality, an organization of power mediated textually.[11] And of course we can't do without it. Societies, the global economy itself, would disintegrate if some magical or extra-terrestrial power were to obliterate every text (computer hackers' vandalism of corporate records gives us some notion of what this might mean, but it's still only a taste).

CLASS IN THE COMMUNIST MANIFESTO
AND IN CONTEMPORARY MARXIST THEORY

There is a standpoint, then, in the relations of ruling appearing through the varieties of disciplines, focuses, relevancies, interests, specializations, textual technologies, and the like. It is a standpoint which objectifies society, social relations and what people do. It is a standpoint evident in texts that conceal in their methods of telling that world, a subject, an 'I' a 'we', outside what is looked at; it is a standpoint producing a consciousness of society as if she who reads and speaks can stand outside it;[12] it is the celebrated Archimedean position so long and fruitlessly desired by sociologists. ("You can't have that wish, little bear," says Mother Bear.[13])

When I was teaching a course on women and class a few years ago, I had this experience: We did a critical review of some of the major contemporary Marxist theorists of class, Olin, Wright, Poulantzas, Carchedi and so forth. Then we read Marx's and Engels's *The Communist Manifesto*.[14] There was a startling difference. The latter locates the reader in the movement of history; classes are not mapped out as a structure consisting of categories of persons or positions; the reading subject is located at a moment between a past, in which classes have arisen that subjected society to their conditions of appropriation, and a future, in which the proletariat abolishes previous conditions of appropriation and thereby appropriation itself. Readers are placed pronominally; the bourgeoisie is directly addressed as an other, in opposition to the "we" situated on this side of the struggle, our side. You are horrified, Marx and Engels write to that other subject, "at our intending to do away with private property." "You reproach us with intending to do away with your property" and "that is just what we intend." The irony is heavy here. The "you" and "yours" are the bourgeoisie, addressed directly. "We" are the communists whose position is stated in the *Manifesto* by the communist authors; "we" creates a position for a subject in the text that is home for whoever takes our side; "we" are placed by this textual act *in* class struggle.

The text places the reader historically; class struggle is going on and you are in the middle of it. The sides are drawn up in the text itself as subjects are directly summoned and addressed. We can enter ourselves directly into its drama. Class is not objectified in the text as it is in the elaborate theoretical constructs of the contemporary Marxist theorists, needing rather careful fitting to the actualities of contemporary social relations. Rather, class emerges as a great historical process of struggle *in which the pamphlet and its analysis are situated*. The time of the text is just exactly that hinge where the past turns on a present that will be the making of the future. This is where you, as reading subject, are placed by the pamphlet. The polemic of the text is a call on you to act at precisely this juncture. But the temporal siting of reading and writing subjects in an historical trajectory of which the text itself is part isn't just a polemical effect. Though the reader isn't always being called on to act as he (I use the pronoun advisedly) is here, Marx's and Engels's analyses have generally this historically situated character; the time of the text isn't separate from the historical time of which it speaks.[15]

Contemporary Marxist texts on class locate the reading subject very differently. Characteristically they take advantage of the elaborate textual devices developed in the social sciences since Marx and Engels wrote. These constitute social and economic relations as if they went forward without the presence of actual subjects;[16] characteristically they construct a temporal order that does not situate the reader in a historical trajectory from past to future; characteristically the reading and writing subjects, if they are explicitly present, are external to the phenomenon of which the texts speak. Class is a theoretically constituted entity that will classify positions or individuals. To use the language of class to speak of the everyday/everynight world that we experience directly involves entering ourselves into discursive space and interpreting our own lives, friends, political associates from its standpoint. Such practices of objectification are constitutive of modes of organization in the relations of ruling, creating forms of consciousness that are properties of organization and discourse rather than of individuals, and they are essential coordinators of processes of ruling.

I'm suggesting that it is the emergence of the relations of ruling as a standpoint, as institutionalized practices of knowing within texts, that makes possible the objectification of processes known, lived and experienced only from within. Sociology has attempted to deal with this in its critique of positivism, but its interpretive substitutes preserve the same relation to actualities. Political economy appears never to have seriously addressed such issues. Perhaps political economy borrows from economics its confidence in the reality of the entities, objects and relations given presence in its discourse. But such discourse is deeply rooted and deeply dependent upon the elaborately evolved texture of texts mediating the relations of ruling. The intertextuality of our work as social scientists is wholly taken for granted in how we proceed.

Take the notion of 'position' for example which is so central to contemporary Marxist theorizing of class. Its force and intelligibility are grounded in multiple, textually-mediated sites in the organization and management of ruling in state and capitalist enterprise. For example, the occupational categories of the Canadian Classified Dictionary of Occupations is a constituent of state accounting that is part of the management of a labour force;[17] systems of job description and formally designated positions are formal properties of the organization of large-scale corporations and government bureaucracies. Positions arise in an organization of management through texts. Categories such as 'skill', 'occupation', 'industry', and so forth are constituted in textually-concerted organization lodged in the relations of ruling.[18] Contemporary Marxist conceptions of class, grounded in forms of knowledge generated by the relations of ruling, contain and conceal a basis in an organization of class (in state and management) that they are incapable of explicating. The entities incorporated as taken-for-granted presences in the discourses of political economy evidence their intertextual embedding in the relations of ruling. The relevancies, conceptual frameworks, as well as the informational bases, of political economic discourse are profoundly dependent upon the textually coordinated processes of ruling.

At the same time an institutionalized discourse such as political economy comes to constitute its own relevancies, concepts, entities, critical standards, and so forth. A textually-contained world comes into being. "[G]roups of texts, types of texts, even textual genres, acquire mass, density, and referential power among themselves and thereafter in the culture at large."[19] A sphere of work and inquiry is created with its own internal logic, its agreed upon objects and categories, its recognized authorities and referents. These constitute it as political economy; an object world is created which members of the discourse have in common; the actualities of social, economic and political process are interpreted through this prism. A textually-contained world is created, standing as object, external to the writing and reading subject; the lived world is to be interpreted through the medium of the textually-contained.

Such structuring isn't just a matter of will and intention; it is a matter of how our work gets taken up, who responds to it within discursive or organizational processes and hence of the part it comes to play within the division of the labour of ruling. Discourse establishes canons of relevance and validity, reproduces judgments and values, incorporates experiences and perceptions introduced by its participants as themes and topics that have become properties of discourse institutionalized in relations and apparatuses of ruling. We come to reflect on the world in terms of such relevancies, through the interpretive practices it provides, and indeed the constituents of the world we recognize as such are given to us by its categories. Most important of all, we come to be related to the world in which we are politically active (in whatever way) in its terms; thus class is constituted as external to us, an object to be investigated; political questions as to who are the working class arise as problems of the relation between a theoretically constituted entity and finding how to build its textual correlates through a selective investigation of the already textual (census, department of labour statistics, economic reports of task forces, commissions, think-tanks, and so forth) and the extra-textual world mediated by interviews, observation, personal reports.

FEMINISM, POLITICAL ECONOMY AND THE 'MAIN BUSINESS' OF RULING

Feminism has made important inroads on political economy. There have been very substantial achievements. At the same time there are barriers to our further advance. As the discursive domain of political economy has been institutionalized in the relations and apparatuses of ruling, it has acquired their relevancies. It depends upon their habits of thought and conceptual organization through the unexplicated incorporation into its discourse of the categories institutionalizing the 'main business' of ruling — to facilitate the self-expanding dynamic of capital.[20]

The feminist critique of political economy clearly marks the boundaries of the agenda comprising the 'main business' of ruling. Important theoretical work has established women's place in political economic discourse; the domestic labour debate wrote women into the classical categories of political economy — surplus-value, exchange-value and use-value. And even though the debate has been inconclusive, it has created an official door to a range of topics concerning the household and its organization that had not formerly been received as a legitimate discursive presence. The gendered organization of political economic processes has been insisted upon; issues of biological reproduction and of sexuality have been incorporated; important studies of women's paid work, women in the trade union movement and of the development of state management of women's domestic lives, have been done. The insertion of such topics into political economy (as evidenced, for example, by two recent Canadian anthologies, one edited by Heather Jon Maroney and Meg Luxton, the other by Michèle Barrett and Roberta Hamilton[21]) mark, through the absences and gaps they highlight in traditional political economic discourse, the contours of its relevancies.

The traditional relevancies are shaped, I suggest, less by 'sexist' practices, than by a deeper relationship between the gendered organization of ruling and the central and centripetal focus of the relations and apparatuses of ruling on the 'main business' of a capitalist economy. Embedded in the textual mediations of the relations of ruling, and therefore built on the textual forms integral to the governing of the society in relation to its 'main business,' the discourse of political economy operates within their parameters. The 'main business' defines the central position from which topics introduced by feminism are marginalized. The topics of feminism inscribe the contours of the 'main business' by marking what is excluded.

This exclusion corresponds to that divide introduced by capitalism into the productive organization of society. In the earliest pre-capitalist societies there is no separation between 'production' and 'reproduction'. Producing food, shelter, tools and so forth produces the subsistence and provides for the childbearing and childrearing of those who do the work of production. There is no economic organization that is not also an organization of gender. Indeed to speak of economic organization is to make an abstraction unwarranted in simpler social forms. Capitalism breaks the integration of production and reproduction. Production no longer produces the subsistence of those who do the work; nor does it provide for childbearing and childrearing; production is governed by the relations of capital accumulation; those who can earn a wage by selling to capital their capacity to labour may buy the commodities on which household members, including children, can subsist. The direct relationship between production, producers and reproduction has been ruptured. What we call the 'economy' emerges thus as a differentiated order of activity. Indeed what is commonly known in political economy as 'the capitalist mode of production,' is constituted as an internally driven sphere of dynamic relations mediated by money and commodities. Subsistence enters this sphere only insofar as it is given economic presence by the uses of the wage to buy commodities and hence also as 'consumption'. The other dimensions of household work and of childrearing, on which feminist political economists have insisted, don't become visible.

The central relevancies of political economy are the 'main business' of ruling, servicing, regulating, planning, criticizing, managing, organizing, the process of capital accumulation. It is a mistake to see the 'main business' as having to be constantly enforced by a ruling class. Over time, the 'main business' has become thoroughly built into the division of labour within ruling and the relations concerting it. It is institutionalized. Let me give one example: Sylvia Ann Hewlett is an economist who worked for the Economic Policy Council in the United States. During the 1980s she tried to set up a committee to study problems of women's work, family and daycare with a view to making recommendations to the President and to Congress on this topic. She had, however, the utmost difficulty in establishing the committee, for while both women and men were willing to work on committees investigating topics to do with the World Bank, etc., childcare and family was clearly a topic that was peripheral to the 'main business'. Participation would not lead to career opportunities or appropriate and advantageous connections, nor would it enhance a participant's professional reputation, and so forth. Hewlett writes of this episode thus:

> ...when I attempted to convene my panel in the spring and summer of 1983, I got a rude awakening. Most of my distinguished male members were simply not interested; they either yawned or raised their eyebrows when I insisted on explaining to them why they should get involved. After listening to my pitch, one eminent banker looked embarrassed and told me rather lamely that he was not "up to speed" in this policy area, and couldn't he join one of our other panels? I should point out that these men were not, in general, shrinking violets and had no problems in speaking out on Japanese defense policy or third world debt even when they had no fine-grained expertise in the area. Somehow issues like maternity leave and child care made them very nervous. But it was not just nerves; I could have overcome an attack of nerves. When pushed, they revealed another reason behind their reluctance to get involved: Family policy had no standing in their world. Being involved in this project would get them no brownie points in boardrooms or at cocktail parties. It seemed clear that

while they might sacrifice precious time getting up to speed on Japanese defense policy, they were not prepared to do so for "women's stuff" — as one member called it.

If the male reaction was bad, the female reaction was even more difficult to take. I discovered that most of my distinguished women members weren't interested either. I remember feeling almost numb when one woman, a senior vice-president at a major manufacturing corporation, excused herself on the ground that she could not afford to become identified with this panel. She explained, "It has taken me fifteen years to get a hard-nosed reputation, and I just daren't risk it. If I were to get involved in these messy women's issues, it could do me a lot of harm in the company."22

Childcare and family are not articulated to the 'main business' organizing career processes in government and economy. The interests and relevancies institutionalized in the social organization of the relations and apparatuses of ruling marginalize topics such as childcare and family. Marginalized politically, they are correspondingly marginalized in academic settings. The pull of academic status is towards the categories identified with the institutions sustaining the 'main business'. Even a critical discourse such as political economy has its agenda set by 'the main business'.

The 'main business' is built into the categories and concepts organizing what we treat as 'information', news, statistical data of all kinds, and so forth — *these are integral to getting the 'main business' done* and are, of course, shaped to their uses.23 It is built into the categories and concepts that are the working currency of discourse. The centripetal effect of discourse around the 'main business' is sustained by academic practices restricting the ways in which knowledge can be developed as a service to those outside the relations of ruling. The institutionalized practices restricting the access of the ruled, the marginal, the excluded to knowledge are deeply built into the ordinary working practices of academia, and are, for the most part, below the level of consciousness. They include the normal methodological procedures of sociology, indeed precisely those that my experience with a women's research centre called into question. They also become visible in the requirements imposed on those seeking research funding, less as a matter of topic than of the methodological and evaluative criteria reproducing the objectifying practices of academic, professional and state discourse.

The institutions of ruling themselves are taken for granted as the ground on which political economy operates, and women have been marginal to these. Thus the topics of political economy have marginalized women not only as an effect of sexism, but as an effect of how the discourse has built itself upon the textual accounting and information practices of 'the main business' and thereby taken over its parameters and its bounding assumptions. Issues concerning women don't seem somehow to be there when general topics are undertaken. An example: Goran Therborn's "Classes and states: welfare state developments, 1881-1981"[24] is a comparative account of welfare state development. It is concerned with the question of what labour movements have contributed to the making of the welfare state. The venue of struggle is the political process of the state. Class analysis is rendered into the perspectives of business and trade unions. Women are naturally absent though Therborn makes an appropriate gesture recognizing the gendered nature of the working class and providing a reason for their absence from his account in terms of male dominance of working class organization. The actors and entities on his stage — state, trade unions, a masculine version of class, the political process, business, and so forth — are the natural players on the stage defined by the 'main business' and they naturally marginalize women.

But suppose we shift to a standpoint from which women's experience becomes visible. New actors, institutions, and organization come into view: the extensive charitable and voluntary work of women of the middle and upper classes in the later 19th and early 20th centuries in providing the organizational foundation for social services in what later becomes integrated into the welfare state; the development of systems of managing the domestic and reproductive lives of working class women; the emergence of professions such as social work, public health nursing, teaching, as essential aspects of the development of the welfare state; the class relations among women that were set up in these ways. Such aspects are missing when the procedures for collecting historical instances are governed by the institutional forms central to the 'main business'. An undertaking, such as that made at one time by *Studies in Political Economy*, to incorporate women's issues in general papers, turns out to be awkward and difficult to adhere to, because it's hard to see how to fit them in when the very presuppositions of discourse have already denied them presence.

One aspect of the problem is the tendency to identify class struggle with trade union organization. This too marginalizes women and in particular women's distinctive experiences of work outside and inside the home. I recognize, of course, the important changes in trade union policies which women trade unionists have been able to bring about as well as the significant shift in organizing policies impelled by the changing proportions of the manufacturing and service industries in the economy. Nonetheless women's work force situations can't be cut off from their special relationship to childcare and childrearing as well as housework. To treat 'trade unions' as a textual stand-in for class is an illustration of the kind of centripetal pull of the 'main business' and its marginalization of women that I'm explicating here.[25] Though the political economist may recognize class as gendered, in practice, when the point of production is treated as the exclusive site of class and class struggle, major dimensions of women's lives are dropped from view.

The site from which issues relevant to women have been brought into view is at the margins and not at the centre. Feminist corrections to the discursive relevancies of political economy struggle within, more rarely against,[26] existing contours. Women's issues are organized in terms of an agenda defined from that centre. Assertions of women's presence in class, of the significance of domestic labour in economic relations, let alone of the need for representation within political economy of the neglected areas of sexuality and motherhood, have not yet succeeded in shifting the central determination of the focus of political economy from the 'main business' dominating the relations of ruling.

A STANDPOINT OUTSIDE THE RELATIONS OF RULING

The central relevancies, assumptions, methods and conceptual practices of political economic discourse remain largely unchanged by attempts to embed feminist topics in the discourse. The contours of the discursive barrier are perhaps most strikingly displayed in our failure as feminists working within the political economic tradition to come to terms with a racism implicit in our practices and arising less from attitudes we hold as individuals as from just the ways that we participate in and practice the discursive assumptions and the structuring of the 'main business' within the relations of ruling. As we latch our feminist work to the discourse of political economy, we latch it to the structures organizing and managing class and race as well as gender. Edward Said's study, *Orientalism*,[27] describes the development of a body of knowledge and scholarly study, the apparent objectivity of which conceals its profound structuring from a centre inside the Western capitalist powers and their imperialist enterprise, constituting the Orient and Oriental as Other. "[P]olitical imperialism governs an entire field of study, imagination, and scholarly institutions — in such a way as to make its avoidance an intellectual and historical impossibility." The disciplines organized from this centre claim to stand outside such effects but do not.[28]

The parallels are obvious here. Indeed the structures are the same. The relations and apparatuses of ruling constitute other Others — of class, of gender, and of race. This statement is to be taken quite literally. The divisions between gender, class and race don't exist at the level of the everyday/everynight world of people's actual lives; to be black, a woman and working class are not three different and distinctive experiences. Himani Bannerji has dissected the constitution of gender, class and race as realized abstractions as follows:

> In this method of operating, the abstraction is created when the different social moments which constitute the "concrete" being of any social organization and existence are pulled apart, and each part assumed to have a substantive, self regulating structure. This becomes apparent when we see gender, race and class each considered as a separate issue — as ground for separate oppressions. The social whole — albeit fraught with contradictions — is then constructed by an aggregative exercise. According to this, I, as a South Asian woman, then have a double oppression to deal with, first on the count of gender, and second on the count of race. I am thus segmented into different social moments, made a victim of discrete determinations. So it is with the moment of gender, when it is seen as a piece by itself, rupturing its constitutive relationship with race and class. Needless to say, race and class could also be meted the same treatment. What this does is to empty gender relations of their general social context, content and dynamism. This, along with the primacy that gender gains (since the primary social determinant is perceived as patriarchy), subsumes all other social relations, indeed renders them often invisible.[29]

The objectified and objectifying practices constituting the systematically developed forms of social consciousness of contemporary society — among them political economy — conceal the 'subject-other' relationships structuring the centre from which that consciousness 'looks' out. As political economic discourse participates in and is structured by the relations of ruling it participates in this ground and walks the same circumference. So do our feminist riders to the theorems of political economy.

Issues of racism confront, I believe, the same barrier, a barrier confining thinking and analyses to the racist tracks of the ruling of contemporary capitalism. The problem isn't to make third world women a topic within a feminist political economy, nor yet to invite third world women to speak in this zone of discourse. Of course they have already seized that initiative. The problem I am explicating is of a different kind; it is a problem of the concealed standpoint, the position in the relations of ruling that is taken for granted in how we speak and that bounds and constrains how a political economy of women can speak to women, let alone to third world women. It is a problem of the invisible centre that is concealed in the objectifications of discourse, seeming to speak of the world dispassionately, objectively, as it is. For third world women, nothing is gained by being entered as topics into the circumscriptions of white, male grounded, or of white female grounded, discourse. The theoretical expansions of political economy introduced by white women have merely rewritten the boundaries, the centre still remains, the standpoint within ruling is stably if invisibly present. Nothing will serve but the dissolution of objectified discourse, the decentring of standpoint and the discovery of another consciousness of society systematically developed from the standpoint of women of colour and exploring the relations of political economy or sociology from a ground in that experience.

The logic of the feminist critique as I understand it, opens up not only the issue of women's absence, nor only of the agenda of the 'main business,' but also of the making of a political economy from standpoints outside the relations of ruling. Back then to the issue of how *The Communist Manifesto* relates the reader to the world in which she lives and reads. Obviously we cannot reconstruct the relations characteristic of an earlier stage of capitalism when the emergence of what I'm calling apparatuses and relations of ruling was only in its infancy.[30] We can't return to that relatively pristine state (so far as political economy is concerned).[31] But we want, I want, a political economy exploring the world in which I live, in which we live, and exploring it in ways that do not objectify it or relate us to it through the medium of ruling. I want a political economy that explicates and analyzes just how our lives are caught up in political economic processes, including of course the relations and apparatuses of ruling in which our own work as social scientists is embedded.

This, as I see it, is the next step in the feminist critique. It calls for methods of thinking, methods of writing texts, methods of investigation that expand and extend our knowledge of how our everyday/everynight worlds are put together, determined and shaped as they are by forces and powers beyond our practical and direct knowledge. It calls for an openness to the multiple sites of experience in contemporary capitalism and the evolution of a systematically-developed social consciousness (a political economy, a sociology) that does not depend upon collapsing them into a single over-riding standpoint. Taking up the standpoint of subjects outside the relations of ruling means evolving a political economy not confined to the 'main business', nor assuming a single standpoint, nor that the relations and forces of capital, including those of ruling, are going to look the same from every standpoint. Different sites, different experiences, provide different perspectives and propose different strategies of exploration; they enhance and expand our capacity to grasp the nature of the beast.

    This doesn't mean an endless relativism of perspective, a multiplicity of 'truths' for we are addressing relations, practices, powers and forces which are actual, have consequences, need exploration, can be discovered, are there. But we are addressing that complex from the sites and standpoints it has constructed. In exploring how we are related through its determinations, the concept of class has an essential role as a method of analyzing and explicating the actual organization of relations in which our lives and struggles are embedded. Our concept of class can't be identical to that of Marx and Engels, for the analytic capacity of such concepts is firmly articulated to the social relations of their time. Nonetheless inheriting the tradition of analysis they founded, entering at a later stage the same historical trajectory, and caught up in the same historical struggles that they charted, their work is the original and the model for ours. We want the analytic powers of a concept of class that will display our site in a trajectory of struggle in which we are necessarily already implicated and already act. Women's struggles for liberation and equality are already deeply embedded in these relations; we need a political economy that will explore and display the properties and movement of the complex of powers, forces and relations that are at work in our everyday/everynight worlds.

ENDNOTES

I am indebted, as so often in the past, to Nancy Jackson's exceptionally intelligent and critical reading.

1.   In much of what I've written, I've used the term 'ruling apparatus'. George Smith and Lorna Weir have convinced me that 'relations of ruling' is in many respects a more appropriate term. However I find I sometimes want the notion of 'apparatus' in there and so have arrived at this compromise.

2.   See Dorothy E. Smith, "Sociological theory: writing patriarchy into feminist texts," in Ruth Wallace (ed.), *Feminist Contributions to Sociological Theory*. (New York: Sage Publications, forthcoming).

3.   Michel Foucault, *The Archaeology of Knowledge* (London: Tavistock Publications, 1974).

4.   It is true, of course, that if we'd read Simone de Beauvoir's *The Second Sex* more attentively we might have become aware of this sooner. Perhaps because we were first necessarily preoccupied with the problems of developing a discursive space among women, we did not attend to the realities of the power relations within which our enterprise was undertaken.

5.   See Marilyn Frye's marvellously lucid discussion of 'sexism' in her *Politics of Reality* (Trumansburg: Crossing Press, 1983), and Sandra Harding's treatment of rationality in her essay "Is gender a variable in conceptions of rationality? a survey of the issues," *Dialectica* 36: 2-3, 1982, pp. 226-242.

6.   Kate Millett's, for example, in *Sexual Politics* (New York: Avon, 1971).

7.   Albert Chandler Jr.'s *The Visible Hand: The Managerial Revolution in American Business* (Cambridge: Harvard University Press, 1977), is a remarkable study of this transition.

8.   See David Noble's study of the emergence of the engineering profession in the United States at this period, *America by Design: Science, Technology and the Rise of Corporate Capitalism* (Oxford: Oxford University Press, 1979).

9.   Thorstein Veblen's *The Higher Learning in America* (New York: Hill & Wang, 1957), must be seen in "performative" terms as contributing to prying universities free from local controls and organizing them at an extra-local level. Veblen wrote at a watershed point in these developments and his study *Absentee*

Ownership (Boston: Beacon Press, 1967), is also preoccupied with these themes, though it was, perhaps for obvious reasons, never taken up in the same way as *The Higher Learning* was.

10. See Ben Bagdikian's *The Media Monopoly* (Boston: Beacon Press, 1983), for a very useful account of the relation between the resiting of newspapers and the institutionalization of objectivity in reporting.

11. See in particular his *Discipline and Punish: The Birth of the Prison* (New York: Vintage Books, 1979). In this work Foucault argues, though the argument isn't fully worked out, that the social sciences are grounded in technologies of punishment and discipline, subduing people to the status of objects. As may be seen, my argument here is somewhat different for I have emphasized the emergence of the textually-mediated relations of ruling as a distinctive level and mode of organization, not merely grounded in technologies of punishment and discipline (in any case rather broadly interpreted by Foucault) but active in organizing and reorganizing them. My own view is that objectification is a distinctive mode of organizing social consciousness as a property of organization rather than of individuals — see my *The Conceptual Practices of Power: A Feminist Sociology of Knowledge.* (Boston: Northeastern University Press, forthcoming).

12. In my "Sociological theory..." in Wallace (ed.), *Feminist Contributions.* I've explored sociological theory as a set of conventions for writing this standpoint into sociological texts.

13. The reference here is to children's books by Maurice Sendak, about Mother Bear and Little Bear, full of wise sayings.

14. I don't now remember why we did them in that order; it may have been because different subgroups in the class took responsibility for a critical presentation of the different theorists and that the group responsible for this one, for some reason got out of phase.

15. Indeed it can be argued that Marx's method took very strong advantage of this in proposing that the very categories capable of displaying the properties of political economic relations awaited the development of capitalism for only capitalism differentiates, and hence makes visible, the effects addressed by political economy.

16. see Smith, "Sociological theory..." in Wallace, (ed.), *Feminist Contributions.*

17. See George W. Smith, "Occupation and skill: Government discourse as problematic," Occasional Paper No. 2, *The Nexus Project: Studies in the Job-Education Nexus.* Toronto, May, 1988.

18. Joan Acker has made precisely the same point in a paper that must have been in the writing at the same time as this. (We have a history of such happy coincidences in our work, speaking for an intellectual and political companionship, though at a distance, of long-standing.) I don't quote because it is still in draft, but she writes of the job as a specific property of contemporary formal organization and of how structural accounts of class using notions of positions or places would seem to be grounded in that form of the organization of power in contemporary capitalism. See Joan Acker, "Hierarchies and jobs: notes for a theory of gendered organizations," paper presented at the American Sociological Association Meetings, Chicago, Ill., August, 1987.

19. Edward W. Said, *Orientalism*. (New York: Vintage Books, 1979).

20. I don't want to give the phrase, the 'main business,' any particular theoretical weight. It is a preliminary conceptual sketching of a property I'm trying to bring out as a way of seeing some of the problems women have in becoming full political subjects in contemporary society.

21. Heather Jon Maroney and Meg Luxton (eds.), *Feminist and Political Economy: Women's Work, Women's Struggles* (Toronto: Methuen, 1987); Roberta Hamilton, and Michèle Barrett (eds.), *The Politics of Diversity: Feminism, Marxism and Nationalism* (Montreal: The Book Centre, 1987).

22. Hewlett continues, "She was a kind woman and followed this up with a piece of personal advice: 'You know, if I were you, I would drop this whole project. You are an economist who has had enough sense to build a career in serious fields such as development economics. Why risk all that by getting everyone's back up?' The most depressing thing about her response was that I knew enough about her personal history to understand that she herself had encountered difficulties in bearing children mid-career. If she wouldn't take these issues seriously, who would?" Sylvia Ann Hewlett, *A Lesser Life: The Myth of Women's Liberation in America* (New York: Warner Books) 1986, pp. 369-370.

23. See Robert Sterling and Denise Khouri, "Unemployment indices: the Canadian context" in John Fry (ed.), *Economy, Class and Social Reality* (Toronto: Butterworth, 1979) on the Keynesian presuppositions of national economic statistical measures, such as the GNP.

24. *Studies in Political Economy: A Socialist Review* No. 14 (1984) pp. 7-14. This paper was picked at random and without prior testing of its responsiveness to a gender analysis.

25. See Gilles Malnarich and Dorothy E. Smith, "Where are the women?" paper presented at the Conference on the Centenary of Marx's Death, University of

Manitoba, Winnipeg, 1983.

26. Recent instances are Diane Elson's strikingly original "Socialization of the market," *New Left Review* No. 172 (Nov./Dec. 1988) pp. 3-44 and Nicky Hart's equally striking analysis "Gender and Class in England," *New Left Review* No. 175 (May/June 1989) pp. 19-47.

27. Said, *Orientalism.* (1979).

28. *Ibid.,* p. 14.

29. Himani Bannerji, "Introducing racism: notes towards an anti-racist feminism," *Resources for Feminist Research: A Canadian Journal for Feminist Scholarship* 16: 1 (March 1987). [Special issue on Immigrant Women edited by Roxana Ng, Joyce Scane, Himani Bannerji, Didi Khayatt and Makeda Silvera.]

30. In Marx's critique of the ideological practices of the German ideologists we can find a preliminary isolation of some of the conceptual practices that are now integral to the organization of the relations of ruling. Karl Marx and Friedrich Engels, *The German Ideology* Part II (Moscow: Progress Publishers, 1976).

31. We wouldn't like the plumbing either.

CHAPTER 2

CLASS AND GENDER IN FISHING COMMUNITIES IN NOVA SCOTIA

MARTHA MACDONALD
M. PATRICIA CONNELLY

This paper explores the complexity of class relations in Nova Scotia fishing communities, using a conception of class which takes into account gender and household relations. The purpose of any class analysis is to better understand the conditions under which people live and work, and the way they act in their lives. Workers often behave in ways that surprise and frustrate Marxist theorists — being passive where they should act, and rising up and resisting in the most unlikely circumstances. It is our view that an understanding of gender and household dynamics as they relate to class would help make sense of such behaviour. There is always a danger, however, that attempts to clarify class positions degenerate into static exercises in labelling and filling boxes.[1] Our purpose in this paper is to show that a more complex, gendered class analysis can illuminate otherwise anomalous characteristics of the pattern of labour relations and capital accumulation in an industry.[2] We use a specific case study of the fishing industry to illustrate our general point.

We find that the literature on class, both theoretical work and applied work on the fishing industry, has two problems: it tends to focus on the individual, ignoring household dynamics and gender, and it is static, focusing on an individual's work at a single point in time. In traditional analyses, class position is determined solely by an individual's own direct relationship to the means of production,[3] or for dependent individuals by the class of the (male) head of household.[4] When the mode of production is understood to include relations of reproduction as well as production, then the conceptualization of class must change. Household and gender relations must be taken into account. Both life cycle work patterns and spousal work patterns will affect a person's current class identification. This is crucial for understanding class struggle. After some theoretical discussion of these issues, including an examination of attempts in the feminist literature to come to terms with class, we illustrate from our research in Nova Scotia fishing communities how an expanded interpretation of class provides a better guide to understanding relations in the industry. We focus on the behaviour of family household members in relation to each other, exploring the use of the family household as a crucial unit in class analysis. The actual dynamics of the formation of family class consciousness and decision making are not directly analyzed, though this is an important part of the overall feminist project of reevaluating the traditional concept of class.

CLASS REVISITED

In recent years a considerable effort has been put into a reevaluation of orthodox Marxist class categories, primarily in order to understand the position of the expanding "middle class" (such as managers and professionals). Attempts to locate these predominantly white collar workers have led to debates over the key defining elements of Marxian class positions and the notion of contradictory class location. A number of schemas for revised class categories have been proposed.[5] In this literature renewed attention has been paid to the category of petty bourgeois. However, petty bourgeois is itself a problematic category in the literature.[6]

Issues surrounding the petty bourgeoisie and contradictory class positions have been at the heart of the literature on class structure and struggle in the fishing industry of Atlantic Canada. The main problem in this literature is the position of fishers, for processing workers are seen as clearly working class, and owners of fish plants with employees seen as capitalists.[7] There is general agreement in the literature that offshore crew are essentially working class, though in terms of ideology they may identify as petty bourgeois, holding onto the notion of the "independent" fisher. Crew on inshore and nearshore boats are argued by the unions and most analysts to also be working class, though through kinship ties many can also be members of family businesses. Furthermore, many aspire to become boat owners themselves, which affects their class identification.

The main debate in the literature and in organizational efforts in the fishery has to do with the status of fishers who own their own boats. Are they small scale capitalists, or petty bourgeois, or in a contradictory class location? Williams and Sacouman were early writers on this issue.[8] More recently,

Clement[9] identifies five patterns among fishers: subsistence production (no exchange); capitalist commodity production (both company owners and owners of longliners with four or more crew would be considered capitalist); independent commodity production (the fisher has formal and economic ownership of the means of production, has non-exploitive labour relations, faces prices determined by supply and demand, and, therefore, is part of the traditional petty bourgeoisie); dependent commodity production (the fisher is tied to buyers in a relationship of unequal exchange, having formal but not economic ownership); and cooperative commodity production (where the boat owner is either capitalist or petty bourgeois). Williams[10] has a similar scheme but includes an additional category of semi-proletarian, or semi-proletarian dependent commodity production, where fishers engage in wage labour to help make ends meet. He also recognizes that this wage labour may be sequential, not seasonal, and that the wage labour of other family members may also be involved. We elaborate on this point in this paper.

The class position of dependent commodity producers is considered to be either contradictory,[11] inherently unstable, or transitory.[12] The debates on this are part of the larger debate about underdevelopment and the future of independent commodity production within capitalism. Sacouman and Williams argue that part of the process of underdevelopment is the distorted maintenance of this mode of production, while Fairley argues that straightforward capitalist development is occurring in the industry, with some fishers becoming small scale capitalists.[13] Certain concerns have been clearly manifested in the debate: the implications for class struggle, and the potential for progressive action on the part of fishers' organizations.[14]

In general, the literature on the Atlantic fishery is very rich, and tends to be grounded in concern for political struggle rather than academic classification. However, it is our view that important implications for understanding class struggle are missed by inadequate attention to gender and household in most analyses.[15]

As Marxist feminists have reiterated over and over, mostly to nodding heads with deaf ears, there are problems with Marx's original analysis of class, based as it is on an individual's relationship to the means of production. They have tried to sort out the interrelationships of class and gender, arguing for a gendered analysis of class and a class analysis of gender.[16] The process of developing an integrated, comprehensive theory of gendered class struggle is long and difficult, with work proceeding on the level of grand theory and through empirical studies.

Feminists have strongly criticized Marxist theory because its concepts don't apply to the household, which is the traditional area of women's work. Among feminists, there has been more unanimity in the critiques than in the proposed revisions to received theory. Much intellectual effort has been expended in trying to integrate women's work in the home into the Marxist class framework through the "domestic labour debate."[17] Radical feminists have argued that the "domestic mode of production" has its own mechanisms of exploitation, creating sex classes which coexist with the classes of the capitalist mode of production.[18] Walby argues that gender interests operate independently and often in contradiction to class interests, and that gender subordination is independently created in the workplace as well as in the home.[19] Others disagree with this "two systems" approach, arguing that the concept of mode of production should be expanded to include both the reproductive and productive spheres, with relations of reproduction and production seen as interactive and dialectically related. There is continuing debate over the extent of autonomy of the spheres of social reproduction and production.[20]

Others have posed the problem in terms of women's relationship to the wage in capitalism, focusing on the contradiction between women's roles as wage labour and domestic labour. This dual relationship to the class structure, it is argued, has important implications for consciousness and forms of resistance.[21] Along these same lines, it has also been argued that the working class should be defined not as those with a particular relationship to the means of production but as all those who are dependent upon the sale of labour power — directly and indirectly. As wage earners women have a direct relationship to the wage, but as domestic workers they have an indirect relationship to the wage experience through their husbands' wage labour.[22] In this approach women's relationship to the class structure is, at least partially, mediated by the family household, domestic labour and dependence on men. Even when women are themselves wage workers, the integration of gender and class relations gives a distinct meaning to their experience of class in the workplace.[23] Thus, in the feminist literature, as in the Marxist literature discussed above, there is an emphasis on contradictory aspects of class position. The contradictory forces identified by feminists analyzing the class positions of women (i.e. both direct and indirect relations to the means of production) must also be applied in a revised class analysis of men.

Recent feminist work has focused on demonstrating theoretically and empirically the centrality of women's household labour and the relations of reproduction to any analysis of the economic system. This is especially true in the literature on gender and development, which shows that women's work, gender relations and household forms are integrally related to the accumulation process. In a variety of ways they both affect and are affected by the specific form accumulation takes in particular countries and regions.[24]

The literature on gender and development reminds all political economists of the need for an "analysis of the interconnections between capital accumulation, class formation, and gender relations."[25] The feminist agenda includes showing that gender analysis is not something to be done separately, but is something that profoundly affects the "main business" of Marxist analysis.[26] Ignoring issues of gender and household may quite simply lead to a wrong understanding of the world. "Gendered class analysis" does not mean class analysis of women; it means a new approach to all class analysis.

How can we begin to revise the standard class analysis to take into account these concerns? Feminists have strongly criticized the common sociological approach in which women's class position is assumed to be the same as that of their husbands.[27] The class position of women must take account of both their direct and indirect relation to the means of production — their own productive and reproductive labour as well as that of their husbands. By implication, the class position of husbands must take account of the work of their wives.[28] An excellent attempt to analyze the joint determination of the class positions of family members is the work of Beneria and Roldan, which analyzes the class trajectories of wives and husbands and their interactions in Mexico city.[29] They show that advances in the class position of the males are facilitated by downward mobility of their spouses, and they relate this to the general process of capital accumulation.

There have been attempts to assign class locations to households by taking account of the work of both husbands and wives, such as that by Britten and Heath using aggregate data for the United Kingdom.[30] There are many conceptual and empirical challenges in such undertakings. It is our view that such revisions are better explored at the level of local data, with particular issues of class struggle and economic change in mind. In the next section we outline some of the elements involved in this expanded class analysis, and suggest why it should make a difference to the analysis of the fishing industry. Later sections use specific examples from our research to explore how such an analysis could be used.

THE FISHING INDUSTRY REVISITED

As mentioned above, most of the class analysis of the fishery has focused on individuals at one point in time, while ignoring their work histories and family work patterns. But class identification is affected by both, as well as by gender. Rick Williams devotes some attention to the work history aspect in his sketch of a "typical" inshore fisher.[31] He describes a person who began fishing with his father then decided he wanted to be a fisher. He then spent five years crewing in B.C. (working class) to raise capital to buy a boat. Now he owns a boat, is a "highliner," sells competitively and employs no labour (petty bourgeois, or independent commodity production). However, if the fishing is bad he occasionally still goes to Prince Rupert to crew for a season. His experience on the west coast gave him a belief in unions, and he is active in the Maritime Fishermen's Union, though his concerns reflect a mixture of working class and independent business ideology.

One can imagine another equally "typical" fisher who inherited his father's boat and never had the wage-labour experience, or one who worked on offshore boats for awhile, or one who drove a cab in the city for years. Each of these would have a different identification and orientation towards the struggles in the inshore fishery. Understanding the patterns that operate should enable us to better understand class behaviour at a given point in time.[32] Furthermore, work patterns may differ by community, or may be changing over time, which will help us understand the changing class dynamic across communities.

Women's work histories also affect their current work behaviour.[33] Women may move between formal wage labour and informal activities such as babysitting, selling handmade goods, taking in boarders and so on. The class position of these informal sector activities is seldom examined. For women there is also the ever-present work of reproduction, the class position of which has been subject to scrutiny in the domestic labour debate.[34] The combination of productive and reproductive work undertaken by most women adds complexity to their class position and class consciousness.[35] In fishing communities there is another kind of women's work activity that is often ignored, and that is the work that wives of fishers do for the family enterprise, generally without pay. There are certainly implications for class analysis of women who are not only fish plant workers but are also working for their husbands' fishing operations. Most of the research on the fishery has ignored the implications of the complex work histories and pluralistic work patterns of the individuals involved in the industry.

For the most part, household/spousal work patterns have also been ignored in analyses of class relations in the industry. One of the questions that motivated our own research was 'Who works in the fish plant?' It seemed to us that it made a great deal of difference whether it was wives of fishers, wives of fish plant workers, single people, people whose spouses were unemployed, or those whose spouses worked in unrelated industries. The employees' class identification and the terms of struggle in the plant (and in the fishery) should be profoundly influenced by the answer to this question. For example, analyzing the relation between fishers and plant owners, and separately analyzing the relationship between plant owners and processing workers makes little sense if the fishers are married to the plant workers. Their interests are intertwined. Higher prices for fishers may mean lower wages for plant workers. This may be acceptable to the wives of fishers, given unequal gender relations; it may not be acceptable to women plant workers whose husbands work outside the fishing industry, or alongside them in the plant.

There are many examples which illustrate that spousal work patterns should be an essential part of the analysis. For instance, Clement tries to explain the internal dynamics of co-ops in the fishing industry by analyzing the complex class relations within the co-ops.[36] He points out that co-ops contain within them all the classes of capitalism, creating internal class struggle. He emphasizes that the member fishers may be independent commodity producers in their own fishing enterprises, but that in their role as co-op members they function as capitalists in relation to the processing workers. This helps explain why co-ops have a very bad record as employers, in terms of wages. However, gender relations are ignored, even though most fishers are men and many processing workers are women. Nowhere, furthermore, does Clement take into account the household relations between co-op plant workers and member fishers, or between crew and boat owners for that matter. How this complicates the class struggle within the co-ops, and how it affects their potential for progressive action, is illustrated in the final section of this paper.

Spousal work patterns and gender relations also need to be more closely addressed in the analysis of semi-proletarianization of fishers (dependent commodity production). We expect it makes a difference whether it is fishers who take wage jobs, or their wives, or even their children. If it is the fisher himself, it may give him a contradictory sense of his class, and may incline him more to a working class analysis of his situation, with implications for the kind of political action in which he will engage. If it is his wife, given asymmetrical gender relations in the household, her proletarianization may facilitate his acquiring a purely bourgeois class identification, which of course may also limit his wife's political action. We would expect differences in the struggles over time and by area, depending on the form this so-called semi-proletarianization of the fishing household takes.

A final general point about the importance of household and gender relations to a class analysis is that the terms of struggle are both shaped by, and in
turn shape these household relations. How do household strategies for survival, individual strategies regarding work, and strategies of capital interact
over time? Does capital encourage (or benefit from) a particular spousal work
pattern rather than another? Do households choose a pattern of labour allocation as a conscious part of class struggle?[37] If so, what are the gender implications of this choice? We can look for evidence that capital has consciously
tried to manipulate family work patterns through hiring practices, for example,
to strengthen its hand. The state has of course also played a role in altering
the work patterns and this has changed the class and gender relations in the
fishing industry.[38]

In other words, an expanded class analysis enables us to take a fresh look
at the processes of struggle and economic change in the industry and in the
communities. In the remainder of this paper we use two types of data from
our research to examine some of these issues. First, we document the family
work patterns, exploring the combinations of individual class positions and the
question of a family household class position. Second, we examine changes in
industrial relations in two communities, showing that using the household as a
unit of analysis helps clarify our understanding of the struggles.

HOUSEHOLD AND LIFECYCLE WORK PATTERNS
AND THE COMPLEXITY OF CLASS

In this section we examine household survey data from a sample of six
Nova Scotia fishing communities.[39] We are interested in individual work history patterns and spousal work patterns.[40] The purpose is to show the complexity of the work patterns and therefore of class positions. We suggest implications for class relations in the industry, which are more fully explored in the
next section. The six communities include two larger fishing centres, dominated by National Sea plants, three medium size communities with independent-
ly-owned fish plants, and one small community with a co-op buying station but
no processing plant. With these data we are able to examine overall trends
and differences in patterns by age group and by community.[41] First we look at
the individual work histories, then we examine combined work patterns of
wives and husbands.[42]

Approximately 30 percent of the male spouses had fished, 30 percent
had worked in the plant, and 15 percent had done both. We are interested in

movements among boatowning (petty bourgeois), crew, and wage labour (particularly in the fish plant). We found that 70 percent of men who had owned their own boat at some time had also worked in a crew position and three-quarters of them had other wage work experience, with 17 percent having worked in the fish plant. Typically those who owned their own boat had spent only 60 percent of their working lives self-employed and a pattern of multiple job holding throughout the year also characterized about 40 percent of them at least some of the time. Of men who had ever worked in the fish plant (45 percent of our sample), 40 percent had also fished at some time and a quarter of those had moved between plant and fishing more than once. While the most common direction of move was from the plant to crew, 15 percent had owned boats before going into the fish plant, and 10 percent left the plant to buy their own boats. For these men, it is likely that the experience of owning a boat, or the aspiration to become a boat owner coloured their consciousness while they were in a working class position.

In general, then, there is considerable evidence for complex individual class positions of male fishing industry participants over the course of their lives. Interpreting male fish plant workers as strictly working class, or boat owners as petty bourgeois will limit our ability to explain their behaviour.[43] We found considerable variation in the patterns by community. For example, in the largest port all of the boat owners had wage work experience, whereas in the smallest, most traditional community, only 25 percent had done anything other than fish. The pattern of multiple job holding during the year was particularly common in the Eastern part of the province, where the fishing is poorer. We also found differences by age group, with the younger cohort less likely to hold multiple jobs, or move from one class position to another.

Turning now to the work patterns for women in the communities, we found them to be equally complex. Approximately three-quarters of women have done wage work at some time since marriage, typically for about a third of their married lives. Much of this wage work experience was outside the fishing industry, primarily in the service sector; however 40 percent have worked in the fish plant at some time. Women have also been active in various forms of self-employment, such as babysitting, selling crafts, or selling Avon products. In addition to doing most of the domestic labour for their households (wives of fishers do essentially all the household work), women engaged in subsistence production of various sorts, including keeping gardens, making clothes and preserving food. These activities, which are often associated with independent commodity production, have declined rapidly in recent years, with the younger cohort more likely to substitute wage work for subsistence activities. We also found that subsistence activities remain more common in the Eastern part of the province where, as mentioned above, the fishing is poorer. Women whose husbands have been boat owners have also engaged in a variety of work (generally unpaid) that supports the fishing enterprise. This adds another dimension to the class fabric of their work histories. As emphasized above, in our view it is critical to class analysis to link up the work experiences of household members, and in this paper we focus on the spousal work combinations. In examining spousal work patterns, we are particularly concerned with combinations of work which are relevant to understanding class relations in the fishing industry, in both the harvesting and processing sectors. Therefore we focus on the work of wives of fishers (owners and crew), wives of male plant workers, and husbands of female plant workers.

We found that almost half of the wives of boat owners worked for wages during at least part of the time their husbands owned the boat. In fact, one-quarter of the wives of boat owners worked at the plant at some time while their husbands owned boats. We found this to differ by community and by age group. In the larger fishing ports the recent trend has been away from wives of fishers (both crew and owners) working outside the home. This implies more consistent family class positions emerging. In smaller communities it is still common to have wives of fishers working in the plants, which affects the struggles of both fishers and plant workers against the plant owners.

We also collected data on the extent to which wives of boat owners contributed labour directly to the fishing enterprise. We found that the amount and kind of work contributed by wives has changed over the years. Since World War II they have become more involved in the bookkeeping tasks and less involved in production of supplies or processing of the catch.[44] Among the wives of the current boat owners, the most common involvement was in bookkeeping work (50-60 percent do books and bills) and running errands (50 percent). One quarter of the wives also arranged sales. Only 25 percent of wives now prepare meals for the men or ever fish with their husbands. Interestingly, in our sample we found no differences in the extent of involvement in the fishing enterprise between those wives who also held paid jobs and those who did not. From interviews with key informants in the communities we know that many of the larger independent fishers have their wives working as partners (often unpaid), running the business side of things. These households fit the traditional model of petty bourgeois, though of course the class position of these wives is still problematic.

When we examined the spousal work patterns for men who have been fish plant workers, we found that their wives were more likely to have a history of work outside the home than the wives of fishers. Almost three-quarters of the wives worked outside the home during the time the men were in the plant and almost forty percent worked in the plant at the same time as their husbands. The class position of most of these households thus appears to be working class, although as mentioned above many of the men would have also fished and some would have been boat owners, affecting their class identification.

It is also crucial to know the work patterns of the husbands of female plant workers. In our sample, 40 percent of the wives had worked in the fish plant at some time. There was great variation in the pattern of their husbands' work by community. In the larger ports (dominated by National Sea), the more common pattern was for husbands of female plant workers to work in the fish plant or do other wage work, whereas in the smaller ports the husbands were more likely to be fishers. We also found variation by age, with the younger generation more likely to have both husband and wife working in the fish plant.[45] This is particularly significant for class struggle in the processing sector, which we examine in the last section of the paper.

When we examined the current family work patterns in our sample,[46] we found that none of the wives of current boat owners were in the plant, though 63 percent were doing wage work.[47] This differed by area, with the wives of owners on the more prosperous South Shore more likely to be at home. We found that 18 percent of the wives of crew and 21 percent of the wives of male plant workers were in the plant,[48] again with differences by community.

Looking at the husbands of female plant workers, 46 percent were also in the plant, none were owners, 23 percent were crew, and 8 percent were unemployed or retired. In one medium size inshore port none of the female plant workers' husbands worked in the plant, and 75 percent were crew, whereas in the large National Sea dominated ports 67 percent and 80 percent of the husbands were also plant workers and none were crew. These differences by community should help explain observed differences in industrial relations.

In conclusion, our data illustrate the complexity of household class positions in the fishing industry. We find differences by community, which seem to be related to the nature of the fishery in each area (inshore/offshore, prosperous/marginal, corporate/independent). These differences also reflect the stage of capital accumulation, since the ports studied represent the spectrum from traditional small scale fishing to monopoly capital. We find some evidence that male work patterns have become more stable, with less movement between fishing, plant work and other work, at least in the more corporate communities. The evidence also suggests that clearer family class positions are emerging in the more corporate sectors of the industry. This means that the class interests of family members are compatible; for example, both are wage workers, or both are dependent on one income, whether it be from wage work or self-employment. Contradictory household class positions characterize the more marginal sectors of the industry, with the class interests of family members potentially conflicting. In such cases, the class identification of either spouse can deviate from what one might predict by observing only their individual relationship to the means of production. Unequal gender relations in the household and the workplace will affect what the dominant class interest in the family household will be and what the household strategy will be regarding the allocation of labour.

ANALYSIS OF PARTICULAR STRUGGLES

In this section we use particular examples from our community case studies to demonstrate that an expanded class analysis helps clarify the state of industry relations. In our first community, a medium size port, the fishers co-op built a processing plant in 1950. Fishers earned low incomes and their wives worked in the plant for low wages. The benefit of the co-op was that the people felt they were working for themselves and they were keeping some surplus in the community. Since the fishers owned the co-op and their wives worked in the plant there was a perception of it as a family affair; men caught the fish, women processed them. Therefore, despite the fact that women were doing working class jobs and earning low wages under poor conditions, the petty bourgeois class consciousness of the husbands prevailed and there was no talk of unionization in the plant. Women essentially saw themselves as family help (processing the catch) in a petty bourgeois enterprise.

In the early 1970s, as a result of untimely expansion followed by a refusal of the Nova Scotia government to provide support, the co-op was sold to private interests. This was a period of crisis in the fishery. Many fishers sold their boats and more women entered wage labour. Conditions in the plant worsened, if anything, under private management. But fishers needed to sell their fish to the plant and their wives, along with other women, needed the wage, so unionization was still not on the agenda. A fight for higher wages could have negatively affected the price of fish and even the sale of fish to the plant. Once again the family household work patterns affected the potential for working class consciousness and militancy of women wage workers.

When fishing improved and fishers' incomes rose in the late 1970s, it no longer made economic sense for wives of fishers to work for low wages in the plant. Rather than raise wages to keep the labour force, the owner (thanks to a government-supported ferry) was able to use a more marginal female labour supply in a nearby community. These women were married to men who had low paid, often seasonal jobs outside the fishery, such as cutting pulp or working on the roads. At first there was no sense of class consciousness among these women and no sign of resistance. They were grateful to have the work. The fishers' wives, as part of their household strategy, withdrew from the labour force even though some said they would have preferred to stay. In this case, the household strategy and gender relations within the household took precedence over women's wishes and employers needs.

In the 1980s the plant ceased buying fresh fish from local fishers and began to process northern cod to supply a fast food chain in the USA. A new manager was hired to double productivity and increase the quality of fish, with no corresponding increase in pay for the workers. Women on the line bore the brunt of these changes. Most of the women from the nearby community were the most stable, if not the main, breadwinners in their households. They were unprepared to continue working under deteriorating conditions and they sent for a union organizer. The employer's response was to threaten to close the plant. The women called the employer on his threat and after a lengthy struggle the union was certified.

When we first interviewed these women several years ago they showed no signs of militancy of any sort. In this case, however, the women's class position was not only the dominant one in their households, but as well the position of their husbands was not in conflict. As a result, their household strategy reflected a working class consciousness and led to working class struggle.

We next illustrate the implications of this approach for clarifying class relations in the industry with a brief case study of another community, a larger fishing port which has been an industry centre for over a hundred years. It has had two large processing plants since the early nineteen hundreds, one of which is a National Sea plant, recently modernized. The plants have been the largest employers for the town and surrounding area. It had an offshore fleet until the early 1970s when National Sea consolidated its fleet in other ports. Recent years have seen the rise of a few successful midshore boats, owned by independents.

Up until World War II, no women were employed in the fish plants, though they worked in the service/trade sectors. Most married women did not work outside the home. The early pattern for men, when processing was minimal, was to crew on the schooners and then do small boat fishing as part of a package of subsistence activities. This pattern seemed to follow both seasonal and cyclical lines, with men doing a combination of inshore and offshore fishing over a period of years, including going away to fish. In the period between the two World Wars, the men were increasingly involved in processing (wage work), and there was also an increase in small boat fishing as well as a continuation of work in company-owned offshore boats. The incomes and social standing of the fishers (inshore and offshore) and the fish-handlers seems to have been equally low, and men moved between these two types of work. In this context, it is not surprising that in the organizing efforts of the 1930s, fishhandlers and fishers (offshore) formed one union and waged an ardent, lengthy, but ultimately unsuccessful, struggle for recognition. These men had a shared class consciousness. Furthermore, they were strongly supported in their fight by their wives.

After their bitter defeat, and after World War II, relations changed in the industry. More men turned to inshore fishing, moving between crew and owner status. Increasingly, once they got their own boats they were almost exclusively self-employed, though a few ended their working lives in the plant. At the same time, the companies began hiring women in the plants, a change variously explained by the labour shortage of the war and by technological changes in processing. It is our opinion that the change had also to do with the bitter labour struggles which had just occurred and the companies' desire to maintain its cheap (docile) labour policy.

The ensuing period saw much more passive labour relations in the community. Many wives of the fishers who sold to the companies now worked in the fish plant. These fishers were in dependent commodity production, tied to the companies who had monopsony power as buyers.[49] They were further tied by their wives' wage work in the plants, and often by the work of their children.[50] The companies had considerable leverage over these families. In terms of consciousness, it seems that these inshore fishers developed more of a bourgeois consciousness of "independence," facilitated by their wives' proletarianization. The combination was not conducive to political action on either front — in the plants or on the boats.

When we look at changes in the community in the last twenty years, we find that gradually less and less wives of fishers worked at the plant. This is partly due to higher incomes for fishers in the area. More and more the male labour force is being divided between boat owners, crew and plant workers, with less movement among these positions. A further trend is for the number of boat owners to decrease, so that more and more men are in a working class position in terms of their own relation to the means of production. The men who remain as boat owners have been able to achieve more independence from the companies, due to the rise of the fresh fish market and independent buyers. They are also less tied to the companies through family links, for increasingly their wives do not work in the plants.

Most male plant workers' wives worked outside the home throughout the post-War period; however, only in recent years have they tended to work in the plant. Increasingly the trend has been towards husband/wife teams in the plant, and for the female plant workers to be married to plant workers rather than to fishers.[51] There are also many female plant workers who come from outside the community and who are typically married to men not involved in the fishing industry (working at low-wage jobs), or are single parents. In terms of the family class orientation of the plant workforce, then, it has become more clearly working class in recent years.

How has this affected relations in the plant? Relations between workers and management have been very bad in recent years. The paternalistic strategy which the company successfully employed in the past is no longer used, nor is it workable. The withdrawal of fishers' wives from the plant probably contributed to this, as it did in the community discussed above. The corporate strategy as described by both the company and the workers is much like any capitalist labour strategy. Class struggle in the plant has become more pronounced, the lines more sharply drawn. The company's strategies include technological change, speed-ups and dividing the labour force through recruitment strategy. During one of our visits, this seemed to be working in capital's favour, for the workforce was demoralized and frightened for their jobs. However, a later visit reassured us that class struggle was alive and well, and there was more sign of resistance by the workers who, as analyzed above, have a fairly clear class position.[52] Resistance has mainly taken the form of turnover and individualized responses to the bad conditions. The company is feeling the effects.[53] These workers have a great deal of potential power, although, as usual in an underdeveloped region, this is offset by the pressure of a reserve labour force. Management is looking for a more desperate workforce (single parents, women whose husbands are unemployed). They also have the ever-present option of closing the plant. At the time of writing, after our fieldwork was completed, there was a strike in this plant, confirming our expectation that clearer household class positions should facilitate increased worker resistance.

CONCLUSION

The theoretical debates about class and the literature on class structure and struggle in the fishing industry focus on the individual at one point in time and ignore both women's unpaid and paid work, the family household and gender relations. Feminist research, on the other hand, has shown the importance of these issues to class analysis. In this paper, we have argued that women's work, gender relations and household strategies are necessary to understanding class relations and class struggle in the fishery.

Using data from our study of fishing communities we have explored ways of modifying class analysis using the family household as a unit of analysis. Class is a dynamic and complex relationship affecting, in the majority of cases, women and men who live together in unequal gender relations within households. By looking at women's and men's work histories (domestic and wage labour) and their family work patterns and strategies, we are better able to understand their class position and their class consciousness. Using the household as the unit of analysis, it appears that class conditions gender relations and gender conditions class relations. The challenge for political economy is to more fully understand these processes. Research is needed on the dynamics of family decision-making, the formation of class consciousness, and the interaction of class and gender interests at the level of the family.

In this paper we have illustrated in a preliminary way the implications of class positions and class struggles in the fishing industry. We have demonstrated that an expanded class analysis clarifies the state of relations in the industry. Insights are gained which go beyond those possible using the traditional, individually-based class framework of most Marxist analysis.

ENDNOTES

We would like to thank the people in the communities we studied and the members of our research team, Joyce Conrad, Suzan Ilcan, Beth McIsaac, Kathy Moggridge and Daphne Tucker for their contributions. This research was supported by a Social Sciences and Humanities Research Council Women and Work Strategic Grant and by the Donner Canadian foundation. All papers out of this joint research are co-authored, with alternating order of names.

1. This accusation has been made of much of the debate over the proper class location of the "new middle class." It has also been made of the "domestic labour debate"; see, for example, Eva Kaluzynska, "Wiping the Floor With Theory" *Feminist Review* 6 (1980).

2. There are, of course, many class-related issues in the feminist literature which we do not address in this paper. For example, we focus more on struggles in the sphere of production than on intra-family relations and domestic labour.

3. We are referring particularly to the literature on a reevaluation of Marxian class categories, such as Eric Olin Wright, "Class Boundaries in Advanced Capitalist Societies," *New Left Review* 98 (1976) pp. 3-41 and *Class, Crisis and the State* (London: 1978); as well as Nicos Poulantzas, *Political Power and Social Class* (London: 1973). See also attempts to enumerate the class composition of Canada, such as Wallace Clement, *Class, Power and Property: Essays on Canadian Society* (Toronto: 1983); and Henry Veltmeyer, *Canadian Class Structure* (Toronto: 1986). The literature on class consciousness takes more account of formative factors such as father's occupation. For an interesting example of such work on the fishery see Trevor Lummis, *Occupation and Society, The East Anglian Fisherman, 1880-1914* (Cambridge: 1984).

4. See John Goldthorpe, "Women and Class Analysis: In Defence of the Conventional View," *Sociology* 17/4 (November 1983).

5. Veltmeyer, *Canadian Class Structure*, summarizes the positions. One approach is to add all these workers to the traditional working class, since all are dependent on selling their labour power. However, it seems that the identification and interests of these workers is often more similar to the capitalist class than the working class. Some writers thus emphasize the similarities between this group and capital, either in terms of their real economic control (though not ownership) of the

means of production, their ownership of significant "human" capital, or their control over their own or other people's labour. Depending on the factors emphasized, the group is then viewed as forming a new class (either a professional-managerial class, as argued by Barbara and John Ehrenreich, "The Professional-Managerial Class" in Pat Walker (ed.), *Between Capital and Labour* (Montreal: 1978), or a new middle class, as argued by G. Carchedi, "On the Economic Identification of the New Middle Class," *Economy and Society* 4/1 (1975), or occupying a contradictory class position, as in Wright, "Class Boundaries," or being part of the petty bourgeoisie, as in Poulantzas, *Political Power and Social Class* and Judah Hill, *Class Analysis; United States in the 1970s* (San Fransisco: 1975). Veltmeyer, *Canadian...*, and Clement, *Class...*, essentially take the latter position, at the same time acknowledging the contradictory aspects of their class location.

6.   There are debates about the definition of petty bourgeois, for example, whether they may purchase any labour power; there is some disagreement about their relation to the working class and whether they can be part of a progressive alliance for social change; there is also interest in the evolution of this class, whether it would whither away or stubbornly persist.

7.   The problem of classifying fishers on the East Coast is reflected in the law, where until recently all fishers were excluded from trade union legislation and classified as co-adventurers (self-employed), based on the fact that crew are paid on a share basis rather than with a wage. Newfoundland was the first to change the law, so that all fishers (other than captains on big company trawlers) are now able to be members of the union. Nova Scotia changed the law in 1971 for crew on large trawlers.

8.   Rick Williams, "Inshore Fishermen, Unionization, and the Struggle Against Underdevelopment," in R.J. Brym and R.J. Sacouman (eds.), *Underdevelopment and Social Movements in Atlantic Canada* (Toronto: 1979); James Sacouman, "Semi-Proletarianization and Rural Underdevelopment in the Maritimes," *Canadian Review of Sociology and Anthropology* 17/3 (Spring 1984).

9.   Wallace Clement, *The Struggle to Organize: Resistance in Canada's Fishery* (Toronto: 1986).

10. Rick Williams, "Implications of Political Economic/Class Position of Inshore Fishermen for Development of the Maritime Fishermen's Union," Unpublished paper, Halifax, 1982.

11. *Ibid.*

12. Bryant Fairley, "The Struggle for Capitalism in the Fishing Industry in Newfoundland," *Studies in Political Economy* 17 (1985), pp.33-70.

13. Sacouman,"Semi-proletarianization..."; Williams, "Inshore Fishermen..."; Fairley, "The Struggle for Capitalism...."

14. Fairley, "The Struggle for Capitalism...," argues that the NFFAW is dominated by the larger boat owners and the union's agenda has become the development of capitalist production in the fishery. Most other Marxists argue that the contradictory class position of fishers means there is the potential for more progressive organization and struggle in the industry. Both Williams, "Implications of Political Economic...," and Clement, *The Struggle to Organize*, emphasize the mixture of working class and independent commodity producer ideology in fishers' attempts to organize and in the issues they pursue. Peter Sinclair, "Fishermen of Northwest Newfoundland," *Journal of Canadian Studies* 19/1 (Spring 1984) argues that for Newfoundland the direction of development seems to include both an increase in small capital (as emphasized by Fairley) and a growth of dependent commodity production (as emphasized by Sacouman and Williams).

15. A literature on women and fishing that begins to redress this imbalance, and of which this research is a part, is now emerging. Gradually all researchers working on the political economy of the fishery are being sensitized to the need to include gender in their analyses.

16. See, for example, Pat and Hugh Armstrong, "Beyond Sexless Class and Classless Sex: Towards Feminist Marxism," *Studies in Political Economy* 10 (1983) pp.45-72.

17. See, for example, Bonnie Fox (ed.), *Hidden in the Household: Women's Domestic Labour Under Capitalism* (Toronto: 1980).

18. See Christine Delphy, *The Main Enemy* (London: 1977) and *Close to Home* (London: 1984).

19. Sylvia Walby, *Patriarchy at Work* (Cambridge: 1986).

20. See Jane Humphries and Jill Rubery, "The Reconstruction of the Supply Side of the Labour Market: The Relative Autonomy of Social Reproduction," *Cambridge Journal of Economics* 8/4 (1984).

21. See M. Coulson, B Magas and H Wainwright, "The Housewife and Her Labour Under Capitalism — A Critique," *New Left Review* 89 (1975).

22. See J. Gardiner, "Women's Domestic Labour," *New Left Review* 89 (1975) and Joan Acker, "Class, Gender and the Relations Of Distribution," *Signs* 13/3 (Spring 1988).

23. This is well illustrated in Anna Pollert, "Women, Gender Relations and Wage Labour" in Eva Gamarnikow *et al* (eds.), *Gender, Class and Work* (London: 1983).

24. See, for example, the studies in Eleanor Leacock and Helen Safa (eds.), *Women's Work: Development and the Division of Labour.* (Massachusetts: 1986).

25. Lourdes Beneria and Gita Sen, "Accumulation, Reproduction and Women's Role in Economic Development: Boserup Revisited," *Signs* 7/2 (1981) pp. 279-99.

26. Dorothy Smith, "Feminist Reflections on Political Economy," paper presented to the Political Economy Sessions, Canadian Political Science Association, Learned Societies Conference, McMaster University, Hamilton, 1987.

27. See, for example, Acker, "Class, Gender..."; Delphy, *Close to Home*; Michelle Stanworth, "Women and Class Analysis — A Reply to Goldthorpe," *Sociology* 18/2 (May 1984); Marilyn Porter, *Home, Work and Class Consciousness* (Manchester: 1983).

28. This continues to be resisted, and the traditional approach defended, by some leading class theorists (Goldthorpe,1983). See Anne Phillips, *Divided Loyalties: Dilemmas of Sex and Class.* (London: 1987) for a discussion.

29. Lourdes Beneria and Martha Roldan, *The Crossroads of Class and Gender. Housework, Subcontracting and Household Dynamics in Mexico City* (Chicago: 1987).

30. Nicky Britten and Anthony Heath, "Women, Men and Social Class" in Gamarnikow *et al* (eds.), *Women, Men and Social Class*, pp. 46-61.

31. Williams, "Inshore Fishermen, Unionization...," p 162.

32. One relevant determinant of class consciousness is of course class of origin, routinely decided with reference to father's occupation. The influence of mothers on children's future class identification should equally be investigated.

33. This is sometimes recognized in the literature on unionization, for example. The point is often made that women are not interested in unions because of their short commitment to the job, or because their experience in household work gives them an ideology of "independence."

34. Fox, (ed.), *Hidden in the Household.*

35. This has been explored in many case studies of women and the labour process. A good example is Anna Pollert's study of tobacco plant workers in Pollert, "Women, Gender Relations..."

36. Wallace Clement, "The Limits of Cooperation: Strategies for Fisheries Development," paper delivered at Social Research and Policy Formation in the Fisheries: Norwegian and Atlantic Canadian Experiences, An International Working Seminar, University of Tromso, Tromso, Norway, 1986.

37. Jane Humphries, "The Working Class Family, Women's Liberation and Class Struggle: The Case of Nineteenth Century British History," *The Review of Radical Political Economics* 9/3 (1977).

38. Patricia Connelly and Martha MacDonald, "The Impact of State Policy on Women's Work in the Fishery" in Hugh Armstrong (ed.) *Women and the State.* (Montreal: forthcoming).

39. The data was collected from 1984 to 1986 and included a household survey which focused on family work patterns, including paid and unpaid work (n=150). In addition we conducted oral history interviews and interviews with key informants, including fish plant managers.

40. We focus on spousal work patterns both because of their theoretical importance in discussions of class and gender and for empirical reasons. Our data is from a project focusing on women, and our universe for sampling purposes was all households with adult females. As it turned out, only one of our respondents was a single (never married) woman.

41. We divided our sample into three age cohorts, those born since 1950, those born between 1930 and 1949, and those born prior to 1930. Our interest in community in this paper is to document that there are community differences in work patterns which relate to community differences in observed class relations. Given the primary focus of this paper and limitations of space, we are not able to discuss the detailed differences among communities, or the theoretical role of community in class analysis.

42. Our sample was a random sample of households (with adult females) in each community, therefore not every household was necessarily involved in the fishing industry. However, of the male spouses in our sample, only 25 percent had no work history involvement in the fishery.

43. Lummis, *Occupation and Society...*, in a study of East Anglia fishermen considers the boatowners to have a predominantly working class consciousness.

44. Wives of men who owned boats prior to World War II mainly knit lobster heads (75 percent), cooked meals (75 percent), cleaned and salted fish (38 percent) and sometimes fished with their husbands (63 percent). In the period from the War to 1970, 25 percent helped with bookkeeping, while running errands, knitting lob-

ster heads and salting fish declined in importance. Preparing meals remained an important job (77 percent). Fewer women fished with their husbands in this period (31 percent). The pattern remained similar from 1970 to the present for wives whose husbands owned boats during that period.

45. Other papers based on this research examine the sexual division of labour in the plants. There are many differences in the way the husbands and wives experience the labour process, even if they work together in the same plant.

46. Of the men, 22 percent are in the plant, 22 percent are fishing, 29 percent are in other wage work, and 27 percent are retired or unemployed. Of the women, 10 percent are in the plant, 27 percent are in other wage work, and 62 percent are at home (including retired). There is considerable variation in the labour force participation rates of the women under age 65 by community, ranging from 25 percent to 60 percent.

47. Our sample of current boat owners is very small. Our key informant interviews in the communities indicated that in the smaller communities many fishers' wives do still work in the plant.

48. There is wide variation by type of crew in whether wives of crew work outside the home. Wives of offshore crew, who earn good money and are away for extended periods, tend to stay home, whereas wives of inshore crew, particularly in the smaller ports, have a high labour force participation rate. There is also a life cycle effect, of course, with younger wives more likely to be home with small children.

49. Williams,"Implications of Political Economic/Class Position of Inshore Fishermen..."; and Clement, *The Struggle to Organize.*

50. It is our estimation that only 20 percent of the fishing families in our sample from this community who were born before 1930 and had their own boats after the War survived solely on the income from "independent" inshore fishing. There was often a seasonal pattern to the work of wives and children in the plants, with older children working in the summer while mothers stayed home to look after the younger children who were out of school at that time.

51. Today we see a situation in which all the young male plant workers' wives in our sample have worked in the plant in the last two years; furthermore, two-thirds of the husbands of the female plant workers in our sample also worked in the plant.

52. There are still gender differences in the experience of class of the men and women, which affect the possibility of unified action. See, for example, Pollert, "Women, Gender Relations..."

53. One manager gave an analysis of the power that two-earner families have. He

said that neither one feels the responsibility of a primary earner — the women quit for periods of time and want their jobs back, and the men are increasingly slacking off in other ways, such as absenteeism.

CHAPTER 3

FIFTY YEARS A FEMINIST TRADE UNIONIST: AN INTERVIEW

MADELEINE PARENT

Madeleine Parent's long career as feminist and activist began when, as a student at McGill University in the late 1930s, she campaigned for scholarships for both poor women and men. She went on to become a union organizer in war industry and in the textile industry in Quebec, where her activities led to her arrest on a number of occasions. In the 1950s, along with Kent Rowley (her long time associate in union organization and her spouse) and other working people, she co-founded a Canadian textile workers union, and, in 1969, a Canadian union centre, the Confederation of Canadian Unions. In 1972, she attended the founding meeting of the National Action Committee on the Status of Women and continues to be active in that organization. In 1983, at age 65, she retired from her union position. At present, she is Quebec representative to the National Action Committee (NAC) and co-chair of its committee in support of Native Women. She is also a member of the Coordinating Committee of Solidarité Populaire Quebec, a coalition of community organizations, church groups and unions.

Madeleine Parent has made and continues to make an enormous contribution to the improvement of women's position in Canada. From her long history of involvement in the student movement, the union movement and the women's movement, we can learn a great deal about the struggle for gender, class and ethnic/racial equality. In this new conservative era, when there are fewer new victories and hard won gains are being eroded, learning from the knowledge and experience of people like Madeleine Parent in order to develop future strategies becomes more important than ever. With this in mind Pat Connelly, assisted by Marilyn Keddy of the Women's Action Coalition of Nova Scotia, interviewed Madeleine Parent for SPE. The interview focused on Madeleine's experience and her ideas about where, with whom and on what issues to struggle.

SPE: When did you begin to think of yourself as a feminist?

MP: I, like most women, learned by my experience in life to become a feminist. I can be sure I was a feminist during my years at college in Montreal, when it was quite clear that on the campus at McGill University, men were the predominant force and of predominant significance and women took second place. I joined the student movement at a time when we were fighting for free scholarships for young men and women of poor families. That in itself was quite radical and I, like some other women, insisted that the scholarships, if they were won, should go both to women and men because women had a right to an education and they had a right to learn to make a better living for themselves just as men did.

There was a concept then that boys would have to be the providers for their families. Lawyers, doctors, and politicians were men and therefore, wasn't it a waste to educate women who were going to grow up to marry, stay home and bear children? Within the student movement a growing number of feminists amongst us were very clear that bright girls must have the same opportunity to free scholarships as bright boys did. It was also clear that, except in particular women's organizations, males were expected to be the spokespersons for student groups. If my memory serves me, all the co-educational student clubs or associations on campus were presided over by males.

When the Second World War started, the position was that you had to sacrifice everything for the war. The whole movement for free scholarships for poor students was gravely assaulted. It dwindled down to a small, but strong core of people who retained their convictions. It became obvious to me that the idea of higher education that prevailed in our society was that sons of the rich or families of professionals had a right to a higher education but others did not have that same right. Women, whether from rich or poor families, but especially from poor families, did not have a right to a higher education and it would be a waste to give it to them. Of course, if one's parents could and would pay the high cost of their daughter's education, it was different.

SPE: So as a student you were already fighting for poor women and men.

MP: Yes. I was, of course, also part of the French minority on McGill campus and that was interesting because a lot of those amongst the minority of French students tended to be discrete about their French identity. To assert your position as a francophone, which I did, was far from being prevalent on campus. Many of us francophone students met with Irish Catholic students at the Newman Club, the Catholic student club. It was in identifying yourself as a francophone that you ran into racial prejudice and realized the arrogance of a fair number of anglophone people on campus.

SPE: This was a very strong position for a young woman to be taking in those days. Was this difficult for you to do?

MP: I was sent to convent when I was very young and was educated continuously in convents. It was just in the last two years before college that I attended an English school to prepare for McGill. One could not go to Laval or to Montreal University to earn a B.A. at that time. There were no co-educational schools in undergraduate studies under Quebec's then Catholic school system. I would have been obliged to continue those studies with the nuns, where Voltaire, Rousseau and others were forbidden reading. I had found the constraints of convent life unacceptable so I decided to go to McGill. By the time I reached McGill it was quite natural for me to want to be myself and that meant standing up for what I believe in.

SPE: Did your parents support and encourage you?

MP: My parents were quite proud and always felt that nobody should lord it over anyone else. They made me feel the same way. They respected my independence of thought, even though they didn't necessarily agree with my approach to things. In the 1940s and 50s, when textile workers came under attack from the bosses and Quebec Premier Duplessis, my arrests and trials were painful to them but they supported me and refused to submit to pressures from government to denounce me.

SPE: After your student days did you go directly into the Union movement?

MP: I decided when I was on the McGill campus that I wanted to work with working people, especially with factory, blue collar workers. I realized that if I did not organize I would be limited to a secretarial job or a technical job where I would not be with the rank and file. I did not want that. As a student, I was involved in the youth movement which had within it a strong component of union people (of young women's groups and of students' groups). I first taught evening classes, with the Workers Educational Association, for trade unionists, women in the garment industry. Some time after war broke out, I joined the organizing drive in war industry. That was in the spring of 1942. The AFL unions, which were the predominant unions in Quebec at the time, launched this drive following the organization of some 25,000 aircraft workers in Quebec. I helped to organize workers in the munitions, shell filling, and gun powder industry in Quebec. The companies exploited a large number of women. The largest was at St. Paul l'Ermite, east of the island of Montreal which at its pinnacle had over 13,000 workers.

From there, I joined Kent Rowley in organizing amongst textile workers, especially cotton-mill workers. Women were not the majority but they were a strong component making up 40 percent or so of the workforce. I also helped in organizing women amongst the tobacco workers, and in other sectors but textile was my concern. I still keep in contact with textile workers and occasionally run into daughters and sons of old textile union members, in community activities and demonstrations. They tell me of their pride in parents who fought for social justice before them.

SPE: Did you focus mainly on women in your organizing work?

MP: I worked with both women and men but a special effort was required to ensure the presence and the indispensable participation of women in the unions and to have them appreciated by their fellow workers. Women needed to be encouraged to join, to feel at home within the union and to feel that they did not have to take a back seat to anyone. It took particular efforts for women to recognize that their experiences at work, in the factory and even in their daily lives, were just as important as those of men and that they should be equal in the work place and in their union.

SPE: Were the men supportive of your efforts to organize women?

MP: They were supportive but in the beginning some of the mechanics in the factories took for granted that they would have the leadership in the union. The mechanics were the highest paid. They were the skilled tradesmen in the industry. Fortunately in Valleyfield, where Kent Rowley started the campaign, he found one particular mechanic, Treffle Leduc, who appreciated the role women textile workers had played in the 1937 general strike of cotton mill workers in Quebec. He was strongly in agreement with Kent and with myself that women had to be encouraged to organize. He became president of our largest local union and gave good leadership on this issue.

I started off the organizing drive in the Merchants' Mill of the Dominion Textile Company, located on the Lachine Canal in Montreal. Skilled tradesmen and mechanics tended to assume that they would have the leadership. I got them around to telling the story of how women fought on picket lines in the strike of '37 and I got them to give me names of some of those brave women. With this information, I was able to visit the women individually. They were motivated to get into the organizing campaign and soon felt at home. You had to consciously work at involving women and then follow through.

SPE: The women did not stand back because they thought it was the men's role to run the union?

MP: Oh, no! They realized the men thought it was their role, that is, not the young men, but the mechanics and the skilled tradesmen. Women who had picketed in the 1937 strike understood that there was a place for women in the unions and they had to make that place for themselves. They had a lot of staying power, partly because women do not have that many choices in jobs. Once into it, they had the feeling that it was their union. They stood their ground.

SPE: Did women have difficulty participating in the union meetings?

MP: Yes, but women came in groups. If the union meeting was in the evening or in the daytime, after work or before the night shift, men could walk into a union hall individually but women would come to the hall in groups of threes or fours or by departments. They sat together because they wanted to consult with each other. When they spoke, you had a feeling that they were not asking for themselves individually but as part of the group they sat with. Women were also very effective at organizing young people. We had children in the mills. The legal age to go to work was 14 in Quebec in the 1940s, but there were in fact many children who were 12, 13 years old. There were even 10-year-olds working in the factories! They would borrow the birth certificate of an older sister or brother to get a job and they came to union meetings. Women, who were very good at teaching the children how to work, were good at recruiting them into the union and at explaining issues to them. The women already had their confidence and used to look out for them in the face of industrial hazards.

SPE: There must have been unions that didn't put any special emphasis on the role of women.

MP: Of course that was the case even in unions where women had organized, for example the International Ladies Garment Workers Union. Women were deeply involved in the organizing drives and strikes that made that union. Once the union had its contracts and had in fact a closed shop, women became second class members. I'm not speaking about the Rand Formula which didn't exist then. The closed shop meant that the union hall was in fact the hiring hall and any worker who had been laid off was not recalled to a job in a factory unless the union recommended that worker for the job. The union, once it had achieved that power, relegated the women to a very secondary position. For example, women, who made up about three-quarters of the work-force in garment factories, were nearly all on piece-work. The speed and accuracy of their performance was the greatest immediate factor in increasing the company's profit. Therefore, women who resisted the speeding-up of work, increasing work-loads, and cut-backs in piece-rates were to be discredited among their sisters, or removed. Garment bosses, once obliged to accept the union, found a thousand ways to endear themselves to a few (mainly male) union business managers and agents, to ensure they did not support women who fought the injustices of the piece-work system. Thus, a bureaucratic leadership in the union tended to discourage and disperse women activists and to make things more secure for themselves and more profitable for the employers.

SPE: For 41 years you worked within the union movement. In general, how would you describe the role of women over these years?

MP: Where you had councils of unions, for example, a central labour council in the city, a provincial federation of labour and a labour congress Canada wide, the higher you went, the fewer women you found, and the less power they had. A few women would be delegated to certain councils within a union, but the elected body was usually made up mainly of men. It was about 1944 or so that I became the first woman elected to the Montreal Trades and Labour Council executive. The argument against my election was that the Council was no place for a woman because some men came in drunk to meetings and they swore. My position was, that's the men's problem not the women's problem. I was elected. The Central labour bodies were known to be a place for men. On the provincial federation of labour bodies and in their conventions, the International Ladies Garment Workers, for example, would tend to bring in women to that convention not on a Friday, and not so much for Saturdays deliberations, but for the Saturday night dance and for the Sunday morning vote. The women heard very little and participated very little in the actual debates on the issues in those conferences and conventions, so they were expected to vote under their leaders' direction. When we went to the Trades and Labour Congress convention, there were even fewer women and no women were elected to the main bodies. If you wanted to get up and speak on an issue at a conference, your first words had to attract people's attention right away. If they didn't, you were given the hook. You had to count on the audience getting your point immediately and supporting your right to speak. It was difficult, but it turned out to be good training for those who survived.

SPE: Were there no women's groups within any of the unions at that time?

MP: There were no Women's Committees. If the union had a lot of women members, and if, as in our case, those women were a strong part of the delegation, then we fought for our right to speak up. I was the only woman on the Resolutions Committee of the Quebec Federation of Labour. I was on the committee from the late 1940s. I was on it because our textile union, in alliance with delegates from other unions, such as the Tobacco Workers' Union and the Canadian Seaman's Union and others, supported my being there as a woman and also because it was the only way to get a progressive on the Resolutions Committee. Union leaders in the garment industry tried to influence the choice of token women as delegates. In debates, these token women just couldn't stand up. They had to be rescued by their male leaders, and when the issue was a feminist one, they were a pretty sight!

SPE: But as the years went by more women did get included in the various committees and councils of their unions.

MP: Many women did get included in these bodies because we were fighting on certain issues and members wanted us there. Some of the things we fought for, for example, were the single wage classification lists. Prior to our winning that, factories had a wage classification list for men and a wage classification list for women and for children. We wanted one wage, one job and that issue was won in Quebec cotton mills, as a result of our 1946 strike. This still did not give us equal pay for work of equal value but at least it was equal pay for equal work. Even though it was not written into the law or in the contract, we often won maternity leave in practice. Paid maternity leave is a different issue, but we won *de facto* maternity leave by united action on the shop floor. For example, in a given department, women would stage a going away party for a sister who was getting ready to leave to have a baby. They would put the boss on the spot and make sure that the pregnant woman had a job to return to. In war time, because the government needed female labour everywhere, we had won six weeks maternity leave. That was an early recognition of the principle of maternity leave. Employers had to encourage women to go back to their jobs, because they needed their labour. War time was no time to bring in immigrants to fill job vacancies, so they had to make do with what they had. What they had was the reserve labour pool constituted by those women who stayed at home or who were in domestic service or in other low paid jobs.

SPE: What happened in the unions after the war?

MP: First, there were huge layoffs in war industry. Then, the boys returned from the armed forces. They were given places again in industries, often at the expense of women. Women suffered most from post-war layoffs and from having to give up their non-traditional jobs to the veterans in the midst of a massive re-structuring of Quebec industry. There was a tremendous drive to prevent women from holding on to their war-time gains.

SPE: And the unions supported this?

MP: The lay offs coincided with the development of a witch-hunt. The witch-hunt in the labour movement was directed at taking union labour down a peg, taking away from them a new bargaining strength that they had gained in war time, making it costly to strike and trying to force workers to go backwards or at least to stop their progress. In the United States, Joe McCarthy and his House Committee on "Un-American Activities" led the attack on all militants, in unions and in other democratic organizations. As a majority of union members in Canada belonged to US unions in those days, the witch-hunt extended to the North. Those Canadian union leaders who were subservient to their US officers supported the witch-hunt, some of which was directed at women's rights. In Quebec part of this witch-hunt involved a renewed drive against abortion, and the persecution of doctors who performed abortions illegally but who had been quietly tolerated during war time because industry needed women's work. War-time childcare centres were mostly shut down. There was a regressive trend, fostered by the Duplessis Government in Quebec, encouraged by the Mackenzie King government, for the benefit of large corporations. Women were encouraged to go back home. Many did not have much choice but to go back. Some women, in what were higher paid war industries, were pushed back to lower paid industries such as textiles, tobacco, food preparation or to domestic service. Domestic service didn't work out as well as wealthy people would have liked because once you have worked in a factory you don't like to go back into quasi bondage.

SPE: How did the men in the unions at this time deal with the fact that it was women who were experiencing so much of the pressure that was applied in this regressive period?

MP: That depended on the union. It was a period of general attack on union rights; in some unions the leadership tried to win the acceptance of corporations and governments. In these unions men were encouraged to accept what was happening, and not to defend the lowest paid people in their ranks — that is the women and the young people and, later, post-war immigrants. Whereas, in unions like our own the women had a strong position and were very vocal. We went out on strike when we considered it necessary. In the strike the women shone brightly; they were persistent fighters. When picketers' ranks declined because a strike lasted longer than was expected, it was mainly young men and some skilled men who would go and find jobs elsewhere. The women tended to stick to the picket lines until the end. In these unions, the women gained the respect of men and the witch-hunt against the lower-paid did not succeed. Many unions in Quebec at that time fought against the repression.

SPE: So in unions where women had already achieved strong positions during the war, men tended to be more supportive.

MP: Yes, but of course some industries which had been converted to war production were reconverted for much smaller production in peace time. These industries had huge layoffs, mainly of women. The unions in these industries found themselves with a much smaller contingent of women and some of the men forgot what the women had done during the war.

SPE: What has happened in the union movement in more recent times?

MP: Women, though they've been paid precious little, have, of course, always earned their living while looking after their family, bringing up children, and doing the unpaid work in the home. But over the years more and more women who had depended on a man found their marriage breaking up. These women were thrown onto the work force with very little preparation and few skills that were helpful in getting a decent job. It became clear that women had to fight for better rights and conditions on the job and for equal pay. They recognized that they needed to fight for maternity leave, that is, the right to go back to their jobs and eventually, for paid maternity and parental leave.

There are, then, several factors for increasing numbers of women going into the workforce. First, there is their own need to earn a living for themselves and for their children. Then, in the 1950s and into the 60s, labour's persistent demands for greater social security, finally brought us social programs such as free public health care, better social welfare benefits, universal old age pensions and eventually, the Canada Pension Plan and the Quebec Pension Plan and pension supplements for the needy. This increase in social programs meant that there were many more jobs created to administer these programs, especially in health care and in welfare, and there were more government jobs required to deliver and monitor these programs. These new jobs were in the majority filled by women. The public sector in Quebec is now made up of nurses and health care workers, of teachers from elementary classes right up to Ph.D.s, of social welfare workers and provincial civil servants. Two thirds of this work-force of some 350,000 are women. There was a huge development in union organization particularly in the latter part of the '60s and on into the '70s in the public sector.

The public sector mainly organized into Quebec unions or Canadian unions. This meant that the leadership was within our country, and therefore power within those unions was more accessible to the members. The possibility of criticism and of changing the direction of the union, even in shaping the constitution, was more accessible to the workers. That helped to build a greater presence of women within our union movement. From then on women were much more visible. Of course, some powerful male union bureaucrats, as they saw the participation of women and the strength of women within unions grow, tried to influence the situation by favouring token women and pushing them forward. Some of these token women did go forward and still are in the administration and leadership of a few unions. But increasingly, women are chosen by women within the trade union movement, and have the support of men. In the lower echelons, rank and file women have more say, women are taking responsibilities and women are taking office. This is moving up the scale as well. Today we have some outstanding women who are spokespersons within the trade union movement. Women are the main leaders and spokespersons of the three main unions involved in public sector negotiations with the Quebec government this year. It is an historical landmark.

SPE: Do you think it is important for women to work within today's union movements even though many of the unions are still male dominated, or do you think women should develop their own unions?

MP: I don't think women should develop separate unions. That would be dividing the ranks of the working people. Working people have to develop and maintain unity and the bargaining power to negotiate the best conditions with their employers. But I think it is very important that within unions, women set up women's committees so that they can get together to exchange views about their own experiences at work, to discuss their particular problems as child bearers, and to be united on the demands they want their union to make. By being more united themselves, women can have a stronger and more consistent voice within union meetings where decisions are made. They can also decide who amongst the women members they will support for office. They will want women officers who will address the issues of particular concern for their gender, such as paid maternity leave, paid parental leave, equal pay, job equity, discrimination against minority women in their ranks and other issues. Every union, even if it is a predominantly female union should have a Women's Committee. With a Women's Committee they can develop the issues and bring them to the membership. Certainly, where women don't already hold equal power, it is very important that they have a Women's Committee. Women very often will not address issues that make for their greater exploitation unless they can get together to do it. I find also that a Women's Committee tends to give younger women the opportunity to learn something about the history of their union and how they achieved maternity leave and equal pay, if they have achieved it. If there is no Women's Committee, women who are new will tend to take their union's achievements for granted and will be less watchful about maintaining gains when employers try to force them to take cut-backs. A strong Women's Committee will also alert and organize women members for action when bureaucratic tendencies among the officers are destroying the democratic process within the union itself. This could result in changes where more women are elected to responsible positions by the rank and file.

SPE: What advice would you give to women in groups, like transition houses, who want to unionize?

MP: I think it is true to say that many of the social services that are established and accepted, mainly or partly financed by governments today, originated with the volunteer work of women. Women knew that there was a need for these services and they just got together and provided them. Most of these women were unpaid. But where they could, they raised money and worked on very, very low budgets. Transition houses are still at the stage where they are not recognized as a necessary social service for women who are victims of family problems or of male violence. Women may have to go there for shelter or to reorganize themselves. Mothers may have to go there to protect their children. To operate these shelters, many women provide a lot of volunteer work and the women who are the workforce in these transition houses tend to get very low pay. Houses are generally understaffed and are small units. The administrators of these transition houses, while they mean well, often are people who live in comfort themselves and expect the women workers to give of their time and effort as they do for their own families. There is a great need for these workers to organize. Childcare workers today are also grossly underpaid, considering the value of their work and the care given to the children. Zookeepers get much higher pay than do childcare workers.

There is a need to organize, but organizing is costly. It often takes a long time and is difficult. It takes a lot of effort on the part of the workers themselves. They need constant support and it so happens that most of the big unions that have the money, but tend to be bureaucratic, don't give these groups the support, time and technical assistance they need to organize. Neither do they want to be involved in long, difficult strikes for a small unit of six, eight or even twenty workers. Many of these groups feel that they have to organize on their own. In the future, I am sure that as the struggle continues, transition houses will be part of the social service network, paid by government; But in this neoconservative era, there are slim chances of their soon becoming part of that network. Therefore, it is a great struggle just to exist and a greater struggle for the women employees to organize. Where a larger union is willing to give them support and direction with respect for their needs and their wishes, that is fine. Where that is not available or where they just decide they wish to organize as an independent union, then they should do so. In that case, they need a great deal of support from women's groups within their region in order to sustain the struggle. These workers also need help from feminists in their relations with the administrators and boards of these transition houses. These latter must understand that while they are doing good by financially supporting a transition house for women in need, they must also respect the needs of the women who are carrying the burden.

SPE: Since you retired five years ago you have been working primarily with women's groups. You are a founding member of NAC for example. Why is it important for women to work in organizations like NAC?

MP: I went to NAC's founding meeting in 1972. I knew that some professional women, and others who were well-off but socially aware feminists, were planning to organize in order to put forward changes in our sexist laws, changes recommended by the Royal Commission on the Status of Women whose report was tabled in Parliament in 1970. Their aim was to achieve greater opportunities for women to be equal in our society. I felt that it was terribly important that a much broader spectrum of women be involved in this undertaking. I felt that working class women, blue collar women working in factories, should also be there, as well as women from various minorities, so that our particular needs would be considerations in the battle. It was important that working class women be a voice in that movement.

SPE: Has that worked out?

MP: Well, it is not without its tensions and difficulties. Certainly women who are well educated, and who are favoured by their economic conditions, tend to assume a leadership role more easily. It is intimidating for a lot of working women — who have struggled all their lives and have not had the opportunity of a better education to articulate their demands — to bear the brunt of debate and criticism within a group. But these women must be there, they must earn respect, make others aware of their particular conditions and win support for the demands they make to improve these conditions. Working women must be an articulate presence within the women's movement. That's why I go to the NAC meetings. Even with the tensions, we are a presence.

SPE: Madeleine, there are some who feel that women should only work in women's groups because that's where they can achieve the kinds of goals they set for themselves. Given your experience, how do you feel about that?

MP: In answer to that I would refer back to the discussion on women in unions and my advocacy of women setting up women's committees within unions so that together they can be a greater force within the larger union movement. I think that principle applies to women within the community as a whole. I believe we have got to develop women's groups and a women's movement so that together we can share our experience in society. We must look at and assess our economic conditions, our social conditions, and our political situation. Together we can decide on taking a stand on those issues which will equalize our position with that of men. We can go ahead and fight to win on those issues. At the same time, we cannot abstract ourselves from the whole of the community, we need the support of others and they need our support in the cause of social justice. I think it is important that women who are part of the trade union movement, also be part of the women's movement and bring to it the demands and the needs of women in the workforce. We work some eight hours a day — some more, some less — to earn a living and that is roughly one-third of our life. So it is important that we be involved in the unions and in other struggles, along side of men. We must do so in a very articulate manner and in our own interests. But we must also see our common interests with men who are fighting for better conditions, and who will respect us if we are knowledgeable, vocal and active in those movements.

I believe that women's groups that are united on feminist objectives should join in social solidarity with other groups in the community if we are to be more effective. We are fighting for ourselves but we have to take an interest in others such as the elderly — both women and men — and children, all of whom have a right to live in security rather than in poverty. I think we should work with the student movement. The pressure on social programs and educational programs are such nowadays that unless we are constantly vigilant, active and united, governments will increase the costs of education and only the children of the rich will receive a higher education. In the 21st Century, that would be catastrophic! Those without education will have the greatest difficulty in making a living in our society. Their own children will grow up in life handicapped and incapable of learning and living well enough to be productive. I think it is terribly important that we work in social solidarity with men, with young people, with the elderly and with the disadvantaged minorities in our society who are also suffering injustices which cry out for redress. In this kind of social solidarity we would be fighting for an alternative society, not one based on the market economy where the profit of a few large corporations is supposed to be of benefit to the whole of society. We would be fighting for an economy based on the greater need and the greater security and ability of all to produce and to live in comfort in an environment that would be improved, instead of steadily destroyed as is happening today.

SPE: How do you think that organizations like NAC should relate to women of colour, aboriginal women, immigrant women and disabled women?

MP: I think there is still a great deal of progress to be made in NAC and in other feminist organizations in terms of their attitude to and respect for aboriginal women, women of colour, immigrant women, and disabled women. There are many organizations of women in these minority groups. For example, there are organizations for aboriginal women throughout the country. There is the Black Women's Congress which has chapters across the country as well. Some immigrant women's organizations cut across ethnic lines. There is in Montreal, for example, the Collectif des femmes immigrantes which has Haitian women, Italian women, Latin American women, Greek women and others. Disabled women have organized to be more autonomous, to have a better chance to earn a living, to have housing, living conditions and services which are appropriate for them. They have tremendous battles just to overcome their disability. They need support as do the other minority groups.

We must consider the fact that many women face the effects of racism and racial discrimination in a way that we cannot appreciate fully because we do not live under those conditions. We must learn from them about the injustices they face and the needs they have. When we have learned about the issues that they are fighting for, then we should support them to the hilt. For this, we must make them welcome in our ranks. This is not always done. As anglophone or francophone white women, we are inclined to think that we know what other women's lives are like and what their needs are. We do not really know this unless we know how the most highly exploited women live. We can only learn that from them; book-reading is not enough.

In NAC from the founding convention, we were fortunate in having the presence of Mary Two Axe Early, a Mohawk woman from the Kahnawake Reserve in Quebec. She told us about the conditions of native women who married non-native men. They lost their Indian status and could be expelled from the reserve and the community, as indeed some were. She asked us to fight with her and her companions to change the Indian Act. This act was passed by white men in parliament in the days of Sir John A. MacDonald; it was not passed by native people. According to this Act, a native man who married a white woman retained his native status which he conferred on his white spouse and on their children. Meanwhile, the native man's sister who married a white man lost her status. We pledged to support Mary and other native women who were fighting for this change. In 1985 Bill C31 was adopted. It was an amendment to the Indian Act whereby henceforth, when a native woman marries a white man, she retains her status, and native women who lost it in the past will have a right to regain it. I must say that the government has been very remiss about granting them status quickly and still more remiss in its provision of housing which would permit women to go back on the reserve and become active members of their native bands.

In the case of black women, we have had some black women on the executive board of NAC, and we still have at least one at this time. We have to convince them that we want to understand their conditions and we want to support them in their fight. In the case of immigrant women, if they arrive in Canada as part of a family group, as do many of the southern European women, Portuguese, Italians, Greeks, Yugoslav, and some Latin American women, the husband is expected to go and look for a job and he gets trained in the prevailing language, be it French or English. He gets assistance, not as much as he should, but some. The children go to school and learn the prevailing language. The woman is at home looking after the husband, looking after the children, working hard and she feels that she is lucky if she can run out for eight hours to a job in the garment industry, toy making or whatever consumer industry, or in service. She doesn't have time to go out and learn languages and other skills. Often, she is stuck with a precarious factory job. If the factory closes down, it will be very, very hard for her to move around in the economy, to find another job. For some, it is even hard to go downtown and do shopping. A number of these women must be accompanied by a child, or by the husband, who will translate for them and help them get around. It is up to us to go out to these women, to listen to them and find out what their needs are, and, where we can agree, to back them up. We have to get them to represent themselves in our organizations and in our communities. It is not easy to do, just as it is not easy to bring blue collar working women into NAC. It does not happen without tension. Women who are used to assuming leadership within the women's movement have to learn that they must share it with these other women who have greater needs. That will strengthen the movement itself and we will be fulfilling our role much more fairly as we do that.

SPE: What do you think is needed to make a stronger women's movement in Canada?

MP: I think we are already working in that direction and have been for a number of years. We should continue to intensify our efforts while making significant corrections on the way in some of our working methods. We should continue the organizing work of bringing together women's groups, emphasizing the work within the context of each province and each territory and of different areas within each larger region. We must be respectful of, and concerned for, women from the various minorities be they native women, women from visible minorities or others.

A weakness in our present work is insufficient linkage with women working on farms. In the past several years, Quebec has seen remarkable union organization among women farmers. Les femmes agricultrices du Quebec, UPA (Union des producteurs agricoles) is a vibrant union of women struggling to make ends meet on farms which tend to be of modest size. They are very concerned about the Canada-US Free Trade Accord and respond sympathetically to coalition work with other democratic forces in the community. We must explore possibilities of working more closely with rural women. On the other hand, we should be more outgoing with young women and not expect them to come to us on their own. Every new generation of women students has a greater immediate stake in abortion rights than has the previous generation of women who carried the free choice fight before them. If we appreciate this fact, we will be more sensitive to their needs and we will have more credibility in helping them to understand how precarious are those rights, so long as they are not enshrined in strong legislation. We must make a generous place for women students within the feminist movement, on the basis of our common action, first on the community level. Tensions that are too great between generations of feminists narrow down and weaken our common struggles. In a way, the same can be said of our relations with women in democratic senior citizens' organizations.

At the same time, we should encourage and respond to initiatives by women in their respective local communities who carry feminist issues (expressed in terms that reflect the living experiences in their own areas) to MPs, MPPs, to Cabinet Ministers or even to Senators in their province or territory. This aspect of women's work is effective with politicians and adds considerably to women's experience and influence in non-partisan, coalition politics. It also gives them a sense of their own collective power. If we show continuity in this work, irresponsible politicians who make lots of promises but fail to deliver, will lose credibility and could be replaced by candidates from the ranks of feminists or from other democratic organizations in the community.

We also need more feed-back from feminists on their activities in their own regions. Those reports will improve our understanding and help to make our choice of priorities, our literature and our public statements and lobbying activities more understandable to women everywhere in Canada and in Quebec, as it will reflect more vividly the reality of women's lives.

The leaders' debate, sponsored by NAC in the 1984 federal election campaign, was a recognition of the feminist movement's power. I am not sure that if Pierre Elliott Trudeau had still been government leader instead of Turner, that he would have accepted. In any case, in the 1988 elections, the Mulroney Administration made sure its leader would not be subjected to another leaders' debate, where he would have to answer for all the broken promises made to women four years earlier. The same reasons apply to the refusal of government caucus to meet with the NAC women's lobby in May, 1989. Mr. Mulroney, though seen and heard in the media, chooses his audiences more carefully these days.

In current Quebec elections, government leader Robert Bourassa has so far succeeded in avoiding a general debate with opposition leader Jacques Parizeau, let alone a debate on women's issues

SPE: What do you think is needed to create global solidarity among women?

MP: When we look around we can see power struggles in so many areas of the world. In Nicaragua, elsewhere in Central America, in the Middle East, in Africa — where the people of Angola and Mozambique are being assaulted daily, where the South African black people, who are the overwhelming majority of the population, are being repressed and held in bondage — and elsewhere as well. We realize that our government, the US government and others, are making use of these struggles to build up arms, and our armed forces. They are selling arms to dictators who repress their own people and to mercenaries, killing people in order to upset popular governments. Huge fortunes are being made by trafficking in arms. The US/Iran Contra scandal, in which arms dealers in Canada were involved, is only one significant example of this. We as women must remember that women and their children suffer most in these regional wars. The women's movement in Canada will become more conscious of the need for international solidarity if women from minority groups in our own country are a more active and integral part of our own movement. Black women in Canada can teach us about the struggle of black African women against apartheid. Latin American refugees and immigrant women from Chile, Guatemala, El Salvador, and other Latin American countries can teach us about US militarism and interference in their own countries in Central and South America. Native women and men in Canada are sensitive to the plight of native peoples in Latin America and their opposition to large white land owners, to US multinational corporations who exploited their labour in the tin mines of Bolivia, in the copper mines of Chile, in the banana plantations of Central America, and in countless other areas. When Ronald Reagan spoke of his plan to have the countries of the Americas from Tierra del Fuego to the Arctic come together in one common market, he was thinking of a common market controlled by the large multinationals, mostly American. The people within this common market would be exploited for cheap labour, and countries such as Canada would be exploited for their resources. He was also thinking of the Mexican *maquilladora* where women today in the hundreds of thousands work for about $4.00 a day, for eight hours of work, with no pensions, no paid vacations, no maternity leave, no health care provisions and no safety provisions on the job. Our response to the large corporations and to Reagan's and Bush's dream of controlling people of all the Americas for the greater profit of US-based multinationals must be more exchanges, more information, more support for and greater solidarity with the women of the Americas, women of South Africa, women of all countries who are suffering and struggling against repression. We must support all women who are struggling for the self-determination and freedom, with justice, of their own countries. This is the only road to peace in the Americas, and to world peace, and to the development of a society dedicated to a better life for its people rather than the profit of a few. We must put much greater effort into organizing ourselves, and into building the links with the women of other countries. If given a hearing, the women of minority groups within our own country will help to lead the way.

SPE: If you had one piece of advice to give progressive women today, what would it be?

MP: We should be witness to the hard reality of women's lives in all its aspects. We must be witness to their struggle to survive; to learn; to equip themselves to earn a decent living; to be able to nurture the children they choose to bear; to live and be respected as equal human beings in the community. We must agree to translate these desires into issues and demands and we must, with a united and strong voice, pressure politicians to fulfill their promises on these demands and we should work in social solidarity with other democratic organizations. It is not enough for Brian Mulroney to have promised us in 1984 that he would bring in a proper childcare program such as women demanded. He did nothing for four years and then pretended on the eve of the coming election that he was in a hurry to give us a childcare program. In the old days Maurice Duplessis, the Premier of the province of Quebec used to say that "building a bridge served three elections." In the first election, he promised the people in the area that he would build a bridge across the river. In the second election, he began the construction project. In the third election, he had the Bishop at his side blessing the opening of the bridge. I think we are beyond that. We expect results from our politicians. We must debate and clarify the issues in our discussions amongst ourselves, with respect for each other. We must also guard against emotional issues in our internal discussions. We need a clear head and persistence in pursuit of our goals to make further progress.

CHAPTER 4

CLASS AND ETHNIC BARRIERS TO FEMINIST PERSPECTIVES IN TORONTO'S JEWISH LABOUR MOVEMENT, 1919-1939

RUTH A. FRAGER

The history of Toronto's Jewish labour movement provides a critical context for examining the relationship between feminist and socialist currents in Canada's past. It also illuminates the relationship between these currents and ethnic identity within a key section of the working class. In the 1920s and 1930s, Toronto's Jewish labour movement was not only militant but also had a strong radical cast: the Jewish unions were led primarily by socialists and contained a significant socialist component within their rank and file as well. Furthermore, as in the United States, the Jewish labour movement was concentrated in the garment industry, an industry with a highly unusual gender composition of labour. During most of the period under consideration, women constituted over half of Toronto's garment workers. A significant number of the Jewish women were active not only as trade-union militants but also as socialists. An examination of the Jewish labour movement in the interwar period thus provides an opportunity to study the historical interaction between class and gender in the context of both trade-union and socialist politics.[1]

This interaction was characterized by the systematic subordination of women's issues to class issues. Significantly, this subordination of the interests of female workers *as women* stands in marked contrast to the prominence which the Toronto Jewish labour movement accorded to Jewish workers' specific interest *as Jews*. Because the commitment to ethnic identity within the Jewish labour movement was not only powerful but also considered a *legiti-*

mate characteristic of both trade-union politics and Jewish socialist ideology, it provides a counterpoint to the subordination of women's issues. In addition, the intensity of ethnic concerns provides part of the explanation for the subordination of women's issues. Within Toronto's Jewish labour movement, the emphasis on both class consciousness and ethnic identity inhibited the development of feminist perspectives.

While Jewish women were subordinated within their families, in the factories, in their unions, and within the Jewish left, there was hardly any awareness of this subordination and even less attempt to struggle against it. This was partly a product of deeply held assumptions about a woman's domestic responsibility and a man's responsibility as the primary breadwinner. These assumptions helped ensure that union activists did not fundamentally challenge discriminatory wage structures or the gender division of labour in the garment factories. At the same time, the nature of Jewish activists' class analysis meant that they generally focused on the common oppression of all workers and ignored the fact that female workers encountered special forms of oppression. Moreover, the Canadian women's movement, which was weak in these years and predominantly Anglo-Celtic and middle-class, did not ally with Jewish women workers and thus did not help these women develop feminist perspectives of their own experiences. Jewish women themselves stressed that which they held in common with Jewish men — their deep commitment to Jewish identity, and their experience of anti-Semitism — rather than interests they might have shared with non-Jewish women. For all these reasons, women's issues were systematically subordinated.

In the garment shops, Jewish workers often toiled side-by-side with non-Jews, and both groups frequently worked for Jewish manufacturers. The International Ladies' Garment Workers' Union, the Amalgamated Clothing Workers, the International Fur Workers' Union, and the United Cloth Hat, Cap, and Millinery Workers' International Union were known as the "Jewish unions." While non-Jews constituted a significant minority within these four unions, a majority of the members and most of the leaders were Jews.

Although the term "Jewish unions" was sometimes used as a racial epithet in this period (particularly by the anti-labour English-language press and others who sought to prevent the non-Jewish clothing workers from uniting with the Jews in these organizations), much of the significance of the term lies in its use by Jews themselves. Despite the fact that these unions included non-Jews and despite Jewish labour activists' need to appeal more successfully to their non-Jewish co-workers, the Jews themselves characterized these four unions as the "Jewish unions." The term reflects the distinctive stamp imparted to these particular unions, for Jewishness pervaded and shaped them in fundamental ways. Moreover, the activists commonly used the term "Jewish labour movement" to refer to the movement they forged largely through these garment unions and also through the related cultural institutions, particularly the Jewish socialist fraternal organizations (which did not include non-Jews) and the pro-labour Yiddish-language press (which, of course, non-Jews could not read).[2]

The Jewish labour movement of Toronto, which emerged at the turn of the century and blossomed during the inter-war period, was broadly based in the immigrant community. These immigrants had fled to the New World in the early twentieth century to escape extreme poverty and virulent anti-Semitism in Eastern Europe. By 1931, there were over 45,000 Jews in Toronto, where their occupational concentration in the garment industry, combined with a high degree of residential concentration, helped create a cohesive community basis for the Jewish labour movement.[3]

Women's position within this community, particularly as defined by family roles, significantly shaped their position on the shop floor, in the unions, and in the Jewish left. Within the city's East European Jewish community, as within Canadian society more broadly, housework and childrearing were female responsibilities. Like so many others in this period, immigrant Jewish women and men considered the man to be the family's primary breadwinner and expected most women to leave the paid labour force upon marriage in order to concentrate on domestic tasks. It is significant, however, that women's domestic responsibilities within the family did not change in cases which did not fit this pattern. If the husband's income was not sufficient to support the family (and if there were no older children to help earn money), the married woman would go out to work, while continuing to shoulder the domestic responsibilities.[4] In extended family arrangements where men did not have wives to keep house for them, unmarried female relatives often assumed the double burden of wage-earning and housekeeping. Moreover, although the many Jewish men who worked in the highly seasonal garment industry had considerable free time during the slow seasons, they typically did not use this time to help with the housework.[5]

Within the East European Jewish community, women and men were bound together not only by family ties but also by deep cultural bonds. Even those who questioned certain aspects of Jewish tradition commonly shared the community's commitment to preserving Jewish identity and believed that the family played a central role in cultural preservation. In the context of significant anti-Semitism in Toronto as well as the more severe prejudice encountered before immigration, females and males within this community shared a sense of oppression as Jews. Because of the continuing threat of anti-Semitism and because of the positive valuation of Jewish identity, there was serious concern for the interest of the Jewish community as a whole.[6]

Jewish identity was based on a tradition that was fundamentally patriarchal. In traditional East European Jewish culture, religion, which permeated every aspect of life, assigned women a distinctly subordinate role. Education in particular (especially since it was so closely tied to religion) was a male preserve. Although the traditional way of life had been significantly transformed in other ways, women generally retained their "second-class" status within Toronto's immigrant Jewish community in the inter-war period.[7]

This continuing subordination can be seen, for example, in the life of a Jewish woman who had come to Toronto from Eastern Europe when she was a small child and later went on to become an activist in the Jewish labour movement. During her early years in Toronto, her father did not ensure that she would learn to read or write Yiddish. This was not because her father was an assimilationist. He was reluctant to spend money on a basic Yiddish education for her not only because of tight financial circumstances but also because he felt that it was not important: she would get married, in any case, and that was all that mattered. Then, when she began to teach herself to read the Yiddish newspaper, her brother ridiculed her efforts. This woman had to cope with disapproving male relatives in later years as well, for her first husband would not "let" her be as politically active as she wanted to be. Cases such as hers were not unusual within the immigrant Jewish community.[8]

Jewish women were also at a significant disadvantage on the shop floor. In the needle trades, where so many immigrant women toiled, they were systematically confined to the lower-paying jobs which were deemed to be less skilled.[9] Statistics available for the city's garment industry in 1921, for example, illustrate the sharp difference between female and male wages. At that time, the average adult female worker earned only 58 percent of what her male counterpart earned.[10] Fifteen years later, the average earnings for women in Toronto's needle trades were a scant 52 to 53 percent of the average earnings of men.[11] This differential is mainly attributable to the fact that the women were generally confined to low-paying female job ghettoes within the industry, but unequal pay for equal work was also a factor.

One of the main rationales for this discrepancy in wage rates rested on the view of the woman garment worker as unskilled and temporary. The skills which women brought to the job were generally based on their domestic sewing experience and were devalued not only because these were not scarce skills, but also because work done by women was generally devalued. Most needle trades women were young and single and were expected to leave the paid labour force upon marriage. The married women workers, who constituted a significant minority, were usually expected to leave the shop floor as soon as their husbands were no longer ill or unemployed or earning too little money. The woman worker's temporary status was a rationale for excluding her from training for the better jobs.[12]

Yet this "temporary" status could well last a considerable length of time. For those who did not marry at all, "temporary" status might last a lifetime. But even the young woman who had entered the garment shop when she was fifteen, for example, might not marry until her mid-twenties. One could presumably acquire considerable skills within such a time period, if one were not confined to the less valued jobs.

The significance of gender on the shop floor was graphically demonstrated in William Lyon Mackenzie King's 1897 newspaper report on "Toronto and the Sweating System." When King asked a manufacturer of ready-made clothing what he paid his help, the manufacturer replied: "I don't treat the men bad, but I even up by taking advantage of the women. I have a girl who can do as much work, and as good work as a man; she gets $5 a week. The man who is standing next to her gets $11. The girls, however, average $3.50 a week, and some are as low as two dollars."[13]

In situations where women earned substantially less than men who did the exact same jobs, the perception of women as temporary workers usually meant that they were assumed to be less experienced on the job, so their work was presumably worth less. In the men's fine clothing industry in 1920, for example, there were cases where women and men did the same work and the women earned considerably less. These women did have significantly less work experience. Male button-hole-makers, for example, had an average of 19 years of experience and received an average wage of $36 per week, while female button-hole-makers had an average of only 7 years of experience and received an average wage of $22 per week, which amounted to 61 percent of the male wage for this job. In these shops, women who did basting (i.e. temporary stitching) and women who made collars and lapels found themselves in similar situations.[14]

It is a dubious assumption, however, that women's unequal pay was simply a product of fewer years of work experience. It is unlikely that these women were so much less skilled than their male counterparts as to merit such wide pay differentials. After all, one could learn to be an efficient button-hole-maker in far less than seven years. Indeed, according to a 1920 Ontario government publication on vocational opportunities in the needle trades, "the maximum speed on a single [sewing machine] operation will generally be attained in one or two years."[15]

Moreover, in these men's fine clothing shops in 1920, there were cases where women and men performed the same jobs and where the women had experience equal to or greater than the men in those jobs. The women still earned dramatically less than the men. Consider the case of the pants operators. Men in this job averaged 7 years of experience and made on average $39 per week, while women in the same job averaged 14 years of experience and made an average of $22 per week, which constituted 56 percent of their male counterparts' wages. Similarly, male pocketmakers averaged 8 years of experience and made an average of $40, while female pocketmakers averaged 10 years of experience and made an average of $26, which constituted 65 percent of the men's wages.[16]

A major rationale for the wage discrepancy was, of course, the expectation that male workers would be the primary breadwinners for their families. Women workers were not normally expected to fulfill this role. Instead they were expected to be dependent on men, and these expectations were married to necessity. In Toronto's needle trades, as in many other sectors in this period, low wages for female workers often meant that a woman could not support herself, let alone support children or aging parents.[17] By making economic independence impossible for most women, women's low wages reinforced, even as they reflected, the systematic subordination of women.

The conception that men were the family's primary breadwinners was so deeply ingrained in the thinking of the working-class Jewish community that little thought was given to the systematic super-exploitation of women. The cases of unequal pay mentioned above occurred in the *unionized* shops. There is no evidence that the union attempted to rectify these inequities. Although the garment unions may have sporadically and half-heartedly supported the equal-pay principle at some other points in time, the Jewish labour movement did not seriously criticize the discriminatory wage structure. Indeed, no one within the Jewish labour movement developed a critique of the gender division of labour on the shop floor. After reflecting on this issue during a recent interview, one male Jewish activist (who had been a union leader for years) declared: "Women knew their place" in the inter-war period, "insofar as the hierarchy of employment [was concerned]!"[18]

The unions actually reinforced women's subordination, for union policies frequently *increased* the differential between women's pay and men's pay. In a period when the average female garment worker's wage usually amounted to between one half and two thirds of the average male garment worker's wage, unions such as the International Ladies' Garment Workers' Union and the Amalgamated Clothing Workers often fought for an across-the-board percentage increase in wages for all workers.[19] This common formula meant that the dollar difference between the average woman's wage and the average man's wage would widen. (In 1920, for example, when the average wage in the city's unionized men's clothing shops was $21 per week for women and $34 per week for men, the union demanded an across-the-board increase of 33 percent.[20] Thus although the average woman's wage would have remained at 62 percent of the average man's wage, the absolute gap between her wage and his wage would have increased from $13 to $17.) Because women generally could not enter the better paid jobs, the very structure of these wage demands disadvantaged women further.

An examination of the Jewish unions' arrangements with respect to its own funds makes it clear that the unions were not simply forced to go along with the manufacturers' insistence on gender-based pay differentials. Union fees and strike-benefit payments constituted an area of policy where the unions were able to operate in relative freedom from the constraints imposed by the employers. If union activists had felt that it was unfair for women to earn so much less than men, they could have structured strike benefits so that female strikers received the same as male strikers. This seldom happened.[21] The rationale for lower strike-pay for women was that women earned so much less than men on the shop floor. However, this did not necessarily mean that women paid lower union fees. In many cases, they had to pay the same fees as the men.[22] Although the available evidence is fragmentary, it is clear that union policies in this area were far from consistently fair to female workers. Notwithstanding minor variations between the unions and within particular unions over time, the Jewish unions did not make a point of advancing progressive policies in these areas. The inequitable treatment of women was not imposed by the manufacturers alone; it was imposed as well by the unions themselves.

Women's subordination within the unions and on the shop floor was, of course, closely related to their subordination within the home. Significant household responsibilities on top of a full-time wage-earning job meant that the woman worker had less time and energy left over for union activities and shop-floor struggles. Even if the woman worker was single and not directly responsible for keeping house for male relatives, she often had to help her own mother with the housework, or if she had immigrated without her mother, she usually had to look after her own household needs. Moreover, in cases where the woman had been less well-educated than her male siblings, she was at a disadvantage as a unionist, particularly if she was not literate in Yiddish. She faced further barriers if her father or husband disapproved of her activism.

Women's subordination within the Jewish labour movement was also a product of the male culture of the unions. Although the Jewish men used to drop by the union halls to chat with their friends, sip coffee, and play dominoes, Jewish women did not take part in such informal socializing. This was not just because the woman worker usually had to hurry home from work to make supper or do the laundry. According to interviews with retired male garment workers, this informal social network at the union halls was perceived as a male domain where women did not fit. Since the male culture of the union hall gave the men greater opportunity to know each other and to discuss union issues, it reinforced a male-centred solidarity.[23] The marginalization of women within Toronto's garment unions is also apparent in the fact that the overwhelming majority of the leaders of the different needle trades unions were men.[24]

On the one hand, the unions reflected the dominant assumptions about gender roles: men "deserved" the better jobs and better pay because they were the primary breadwinners for their families, and women's responsibility for household labour remained unquestioned, shaping the women workers' position on the shop floor and in the unions in fundamental ways. The commonplace acceptance of these differences in gender roles helped to mask the discrimination against women. On the other hand, despite these fundamental assumptions about gender differences, union leaders did not distinguish between female and male workers at another level. The nature of the Jewish activists' class consciousness meant that they focused on what they saw as the common oppression of all workers, ignoring the fact that women workers faced special constraints. Thus when retired union activists were asked if the Jewish unions had had special policies to appeal to women workers, the question surprised them, for the notion of the special interests of women workers was foreign to their class analysis. Typically, the unions appealed to each person "just as a worker!," as one retired male union leader proudly exclaimed.[25]

Yet this was not a gender-neutral construct, for the prototype of *the* worker was the male worker. Although men usually constituted less than half of Toronto's garment workers, the "masculine conception of class" (which scholars such as Joan Scott have recently emphasized in other historical contexts) operated even in the labour movement in this sector. Men were able to shape the conception of the "typical" garment worker in their own image, partly because the female workers were seen as temporary and hence less "central" to both the industry and the unions. The male union leaders appeared to speak for and represent working-class interests as a whole, but the definition of class was gender-biased. This was a bias which was not questioned.[26]

The Canadian women's movement was unable to provide a significant feminist counter-force, for it seldom reached the women garment workers. This was partly because the women's movement was weak in the inter-war years, the key period in the development of the Jewish labour movement. In addition, the Canadian women's movement was predominantly Anglo-Celtic and middle-class and hence did not appeal to working-class immigrant women. Although very little historical work has been done yet concerning the attitudes within the Canadian women's movement towards the plight of working-class women, the movement as a whole seems to have exhibited little understanding of working-class women's problems.[27]

In the United States, in contrast, the Women's Trade Union League existed as an explicitly feminist organization, specifically concerned with the plight of female workers. Consisting of a cross-class alliance of women, the League sought to improve the conditions of American women workers, sometimes by organizing them into unions and sometimes by pushing for protective labour legislation. The League also tried to make the American women's movement more attractive to working-class women and to develop their awareness of feminist issues. Although the League's influence was limited, and although class and ethnic tensions emerged within the League itself, this organization had a significant impact on several exceptional Jewish women who were among the few females to enter the leadership of the garment unions in New York. Their heightened awareness of women's issues stands in sharp contrast to the situation in Toronto and contrasts, as well, with the situation of the majority of immigrant Jewish women in the United States.[28]

For a time, the Women's Trade Union League pioneered the development of special methods for organizing women workers in a few American cities, thus helping to pull women garment workers into the unions. The organization's Chicago branch, in particular, emphasized such women-centred organizing strategies as home visits to educate women workers about the labour movement, special social gatherings to help solidify networks of women, personal testimonies of female labour activists, and special training for women unionists. Yet while the League's pioneering work was a fascinating development, its impact should not be exaggerated. In New York, the League's efforts had shifted away from these strategies to a focus on agitating for protective labour legislation as early as 1914, and in Chicago, where League emphasis on organizing women lasted significantly longer than elsewhere, it had shifted focus to protective legislation by 1925.[29]

Yet the League had developed significant women-centred organizing strategies for a time. In Toronto, by contrast, there were no similar concerted efforts either in the inter-war years or in the earlier part of the twentieth century. Toronto's Jewish unions rarely used a woman organizer to recruit women workers, and the general absence of special policies to organize Toronto's female garment workers is striking. Although there were minor exceptions, the activists in Toronto's Jewish labour movement attempted to organize men and women using the same methods instead of developing special techniques for organizing women.[30]

The dearth of women-centred organizing strategies was not simply a product of the nature of the Canadian women's movement and the absence of a women's trade union league in Toronto. Perhaps because Toronto's Jewish women felt more beleaguered *as Jews* than did their counterparts in New York City, Toronto's female Jews may have been less inclined to develop gender-based alliances with Anglo-Celtic middle-class feminists or even with the non-Jewish women workers. Jewish women's close identification with Jewish men may have been heightened in Toronto not only because Toronto's Jewish population was so much smaller than New York's but also because, in contrast to the high proportion of non-British immigrants in the major American cities where Jews congregated, Toronto's population was so overwhelmingly Anglo-Celtic. Moreover, Jews had significant political power in New York City, unlike the situation in Toronto in this period. These demographic and political differences probably increased the feeling of insecurity in Toronto and reduced Jewish women's openness to alliances with non-Jewish women.[31]

In this period, Toronto's immigrant Jewish community faced pressing economic needs, and both the women and the men in the Jewish labour movement depended on class gains to improve their lot. Furthermore, while women faced gender-conditioned economic deprivations, this was obscured by the traditional emphasis on the welfare of the family as a whole. Instead of focusing on their own disadvantaged position in the paid labour force, women commonly focused on the family income, for they often benefited directly from the wages of their husbands and fathers. The authority and privileges of males, predicated on their role as primary breadwinner, were usually taken for granted, and these overlapped with and reinforced a male-centred class analysis.[32]

In contrast to the lack of concern for women's issues within Toronto's Jewish labour movement, there was serious concern about relations between Jewish and non-Jewish workers within the Jewish unions. Whereas women were generally not organized into separate locals, it was usually necessary to organize the Jews and the non-Jews into separate locals not only because of the language problem but also because of ethnocentrism and anti-Semitism. Because of 'the Jew/Gentile problem', union leaders often made a point of using Jewish organizers to recruit the Jewish workers and non-Jewish organizers to recruit the non-Jews. Sometimes the leadership even found it necessary to set up a wholly separate office for mobilizing the non-Jewish garment workers. Furthermore, whereas there was little concern to include women within the union leadership, great care was taken to make sure that some non-Jews were included within the predominantly Jewish leadership of the Jewish unions. In Toronto's Amalgamated Clothing Workers, for example, it was common practice to have a Jewish business agent and a non-Jewish business agent; in contrast, the union lacked similar provisions to ensure that women would have ongoing representation in the leadership.[33]

Since members of Toronto's Jewish left played a key role in shaping union policies, it is particularly significant that their radicalism did not include a critique of conventional gender relations. Instead, they — like the other members of the immigrant Jewish community — viewed men as the primary breadwinners for the family and did not question the assignment of exclusive responsibility for housework and childcare to women. Even the female Jewish socialists shared these assumptions. There was very little awareness of the fact that Jewish women were subordinated within their homes, on the shop floor, within their unions, and also within the Jewish socialist organizations. There was even less attempt to struggle against this subordination.[34]

For the Jewish left, the central issues were class and ethnicity, not gender. Jewish radicalism had, in fact, a double dimension, for most of these Jewish socialists had been radicalized not only as workers but also specifically as Jews. In part, they were responding to the poverty and exploitation which working people experienced on both sides of the ocean. In addition, many had experienced harsh anti-Semitism before emigrating from Eastern Europe. Although less severe in Toronto, anti-Semitism was still significant: Toronto's Jews faced serious occupational, educational, recreational, and residential discrimination not only in the 1930s but in the earlier decades of the twentieth century as well. In both the Old World and the New, poverty and anti-Semitism were closely intertwined since prejudice often played an important role in barring Jews from access to better jobs. Immigrant Jewish radicals were deeply committed to socialism not only as a way to end class oppression but also because they felt that only socialism would bring real freedom and equality for the Jews.[35]

Typically, one woman activist, who had worked as a Toronto cloakmaker, explained that she had become a member of the Communist Party not only in response to the hardships faced by working people but also in response to anti-Semitism. She stressed that she had been radicalized as a Jew:

> I joined [the Communist movement] for [the] reason that
> [at] that time, we thought that the best solution for the Jew
> is in the Soviet Union. That was right after the revolution.
> And I joined for that reason, that I wanted my *people*
> should be equal with every other people. And that was the
> slogan of the Communist Party, that in the Soviet Union,
> all the citizens are the same.[36]

Like many other Jewish socialists, her analysis of oppression was limited to class and ethnicity: it did not encompass an awareness of women's subordination.

This woman's descriptions of her own experiences as a female garment worker and female union member revealed significant differences from the experiences of her male counterparts: throughout her seventeen years in Toronto's needle trades, she remained in a typically female job which was considered unskilled, and she used to rush back and forth between paid labour, union labour, and household labour. Yet her class analysis focused on the common oppression of all workers and denied these gender-based differences at the ideological level, obscuring the discrimination against women.[37]

This courageous woman asserted herself not only as a worker and a Jew, but also as a Communist who disagreed with the other political groupings within the Jewish left. During the 1920s and 1930s, the Jewish left was made up of a number of competing factions whose differences revolved around class and ethnic issues. In addition to Communist Party adherents, there were Trotskyists, Anarchists, and Labour Zionists (who sought to establish a Jewish socialist state in Palestine). There were also many Bundists, i.e. non-Zionists who wanted Jews to preserve their own culture within decentralized, multi-ethnic, socialist federations.[38] Whereas gender was deeply subordinated to class, the same was not true of ethnicity. Among these different factions of the Jewish left, an ongoing debate took place concerning the precise relationship between the class struggle and the struggle to end the oppression of Jews. In contrast to the rich complexity and intensity of this debate, there was no comparable debate about the relationship between women's rights and the class struggle. Gender was simply not considered an important issue.

While not all Jewish socialist women were wholly unaware of women's oppression, the limited awareness of this form of oppression contrasts with the strong commitment to fight for the elimination of class and ethnic oppression. Molly Fineberg, a long-time activist in Toronto's Jewish labour movement, provides an instructive example. In a recent interview, Fineberg emphasized her deep political commitment and her activities in the Toronto branch of the *Arbeiter Ring*, a socialist Jewish fraternal organization which was an integral part of the Jewish labour movement. Within the *Arbeiter Ring*, Fineberg played an exceptional role for a woman, holding various executive positions on key committees over the years. She also worked with other women from this organization to provide picket-line support and food donations for local Jewish strikers. In addition, she supported Labour Zionist efforts and was active in other Jewish causes such as raising money for pogrom victims in Eastern Europe. Fineberg, an immigrant from Poland, believed deeply in socialism and stressed that she became a socialist mainly as a response to the poverty which working people encountered in both Poland and Canada.[39]

During the interview, Fineberg did not bring up the issue of women's oppression when explaining why she had become a socialist. When she was directly asked if becoming a socialist had anything to do with women's issues, however, she replied that one of the reasons she had been attracted to the socialists was because she felt they believed in equal rights for women. Yet, apart from expressing her general belief in women's rights, she was largely unaware of the ways in which women were discriminated against during the inter-war years. When asked, for example, if she felt that women should have been more equally represented on the executive of the *Arbeiter Ring*, she replied that she had not felt this way. She found the question puzzling. Whereas Fineberg's description of her concrete political activities stressed her ongoing efforts to help relieve the oppression of workers and Jews, she did not mention any active involvement in women's rights struggles.[40] Ironically, Fineberg was one of the strongest supporters of women's rights within Toronto's Jewish labour movement.

To an important degree, the very class consciousness and intense ethnic identity of the Jewish socialists inhibited a stronger recognition or analysis of women's subordination and hindered the development of feminism. Oriented toward class, they stressed the common interests of female and male workers, so that at the level of their articulated socialist ideology, there was little if any recognition that women workers faced special impediments. This point of view, taken to its logical extreme, was expressed by the Communist Party of Canada in 1931: "The women workers have no interests apart from those of

the working class generally. There is no room for 'feminism' in our movement. There is only place for unity and solidarity on the basis of the joint
struggle against capitalism."[41] "Exactly right!," exclaimed Joshua Gershman,
the main leader of the Jewish Communist faction in the needle trades, when
recently asked to comment on this quotation in the context of discussing his
union activities in the inter-war years.[42]

Yet, for Gershman and so many others, while their class consciousness
obstructed a strong awareness of women's oppression, it did not obstruct a
forceful emphasis on anti-Semitism. As the quotation from the Communist
press indicates, the critique of feminism, from a class point of view, was that
an emphasis on women's rights would weaken the working class by dividing
female and male workers. Furthermore, any vision of the common oppression
of women, which transcended class, threatened to dilute the class struggle. But
clearly the same argument could have been made about ethnicity. These
socialists might have argued, but did not, that a focus on Jewish rights should
be avoided because it would weaken the working class by dividing Jewish
workers and non-Jewish workers. In fact, most Jewish socialists were intensely
committed to Jewish rights, and they had a profound awareness of ethnic differences within the working class. To a certain extent, Jewish socialists did
fear that an emphasis on the common oppression of Jews, which transcended
class, threatened to dilute the class struggle.[43] Yet this did not stop them from
being deeply committed to the fight against anti-Semitism — a fight which
sometimes saw them allied with the Jewish garment manufacturers.[44]

While the socialists' emphasis on the common oppression of all workers,
regardless of gender, undermined the development of a strong feminist perspective, the ethnic concerns of the Jewish activists also undermined such a
development. Jewish working-class women were less apt to develop a clear
critique of their position as women within the immigrant Jewish community
because they shared a common sense of oppression with most of the men in
this community, not only as fellow workers but also as fellow Jews. Moreover,
since the family was seen as so central to the perpetuation of Jewish culture, a
serious feminist challenge to the traditional norms and role structures of the
Jewish family would have been seen as a dangerous cultural threat.

Yet this emphasis on the welfare of the Jewish community as a whole,
this perceived need for Jews to pull together in the face of serious anti-
Semitism, did not prevent Jewish workers from pursuing their own class interests in opposition to the Jewish manufacturers. Fierce conflicts often broke
out in the Toronto garment industry between these two classes of Jews.
Numerous strikes and lock-outs meant that there were bitter fights between

fellow Jews who, while divided by their class interests, were often relatives, neighbours, and members of the same Jewish community organizations.[45]

The immigrant Jewish activists fought tenaciously for justice for working people and for Jews. Their dedication and courage were remarkable in a situation where such dissidence meant heightened vulnerability to repression. Many of these activists had a radical vision of a new kind of society which, they felt, would truly liberate them from class exploitation and anti-Semitism. Yet their deep two-fold commitment to egalitarianism did not encompass a commitment to women's rights. Both class and ethnicity were definitive in shaping the politics and the identity of Toronto's Jewish labour movement, despite the fact that class issues functioned divisively within the Jewish community and ethnic issues functioned divisively within the working class. In contrast, feminism did not emerge, perhaps partly because of its divisive potential both within the Jewish community and within the working class. Working-class Jewish women sacrificed their own potential for *full* equality to male-dominated, male-defined collectivities of family, nationality, and class.

ENDNOTES

I am grateful to Pat Armstrong, Jane Jenson, and Mercedes Steedman for their comments on a previous draft of this paper. I thank Don Wells for all his help with this project. I am also grateful to the Social Sciences and Humanities Research Council of Canada for financial support.

1. These issues are examined in detail in Ruth A. Frager, "Uncloaking Vested Interests: Class, Ethnicity, and Gender in the Jewish Labour Movement of Toronto, 1900-1939," (Ph.D. Thesis, York University, 1986). In 1921, 62 per-cent of Toronto's garment workers were women, and this proportion dropped to 55 percent in 1931. These calculations are based on the *Census of Canada*, 1921, Vol. IV, pp. 534-535 and 538; and 1931, Vol. VII, pp. 288-289.

2. On the significance attached to the Jewishness of the Jewish unions and the Jewish labour movement, see, for example, *Der Yiddisher Zhurnal*, 1 March 1921, p. 5; 23 Oct. 1924, p. 5; and 3 Feb. 1925, p. 3. See, also, Abraham Rhinewine, *Der Id in Kanade* [The Jew in Canada] (Toronto: 1925), p. 205.

3. On the hardships of Jewish life in Eastern Europe, see, for example, Salo W. Baron, *The Russian Jew Under Tsars and Soviets* (New York: 1964), pp. 52-75, 105, and 113-115. On the emigration of East European Jews, see, for example, Irving Howe, *World of Our Fathers* (New York: 1976), pp. 5-63. The statistic for the number of Toronto Jews in 1931 is drawn from calculations based on the *Census of Canada*, 1931, Vol. IV, pp. 268-271. On the high degree of occupational and residential concentration of Canada's Jews, see, for example, Irving Abella's introduction to Irving Abella (ed.), "Portrait of a Jewish Professional Revolutionary: The Recollections of Joshua Gershman," *Labour/Le Travailleur* Vol. 2 (1977) pp. 184-213.

4. This attitude was stressed, for example, in an interview with Moe Levin, 1984. (In order to protect the confidentiality of the interviewees, pseudonyms and mini-mal citations are used in reference to interviews throughout this article.)

5. This was apparent, for example, in the interviews with Bessie Kramer, 1984, and Sadie Hoffman, 1978 and 1985.

6. On anti-Semitism in Toronto in this period, see Stephen A. Speisman, *The Jews of Toronto: A History to 1937* (Toronto: 1979), pp. 119-122, 318-323, and 332-335; and Cyril H. Levitt and William Shaffir, *The Riot at Christie Pits*

(Toronto: 1987), pp. 9-11 and 34-39. The deep cultural bonds within Toronto's East European Jewish community and the serious commitment to preserving Jewish identity were apparent in virtually every issue of the city's daily Yiddish newspaper (*Der Yiddisher Zhurnal*) in this period.

7. On the patriarchal nature of traditional Judaism, see, for example, Susan Weidman Schneider, *Jewish and Female* (New York: 1984), pp. 33-41. The conclusion about women's "second-class" status in Toronto's immigrant Jewish community is based on interviews with women and men who were active in the city's Jewish labour movement.

8. Interview with Sadie Hoffman, 1978.

9. On the fact that women garment workers were commonly in the unskilled job categories, see, for example, International Ladies' Garment Workers' Union, *Handbook of Trade Union Methods* (New York: 1937), pp. 23-24.

10. This percentage is based on weekly wage statistics listed in Michael J. Piva, *The Condition of the Working Class in Toronto 1900-1921* (Ottawa: 1979), pp. 34 and 40.

11. Canada, Department of Trade and Commerce, *Weekly Earnings of Male and Female Wage-Earners Employed in the Manufacturing Industries of Canada, 1934-1936* (Ottawa: 1940), pp. 68 and 70.

12. In 1931, only one quarter of Toronto's women garment workers were married. This statistic is based on the Annual Report of the Ontario Minimum Wage Board, in the Ontario Legislative Assembly's *Sessional Papers*, 1933, part VI, paper #39, p. 16. However, the proportion of married women in the garment industry was higher than in many other sectors. A mere 10 percent of all women who were in the Canadian paid labour force in 1931 were married. On this, see Canada, Department of Labour, *Women at Work in Canada*, (Ottawa: 1965), p. 21.

13. *Toronto Daily Mail and Empire*, 9 October 1897, p. 10.

14. "Averages in the Toronto Market as in Jan. 1, 1920," Box B, File: "Assoc. Meetings??," Papers of the Associated Clothing Manufacturers, George Brown College Archives, Toronto.

15. The quotation is from Ontario, Department of Labour, *Vocational Opportunities in the Industries of Ontario: A Survey: Bulletin No. 4: Garment Making* (1920) p. 10

16. "Averages in the Toronto Market as in Jan. 1, 1920," Box B, File: "Assoc. Meetings??," Papers of the Associated Clothing Manufacturers.

17. Early evidence of women garment workers' inability to earn a living wage is provided by Mackenzie King's 1897 investigation of government clothing contracts
in Toronto, Hamilton, and Montreal. See W.L. Mackenzie King, *Report to the
Honourable the Postmaster General of the Methods Adopted in Canada in
the Carrying Out of Government Clothing Contracts* (1900) p. 21. Recent
interviews disclosed similar situations. For example, Ida Abel, who worked as a
finisher in the Toronto dress trade from 1926 until she got married in 1933,
could not live on what she herself earned. Her parents had remained in Eastern
Europe, so Ida Abel shared her lodging with another young woman in those
years. Although Ida Abel's life-style was humble, her two brothers had to supple-
ment her own earnings in order to cover her living expenses. This information is
available in the interview with Ida Abel, 1983. Similar information is contained in
the interview with Bessie Kramer, 1984.

18. Interview with Ed Hammerstein, 1984.

19. Many examples could be cited to document this practice. For a few typical examples see: *Der Yiddisher Zhurnal*, 17 April 1919, p. 1; *Der Yiddisher Zhurnal*,
14 August 1919, p. 1; Minutes of the Associated Clothing Manufacturers (in the
private collection at the organization's office in Toronto) 2 August 1933, 19
February 1935, and 27 April 1937; Canada, Department of Labour, *Labour
Gazette*, August 1933, p. 767; and *Labour Gazette*, July 1934, pp. 625-626.

20. Records for 1920, Box B, File: "Assoc. Meetings??," Papers of the Associated
Clothing Manufacturers.

21. This is based, in part, on an analysis of the benefits which are recorded in the
Minutes of the Toronto Joint Board, Amalgamated Clothing Workers Collection,
Public Archives of Canada, Ottawa. It is also based on scattered material in a
wide variety of other sources.

22. See, for example, *Der Yiddisher Zhurnal*, 31 March 1919, p. 1; 27 July 1920,
p. 1; 1 August 1920, p. 8; 30 October 1922, p. 1; 7 November 1922, p. 5;
and 17 October 1924, p. 1.

23. This is apparent, for example, in the interviews with Bessie Kramer, 1984; Ida
and Sol Abel, 1983; and Abe Hertzman, 1984.

24. The minutes of the Amalgamated Clothing Workers, for example, indicate that,
throughout the inter-war period, the union's Joint Board (which was composed
of approximately twenty representatives from the various locals) usually included
only one woman. In fact, at a number of points during these years, there were no
women at all on this Joint Board for months on end. In this period, women con-

stituted about a third of the union's membership. On this, see the lists of Joint Board members appearing regularly in Minutes of the Toronto Joint Board, Amalgamated Clothing Workers Collection.

25. The quotation is from the interview with Moe Levin, 1984. Other relevant interviews include those with: Bessie Kramer, 1984; Joshua Gershman (not a pseudonym), 1984; Ed Hammerstein, 1984; and Molly Fineberg, 1984.

26. For Scott's discussion of the "masculine conception of class," see Joan W. Scott, "On Language, Gender, and Working-Class History," *International Labor and Working-Class History* No. 31 (Spring 1987), pp. 1-13. Material on the Jewish labour movement in *Der Yiddisher Zhurnal* provides some typical evidence that the prototype of the worker was the male worker. See, for example, *Der Yiddisher Zhurnal*, 9 December 1919, p. 6.

27. For a detailed discussion of the class and ethnic composition of the suffrage leaders, see Carol Lee Bacchi, *Liberation Deferred?: The Ideas of the English-Canadian Suffragists, 1877-1918* (Toronto: 1983), pp. 3-12. Bacchi argues briefly that the suffragists "remained suspicious of labour organization" and did not "take more than a token interest in the problems of working-class women." (On this, see p. 123.) There has not yet been much work done on the feminists in the inter-war period, but see Veronica Strong-Boag, *The New Day Recalled: The Lives of Girls and Women in English Canada, 1919-1939* (Toronto: 1988), pp. 24 and 189-190, for relevant material on this period. In general, ethnic women's history is just beginning to emerge.

28. For an interesting study of the Women's Trade Union League, see Nancy Schrom Dye, *As Equals and As Sisters: Feminism, the Labor Movement, and the Women's Trade Union League of New York* (Columbia, Missouri: 1980). See, also, Alice Kessler-Harris, "Organizing the Unorganizable: Three Jewish Women and Their Union," *Labor History* Vol. 17, No. 1 (Winter 1976) pp. 5-23.

29. On the development of women-centred organizing strategies in Chicago, see Colette A. Hyman, "Labor organizing and female institution-building: The Chicago Women's Trade Union League, 1904-24," in Ruth Milkman (ed.), *Women, Work, and Protest: A Century of U.S. Women's Labor History* (Boston: 1985), pp. 22-41. On the New York Women's Trade Union League, see Dye, *As Equals and As Sisters...*, pp. 1, 3-4, 46, 52, 115-117, 122-123, and 162-165.

30. This conclusion is based on a wide variety of sources, including the minutes, newspapers, and correspondence files of the various unions.

31. In 1921, immigrants from continental Europe constituted less than 6 percent of Toronto's population. (At that time, Toronto contained very few other immigrants who had come from outside Britain or the United States.) In a number of major American cities in 1920, the proportions of immigrants from continental Europe were significantly higher than in Toronto. In that year, those who had been born in continental Europe comprised 15 percent of Boston's population and 16 percent of Philadelphia's population. In Chicago, Cleveland, and New York City, at least one quarter of each city's total population had come from continental Europe. These statistics are drawn from the *Census of Canada, 1921*, Vol. II, pp. 364-365; and the *Fourteenth Census of the United States Taken in the Year 1920* (Washington: 1922) Vol. II, pp. 47 and 732-736.

32. These attitudes were apparent, for example, in the interviews with Bessie Kramer, 1984, and Sadie Hoffman, 1985.

33. The quotation is from H.D. Langer to D. Dubinsky, from Toronto, 6 July 1937, Box 88, File 1b, David Dubinsky Papers, International Ladies' Garment Workers' Union Collection, Labor-Management Documentation Center, M.P. Catherwood Library, Cornell University, Ithaca, New York. For a detailed discussion of relations between Jews and non-Jews within the Jewish unions, see Frager, "Uncloaking Vested Interests..." pp. 153-190.

34. The interview with Bessie Kramer (1984) is particularly interesting regarding these issues.

35. The double dimension of Jewish radicalism is examined in detail in Ruth A. Frager, "Radical Portraits: The Roots of Socialism in Toronto's Immigrant Jewish Community, 1900-1939," *Polyphony* (forthcoming).

36. Interview with Bessie Kramer, 1969.

37. Interviews with Bessie Kramer, 1969 and 1984.

38. For a detailed discussion of the Bund in the East European context, see Henry J. Tobias, *The Jewish Bund in Russia: From Its Origins to 1905.* (Stanford, California: 1972). For a detailed treatment of the Labour Zionists in Canada, see S. Belkin, *Di Poale Zion Bavegung in Kanade, 1904-1920* [The Labour Zionist Movement in Canada, 1904-1920] (Montreal: 1956).

39. Interview with Molly Fineberg, 1984.

40. *Ibid.*

41. *Worker* (Toronto), 28 February 1931, p. 1.

42. Interview with Joshua Gershman, 1984. Gershman explained that this quotation

accurately expressed how he, together with the other Communist-oriented needle trades activists, felt about women's issues in this period.

43. This concern is apparent, for example, in the interview with Ed Tannenbaum, 1984. Tannenbaum grappled with this issue in his distinction between "bourgeois Zionism" and Labour Zionism.

44. See, for example, *Der Yiddisher Zhurnal*, 9 December 1919, p. 1; 29 March 1933, p. 1; and 31 March 1933, p. 1. Further evidence is provided in the interviews with Jacob Black, 1971 and 1984, and Ed Hammerstein, 1977.

45. See Frager "Uncloaking Vested Interests..." pp. 110-153, for a detailed discussion of the relations between Jewish workers and Jewish manufacturers in Toronto's needle trades.

CHAPTER 5

BANK WORKER UNIONIZATION AND THE LAW

ROSEMARY WARSKETT

The strategy for a working-class must be, not to uphold the impossible ideals of of the liberal forms of the state and the "rule of law," but to insist on the necessity that it be transcended, in forms which challenge the dominance of capitalist social relations.

Sol Picciotto,
Capitalism and the A Rule of Law (1979)

Well, it starts with the feeling of being powerless. So why do they feel powerless? Well, first of all, the big thing is that we are fighting the government and fighting against the law. So you get the feeling, how can I do something? If you meet with lawyers two or three times a week, they are not going to tell you that you have to fight on the streets. They are going to tell you what the legal avenues are, and so you get directed to that.

Jean-Claude Parrot on union leadership, *SPE* 11 (1983)

In June 1977, a small independent union in British Columbia—the Service, Office and Retail Workers Union of Canada (SORWUC)—broke through the defences set up by the chartered banks and gained certification of several bank branches under the provisions of the Canada Labour Code. This achievement was hailed as the beginning of a movement that would result in the unionization of a previously unorganized sector of the economy. SORWUC was unaffiliated with the Canadian Labour Congress (CLC) and had a militant, feminist ideology.[1] At the same time that SORWUC was successfully organizing bank workers on the west coast, another small union—the Canadian Union of Bank Employees (CUBE)—operating independently, applied for certification of several chartered bank branches in south-western Ontario. It took the Canadian Labour Relations Board (CLRB) almost a year to issue a ruling regarding these applications. But its decision in June 1977 was significant: it revised, on the face of it, the 1959 ruling that banks could not be unionized on a branch basis, thereby opening the door to a new round of bank unionization.[2]

While the CLRB was deliberating on the question of the appropriate bargaining unit for the banking industry, the CLC and its affiliated unions waited in the wings.[3] Following the CLRB's decision to recognize the bank branch as an appropriate collective bargaining unit, the CLC formed the Bank Workers Organizing Committee (BWOC) in an attempt to avoid the mistakes of earlier campaigns. The BWOC was to provide the vehicle for a massive organizing drive by CLC-affiliated unions. The plan was to organize bank employees into CLC-chartered locals called the Union of Bank Employees (UBE/CLC). At the 1978 CLC convention in Quebec City, the BWOC was officially endorsed by all affiliates, with the notable exceptions of the Office and Professional Employees International Union (OPEIU) and the Retail Clerks International Union (RCIU). Each of these unions claimed jurisdiction over the banks and was unwilling to participate in a campaign that would organize these workers into a union other than its own. (Both unions launched campaigns, but have been less active in organizing in recent years.) Consequently, by the beginning of 1978, there were several unions attempting to organize bank workers.[4]

In 1977, bank workers seemed poised on the edge of a radical transformation. The Bossen Report, jointly sponsored by the Advisory Council on the Status of Women and the Canadian Bankers' Association, revealed that 77 percent of all bank branch employees were women and that the policies and practices of the banks towards these women were highly discriminatory. It pointed out that approximately 75 percent of all women working in chartered banks earned less than $10,000 a year, whereas 70 percent of all men in these same banks earned over $10,000 a year.[5] Unionists felt that they had every reason to be optimistic about organizing these workers. However, their optimism was short-lived. Over ten years later, only 62 bank units out of approximately 7,000 chartered bank branches and data centres continue to hold union certification.[6] (See Table I).

Table 1
Chartered Bank Certifications and Revocations
by Bank and Union—June 1977 to September 1986

	Certifications Granted	Revocations Granted	Existing Certification as of 31 August 1985
Bank of British Columbia	2	1	1
Bank of Montreal	49	37	12
Bank of Nova Scotia	26	15	11
Banque Nationale du Canada	41	28	13
Canadian Imperial Bank of Commerce	27	16	11
Royal Bank of Canada	20	10	10
Toronto-Dominion Bank	8	6	2
Banque D'Épargne de la Cité et du District de Montréal	(certified since 1967)	—	1
Banque National de Paris	1	—	1
Total	174	113	62*

*plus 2 earlier certifications which existed prior to 1976
(1 Royal Bank; 1 Montreal City and District Savings Bank)
SOURCE: Figures supplied by the CLRB, October 1986.

This article explores the apparent failure of the recent campaigns to unionize bank workers. During the period 1977-87, unions and bank workers repeatedly found themselves entwined in a legal struggle with the banks, either before the CLRB or the courts. I will argue that the *banks*, not the unions, benefitted from this legal battle, *even* when the decision appeared to favour the workers. To begin with, the decision to permit bank unionization on a branch basis resulted in the formation of small, isolated bargaining units too weak to negotiate successfully with the banks. As a result, the motivation of bank workers to unionize eroded, along with the organizing movement begun by SORWUC and CUBE in 1976. The first section examines some of the important issues that inform the unionization of white-collar workers in general and bank workers in particular. That discussion makes it clear that the unionization of bank workers (and any other workers for that matter) must be examined in the context of the system of labour relations established and developed by the Canadian state, and the contradictions that emerge when workers depend on the law to protect their unions from the power of capital. This sets the stage for an examination of the attempts to unionize workers in branches of the federally chartered banks and helps to explain the high number of decertifications and consequent demobilization of the campaign.

UNIONIZING WHITE-COLLAR WORKERS

The vast majority of chartered bank workers are women who are paid relatively low wages, have few promotional opportunities, and are highly transient. They work, for the most part, in branches that on average employ 14 people.[7] Approximately eighty percent of the 150,000 people working in bank branches today are women; less than one percent are unionized. Their conditions are nearly as poor today as they were when SORWUC first launched its drive. Wages remain low, and benefits such as paid maternity leave and leave for care of sick members of the family, often taken for granted by women working under a union contract, remain beyond their reach. The banks' labour force is highly transient, with a turnover among clerical staff running over thirty percent a year.[8] This high turnover rate, which seems to be more pronounced in the branches than in the head offices, has been one factor singled out to explain the lack of success of bank worker unionization.[9] Employers and some union organizers have assumed that the high turnover rates result from the lack of commitment by women to the workplace, and their desire to return to their traditional role in the home. The evidence for this is very weak. There seems to be no reason to assume that women working in banks are returning to the home in any greater numbers than women working in other sectors of the economy. A more logical explanation is that conditions of work are poor, that the remuneration is low, and that bank workers have little to lose by taking up other low-paying jobs.[10]

Some other explanations that have been offered for the low rate of unionization in banking also relate to its predominately female workforce. Women, it is asserted, have a more passive attitude than men towards management— that "in order to unionize, women must overcome the cumulative effects of a socialization process which emphasizes passivity."[11] Yet if sex and its concomitant socialization processes were critical factors, we would expect a lower degree of unionization the higher the proportion of women in a particular sector. Briskin, White and Eaton have demonstrated that the proportion of women in a particular sector does not correlate with the degree of unionization in that sector. They concluded that the sector of the economy has significantly more impact on unionization rates than does gender. For example, a low degree of unionization has been linked to sectors in which "the average size of establishments is small and employment diffused."[12] Unionization may occur in larger establishments, it is argued, because that is where union organizers place their efforts or because there is more of a possibility that a leader, who will lead the organizing drive, will come forward from a larger group. More importantly, larger groups of employees also have more bargaining power and, therefore, may encounter less opposition from management, or at least present a more formidable opposition to management, thus enabling them to successfully negotiate a collective agreement. This latter explanation may throw some light on an important structural factor that has contributed to the difficulty of organizing branch bank workers.[13]

While there seems to be good reason to conclude that one of the important reasons for the failure to unionize Canadian banks is related to the small size of the bank branch units, it is clearly more than that. In Britain, 75 percent of all workers in clearing-house banks are unionized; in Australia, the percentage is even higher.[14] Small branches are a fact of life in most banking systems that serve the general public. Instead, we need to examine that which is specific to the labour relations system in Canada and which has accentuated the isolation of each certified bargaining unit and allowed the anti-union campaign of the banks to be successful. Much of the work on the unionization of white-collar workers has either been of a general, quantitative nature (such as Bain's work on white-collar unionization in Britain, which attempts to arrive at a general theory of unionization),[15] or has focused on the attitudes of the workers themselves in an attempt to understand their motives for unionizing. This was the approach taken by Lowe when analyzing the recent round of bank worker unionization in Canada.[16] The problem with both of these approaches is that they project an ahistorical view of the process. This disconnects the problem of unionization from the labour relations system and from the historical role of the state in moulding and channelling the labour movement's opposition to capital.

Since SORWUC applied for its first chartered bank units in 1976, there have been 206 applications for certification to the CLRB, of which 158 were eventually accepted for certification (i.e., they were able to demonstrate more than 50 percent support for the applicant union or bargaining agent). Clearly, chartered bank workers have shown a significant interest in becoming unionized. But by March 1985, nearly two-thirds of these certified unions—97, in fact—had been revoked, that is, decertified. This problem of decertification of significant numbers of bank units has received little attention from researchers.

Yet an examination of the reasons for the decertifications tells us something important about the failure of the bank campaign. In order to understand fully the difficulties of organizing this group of workers it is necessary to set the problems of the unionization drive within the legal certification framework of the Canada Labour Code and examine how union organizers and bank workers were channelled into a strategy that was doomed to fail.

THE JURIDIFICATION OF THE CANADIAN LABOUR RELATIONS SYSTEM

The certification approach to unionization, that is, the granting of exclusive bargaining agent status to a union that has demonstrated support from over 50 percent of the employees in the bargaining unit, is the basis of Canada's labour relations system. This system has its roots in the United States's Wagner Act, introduced in response to the unprecedented waves of labour unrest in the mid-thirties. Certification, protection against unfair labour practices, and third-party arbitration of grievances were all introduced into the Canadian labour relations system a decade later in return for labour's agreement to limit the use of the strike weapon to specified moments in the collective bargaining process.[17] This compromise on labour's part followed a period of heightened collective action by the Canadian labour movement, culminating in the growth and development of the large industrial unions such as the United Auto Workers (now the Canadian Auto Workers), the Steel Workers and Rubber Workers. To be blunt, then, legal recognition came only after labour, through its collective action, had presented itself as a threat to capital.[18]

Codifying collective bargaining transferred the decision making regarding the definition of the bargaining unit and, therefore, the future bargaining structure of the union, from the sphere of the union and its struggle with the employers, to that of the labour relations board. The determination of a bargaining unit's appropriateness—its size; the number of occupational groups to be included; the number of work sites to be covered; its geographical area—now falls within the purview of the board. Formation of the unit is not based, therefore, on the extent of the union's ability to organize.[19] For example, it may make sense for a union to define the unit narrowly or broadly depending on the willingness and readiness of members to undertake action in support of their demands. But the requirements of the formal certification process make it impossible for the unit to simply "grow like Topsy," reaching out to workers in other locations, branches or geographic areas, wherever the employer is located, and in response to a growing momentum. Legal certification, therefore, "gels" the bargaining unit into a form that can only be changed by the appropriate labour board. This has been one of the problems in organizing bank workers.

The authority of the labour relations board to define the bargaining unit and to certify the bargaining agent is the basis of institutionalized unionism in Canada and the United States. These legal processes are at the root of liberal ideology concerning unions. This ideology depicts the union as a *third party* to the collective bargaining process (the employer and the employees being the other parties), giving it an institutional set of roles and responsibilities which separates it from the volition and action of the rank and file.[20] This view has far-reaching effects on the way that workers, both unionized and non-unionized, view unions in our society. It lays the basis for the perception that unions are businesses with "union bosses," and of course this is reinforced by the practice of some unions and their leadership. The ideology of the third-party bargaining agent creates enormous difficulties and contradictions for union activists who attempt to organize and mobilize workers in opposition to employers. They are faced with workers who view the union as being external to themselves, who ask what they get for their compulsory dues payment, and who are sceptical when told, "*You* are the union!"[21]

But the institutionalization and juridification of the system extends far beyond the certification process and the limitation placed on the union in structuring and defining its own existence. For the law encircles the actions of unionists; it preys on every action they take or wish to take; it dictates that grievances be settled without recourse to strike; it dictates when strike action may take place, who can strike, and how they can strike. Picket lines that are too disruptive are quickly curtailed by injunctions, and when injunctions are ignored, contempt-of-court charges rapidly follow. Strikes that are too successful, and are deemed to be against the "public interest," are ended by back-to-work legislation. If the law is not obeyed by unionists, punishment comes quickly in the form of jail terms, heavy fines and the threat of legal decertification of the union.[22] Yet ironically, despite the repressive nature of the law regulating unions, the Canadian labour movement has historically looked to the law for protection. For example, both the CLC and the Ontario Federation of Labour (OFL) have called on the federal and provincial governments to enshrine in law such protective measures as the Rand Formula and the imposition of a first contract given recalcitrant employers. However, these protective mechanisms bring their own contradictions. A recent editorial in *Our Times* made the point, in response to the recent call from the OFL for first-contract legislation, that unions "did not appear because of laws, but because of social, economic and political inequalities; victories have come not from law reform (although that may have been one result), but from solid organizing." The editor continued: "If union membership is not strong enough to win its own good collective agreement in the first place, then the membership is usually not strong enough to hold on to a government imposed one."[23]

While this may indeed be the case, the law as a protector of working-class rights is not so easily dismissed. Workers discharged for union activity do get reinstated by labour relations boards; workers involved in a strike that has failed are able, under most circumstances, to return to their jobs; employers who try to prevent unionization may face, if caught, the automatic certification of the union; and third-party arbitration of grievances does, in many cases, result in victory for the union and the individual member. Moreover, labour boards and the courts operate with a certain discretion which allows them the flexibility to respond to pressures brought to bear by the class struggle. It is a discretion that often works in favour of the union.[24] How can the contradictory effects of law be explained?

Law as an institution is an important means of integrating the working class in Canada because it is, for the most part, obeyed and respected. We can argue that law is able to command obedience because of its hidden repression, which is not so hidden for leaders of unions who defy its commands. But this is by no means the whole story. Labour relations law receives the support of trade unionists because it embodies important gains won by the labour movement over time. It is, therefore, a mixture of class repression and compromises which have been enshrined in the law as a result of class struggles.[25] Enforced union recognition by employers, protection against unfair labour practices, and the arbitration of grievances were all compromises made during the 1940s in return for labour's agreement to limit the use of the strike weapon to certain points in the collective bargaining process. In effect, the labour movement agreed to its own institutionalization in order to gain a legally enforced negotiation process. This process was the means of achieving increased material benefits for organized workers, at least during periods of economic growth. The explosion of strikes, both legal and illegal, during the sixties caused new alarm within the Canadian state, resulting in the establishment of the Woods Commission. In studying the industrial relations crisis of the sixties, the Woods task force pointed to the over-regulation of collective bargaining and recommended more flexibility in dispute settlement, Recommendations that were enshrined in the Canada Labour Code included freeing up the strike weapon with regard to technological change issues during the life of the contract, and the addition of a preamble to the Code which positively endorsed the principle of collective bargaining.[26] However, these legislative changes, which followed the militancy of the sixties, did very little to loosen the straight-jacket of restrictions on the right to strike. Indeed, during the seventies and eighties, there have been repeated incidences of the "temporary" removal of this right at both the federal and provincial levels of government.[27]

The juridification of the conflict between labour and capital has had far-reaching effects on the ideology and practice of Canadian unions. The result is a labour movement that relies heavily on "labour relations experts" who spend a significant part of the unions' resources in representation before labour boards, arbitration hearings and the courts. Reliance on the law and its legal processes reduces the need of the leadership for active members who are committed to the policies of the union and are prepared to back them with the use of collective action. Indeed, active, critical members tend to become a liability and a threat to union leaders who prefer to put their trust in legalism rather than risk the uncertainty of attempting to mobilize the membership to undertake collective action. Furthermore, a union that depends continually on legalism loses the potential to develop organizing and mobilizing skills amongst its membership at large, leading union leaders to doubt the possibility of successfully mobilizing the membership, who they often perceive as being apathetic and unwilling to undertake action in support of union demands. In this sense, labour relations laws foster legalistic practice and thought among unionists, creating a situation in which the self-reliance of the membership is sapped and a dependency on technocrats is fostered.[28]

Dependency on the skill of legal experts serves to obfuscate the basis of union power, making it appear to derive from legal process rather than from the collective unity of the membership. This is not to suggest that unions can make a choice about whether or not they will participate in the legal labour relations system. The system is backed by the power of the state, and a union that refuses to participate simply cannot exist. Furthermore, the nature of the process is such that union struggles are often channelled into a legalistic battle without the union's consent. This was the case during the sixties and seventies when the Canadian Union of Postal Workers (CUPW) sought to meet the employer on the basis of its own strength, without the intervention of the law. But CUPW has tended to be atypical and, more often than not, it has been the labour movement itself that has looked to the law for protection, especially when small groups of workers have found themselves unable to challenge successfully the power of the employer.

The obfuscation of the relation of capital to labour is crucially important for the operation of the labour relations system. Labour relations laws are not neutral: their goals and practices are those that are defined by lawmakers and interpreters, who act on behalf of a system that is profoundly political and that has, at the end of the day, the objective of protecting the accumulation system of capital. The perception that the Canadian state acts as a "neutral arbiter" between the interests of labour and capital is an essential element in labour's continued obedience and allegiance to the law. In this role, the state is perceived as enacting laws that "give" rights to labour. This can be clearly seen in the expression, "the right to strike." This right has the appearance of being granted by the liberal-democratic state and enacted in law, rather than arising from a struggle waged by labour; it is, therefore, now enshrined in law, at least in a restricted form.[29] The law and application of the law have reinterpreted the history and significance of the "right to strike." As a result, many workers perceive that granting this right was one way the state "equalized" the power struggle between unions and employers.

The embodiment of class struggle in labour relations law remains hidden because of the "ideology" of neutrality that pervades the liberal-democratic form of law. This law is written and presented as though it enshrines the "rights and obligations" of labour and capital as interest groups that are equal in terms of power. As Anatole France put it: "In its majestic impartiality it [the law] forbids the rich and poor alike to sleep under the bridges of Paris." In much the same way, and with much the same facility, labour relations law treats labour and capital as "being on the same plane," with the state standing neutrally above the conflict to arbitrate "group interests." And, like the poor of Paris, unionists are much more likely to find themselves in jail than bankers, because it is unionists who must urge their members, at times, to "illegally strike"—something bankers need to do as little as they need to sleep under a bridge.

The classic example, in labour relations legislation, of treating labour and capital as if they were equally powerful is the strike and lockout. A strike by labour is represented as being equivalent to a lockout of employees by the employer. Yet they are fundamentally different. Their difference lies in their relation to property. Owners and employers can lock workers out because of their property rights, and they can hire "scabs" to continue production; the only power of workers, in this equation, is to withhold their labour power in an attempt to stop or slow down production. The ability of multinational corporations to relocate capital to countries where the price of labour is lower, thus resulting in the permanent "lockout" of Canadian workers, reveals the extent of this inequality. However, although the power of capital and labour is "equalized" under the liberal form of law, unionists receive differential treatment when they actually break that law. When owners or their representatives fire or lay off a worker for union activity, it is not deemed a criminal offence. It is treated simply as a violation of the Canada Labour Code, and the board can only insist on remedies that attempt to undo the wrong. Unions must ask why the Canadian state does not treat such employers as criminals, yet does exactly that to trade unionists who strike when the law forbids it.

Yet, while making the above argument, it is important at the same time to emphasize that the "neutrality" of the law is not merely appearance and hence simply ideology. It is precisely because laws, as they are written, are free from gross manipulation that the working class, in general, accepts their justness. E.P. Thompson has explored this important aspect of the law in *Whigs and Hunters*. He makes the point that laws are free from gross manipulation precisely as a result of previous class struggles.

In all these senses, the institution of law is crucially important in forging class integration. It commands obedience, not only because of its hidden repression and the ideology of equality and neutrality, but because it does embody gains won by subordinate classes over time. One of the fundamental problems facing the union movement in Canada is the need to take a critical stance in relation to "the impossible ideals of the liberal forms of state," which proclaim that capital and labour are equal entities in terms of law, and develop an understanding that the institution of law is based on the contours of the class struggle. "Law always expresses a vision of society. It also expresses the groups behind this vision and the interests served by conceiving the society in that particular form."[30] In other words, labour relations laws, like other laws, reflect both the strength and weakness of the working class and, in turn, act to both strengthen and weaken workers as a class. This understanding of labour relations law sheds light on the bank workers' struggle and, in particular, on how the law both weakened and strengthened their organizing drive.

BANK WORKER ORGANIZING
AND THE CANADIAN LABOUR CODE

The first hearings related to the attempts to organize bank workers began in April 1977, when the CLRB started to consider the question of an appropriate bargaining unit for the banks. SORWUC had twenty-two branch applications before the board, involving 264 workers, and wanted the board to rule that any branch could unionize in isolation from other branches. Ironically, by that time, SORWUC itself had become convinced that the bank branch was not an appropriate unit for collective bargaining. The union realized that a few unionized branches within a sea of non-union branches would have very little bargaining power, and would not be able to withstand the anti-union attack already launched by the powerful chartered banks. Only the day before the hearings began, a special membership meeting of SORWUC voted to organize on a province-wide basis. Jackie Ainsworth, treasurer of the United Bank Workers (a local of SORWUC), stated that "this motion was the result of intense anti-union pressure in the branches, the difficulty of maintaining majorities in the individual branches, and our feeling that bank workers organized on a province-wide basis would have more bargaining power."[31]

SORWUC was criticized severely by both CLC organizers and board officials for the timing of its criticisms.[32] However, SORWUC found itself caught in this contradiction because of legal certification requirements. SORWUC was aware that branch certification would structure the union in a way that would harm the collective bargaining process. But its leaders felt that it had to be demonstrated to bank workers that it was legally possible to unionize. Unionization in Canada has come to mean legal certification and SORWUC believed that it had to gain certification of the bank branch in order to build the union. At the hearings, the union's president, Jean Rands, argued that the board had to define the bargaining unit in such a way that bank workers would know that they had a right to unionize. As she put it, "no bank employees in English Canada have collective bargaining rights and until they do they're not going to believe that they can have them."[33] This is a further example of where a right—that of collective bargaining—has been "naturalized" by the state and workers now perceive it as emanating entirely from the state and the law.

SORWUC gained the branch certification and won the first "legal round" against the banks. But the technical requirements and restrictions inherent in the labour code and the law in general resulted in an immediate set-back to the organizing drive. Only eight of the twenty-two applications before the board actually achieved certification. Five of the branches were able to demonstrate immediately that a majority of employees were union members and, therefore, automatically received certification. However, in the other seventeen, the board ordered votes to be held and the union failed to gain a majority in all but three of the branches. This result had devastating consequences for the Union's organizing drive. Why did the board order votes when SOR-

WUC had majority support in most of the branches on the date it applied for certification?[34] The answer is complex, but important, and illustrates the ongoing technical difficulties which obscure and complicate the process of legal unionization.

Initially the board had taken the date of application for certification as the date when support for the union would be determined. But on 16 February 1977, the Federal Court of Appeal successfully upheld a challenge by CKOY Limited (an Ottawa radio station which was trying to fend off a unionization attempt by its own employees) that the date should be that of certification.[35] This resulted in the CLRB determining union support in the twenty-two branches in July 1977—nearly a year after the first applications had been made. During that year, many union supporters had resigned or been transferred to other branches. This normal turnover of bank workers was problem enough; however, the banks had begun an intense anti-union campaign right after the first applications were made. As a result, many employees resigned from the union and voted against unionization. Also, anti-union personnel were moved into applicant branches to help defeat the pro-union vote. This tactic was very effective in small branches where one or two votes can be the differences between winning or losing. Later on the banks used this same method to destabilize union branches and start decertification petitions.[36]

The CKOY Limited decision illustrates how technical ramifications—which can develop in any type of legal process—affect the labour relations system. Such technicalities increase the reliance on legal experts, and further limit the possibility for rank-and-file involvement. Union members feel frustrated and distanced by legal process, whether it involves certification, unfair labour practices, arbitration of grievances or collective bargaining. Despite SORWUC's particular philosophy of making unionism accessible to its membership, the branch certification decision involved two lawyers on their side, several days of hearings, and many appeals by the banks to the Federal Court. The banks either lost or withdrew all of their appeals but these appeals nevertheless had the effect of diverting time, energy and money from the organization drive.

Fighting the battle for branch certification was only the beginning of the legal difficulties with the bank workers campaign. Once branch certification was won, SORWUC and the other unions which had entered the fray were immediately thrown into a series of unfair labour practice complaints. Just before the July 1977 hearings regarding the occupational composition of the branch units, SORWUC wrote to its members on an optimistic note:

Hopefully the issue of a union for bank employees is now

> out of the courts and in the hands of the bank employees.
> It is now up to bank employees to decide. If a majority of
> bank employees want a union, we will succeed.[37]

It was a false hope. SORWUC found not only that it was impossible to successfully negotiate collective agreements given the lack of power of the branch units, but also that the unfair labour practice complaints submitted to the CLRB threw up so many legal entanglements that it was to be a long time before the union left the hearing rooms and courts.

The unfair labour practice complaints arose in response to the banks' anti-union campaign. In the initial organizing period of 1977-78, when the organizing drive was at its height, the banks had more complaints laid against them than any other sector under the jurisdiction of the CLRB.[38] The complaints against the banks constituted over one-third of all those received. The banks' counter-union campaign ranged from accommodative to coercive measures. The accommodative measures improved the benefits of the bank employees in an attempt to weaken the attractiveness of unionization. During 1977-78, most of the large chartered banks announced a series of improved benefits. After the anti-inflation guidelines were lifted near the end of 1978, the five largest chartered banks announced a wage increase of nine percent.[39] The largest increase that any of the banks have given previously was eight percent in 1974, when inflation, as measured by the consumer price index, had been running at eleven percent compared to nine percent in 1978. The other thrust of the anti-union campaign was to "punish" those bank workers who unionized and to advertise their punishment as a deterrent to others.

The punishing tactics ranged "from the clearly legal to the clearly illegal."[40] They included captive-audience meetings in branches that had applied for certification or were suspected of being "infiltrated" by the union; dissemination of anti-union literature; manipulation of the branches' employees complement; closing down branches; and discharging or laying off union leaders and members. The anti-union campaign became so blatant that Marc Lapointe, chairperson of the CLRB, was obliged to write, in reference to the Canadian Imperial Bank of Commerce (CIBC), that "it has become apparent throughout the organizational attempts (by several unions) at various branches of the employer across the country, that this employer has embarked on a campaign designed to discourage its employees from exercising their rights under the Code."[41] As noted earlier, the unions filed complaints in record numbers. But even when complaints were upheld, the jurisdiction of the board to undo the harm to the organizing drive was, on the whole, extremely limited. When the CLRB did attempt to remedy the situation, the banks, in some cases, successfully appealed to higher courts and had the board's decision reversed.

A good example of this kind of reversal was the case of La Banque Nationale, which shut down a unionized branch and amalgamated it with another with the sole aim of getting rid of the union. As a consequence, the board, among other remedies, ordered the bank to put $144,000 in a trust fund that was to be used "to further the objectives of the Canada Labour Code as they are stated in the preamble." It further directed the president of La Banque Nationale to sign a letter to employees, written by the board, that announced the trust fund and declared the bank's support for collective bargaining. This was a novel decision for the CLRB, even though it appears to be mild.[42] The bank appealed the ruling, and another two years of legal representation and wrangling ensued. Finally, the Supreme Court of Canada struck down the decision as "totalitarian," maintaining that it forced the president to sign a letter he had not written. Mr. Justice Beetz, acting in the best liberal tradition of the law held that

> this type of penalty is totalitarian and as such is alien to the tradition of free nations like Canada, even for the repression of the most serious of crimes. I cannot be persuaded that the Parliament of Canada intended to confer on the Canada Labour Board [sic] the power to impose such extreme measures....[43]

It should be noted that the court did not dispute the board's findings, and upheld the ruling that the union was to be allowed to represent workers at the branch's new location. Given this, the description of the penalty as "extreme" indicates the narrow limits within which the state acts as "neutral arbiter." The ruling also indicates that the individual rights of the president of the bank were deemed by the Supreme Court to have more importance than the collective right of workers to associate and organize.

The most important and sophisticated tactic in the banks' plan to defeat unionization revolved around the "freeze" sections of the Code. These sections prevent the employer from altering rates of pay, or any other condition of employment, when the union applies for certification (section 124), and again when notice to bargain is given (section 148). These sections, supported and demanded by the labour movement in general, were designed to protect unions from employers who attempt to "undercut" collective bargaining by giving additional benefits to individual employees. The banks interpreted the freeze sections to mean that the annual cost of living increase would only be given to the non-union branches and not to employees in unionized branches or those applying for certification. This illustrates that even when the clear intent of the law is to protect workers, its formal, technical aspect can act as a "doubled-edged sword" and be used against them. The wage freeze caused consternation in branches where union drives were in progress, and the cry went up from anti-union employees, demanding: "Are you for the nine percent increase or for the union?"[44]

The freezing of pay in the unionizing units occurred almost immediately after the first branches were certified and had a devastating impact on SORWUC's organizing campaign. The decline in organizing began with the rumours and actual announcements of the wage freeze. SORWUC immediately filed an unfair labour practice complaint, but the CLRB did not rule in the union's favour. With the failure of the complaint, the number of SORWUC's bank worker members dropped drastically.[45] The detrimental effect of the wage freeze on its own organizing drive led the UBE/CLC to take "another run" at the issue. Informal discussions with Marc Lapointe led CLC leaders to believe that another complaint might be successful.[46] A second freeze complaint was filed, therefore, and nearly a year later the board found in favour of the union. In exercising its discretion, this time in favour of the union, the board was responding to pressures brought both by the CLC and the women's movement.[47]

In its second decision, the CLRB strongly repudiated the banks' strategy of freezing unionizing workers' wages. It noted that the CIBC's "motive was undoubtedly aimed at having a chilling effect on potential organizing." The decision went on to point out that "very harsh corrective measures had to be ordered by the Board in order to restore the balance destroyed by the unlawful actions of the employer."[48] But were the corrective measures harsh? Certainly not compared to the jail terms that some union leaders have received for ignoring the law. Neither were they of a kind that would deter the banks from using similar tactics in the future. The monetary penalty simply restored lost wages to the unionized employees. The CIBC was also required to post a retraction in all bank branches—hardly "a very harsh measure." John Crispo has pointed out that the CIBC might have been happy to write it "because in doing so, in being forced, they were able to convey to their employees that they don't like unions."[49] Certainly the banks lost very little as a result of the decision—particularly when compared to the unions' loss of membership. Furthermore, the momentum of the initial organizing drive had evaporated entirely by the time the board issued the favourable decision in November 1979.

Canada's chartered banks will always be tough employers. They will always fight "tooth and nail" to defeat a unionization drive. They have a lot to lose. With an overwhelming majority of women as their employees, and with these women being paid far less than the industrial average and provided with comparatively few benefits, the banks will apply every strategy and tactic to ensure that they remain union-free.[50] They were able to exploit the lack of power of the small branch units and benefit from the delays inherent in the legal system; they were prepared to violate the Canada Labour Code and risk penalties for unfair labour practices—all this to stop the success of the unionizing drive. They were able to force SORWUC into a set of costly and protracted negotiations; they launched appeals; and they frustrated the unions' organizing campaigns by a wide array of unfair labour practices. The money, time and effort spent by the unions in legal hearings channelled needed resources away from the organizing process. But even more important, the unions' strategy to fight back against the banks' anti-union tactics remained, for the most part, in the hearing rooms of the CLRB and the courts, removed from the actions and volition of workers.

The experience of bank branch organizing required the unions to change their approach to the organizing drive. SORWUC began with enthusiasm, vowing to build a union based on the collective action and decision-making of its membership. Branch certification, however, prematurely removed the struggle between the banks and their employees to the hearing rooms of the CLRB. In other words, the institutionalization of the conflict occurred before sufficient mobilization had produced a union strong enough to fight the banks and strong enough not to need the protection of the law. The state's intervention (which occurred at the demand of the union) limited at an early stage in the conflict the possibilities of mobilizing on a wider basis (e.g., regionally or province-wide). Although SORWUC became fully aware of the limitations of the certified branch unit very early on, its organizers were drawn into the contradictions of seeking branch certification, because they believed bank workers had to be convinced that unionization could legally take place. Instead, the unions witnessed the evaporation of collective action and found itself caught up in the technical details of unfair labour practice cases and in attempts to negotiate collective agreements for each of the small certified branches. The chartered banks consistently refused to conduct joint branch negotiations or even to negotiate a mass collective agreement for all branches of particular banks. The resulting difficulties in achieving viable collective agreements on behalf of the small certified bank branches, located all over British Columbia, were insurmountable and SORWUC applied for revocation of the bank units.

The union organizers working for UBE/CLC were appalled at this action by SORWUC, and went on to conclude collective agreements with the banks. Their bottom line was the inclusion of the Rand Formula, which they viewed as absolutely essential if the units were to have any chance of survival. After a well publicized campaign and the threat of the removal of labour movement money from the CIBC, the contracts were won.[51] In the first round of bargaining, however, UBE/CLC achieved little improvement over the conditions of non-unionized bank workers. The chartered banks have proved to be very tough negotiators and have been extremely reluctant to grant any concessions that would demonstrate that it "pays" to be unionized. When the unions did achieve small gains, the banks quickly passed on the same improvements to their workers in the non-unionized branches. This was the case with the Bank of Montreal in the Windsor area. The UBE/CLC had managed to unionize nine branches out of a possible twelve. In the first round of negotiations, one of the main achievements for the union was an extra day's vacation. The improvement was simply passed on to all employees of the Bank of Montreal.[52] The inability of the unions to achieve contracts that demonstrate to non-unionized bank workers the benefits to be achieved by unionization has been a major stumbling block in the organizing.

Unionized bank branch workers have had little to encourage them to remain unionized. Poor contracts, intimidation by the banks, and an apparent lack of support from their sisters in non-unionized branches have resulted in a steady stream of branch decertifications. Clearly bank workers in the small, unionized branches felt they had gained very little for their pains. As one employee stated, in a newly decertified branch in Ottawa: "Why should I pay one percent of my salary for something I've already got?"[53] The employees in this same branch voted for decertification a few months after the negotiation of their first contract. Furthermore, the smallness of the branches has made it relatively simple for the management of the banks to bring in one or two anti-union employees, thus changing the union's majority in the branch and implanting employees who can be depended upon to launch the decertification process. Persuading a majority of workers in a small branch to sign an anti-union petition is a much simpler process than conducting a decertification drive among large numbers of workers in many different locations.

The effect of branch certification meant that a relatively small number of bank workers, in the certified branches, found themselves in the front lines of the struggle, taking on the battle on behalf of the other hundred and fifty thousand who watched from the sidelines. Even if many of those watching had been ready to join in, the nature of branch-by-branch certification meant that they could do this legally only by unionizing their individual branches and negotiating separately with the banks. This scenario has been repeated time and time again over the past ten years; the result has been little improvement in collective agreements and, therefore, a continuing series of bank branch decertifications. This strategy, as we have seen, has resulted in many legal decisions that have been regarded as pro-labour victories. However, the fact that bank workers have been applying continually for decertification of the union they fought hard to obtain demonstrates that these decisions have done little to build a bank workers' organization capable of surviving, let along capable of effectively confronting the power of the banks.

TOWARDS A STRATEGY
OF ORGANIZING BANK WORKERS

Faced with poor agreements, decertification of the branch units, and the demobilization, in general, of the organizing campaign, those unions remaining in the field began to devise more aggressive strategies and tactics to deal with the banks. There have been two significant strikes of chartered banks to try to break the pattern of poor agreements.[54] The first was undertaken by workers in six branches of the Royal Bank after they were organized by La Confédération des Syndicats Nationaux (CSN) in the Saguenay-Lac St-Jean region. These workers—numbering about 100—demonstrated a militancy and courage that once more gave lie to the argument that women workers are more passive than men when faced with a tough employer. They endured a strike that lasted over twelve months, against a multinational corporation which is the largest financial institution in Canada—the Royal Bank. The bank employed the usual delaying tactic of appealing decisions, but when the workers undertook strike action, the bank engaged in a veritable "orgy" of litigation, initiating "no less than forty-two civil and criminal proceedings ranging from injunctions to contempt of court." There were even more interventions by the CLRB and "the board was seized of no less than sixty-five complaints of unfair labour practices." The high number resulted first from the decision of the workers to go on strike before the conciliation procedures in the Canada Labour Code were exhausted, and second from ignoring injunctions against picketing.[55]

The Royal Bank went to great trouble and expense to fly workers from Montreal and Quebec City in and out of the branches in order to keep them open during the entire period of the strike. Although there was no evidence of any real bargaining by the bank, the CLRB concluded that there were no grounds for imposition of a first collective agreement. Board member Jacques Archambault dissented, and in a minority report recommended that such an agreement should be imposed.[56] The strike continued and was eventually settled by special mediators in September 1980. Although the final settlements in these units brought the same small achievements of other branch negotiations, the two branches that took the leadership role in the strike have remained unionized, while the other Royal Bank branches, certified at approximately the same time, have asked to have, and have had, their union status revoked. It is testimony to the fact that long strikes often engender great commitment and union solidarity even when the material gains may be few or even negative. However, militancy on the part of 100 workers, no matter how dedicated, makes an uneven fight against the Royal Bank. Other strategies were clearly needed.

In 1982, the CSN initiated a different approach. The union organized all five branches of La Banque Nationale in the town of Rimouski and then applied to the CLRB to consider these five branches as one unit for the purpose of collective bargaining. The CLRB moves slowly. *Four years later*, it issued a decision certifying the unit as appropriate, referring to it as a "cluster of establishments." Although small, comprising a total of eighty-six employees, the unit does cover all branches of La Banque Nationale in Rimouski.[57] The CSN has demonstrated its militancy in the past. The bank will have to consider whether or not it is willing to face a possible shut-down, or at least slowdown, of its entire operation in this one town. By adopting the "cluster of establishments" strategy, the CSN has gained more bargaining power for branch negotiations than any other union. Whether it will be enough to conclude a successful agreement remains to be seen. In any event. it is hardly surprising that La Banque Nationale immediately appealed the decision to the Federal Court, thereby delaying and maybe even scuttling the entire process.

The other important development in bank worker unionization occurred from 1983 to 1985, with the organizing of employees in the CIBC Toronto Visa centre by the UBE/CLC. The Visa employees were certified in August 1984, and began the process of negotiating a collective agreement. A year later, very little had been achieved at the bargaining table, so the union, after considerable publicity, went out on strike. The Visa workers were joined on the picket line by mailroom employees working at the head office of the

CIBC. This brought the total number of workers affected to approximately 400. The CLC, aided by the Canadian Auto Workers, put considerable financial and human resources into the fight against the Commerce. Each full-time employee was paid $300 a week to walk the picket line, while part-time workers received $160. The unions enlisted the aid of the rest of the labour movement to demonstrate, picket and boycott the CIBC. The bank remained unmoved and kept the Visa centre open.[58] The CLRB, on the other hand, responded to the pressure. The board imposed a first agreement, something they had refused to do during the Royal Bank's dispute with the CSN in the Saguenay-Lac St-Jean region. A comparison of the two decisions reveals that the Royal Bank's actions in the Saguenay dispute were not very different from those of the CIBC in the Toronto Visa case.[59] However, in the case of the CSN strike, the board members took the union to task for using the strike weapon before conciliation had ended. The decision stated that the use of a strike

> in the cold, calculating manner during the conciliation period before the legal right to do so has been acquired, is totally unacceptable. Such recourse by a party constitutes a violation of its obligation to bargain in good faith.[60]

It would appear that the board used its discretion to adopt a punishing attitude towards the CSN because the union went on strike before the legally condoned moment. It is also clear from the decision imposing the first agreement, that the board was well aware that the CIBC Visa strike had become "a national union cause" and that the labour movement, as a whole, was looking for a positive decision.

The imposition of the first agreement, in the case of the Visa workers, was hailed by the labour movement as an important victory. The first reaction of the CIBC was to appeal the decision of the Federal Court. After a few days of reflection, however, the bank announced that it was satisfied with the imposed contract because it "preserved the bank's right to give workers merit pay above the specified wage scales and [did] not award the workers any improvements in benefit plans."[61] On the positive side for the union, the grievance procedure had been improved to provide for arbitration of a wide number of issues, including the pay merit system. Also, importantly, the bank was prevented from contracting out work during the life of the contract. Given the contract's contents, it appears unlikely that a successful strategy for organizing bank workers will be aided very much by the imposed first agreement.

Such an agreement may, however, provide an important "beach-head" from which further counter-attacks can be launched. It is also significant that, since the beginning of the CIBC Visa struggle, another unit has received certification at the head office in Toronto, bringing the number organized there to approximately 760.[62] It is likely that the relative success of the Visa strike, together with the support shown by the rest of the labour movement, have had a positive effect on the organizing drive in that city.

It appears that the strategy of combining collective action with use of the protection offered by the Canada Labour Code has resulted in the greatest success to date for bank workers unionization. Yet the problem remains that most bank workers are employed in small bank branches. The banks will only likely be ready to negotiate with the unions, in a meaningful way, once all branches and data centres are organized in a particular region, and one ready to strike. This form of organization, together with support from the labour movement in the form of an effective boycott of the bank, backed up with demonstrations and other forms of collective action, offers the best possibility for achieving better collective agreements and the continuing development of the bank worker unionization.

CONCLUSION

At the beginning of this article, it was contended that the last ten years of organizing bank workers have resulted, for the most part, in demotivation and demobilization of branch workers, rather than the development of an organization that has successfully confronted the power of the chartered banks. Certification of the bank branch resulted in a strategy of unionizing small groups of workers, often in branches completely isolated from each other, and led to a recognizable pattern of organizing, certification, attempt at negotiations, poor settlements and then application for decertification. Recently we have seen two important breaks in this pattern. The organizing of workers in the CIBC Visa centre and parts of the head office in Toronto has resulted in the largest grouping of organized bank workers to date, albeit one separated into three bargaining units. In a further development in Quebec, workers in five branches of La Banque Nationale successfully applied for joint certification on the basis of clustering together appropriately located establishments. The question is whether these two newly grouped organizations of bank workers will be able to provoke a serious challenge to the power of banking capital.

The other important and successful ingredient in the CIBC Visa struggle was the mobilization of the whole labour movement in support of the bank workers. While this mobilization did not seem to seriously affect the continuing operation of the CIBC or lead the bank to negotiate meaningfully with the union, it did, nevertheless, place pressure on the state itself, in the form of the CLRB, thus resulting in the imposed first agreement. The support of the labour movement may also have been an important factor in encouraging other CIBC workers, at the head office location, to join the struggle. The experience of organizing bank workers points to the need to develop an organizing strategy that finds ways of grouping larger numbers of workers together when confronting the banks, and that seeks to involve the labour movement as a whole in the struggle.

The organizing of bank workers has, however, lessons for the organizing of workers in general. The certification approach to unionization, although forcing the banks to acknowledge the existence of the unions and thus bringing them screaming and kicking to the bargaining table, has done very little to strengthen the power of bank workers as a collectivity. On the contrary, it can be argued that the institutionalization of collective bargaining, through the certification process, has done much to weaken that power. We saw this very clearly in the case of the branch bank workers. The organizing and certification of workers into small, isolated units without the bargaining power to achieve viable collective agreements provides one example. We also saw the effects of a highly juridified system, which, while offering important protections, nevertheless channelled bank workers into a dependency on the law, reducing the possibility for collective action. It was only when the CIBC bank workers, together with the labour movement, combined collective action with the limited protection offered by the law that some real gains were achieved.

Organizing the unorganized is an essential part of strengthening working-class organization. The large number of unorganized workers (over 60 percent of the total), many of them women and new Canadians, limits the potential of the labour movement both in the short and the long term. For example, the problem of unequal pay is difficult to address in the absence of a union; the use of non-unionized workers as cheap labour places them in opposition to the unionized work force and aids the attack on workers as a whole; the harmful effects of technological change, with its propensity to de-skill jobs, cannot be limited in the absence of a union contract. But more importantly, the project of organizing the unorganized has a significance that goes beyond the mere defence of jobs and the material conditions of workers. The extension of unionization to the majority of workers in the paid labour force would be a step in overcoming the divisions and the fragmentation that cut through the subordinate classes. It would further open up the organized labour movement to the concerns of those workers who have been marginalized in our society—women, indigenous Canadians, immigrants and youth—and to issues that derive from the dominance of capitalist social relations. In this sense, the organizing project stands in opposition to the exclusiveness of business unionism, which narrowly perceives its only purpose as the increase of material benefits for its own exclusive membership.

The juridification of the labour relations system and the certification approach to collective bargaining came into being, in part, because of the demand of industrial workers, in the 1940s, to participate in the benefits of unionization enjoyed mainly by the exclusionary craft unions. The contradictory outcome of that movement was a system that increased the bureaucratic tendencies of the union movement and limited its potential to undertake the kind of collective action needed to organize the unorganized. The experience of bank workers points to the need for a strategy that mobilizes unionized workers in support of the unorganized and seeks to build and support the collective power of these workers. Such a strategy cannot be achieved by relying on the decisions of labour boards and the courts, or by allowing the liberal form of law to structure the action to be taken. It is a strategy that must begin with the collective action of the labour movement as a whole.

ENDNOTES

An earlier version of this paper was presented at the Sixth Conference on Workers and Their Communities at the University of Ottawa, May 1986. I would like to thank Amy Bartholomew, Donald Swartz and George Warskett for their comments, and Roberta Hamilton for her help in making revisions.

1. The story of the United Bank Workers (UBW), a section of SORWUC, is told by the Bank Book Collective in *An Account to Settle* (Vancouver, 1979).

2. Re: Canadian Imperial Bank of Commerce (CIBC), Victory Square Branch see Canadian Labour Relations Board, *Decisions Information* 20 (Ottawa, June 1977) Board File No. 555-614, pp. 319-55; *Idem* for discussion of 1959 decision re: the Bank of Nova Scotia, Kitimat, British Columbia [hereafter CLRB, *DI*]. The unionization of bank workers had been blocked because of the perceived need by union organizers to sign up all workers of a particular bank, from coast to coast. This, in fact, was not a correct assumption, but union organizers tend to be socialized by board decisions and are often unwilling to take time, energy and expense to challenge them. See Rosemary Warskett, "Trade Unions and the Canadian State: A Case Study of Bank Worker Unionization, 1976-1980," (M.A. thesis, Carleton University, 1981).

3. At its 1972 convention, the CLC had established a fund for organizing the unorganized. The same convention sponsored the formation of the Association of Commercial and Technical Employees (ACTE), with the expressed intention of organizing workers in the financial sector. However, the ACTE campaign was a failure. A lot of money was spent on billboard advertising and glossy booklets, but little time and effort was spent on building organizing committees at the level of the workplace. See Graham Lowe, "Insurance Union Squelched," *Ontario Report* (March-April 1975).

4. These included SORWUC, UBE/CLC, OPEIU (and its British Columbian counterpart, the Office and Technical Employees Union—OTEU), RCIU and La Confédération des Syndicats Nationaux (CSN), the independent union central which operates wholly in Quebec.

5. Marianne Bossen, *Employment in Chartered Banks,1969-1975* (Ottawa: Labour Canada, 1984), pp. 13-14.

6. Figures issued by the CLRB effective March 1985 and August 1986. Figures

regarding the number of applications made and the number of revocations granted were available only to March 1985. Included in these figures are two units that
were certified before 1975.

7. Bossen, *Employment in Chartered Banks*, p. 11.

8. Elizabeth Beckett, *Unions and Bank Workers: Will the Twain Ever Meet?*
    (Ottawa: Labour Canada, 1984), pp. 1-9.

9. For decision re: La Banque Nationale du Canada, Rimouski, Quebec see CLRB,
    DI 55 (December 1985) BFN. 555-1685, p. 3.5; Beckett, *Unions and Bank
    Workers*; and Graham S. Lowe, "Causes of Unionization in Canadian Banks,"
    Industrial Relations 36:4 (1981).

10. In a recent decision, Marc Lapointe, chairperson of the CLRB—in an extraordi-
    nary outpouring of conservatism—wrote that the banks and unions attribute the
    high turnover of staff "to the life patterns of women employees." Lapointe then
    went on to describe this life pattern as marriage followed by housekeeping and
    childcare. "Furthermore," he reported, "some of them want only to get a little
    extra income to contribute to a major capital expense (a house) or to replace
    their husband's lost income for a certain period of time. Insofar as this was and is
    a valid view of society, unionizing bank employees is a major challenge. Women
    would not be looking for careers, and would be undemanding in the salaries and
    working conditions they expect from the industry. These are all factors that make
    them an unattractive prospect for a union organizer." See La Banque National du
    Canada, pp. 3.5-3.6. In opposition to the above views, the evidence indicates
    that women are staying in the labour market in greater numbers than ever
    before. The female labour market participation rate rose from 20.7 percent in
    1941 to 51.6 percent in 1981. See Statistics Canada, *The Labour Force, 1981
    Annual Averages*, 71-001 (December 1981). The percentage of women
    employed in banking is among the highest of any sector; however, women are
    found in equally high numbers in public administration. It is unlikely that clerical
    workers in the public sector have a completely different life pattern from bank
    workers, yet these workers are not only highly unionized but have a substantially
    lower turnover rate.

11. Lowe, "Causes of Unionization," p. 872. The reliance on this kind of explanation
    is somewhat surprising given that evidence has long been available from a wide
    variety of research projects which have effectively called into question the con-
    tention that women are less likely to unionize than men. As far back as 1958, D.
    Lockwood, noting that the density of unionization was much lower among
    women than men, was led to conclude that the differences in the degree of

unionization among women and men were attributable "to something other than differences in sex ratios." See D. Lockwood, *The Blackcoated Workers* (London, 1958), p. 151. See also G.S. Bain, *The Growth of White-Collar Unionism* (London, 1970); J.K. Eaton, *Union Growth in Canada in the Sixties* (Ottawa, 1976); Julie White, *Women in Unions* (Hull, Quebec, 1980); and Linda Briskin, "Women in Unions in Canada: Statistical Overview," in Linda Briskin and Lynda Yanz (eds.), *Union Sisters* (Toronto, 1983).

12. Bain, *Growth of White-Collar Unionism*, p. 41.

13. In the context of the campaigns to organize Canadian Banks, some researchers have questioned the employment concentration thesis. See Allen Ponak and Larry E. Moore, "Canadian Bank Unionism," *Industrial Relations* 36:1 (1981), p. 17; and Lowe, "Causes of Unionization," p. 881. However, these researchers based their findings on a small number of certified branches near the beginning of the campaigns. What is important to understand is that legal certification does not necessarily amount to viable unionization. This certainly was the case with most of the small branches that were decertified at a later date. Small branches were the first to unionize in Canada because of the 1977 branch decision. Following that ruling, legal certification could be obtained if over 50 percent of eligible workers in a bank branch (or other viable unit) were members of the applicant union. Therefore, it was easier for a union to obtain a majority in the smaller branches simply because a smaller number of members needed to be signed up.

14. See A. Egan, "Women in Banking: a Study in Inequality," *Industrial Relations Journal* 133:20 (1982), p. 28.

15. Bain, *Growth of White-Collar Unionism*.

16. Lowe, "Causes of Unionization."

17. The roots of the New Deal collective bargaining policy are examined by Christopher L. Tomlins in *The State and the Unions: Labor Relations, Law and the Organized Labor Movement in America, 1880-1960* (Cambridge, U.K., 1985). Tomlins concludes that unions must recognize that many of their problems stem from the laws that purport to protect them.

18. In terms of the history of Canadian labour relations law, from the perspective of class theory, see Paul Craven, *An Impartial Umpire: Industrial Relations and the Canadian State, 1900-1911* (Toronto, 1980). Craven analyzes the introduction of a public interest dispute policy at the turn of the century. Also see Leo Panitch and Donald Swartz, *From Consent to Coercion: The Assault on Trade Union Freedoms* (Toronto, 1985). They give an overview of labour relations law

in Canada and argue that there has been a growing reliance on coercive measures in the 1970s and 1980s.

19. Of course, the labour relations board does receive representation from the union and employer on the issue of appropriate unit, but the final decision rests with the board. When the Wagner Act was first introduced, the National Labour Relations Board based the unit's definition on the extent of the union's organizing. See George W. Adams, Q.C., Canadian Labour Law (Aurora, Ont., 1985), p. 320.

20. Karl E. Klare, "Judicial Deradicalization of the Wagner Act and the Origins of Modern Legal Consciousness, 1937-1941," Minnesota Law Review 62 (1978), pp. 265-339.

21. This refers to Justice Rand's 1946 ruling on union security, in which all employees in the bargaining unit must pay dues, but do not have to be members of the union. The ruling was an arbitral award resulting from a settlement between the Ford Motor Company and the United Auto Workers after a bitter strike in Windsor in the winter of 1945. The Rand Formula, which is the union security found in many collective agreements, has reinforced the ideology of the union as "institutional bargaining agent." The fact that members and non-members benefit equally from the collective bargaining and representation processes produces an insurance-policy view of union process: "You pay your money and you receive protection," and there is no requirement to participate. This view of union process has been heightened by the ruling of Justice White, of the Ontario Supreme Court, in the case of Lavigne. That decision held that the use of compulsory union dues for purposes other than collective bargaining contravenes the Canadian Charter of Rights and Freedoms.

22. This was the case for the Canadian Union of Postal Workers and its leader, Jean-Claude Parrot, 1980, and labour leaders in Newfoundland in 1986.

23. See "Second Thoughts on First Contracts," Our Times November 1985, p. 4.

24. Douglas Hay argues that the use of legal discretion in eighteenth-century England contributed to the ideology that law was just and merciful, and helped "to maintain the fabric of obedience, gratitude and deference" of the labouring classes. Discretion "allowed a prosecutor to terrorize the petty thief and then command his gratitude...." See Douglas Hay, "Property, Authority and the Criminal Law," in Piers Bierne and Richard Quinney (eds.), Marxism and Law (New York, 1982), p. 120. Consent by unionists to the system of labour relations is increased when labour relations boards and the courts find in their favour, but even losses can be absorbed in a system where a "lose some/win some" consciousness prevails.

25. For an elaboration of this argument, see E.P. Thompson's remarkable study of the Black Act in England, *Whigs and Hunters, The Origin of the Black Act* (New York, 1975).

26. H.D. Woods, *Canadian Industrial Relations, The Report of the Task Force on Labour Relations* (Ottawa, 1968). The preamble, recommended by the Woods Commission and enshrined in the Canada Labour Code, expresses a positive encouragement of the principles of free collective bargaining. Marc Lapointe, chairperson of the CLRB, used this preamble as the touchstone for the bank branch decision. He stated that branch certification would give "employees a realistic possibility of exercising their rights under the Code." CIBC, Victory Square branch, CLRB, *DI* 20, p. 349.

27. Panitch and Swartz argue that restrictions on labour have become the norm rather than the exception and are part of "a new era in state policy towards labour." They contend that "what marks this transformation is a shift from the generalized rule-of-law form of coercion...towards a form of selective, ad hoc, discretionary state coercion...." See *From Consent to Coercion*, p. 33.

28. Following Claus Offe and H. Wiesenthal, it can be said that with the juridification of collective bargaining, unions have been channelled into relying on monological practices, in which bureaucratic and individualist elements predominate, rather than on dialogical practices, which rely upon collective action of the membership as the source of power in achieving the union's goals. See "Two Logics of Collective Action," in Claus Offe *Disorganized Capitalism* ed. John Keane, (Cambridge, Mass., 1985). In the context of the juridification of the American labour relations system, Klare argues that the courts fashioned the Wagner Act so that "certain concrete legal inhibitions were placed on worker self-activity." He gives the example of the "sit-down" strike, which was ruled to fall outside of "the right to strike." See Klare, "Judicial Deradicalization of the Wagner Act," p. 319.

29. Stuart Hall has referred to this as the "naturalization of rights." See *Drifting into the Law and Order Society.* (London, 1980).

30. Klare, "Judicial Deradicalization of the Wagner Act," p. 265.

31. Bank Book Collective, *An Account to Settle*, p. 44.

32. Discussions with CLC organizers (September 1978). In a recent decision, Marc Lapointe, CLRB chairperson, took SORWUC to task for its actions and statements, going so far as to refer to the union as "the sorcerer's apprentices." See La Banque Nationale du Canada, Rimouski, Quebec in CLRB, *DI* 55.

33. Bank Book Collective, *An Account to Settle*, p. 44.

34. See Elizabeth J. Shilton Lennon, "Organizing the Unorganized: Unionization in the Chartered Banks of Canada," *Osgoode Hall Law Journal* 18:2 (August 1980), p. 198.

35. CKOY Ltd. v. Ottawa Newspaper Guild, Local 205 [1977] 2 Federal Court 412, 74 *Dominion Law Report* (3d) 229, 77 *C.L.L.C.* 14,093 (C.A.)

36. Evidence of the chartered banks' anti-union campaign is outlined in the following decisions: Bank of Nova Scotia, Selkirk, Manitoba in CLRB, *DI* 27 (February 1978), BFN 745-287, pp. 690-700; the Royal Bank of Canada, Kamloops and Gibsons, British Columbia in CLRB, *DI* 27 (March 1978), BFN 745-300, pp. 701-27; CIBC, Gibsons, British Columbia in CLRB, *DI* 27 (March 1978), BFN 745-293, pp. 748-64; Bank of Montreal, Tweed and Northbrook, Ontario in CLRB, *DI* 26 (March 1978), BFN 745-297, pp. 591-614; CIBC, Sioux Lookout, Ontario in CLRB *DI* 33 (October 1978), BFN 745-362, pp. 432-50; CIBC North Hills Shopping Centre branch, Kamloops, British Columbia in CLRB, *DI* 34 (October 1978), BFN 745-362, pp. 651-76; CIBC, Toronto, Ontario in CLRB, *DI* 34 (January 1979), BFN 745-361, pp. 677-706. Also see Lennon, "Organizing the Unorganized"; and the Bank Book Collective, *An Account to Settle.*

37. SORWUC report to its United Bank Workers membership, June 1977.

38. See CLRB annual reports of 1977-78 and 1978-79.

39. The five largest chartered banks, commonly referred to as "the big five," are the Royal Bank, the Canadian Imperial Bank of Commerce, the Bank of Montreal, the Bank of Nova Scotia and the Toronto Dominion. La Banque Nationale, which is mainly located in Quebec, is the sixth largest bank in Canada. The benefit improvements included a dental plan; no more deduction for teller cash shortages; overtime payments after 37.5 hours of work in any week, plus after 7.5 hours in any day; and two coffee breaks a day. Reference to these benefit increases can be found in the following decisions: Bank of Nova Scotia, Selkirk, Manitoba, and CIBC, Niagara and Scott Street branch, St. Catherines, Ontario, recorded in CLRB, *DI* 35 (November 1979), BFN 745-422, pp. 105-28.

40. Lennon, "Organizing the Unorganized," p. 204.

41. CIBC, Niagara and Scott Street branch, St. Catherines, Ontario in CLRB, *DI* 35.

42. See La Banque Nationale du Canada, Sillery, Quebec in CLRB, *DI* 42 (September 1981), BFN 745-791, pp. 352-97.

43. Supreme Court of Canada, La Banque Nationale, Sillery, Quebec, 1984.

44. Testimony before the CLRB from a UBE/CLC bank member, November 1978.

45. Bank Book Collective, *An Account to Settle*, p. 135.

46. Discussions with CLC organizers, November 1978.

47. The National Action Committee (NAC) had been vocal in support of women becoming unionized and critical of the anti-union activities of the banks. The NAC was followed in 1980 by the Advisory Council on the Status of Women, which issued Julie White's book, *Women in Unions*, together with a number of recommendations designed to encourage unionization in the banks.

48. CIBC, Niagara and Scott Street branch, St. Catherines, Ontario, in CLRB, *DI* 35. p. 105.

49. Reported in *The Toronto Star*, 15 January 1986.

50. With respect to the cost of unionizing for the chartered banks, Burns-Fry Ltd. estimated that every 1 percent increase in wages will reduce bank earnings by 1.6 percent. See Burns-Fry Ltd., "Labour Unions and Chartered Banks," *Investment Notes* (October 1977). In order to defeat the organizing drives, the banks adopted a new form of "union busting" similar to that developed in the 1970s by a New York-based law firm called Advanced Management Research (AMR). AMR advanced the idea of brains replacing violence in the business of remaining "union free." The firm held seminars in large Canadian centres advertised as "Strategies to Stay Union-Free." During the late 1970s and 1980s, the firm emphasized strategies for dealing with "the new wave of white collar, technical and professional organizing." See Waldie, Brennan and Associates, *Labour Commentary* (Toronto, March 1980).

51. In total, this would have meant $850 million in union funds. It was an action that was to be undertaken by CLC-affiliated unions. Reported in *The Globe and Mail*, 19 March 1981.

52. Discussions with CLC organizers, November 1979.

53. Reported in *The Ottawa Citizen*, 15 March 1980.

54. These are apart from the 1980 strike of the Montreal City and District Savings Bank by OPEIU members, and a lockout of RCIU members at a small CIBC branch in East Angus, Quebec, in 1979.

55. See Royal Bank of Canada, Kénogami, Quebec in CLRB, *DI* 41, BFN 675-6, pp. 199-221 (dissenting opinion of Mr. Jacques Archambault, pp. 221-266).

56. *Ibid.*, p. 251.

57. La Banque Nationale du Canada, Rimouski, Quebec in CLRB, *DI* 55.

58. See CIBC, Toronto, Ontario in CLRB, 1986, BFN 675-18. See also reports in

The Toronto Star, 15 January 1986 and *The Globe and Mail*, 29 January 1986.

59. In both cases the banks' negotiators employed similar tactics from the outset of negotiations.

60. Royal Bank of Canada, Kénogami, Quebec in CLRB, *DI* 41.

61. Reported in *The Globe and Mail*, 5 February 1986.

62. CLRB figures, August 1986.

CHAPTER 6

ORGANIZING WOMEN IN THE CLOTHING TRADES: HOMEWORK AND THE 1983 GARMENT STRIKE IN CANADA

CARLA LIPSIG-MUMMÉ

On August 15, 1983, 9,500 members of the American-based International Ladies' Garment Workers' Union (ILGWU), eighty-eight percent of whom were women, unleashed the first industry-wide strike in forty-three years in Montreal, Canada's principal garment-producing centre. The media was full of the strike: the sweatshops, the health hazards, the return of home sewing, the dying industry. Homeworkers were interviewed with their backs to the camera, and the visibly poor and elderly sewing machine operators— French Canadian, Italian, Greek, Portuguese, Chinese, Haitian and Island women—slept out on their first-ever picket lines, "to protect the strike." They called it "la grève de la fierté" — the strike of pride. It began as a rebellion against the homework which was deunionizing the industry, but it soon spread to become a revolt against the union leadership as well.

Eight days after it began, the Montreal strike was terminated by the union leadership, which feared that its members' unsuspected and by now uncontrollable militancy might spread to its membership in the United States and elsewhere in Canada, upsetting the traditional power relations in the garment industry. The only major victory of the Montreal strike was in securing a wage freeze instead of the twenty percent cutback in wages that the manufacturers were proposing. And the overall collective agreement was not signed until almost two years later, in the summer of 1985. Yet, despite its ostensible failure, this strike was a landmark and perhaps a watershed. It revealed the extent of deunionization and deindustrialization in the garment industry, exposed the paralysis of the principal union faced by this widespread destruction of women's jobs, and offered painful lessons for feminists organizing in the low-paid trades—lessons which extend beyond Montreal in 1983.

With the benefit of hindsight,we can see that the strike laid bare the dilemma of feminist autonomy in relation to union power—how are feminists to organize and keep clear sight of their goals while taking responsibility for and leadership in the changes unleashed by their own success? These changes must of needs be internal and external: changes in union leadership, structures and democratic practices, as well as changes in the stance of the union in relation to the state, the employer and the rest of the labour movement. The Montreal strike revealed, painfully, how fatal it is for union feminists to avoid or reject union responsibility and power, and underscored their need to re-examine their (collective) attitudes towards both.

In the paper which follows, I mean to take the Montreal garment strike and set it in context. On a formal level, this paper takes as its subject the recent changes in the organization of production in the Canadian garment industry—in particular, but not exclusively, the renaissance of homework—and the impact of these changes on the power and strategies of the International Ladies' Garment Workers' Union. More particularly, this paper traces the history of the union's inability to confront the changes occurring in the industry, and looks at feminist strategies in Montreal for transforming the union so as to reunionize the industry and reduce the threat that homework presents.

To deal with these questions, we must follow out three fairly separate strands of analysis. The first is homework, its role in the restructuring of garment production and in the process of deunionization of the garment industry. The second is the International Ladies' Garment Workers' Union: the growth and the decline of this legendary union; the expulsion of women from active union life; and the death of militancy. The third is an examination of feminist strategies in a union where women form the majority but have long been disenfranchised—the dilemma of power and autonomy from formal structures. Together, these three strands of analysis weave together to address the following question: as the garment industry is a major employer of blue-collar, minority women in Canada, what happens, in this time of economic restructuring and unparalleled employer offensive, when the principal union fails to protect women's working conditions and their very jobs? What can women workers do in the face of employers committed to rendering the union irrelevant, and in the face of a union which seems not to care?

RESTRUCTURING GARMENT PRODUCTION:
HOMEWORK AND INTERNATIONAL COMPETITION

I think we all recognize by now that the "rationalization" of Canada's industrial sector—the pace of which has quickened in the 1980s—has been catalyzed by long-term structural changes in the international division of labour.[1] Canadian enterprises in the manufacturing and basic industry sectors have found it increasingly difficult to compete with producers in Japan and the low-wage Third World countries. This has led to: a) the transfer of production by Canadian enterprises to cheap labour zones in developing countries, with a corresponding rise in structural unemployment in Canada; b) the introduction of sweeping technological "rationalization" to reduce the labour force permanently employed in the Canadian facilities; c) a generalized decline in employment in the traditionally unionized industries, and an increase in employment in the difficult-to-unionize private sector services;[2] d) an exceptional increase in precarious and fragmented employment, and in homework, at the expense of full-time regular employment, in all manner of industries and services;[3] e) an unprecedented campaign of deunionization, aimed at reducing the influence and the membership of unions in the public and secondary sectors, while convincing workers in the weakly-unionized service industries that the "fat cat" unions are to blame for their conditions.

In sectors and industries where women are an important part of the labour force, the impact of the crisis in international competitiveness on working conditions and job security occurs in two ways: directly, where conditions and security are undermined because the industry, facing international competition, is desperate to cut costs, and does so on the backs of its workers; and, indirectly, in sectors where international competition is not an immediate factor, but where employers have borrowed tactics from the internationally vulnerable industries to cut their labour costs, reduce their labour force, augment "flexibility" and weaken the union presence.

Women workers are suffering acutely from the restructuring process—women bank clerks, supermarket checkers, key punchers, claims evaluators, garment workers, contract cleaners—because directly and indirectly their employers are deploying the threat of the crisis to undermine positions which were never that secure. Women, entering the labour force four times as rapidly as men,[4] are now finding themselves just as rapidly expelled—last hired, first fired—pushed to the margins of that shrinking elite which holds a full-time, unionized job; pushed out to join the reserve army of the precariously employed. Recent developments in the garment industry in Canada permit us to analyze the direct impact of the crisis in international competitiveness on job security and working conditions, as well as to look closely at one gender-specific tactic of economic restructuring: homework.

The garment industry is a major employer of blue-collar women in Canada, and has been for at least a century. But at present, clothing manufacturing (in Europe, as well as in Canada and the United States) is an industry in crisis. It is particularly affected by three of the structural changes mentioned above: competition from Third World imports; transfer of production to the Third World; and the breakdown of the full-time job through contracting and homework. Technological change, unless it is technological regression, does not play a pivotal role. Consider these statistics. Between 1968 and 1977, in the developed market economies, clothing production for export dropped from eighty percent to sixty-three percent of the world total.[5] At the same time, developing countries as a whole gained a larger share of the world market, rising from twenty-three percent[6] to thirty-seven percent, while the Asian portion alone rose from nineteen percent to thirty-three percent. The results of the decreasing viability of legitimate clothing manufacturing in high-wage economies were immediately felt: in the European economic community, 243,000 registered jobs were lost to Third World production and to unrecorded homework and subcontracting between 1972 and 1977.[7]

Thus international competition triggers the transfer of production to cheap labour zones and/or a radical restructuring of the pace and organization of garment producing. It has not led to effective import quotas or to modernizing technological advances. The former requires effective government action; the latter, government commitment and enterprises large enough to underwrite large capital outlays. All these are lacking.

In Montreal—historically the centre of Canadian garment production—manufacturers have responded in one of two ways to their "decreasing competitiveness:" the larger have opened plants in some Asian haven, while phasing out their North American or European operations; the smaller have fragmented their production process, retaining cutting, and perhaps pressing or pattern-making, as factory work, while putting sewing out to homeworkers—the rebirth of cottage industry.[8] The fact that in Montreal, profit margins in clothing production are typically low (2.5 percent) and labour costs, as a percentage of total costs, relatively high (twenty-seven percent), while the average size of a garment enterprise is quite small, makes it not surprising that the majority of garment manufacturers at risk through Third World competition are choosing to restructure garment production through homework.[9]

Let's look more closely at each of these restructuring strategies. Company

A makes dresses in Montreal. With 350 inside workers, it is the largest employer in the industry in the city. In May 1984, it announced that it could no longer afford "the cost of unionization." If the union were not repudiated by the employees, the company would shut down in August, its owners said. Union representatives, offering "to make concessions to save the company," nevertheless noted that one of the company's directors had just returned from Hong Kong, and that the presently-employed cutters had been assured that they would not lose their jobs. Within the following twelve months, the company did close its Montreal factory, did transfer sewing and finishing operations to the Pacific Rim, and did re-employ many of its cutters and pattern makers in a newly-opened, non-union cutting shop. The garments thus produced have been returned for sale on the Canadian market.

Company B is much smaller, with fifty inside employees. It is too small to absorb the one-time relocation and the repeated transportation costs that Company A will incur when it opens a factory in Hong Kong. Instead, Company B closes its multi-process factory in Montreal, laying off all sewing machine operators, finishers, floor girls, cleaners, etc.—the female 80-90 percent of the labour force. It will reopen as a cutting shop under another name. Like Company A, it will retain its (male) cutters and its one or two (female) pattern makers. The new cutting shop will enter into contractual arrangements with a labour contractor supplying sewing homeworkers, or with a subcontractor employing operators in a loft.

In both cases, 80-90 percent of the labour force loses their jobs—the 80-90 percent that is almost entirely female. And the union is dead in the enterprise, for the condition placed upon continued employment for the skilled male workers is employment in the new non-union shop. For the garment manufacturer, transferring production to the Third World or to the home of former factory workers is highly cost-efficient. The former allows the manufacturer to pay a fraction of the wages and benefits paid in North America, while enjoying the protection of sympathetic, authoritarian governments. The latter allows the manufacturer to reduce labour costs by shucking off responsibility for minimum wages, vacation pay, sick benefits, maximum hours, pensions, maternity leave, overtime and assorted production costs.[10] Thus in place of a relatively centralized employment situation characterized by a manufacturer constrained by ordinary legal and financial responsibility for his employees, we now have either jobs that vanish overseas, or increasingly decentralized and complex subcontracting arrangements where the vulnerability of the worker increases with her distance from her real employer.[11]

Because of the 1983 strike, we have been made aware of statistics which

reveal the magnitude of deunionization brought about through these strategies. Montreal, as has been mentioned, produces sixty-five percent of all
Canadian-made garments. In 1981, rank-and-file union members (who were
active in the Women's Committee) revealed that in the first six months of
1981, 2,000 factory jobs had been lost to homework in Montreal and the surrounding province of Quebec, while 150 shops had closed.[12] It was unknown
how many of these reopened under other names or moved overseas. For
1981, it was also estimated (with difficulty) that 20,000 women were sewing
women's and children's garments at home.[13] In Quebec, membership in the
ILG declined from 17,5000 in 1976, to 13,000 in 1981. By 1983, it was
down to 10,000; and in 1985, 7,500.

The Montreal experience is not atypical, if better documented than most.
To understand the implications of the restructuring strategies and measure the
impact made on union jobs by cheap imports, the transfer of production, and
homework, we have to set the Montreal experience within the context of a
continental crisis in the structure of garment producing. Beginning in the late
1960s in the United States, several unions in work clothes, men's, children's
and women's garments, fur, millinery and related industries (long organized
around factory or shop production and tacitly accepting the domiciling of a
small and controllable portion of sewing operations) began noting an unspec-
tacular but steady growth in manufacturers' use of homeworkers, and a more
spectacular drainage of "runaway jobs" to Mexico. The growth of homework
had ethnic, gender and geographic dimensions, as well as long-range implications for the organization of garment production itself.

Growth in homework was noted in depressed economic areas where
unionism was or had become weak, and where women were the principal
wage earners: in the United States, the depressed mining areas of Appalachia,
as well as Vermont, and New Hampshire; in Canada, the depressed rural and
mining areas of eastern Quebec, as well as northern British Columbia. In these
areas, women sometimes began sewing cooperatives which failed to survive
the exigencies of the market, leaving the women particularly vulnerable to
contractors looking to employ homeworkers. Sometimes, as in eastern
Quebec, women sewed at home because their mothers had; there were few
daycares and no options. At this time, no one had systematically identified the
source of the homework labour force or the varieties of legal arrangements by
which the homeworker might be exploited. Homework also returned to the
residential slums of all the big cities which housed the immigrant underclass,
and hid what the Americans endearingly call "illegal aliens": immigrants without legal residence permits.[14]

In addition to homework, the chronic problem of runaway shops became acute in the late 1960s and early 1970s. Historically, clothing and textile unions in the US and Canada had to contend with companies which, when facing unionization in towns where the union was strong, would transfer production elsewhere. The "elsewhere" varied according to the decade and the geographical expansion of union strength. In the United States, from the 1930s to the 1950s, runaway shops from New York, Boston, Philadelphia, Chicago and the Mid-West moved to the southern states to protect their union-free status. In the late 1950s, the far West became a haven, as did outlying suburbs of the cities to which garment production had come more recently. In the 1960s, Mexico and Puerto Rico drained jobs from New York and the other major garment cities through the Pronaf or Twin Plants Agreement.[15] And by the 1970s, runaway shops had gone as far as the Pacific Rim. At the same time, the wheel turned full circle: companies seeking to divest themselves of their union returned to the impenetrable jungle of the big city, ethnic suburbs to establish sweatshops anew, and to seek homeworkers. What made the ethnic suburbs impenetrable to unions like ILGWU were race, class and power; for by the 1970s, membership and leadership neither spoke the same language nor occupied the same class position in society. (To open a parenthesis, it seems necessary to underline the point that the evil of runaway shops resides not in the fact that they take jobs away from "our" in-group, but rather that they employ weaker workers in more vulnerable conditions, thereby weakening collective economic defence in general.)

Together, homework, imports and runaway shops reduced union membership and wages among the visible labour force—the legally employed—in the women's garment workers and steelworkers averaged the same wages annually. By 1970, garment workers' wages had dropped to fifty percent of steelworkers'. In 1965, the ILG, with its 442,000 members, claimed to represent forty percent of the visible labour force in women's clothing production. Today it has no more than 300,000 members.[16] And while we are unsure as to where those 150,000 members have gone, we do know—because union and government and independent analysts have so indicated—that there has been a commensurate growth in home sewers, as indicated earlier in this paper.

Thus emerges a grim portrait of deunionization caused by the restructuring of production in the women's garment industry. Not only do the wages and benefits of the visible labour force deteriorate under the impact of these long-term structural changes, but the percentage of workers who pass from the visible to the invisible labour force—from legal to clandestine employment—increases as well. It is not surprising that garment workers erupted into strike in Montreal in 1983. What is surprising, rather, is that they waited so long, and that their union was—and is—so reticent in coming to grips with the transformation of its industry.

THE INTERNATIONAL LADIES' GARMENT WORKERS' UNION AND THE CANADIAN LABOUR MOVEMENT

The second strand of analysis is to be drawn from the 1983 Montreal strike concerns the union itself, the International Ladies' Garment Workers' Union, for while the strike began as an uprising against unemployment in general and homework in particular, it ended as a profound, unsparing indictment of the union by its members.

I think it is generally recognized—in light of the growing spate of "trade union crisis" literature—that while the same international processes of economic restructuring have been present in the US and Canada, their impact on the respective national economies has been quite different, as has the response of trade unions in the two countries. Within the private sector, several factors have served to crystallize the divergent union responses in the two countries. First is the attitude of the law towards conserving existing union rights and permitting unions to adapt to new developments in managerial strategy. If the law is generally seen to have abdicated its historic responsibility in the United States, it is not seen to have done so in Canada.[17] The posture of the law has affected the impact of a second factor serving to distinguish trade union response in Canada from that in the United States. This factor is the scope and effectiveness of new managerial strategies aimed at reducing the ability of unions to influence corporate policies and costs by reducing union power and membership. In the United States, the managerial offensive is seen as a tidal wave, successful in weakening unionism in the traditional sectors while blocking union penetration into the private service sector. In Canada, the success and radicalism of the managerial offensive varies from industry to industry, and has not had the devastating, across-the-board effect seen in the private sector in the US. Numbers are eloquent in this regard: union membership in the US is only a little over eighteen percent of the non-agricultural labour force, while it remains at a bit more than thirty-seven percent in Canada.

The third factor which has contributed to the articulation of differing Canadian and US union responses to the restructuring crisis is the growth of a

Canadian national labour movement and the move away from the affiliation of Canadian workers to American unions. Admittedly complex, the process of repatriation of Canadian unionism in the private sector, coupled with the growth of a strong public sector unionism, has meant that Canadian workers are freer to articulate Canadian responses to the crisis. But it has also meant that the protectionism of certain US unions will now be given free rein; the international coordination of union strategy in continentally integrated industries will be harder to organize; and that within the Canadian labour movement, a difficult process of amalgamation and realignment of the recently repatriated Canadian private sector unions will now have to occur. Thus the third factor influencing divergent Canadian and American union responses to the international restructuring process has an impact on both Canadian and US unions.

The process of Canadianizing private sector unionism is, however, far from complete. In 1983, American unions continued to represent about two-fifths of the unionized Canadian labour force. In coping with restructuring during the 1980s, these remaining American unions articulated two divergent policies towards Canadian autonomy: 1) either the American union allowed its Canadian branches considerable autonomy on condition that Canadian strategy not undermine or threaten the American unions' position within the US; or, 2) it imposed American strategy (or strategy that served the needs of the American component of the unions' membership) upon its Canadian affiliate without adaptation to the Canadian context. Which approach a particular union took was a product of tradition, ideology and structure, particularly as these had evolved since the swell of Canadian nationalism within the union movement began in the mid sixties.

The ILGWU took the second option: more than most other American unions operating in Canada, the ILGWU has been unwilling to permit the specificity of Canadian and Quebec members to be expressed. It has imposed on its Quebec and Canadian branches its American history, the lessons learned from its American struggles, and an ideological tradition that has not evolved since communists and social democrats fought for control in New York City in the 1920s. From American struggles and an ossified American ideology came the unions' remarkably undemocratic structures—and these too have been imposed on Canadian garment workers. Thus far more directly than is the case for other unions, if we are to understand the workings of the ILGWU in Canada and what led to the 1983 strike, we must return to an analysis of the ILGWU tradition and practices in the United States.

The ILGWU was first organized among women and men immigrants on

New York's Lower East Side in the years before 1914. It has become a legendary union, not only in North America but elsewhere, I suspect, for two reasons. First, it is a long-standing union of women in which women (at least in the early years around World War I) took a visible, militant and autonomous role in organizing themselves. Second, the ILG was a pioneer in social unionism—pre-World War I European socialist ideas combined with a particularly American emphasis on individual intellectual and social self-improvement. Together, the profile of immigrant women organizing for a better tomorrow suited the American self-image at least until the 1960s.

Yet the reality is quite other. The central fact about the ILGWU today, and for at least two generations, is that it is a two-class union. In both the domain of ethnic/racial discrimination and gender discrimination, there are two classes of citizens. If you are a woman, hispanic or non-white in the United States or, a woman, Québécois, Portuguese, a member of a "visible minority" in Canada, it is most likely that you be will employed in the skilled trades remunerated on an hourly scale. You are likely to be paid by piece rate and clustered in the lower-paid, less secure, semi-skilled and unskilled trades and subdivisions, i.e., operator, floor girls, trimmers in swimsuits, belts, lingerie, children's wear, etc.

Gender and ethnic discrimination, as reflected in occupation, job security and remuneration, are also reflected in access to leadership positions. Over time, clothing manufacturing (that archetypal industry of the national underclass and recent migrants) absorbed successive waves of immigrants and one group followed another, either up the ladder and out of the shops or permanently blocked on the lower rungs. Between 1910 and 1940, the industry in the United States was the preserve of Jewish and Italian immigrants; in Canada, of Jews and French Canadians. Post-World War II in the United States, blacks followed Jews and Italians into the unskilled and semi-skilled occupations they vacated. Today, the American membership is one-third black and one-third hispanic. In Canada, Italians in the 1950s, and then Greeks, Portuguese and Haitians in the 1960s, joined the original French Canadians, while Eastern European Jews virtually vanished from both the men's and women's trades. But in the United States to this day, and in Canada until 1971, the original migrant elites of the 1910-1940 period (long since vanished from the shop room floor) continue to dominate union leadership, long after the membership speaks other languages and dreams other dreams.

Women, too, are excluded from leadership of this union: women comprise eighty-eight percent of the membership. A review of the holders of principal offices of the ILGWU since 1910 indicates that no president, secretary-treasurer or executive secretary has ever been a woman. Almost all holders of these posts have come from the cutters, pressers or shipping clerks. All, to this day, have been members of one of the two original ethnic groups which founded the union in the United States: the Italians and the Jews. The union's general executive board (its chief governing body between congresses) has never had more than two women vice-presidents at a time, while the number of vice-presidents sitting simultaneously has varied between 16 and 30.

Why? Why has this legendary and once-courageous union developed a self-perpetuating elite using gender and ethnic exclusion to protect itself? What has been the relationship between institutional racism and sexism and the death of union militancy? In the early 1960s in the United States, militant black groups brought charges of racial discrimination against several ILG locals, charges subsequently heard by the United States House of Representatives. The 1960s investigation offers some interesting insights which lead one to suspect that the purposes served by racism and sexism in this union are similar and interdependent.

Herbert Hill, one of the ILG's most unsparing critics in the United States, argued that the union elite had many years back decided that it was necessary at all costs to keep garment jobs in locations where they were unionizable.[18] Effectively, this meant that the union took on the responsibility for providing, disciplining and controlling a cheap labour supply in the metropolises. The two-tier system crystallized with this decision. Labour costs were kept low for the vast majority of the labour force: women and other semi-skilled and unskilled workers. But they were allowed to rise for the skilled white males.

While we cannot date this decision exactly, we can find early expressions of it. Throughout the 1920s, social democrats battled communists for control of the ILGWU. David Dubinsky's accession to the presidency (1932-59) signalled the final victory for social democracy, and in 1935 he uttered his celebrated remark: "The worker needs capitalism like a fish needs water." Four decades later, S. Chaikin, the current president of the union, stated:

> (O)ur union was then and still is stronger than any single
> employer or reasonable combination of employers. When a
> union had that kind of position in an industry it has to
> inhibit itself, to control itself...we negotiate with the under-
> standing that we must not do too much damage to each
> other.[19]

So as early as the 1930s, social unionism had been transformed into corporatism in the original sense of the term: a system of sectoral regulation and control in which the principal institutional participants concur as to their respective roles, objectives, and the means of attaining these objectives. At the same time as the ILG turned to corporatism, it abandoned attempts to restructure garment production along lines which permitted progressive unionism to expand its gains, leaving the organization of both work and ownership to be shaped by the exigencies of profit and the market. Today, corporatism within the ILG takes the form of passive abdication: the union leadership (long captive to the logic that its chronically ill industry must be saved through whatever sacrifices the employers deem necessary) has come to take as immutable the employers' view of the structure of the industry. Corporatism has many faces in the everyday life of a garment worker. It takes the form of allowing employers to renege on their contributions to the pension fund if they say times are rough ($500,000 in debts excused to one employer, and $6,000,000 to the garment contractors in Montreal); of allowing employers to pay workers less than what the contract stipulates; and, of allowing homework to flourish in unionized companies whose contracts specifically forbid it. And all of this is done in the name of helping out desperate employers in an industry they have been calling sick since the 1930s.

In his analysis of the causes of racial discrimination, Hill argued further that non-whites represented a growing minority of the union, a minority whose interests and priorities were not the same as those of a leadership which "has grown contemptuous of its younger, less educated, less sophisticated—its altogether different—newer members."[20] Surely an analogous argument may be made concerning the reasons for gender exclusion. The fact that women are a majority is treated in the triennial Congress Reports as a source of the union's exceptional weakness. Women, as eighty-eight percent of the membership, represent a majority which could, if mobilized, not only topple or challenge the male hegemony in the skilled trades, not only smash the captive labour supply of machine operators, not only supplant men in the leadership positions in the union, but might even scrap the corporatism which for decades has made the union the supervisor and policeman of a reservoir of underpaid women workers.

Hill's argument, that for the union's elite, racism serves as a crucial element in maintaining the cheap labour supply employers require, applies equally well in explaining sexism. But we need to go further and look at the historical origins of gender discrimination in this union, because it is possible to demonstrate links between sexism, racism and the death of union democracy and militancy. In the paragraphs which follow, I mean to argue that in the face of a crisis of the proportions that the garment industry is now facing, any union must call upon the whole of its membership in the struggle to reunionize the sector. But the ILG cannot call upon this crucial resource—its membership—because it destroyed the conditions for membership militancy many years ago when it suppressed active and democratic union life—in the 1920s in the United States, and in the late 1930s in Canada. And it is the inability of the union today (or perhaps its unwillingness) to mobilize the membership that makes the union unable to withstand the crisis generated by the renaissance of homework and the competition of the Third World.

Following World War I, a protracted struggle between social democrats and communists within the ILGWU broke out in the United States, only to be resolved in the late 1920s. This struggle mirrored similar confrontations in other unions between communist parties and union groups, which formed out of the ruins of the Second International and the founding of the Third, and drew to themselves diverse and scattered opposition elements from the Wobblies, the anarchists and the other democratic dissidents whose existence had, in many cases, predated the creation of the Third International. Within the ILG, each ideological camp used muscle against the other to protect its organizers and safeguard the transportation of bundles from 'its' shops, thus opening a door for organized crime in the industry, a door which has never been shut. Shops and union locals in the 1920s tended to be communist or social democrat; and in the struggle to oust the communists, the social democrats encouraged contracting and subcontracting as a way of hiding workers from rival organizers. In other words, the ideological struggle stimulated the first wave of decentralization of production.

Again, social democrats and communists represented very different ideologies of class relationships within the garment industry, and of structures of institutional power within the union. Joel Seidman, an authoritative early analyst, summarized their differences this way:

> In all the needle trade unions, the leftists proposed a pro-
> gram of militant class struggle in place of the policy of class
> collaboration that they accused the right-wing leadership of
> following. They also proposed amalgamation of all unions
> in the needle trades and their reorganization to make the
> shop the basic unit, with the higher governing body made
> up of delegates from the shops...in addition the leftists pro-
> posed union reforms that won them wide following.[21]

With historical hindsight, we may note that because of the peculiar combination of craft and industrial locals within the ILG (craft locals for skilled men, industrial locals for semi-skilled women) the women's locals within the union were large. They had become a source of militancy and rank-and-file democratic dissidence even before the ideological conflicts of the 1920s. One local, the huge New York Waist and Dressmakers Union—the largest women's local in the union—became a pole attracting the whole spectrum of rank-and-file opposition in the 1920s. This local called upon the union's national office to affiliate with the Red International of Trade Unions when it was founded; initiated a shop delegates' movement on the British model;[22] and encouraged a whole range of revolutionary and syndicalist ideas which transformed social unionism into both a radical critique of the post-war American order and a school for young immigrant socialists. By 1920, the Waist and Dressmakers' local had become a stronghold for the Trade Union Educational League and for communist influence within the ILGWU. Social democrats, in control of the union's national office, responded by splitting the women's local in two. Later, when social democratic victory was consolidated, the two locals were submerged in joint councils dominated by male cutters, in which women militants gradually gave up trying to regain autonomy. But at the beginning of the 1920s, as the ideological struggle reigned and the several visions of trade unionism crosscut the issue of women's organizing, the social democratic leadership defined the women's locals as among the most threatening. Expulsions of key women militants, revocation of the charters of smaller locals, and the barring from office of visible left-wingers followed the splitting of the Waist and Dressmakers Union. Between 1926 and 1932, when the social democrats consolidated their hold over the local as well as over the central structures of the ILG, they enshrined in the union constitution the exceptional powers they had used during the civil war.[23]

In the United States, then, by the beginning of the 1930s, women's locals had been split and submerged in organizational forms which discouraged autonomy; caucuses had been outlawed; key women leaders expelled; and the power to control and destroy rank-and-file dissidence by labelling it communist, enshrined.

In the 1930s as well, under the aegis of the American New Deal, the ILGWU turned its attention towards becoming the dominant needle trades union in Canada. It organized in Toronto, Montreal and Winnipeg between 1934 and 1940 as if these were outlying American cities, showing little concern for the separate histories, language (in the case of Montreal) or trade union traditions. In Montreal, as in New York, the ILG's organizing drives supplanted and then absorbed existing radical industrial unionism.[24] Important strike victories (in this case, in 1937 and 1940) were followed by a leadership policy of deflating the militancy the strikes had engendered, so as not to "endanger the industry." After the 1937 and 1940 strikes in Montreal, militants were expelled on suspicion of being communists, thereby losing their right to work in the industry. Caucuses were outlawed.[25] Rose Pesotta, a leading organizer of women dressmakers in 1936, was discredited, marginalized and returned to the shops. Lea Roback (today an 80 year-old peace crusader) found it necessary to resign as ILG Education Director for Quebec. While there was no attempt to break up the big women's locals as a way of extirpating democracy in Montreal (as had happened in New York) the marginalization of Pesotta, the resignation of Roback, the expulsion of dissidents, the refusal to hold union meetings or distribute copies of the contract, and the willingness to label any opposition as communist destroyed the will of average women workers in this Catholic and then-conservative French Canadian province. In 1939, the Montreal leadership itself estimated that no more than one-third of the women dressmakers still supported it.[26] Should we be surprised, then, that there were no garment strikes in Montreal between 1940 and 1983? Or, perhaps, should we have expected the mass uprising that did occur when, at last, the membership was allowed to speak for itself?

RANK-AND-FILE OPPOSITION, FEMINIST STRATEGIES, AND THE 1983 STRIKE

The third strand in our analysis concerns the present and Montreal. In the twenty years preceding the Montreal strike in 1983, successive waves of dissidence had risen, crystallized, and been smashed within by the International Ladies' Garment Workers' Union. The feminist opposition which developed between 1980 and 1983 drew on these earlier movements and transcended them, but was ultimately broken by some of the same forces which destroyed the earlier movements. If our third strand is an analysis of the 1983 Montreal strike and its lessons for feminist organizing within the low-paid trades in Montreal and elsewhere, let us begin by setting this strand in context.

The declining wages and working conditions of the ILGWU members, coupled with the destruction of internal union democracy and the oligarchization of power, stimulated the crystallization (appearing first in the United States) of a black and hispanic challenge to the union's racism. In the 1960s, black and hispanic nationalism was part of a wider rising of the American underclass. But in the unions. the struggle against racism was defined by rela-tively narrow objectives. Black pressers in New York, for example, took the union to court over exclusion from the trade of skilled presser and from the pressers' local. But they neither raised basic questions about the union's will-ingness to defend its members nor attempted to spread their protest to a broad rank-and-file movement.[27] For non-white workers in the 1960s, the objectives were primarily economic: they sought to break open access to skilled jobs. Confronting racism in access to union leadership positions was secondary. While legal proceedings against the ILG and new legislation at the end of the decade led to a democratization of the union's constitution con-cerning eligibility for elected positions, this changed nothing of the union's de facto exclusion of non-whites and women, The ILG's structures and practices remained remarkably impermeable.

In the late 1960s, as racial militancy in the United States waned generally and disappeared within the ILG, a new source of rank-and-file discontent moved to centre stage: Québécois nationalism. During the 1960s, Quebec had moved into a period of rapid, state-sponsored modernization and secular-ization, which gave rise to a nationalist (and eventually, a separatist) move-ment that touched every aspect of social and union life. As with certain strands of the black movement in the United States, the Quebec movement combined nationalist themes with a socialist critique of Canadian society. And as with the black movement in the United States, Québécois nationalism with-in the unions also expressed relatively narrow, if different goals. Inside the ILG in Montreal in the late 1960s, French Canadian male pressers formed a pres-sure group to force the union's leadership to legitimize the use of French in union meetings, to translate the union contract and constitution, and to democratize union elections.[28] In other words, the Québécois reform group emphasized 'union' discrimination rather than 'job' discrimination.

The retirement in 1971 of American Bernard Shane, who had headed the ILG in Canada since 1936, coupled with wide societal support (within Quebec) for any movement aimed at 'Francising' a foreign organization, effec-tively pressured this American union onto the defensive. French became the working language of the ILG in Quebec, and the reformers became paid union staffers. With the absorption of the reform leaders into the union establish-ment, the agenda for educating the membership and reforming the structure quietly dissolved. In due course, a 'democratic action group' crystallized in 1975. Comprised this time of Italian, French and Greek male cutters and pressers, it picked up the theme of democratization of the union. But like its predecessor, it did not question the structures of the industry, the growth of homework, or the union's policies towards either of these. In due course, its leaders too took paid jobs in the union, and by 1979 it had disappeared without a trace. In both cases, women workers had not been involved.

In other words, in Quebec before 1980, each reform group drew its membership from the union's male aristocracy and focused on democratizing union structures, but failed to raise issues about organization, deunionization, homework or the exercise of power in the industry. Each reform group had begun informally, crystallized solely within the union's ranks, defined its issues narrowly, and dissolved as its leadership was integrated into the union's permanent staff.

After 1980, however, the rank-and-file reform movement changed form. Homework became the catalyst, and semi-skilled women operators the leaders. The multi-ethnic Action Committee for Garment Workers (CATV) articulated the issue of homework as a threat, attacked the union's disinterest, educated the membership on the spread of homework, and prepared the ground for 1983 and the strike. Goals, tactics, strategies—and feminism—make this group different.

CATV was formed in 1980 by about 50 garment workers in Montreal. Most were women and operators, some were pattern or sample makers, and there were a few male cutters and pressers involved. The women at the core came from varied ethnic backgrounds and ranged from 20 to 55 years of age. They had been born in Haiti, Portugal, Greece, Italy and French-speaking Quebec. French was their lingua franca. Two movements external to the ILG nourished their vision: feminism as it had developed in France and Quebec; and, the left-wing socialism of the sects or 'groupuscules' articulated in Quebec in the 1970s.

The CATV women crystallized a deep-seated rejection of the patriarchal aspirations of typical union elites. They were cynical about the earlier reform movements and the personal ambitions of their leaders. And they linked the authoritarian practices which predominated in the shops with the authoritarian practices which ran their union. The case of Fatima Rocchia, one of CATV's founders, is typical of the way CATV brought home to women workers the idea that it was possible to fight back.

> Fatima Rocchia has been fired six times between October 1980 and January 1981, because she went to the bathroom too often. In her letter of dismissal, however, no reasons were given.
>
> Fatima is a unionized sewing machine operator, a mem-

ber of Local 262 of the ILGWU. She asked the union to grieve her dismissal, but without success. Her business agent, Isabelle Bittichesu, did not know how to file a grievance. Anyway, the union had no grievance forms. So Fatima filed her own. But just before her hearing her employer, Sample Dress, rehired her.

In the following week, Fatima continued to defy Sample's rule that you can only have one toilet break in the morning and one in the afternoon. Moreover, at Sample, the operator is forbidden to move from her machine even to take a drink, even when it is 108° in the shop. On the day it was 108°, there were three pregnant women in the shop. Fatima took two toilet breaks a morning, two in the afternoon. Worse, she began unofficial translation into Portuguese of the debates in union meetings and she signed up for a union education course and began holding informal classes to explain the contract to her sisters at Sample. Her supervisor did not like this at all. He took to waiting for her at the door of the toilets, timing her, and abusing her verbally.

From the time Sample rehired Fatima (following her grievance) they tried to force her out. The manager regularly called the union, pretending Fatima was ill, and requiring a medical examination. The president of her Local 262, Micheline Parkin, called a meeting with Fatima and the boss, and in his presence told Fatima that she didn't have to go to the bathroom at all during the day.

Parkin offered Fatima a transfer to another shop. Fatima refused. Shortly thereafter, she was elected shop chairlady at Sample.

Things rapidly changed at Sample. The manager no longer felt free to yell at the top of his lungs, hit the machines to make the operators jump, dock them 15 minutes pay for forgetting to punch in. Nor are they searched in leaving the shop any longer. "The women have the feeling now that they have some power," says Fatima, "but they also know that I don't have the backing of our union."[29]

This was recounted in 1981 and there is a postscript. Sample was the largest manufacturer in the city, with 350 employees. Its workers were the backbone of the strike. It is the company, mentioned earlier in the paper, which closed down and moved operations to Hong Kong. What price fighting back?

A second example is the Marbrooke Corporation, where in the spring of 1981 CATV again exposed collusion between the ILGWU and its manufacturer, collusion which allowed the employer to use homeworkers and fire unionized machine operators. CATV succeeded in getting an illegal strike started: they managed to get 6,000 workers to support them for one day. After the first day, Robert Fontaine, then union director, and Micheline Parkin, then president of Local 262, threatened them with the police. They went back to work.[30]

But at the end of the summer of 1981, CATV leafleted the garment centre with information on the cancerous growth of homework. And in December 1981, they used the opportunity offered by a biennial congress held by the ILG's parent, the Quebec Federation of Labour, to ask that their union be taken over by the parent Federation. At that congress, they published *The Black Book on the ILGWU* which detailed, in addition to the two cases already mentioned, the fact that union director Fontain had bought a manufacturer's collaboration by cancelling the manufacturer's debt of over $500,000 to the union's welfare funds, and that the union was presently under investigation by the Commission of Organized Crime. Perhaps more disgracefully, the *Black Book* exposed the fact that in the 47 years the ILG had been in Quebec, it has only paid full pension to 1,850 people. The diverse welfare funds hold more than $80,000,000. The pension pays $185.00 per month.[31] Another section of the *Black Book* pointed out that homework had taken 2,000 jobs out of the shops and into homes in six months.[32]

A postscript here too: the Quebec Federation of Labour refused to put the ILG into receivership. Within a week of that decision, nine CATV militants had been fired from their shops. But organizing work continued nevertheless. In 1981, CATV formed an informal Women's Committee. It did not hold elections, and had no formal leadership. It was open to all women, and offered a legitimate organizational base from which to confront the union's leadership.

Following their victory with the QFL, the ILG leadership moved to destroy the CATV Women's Committee by creating a formal Women's Committee whose members would be appointed by the union director. The CATV Women's Committee struck back by organizing activities in the garment centre for a whole week around International Women's Day, 1982. Activities included leaflets on homework, a showing of "With These Hands," evening information sessions on health and safety, and on the union's history—the impact was immense and diffuse.

It had half of the desired effect. Within a week, under the combined pressure of the revelations in the Black Book and the Women's Committee's unrelenting exposure, two members of the union executive, Parkin and Fontaine, were transferred back to the United States or took early retirement. And yet another reform leadership was chosen—this time a group of male cutters and pressers who had been part of the 1970s reform group under Gilles Gauthier. For the first time, a woman headed the pressers' local. Structural reforms were announced. Several of the CATV women were offered paid staff jobs but all refused. They felt more effective and freer outside of the official structure. Noting that the problem of homework was being avoided, they expressed reservation at the effectiveness of the reforms proposed. Soon enough, their suspicions were born out. In the summer of 1982, the new reform leadership allowed the garment contractors to cancel out $6,000,000 they owed in welfare funds. The times, the union said, were rough.

Come the summer of 1983, the three-year contract expired. The Manufacturers' Guild arrived at the bargaining table with proposals for a twenty percent wage cut and a reduction in paid holidays. The Gauthier leadership called for a strike vote, hoping to win the vote, frighten the employers and not have to hold the strike. Some 9,500 workers were covered by expiring agreements. On Thursday, August 11, some 8,000 members showed up for a vote to strike—in a union which rarely holds meetings and will not translate contracts into the languages of its members. The executive, without realizing it at the time, had opened the floodgates. (There is some evidence that the parent QFL did understand what was happening. It loaned the ILG several "advisors" whose role was later to become controversial.) On Sunday, August 14th, with the strike due to begin at midnight, Gauthier asked the executive to put the strike off—and was voted down.

On Monday at dawn, the picket lines were already packed. In the garment district on Chabanel, in the scattered shops along the north-south streets in the north-centre and elsewhere in the city, if it was a union shop, its workers were out. No picket signs from the union headquarters? The women made their own. At some shops, a five-language team wrote each sign in all their languages. No picket shifts? By the third day, the women had set up their own. It was remarked that the union porkchoppers probably didn't know how to organize a strike—after all, they hadn't had one in forty-three years. And women from different shops began to meet each other and talk about their common experiences for the first time. In the garment district this was easy;

but where the shops spread across the centre-north of the city, as soon as the workers had shut down a shop for the day, the women would leave a skeleton picket crew and the rest would take their picket signs and walk up to another shop to meet other workers they didn't know, to exchange conditions and stories. And then both teams would move on to meet others.

The strike also united the skilled and semi-skilled. "For the first time," one middle-aged woman remarked, "the cutters are with us. They know we have nothing more to lose." The signs, in all those languages, demonstrated the depth of anger and the strength of determination. "Not just a living wage, but a living," said one, carried by a man close to retirement. "Underpaid workers make underfed children," said another, carried by a young Haitian couple who daily brought their three-month old girl to the lines. Picket signs reading "Homework is killing us," and "Stop homework, save our jobs," one saw repeatedly. And "La grève de la fierté" became the strike's central rallying cry.

By Day Two, union headquarters was receiving constant calls from non-union workers asking the union to come and unionize them. (To my knowledge, the union never followed these calls up, in an industry were unionization has dropped to twenty-five percent of the visible labour force.) The retirees came to picket as well. Lea Roback, the veteran of the 1937 strike mentioned earlier in this paper, came daily. She organized a flying squad of women from the Jewish Old People's Home.

On Day Four, Gauthier and the executive again recommended a return to work. A bitterly-divided Shop Delegates' Council turned it down. But the executive chose to put their recommendation to a membership vote, to be held on the Saturday. By Friday morning, young women strikers from shops in the same building as the union headquarters attacked Gauthier on his way to work. Thereafter, he had a bodyguard.

On Saturday, 3,500 members showed up on a blazingly sunny day to vote on the return to work. The executive was howled down and Gauthier was not permitted by the hall to chair the meeting. Another chairperson had to be chosen. The members voted twice on the return to work, chanting, "No, no, no." And then they walked out of the hall.

Faced with what was now an open rebellion against a leadership that had lost control, the leadership called a press conference on Sunday, charging that outside agitators were exerting influence, and insisting on retaking the vote on the following Tuesday. Only after extreme pressure was applied were neutral observers allowed to supervise the new vote. On Tuesday, Day Nine, the vote was held. Out of 6,500 who voted, 50.2 percent voted to return to work and 49.8 percent voted to stay out. The strike was over, broken. Militants were again fired in the wake of the return to work, because no "protocole de retour" had been signed to protect them. The contract was not signed until two years later, at the end of the summer of 1985, by which time the union had changed leadership again. The contract terms follow the demands the employers had tabled in 1983, and it has been claimed that this is the worst contract the ILG has signed in Quebec since the 1950s. Among other things, the issue of the growth of homework at the expense of inside jobs was not confronted. In August 1983, at the time of the strike, the ILG membership in Quebec stood at 10,500. Today it is 7,500 and dropping.

Where was the CATV and the Women's Committee during this strike—this strike they had laid the groundwork for? They were running the strike's day care centre. CATV members refused any formal responsibilities in organizing the strike, except those held by individuals acting as shop delegates. The 1982 choice of a "reform leadership" had not reduced CATV's chronic distrust of union elites. Refusing to become part of the official strike machinery, they felt, left them freer to mobilize and criticize. Running a day care centre in strike headquarters, they felt, would give them excellent and widespread contacts with rank-and-file women. Indeed, it did. Except that when the membership swept beyond the formal leadership at the very beginning of the strike, and then openly moved into rebellion against the leadership, spontaneity could not carry an inchoate, aroused membership far enough to maintain its rebellion. In the face of the quickly reassertive union establishment, and in the absence of a rank-and-file spokesgroup, the new militancy of garment workers was quickly smashed—typically, by its own union leadership. CATV would have had to be able and willing to step into the first week of that strike and speak for the women it had helped to educate over the past three years; speak first to the leadership, and then to the bosses. It refused. Why? Because refusal was consistent with CATV's own ideals.

Over the three years since its founding, the Women's Committee and CATV had always refused to buy into, or oppose in order to supplant, the union establishment. CATV's feminism was profoundly anti-bureaucratic and suspicious of patriarchal ways. It had focused its tactics, over the years, on four methods: first, informing and educating the members as widely as possible; second, using whatever formal protections existed in the contract as militantly as possible; third, exposing the collaboration and cynicism of the union leadership; and fourth, raising, at a time when no one else would, the deeper, harder issues about homework and the future of the garment industry.

In its early years, CATV and the Women's Committee had a precarious but simply-defined position: they were to be institutional homes for rebels against the union leadership's whole way of operating. However, once the ostensible reform slate under Gauthier came into office in 1982, the Women's Committee's position became much less clear. It faced what Debbie Field has recently called "the dilemma facing women's committees."[33] That dilemma concerns the committee's relationship to, and autonomy from, the official union structures.

> Unions as they exist today cannot tolerate intense or prolonged mobilization, which in itself challenges the tradition of business unionism. As a result unions often try to incorporate, co-opt or control women's committees...[In this] women's committees face a problem: Can we keep our focus on the mobilization of rank-and-file women and risk losing credibility with the leadership?...As women's committees become a fixed component of the union organization, their relationship with rank and file women inevitably becomes attenuated.[34]

CATV's choice, at the beginning of the strike it catalyzed over issues it had forced out into the open, was to refuse leadership in order to retain credibility. The reasons for that choice were ethical, but they also reflected a complex blending of organizational tactics and personal styles. For many members of the core group of CATV, leadership—or power—was defined in Manichean terms. As feminist trade unionists, it was acceptable to harass, expose and mobilize against patriarchal union leadership. But it was not acceptable to take the leap towards leadership in those structures, to take responsibility and take power. In other words, it was feared that even partial power would corrupt absolutely, would transform feminists into "apparatchiks" and grind them up in the union machine.

Power itself, in other words, was at the heart of the dilemma. CATV conceived of only two ways of exercising power: as the male union leaders did; or, in negation, in guerilla warfare against this corrupt but entrenched opponent whom one did not expect to dislodge.

Yet there are two other ways of exercising power in a union, and particularly during such unstable and promising times as the 1983 strike. During strikes, particularly when the leadership is perceived to be unsure of itself, even the most impermeable of union power structures suddenly becomes permeable, and changes can be made that will survive into the post-strike period. Feminist militants, enjoying widespread credibility and visibility, might, in the heat of the strike, have challenged the negotiating team and/or the executive, replaced them, and faced the manufacturers with a new agenda. Or CATV might have moved instead to organize parallel power, to create situations and institutions in which it could be seen as the voice of the union membership, thereby undermining the existing leadership and providing a credible alternative to it, without challenging the entrenched leadership in its own power structures or forming a rival union. Eventually, the pressure on the inadequate leadership would become unbearable, and the old guard would crack apart.[35] The definition of a new agenda, of new demands, and of new trade union practices would fall to CATV as the only inheritor of the union's future. But CATV recognized only the first two forms of power, and thus let the unique opportunity presented by this strike slip away.

CONCLUSIONS AND THE QUESTIONS THEY RAISE

What can be learned from the 1983 strike, and how are these lessons pertinent to other low-paid industries in which feminists organize? Unions—anywhere, I suspect—are remarkably impermeable structures. That is, they are resistant to external and internal pressures for reform, and have developed successful mechanisms for incorporating or marginalizing the reformers. The experience of all three recent opposition movements in the ILGWU (black, Québécois nationalist, and feminist socialist) has been that only a platform of reform linked to a wider social movement will make a dent in institutionalized racism or sexism.

However, the broader linkages are necessary but insufficient. The contrasting results obtained by the three reform movements also demonstrate that only if the larger social movement to which union reformers relate becomes a mainstream ideology, are the union dissidents able to make headway against union practices and institutions. In this vein, black and hispanic civil rights activists were largely unable to penetrate or transform the New York ILG, while Québécois nationalists had greater, though partial success with the Quebec branches.

The linkages with a larger social movement, the deliberate 'overflowing' of narrow union structures and goals, were at the same time the strength and the weakness of the feminist socialists of CATV. CATV was able, both ideologically and organizationally, to call upon feminism in order to protect itself against attacks from the union leadership; but only because it has been made politically dangerous to openly reject the fundamentals of equal opportunity for women. On the other hand, the anti-bureaucratic, extra-structural, cynical-of-power components of CATV feminism allowed CATV to catalyze and educate, but impeded it from taking up the leadership (either within union structures or parallel to them) of the revolution it created. Needing 'unionism with a human face', but not yet in control of the structures that might produce it, CATV militants lost their jobs, dropped out, and burnt out. They went to work in non-union shops, became mothers who no longer worked outside the home, went back to school in Women's Studies. The dilemma of women's committees, caught in the struggle between autonomy and establishment recognition, became an unbearable tension.

The 1983 garment strike in Montreal offers, I think, three lessons for the next generation of women struggling to unionize in the garment industry, and perhaps for women organizing elsewhere in the low-paid trades. First, women organizing *as women* challenge traditional union elites—always. Second, transforming a union agenda requires a delicate balance between reliance on the external, wider women's movement, and building a credible, thorough and resilient organization within the union. And third, once traditional power within the union begins to crumble, feminists must not refuse authority and responsibility for the new unionism struggling to be born. Rather, feminists must take those responsibilities, must learn to humanize power, to feminize it and redefine it collectively.

As the CATV women said, in confrontation with the QFL executive after the strike had been lost: "We are asking you for no miracles. Only—let us fight on."

ENDNOTES

An earlier version of this paper was presented at the Women and Labour Conference in Brisbane, Australia, on 15 July 1984. SSHRC provided travel assistance.

1. Rianne Mahon, *The Politics of Industrial Restructuring: Canadian Textiles* (Toronto, 1984).

2. Hubert Kempf argues that in the Unites States, big industrial enterprises are turning increasingly towards the production of services, thereby further contributing to the decline in industrial employment. "Quand l'explosion des services transforme les entreprises," *Le Monde diplomatique* May 1984.

3. The 1986 Report by the Commission consultative sur le travail et la révision du Code de travail (The Beaudry Commission) states that only 50.5 percent of employed Quebeckers in 1984 enjoyed regular full-time employment.

4. For Canadian data, Julie White, *Women in Unions* (Ottawa, 1976); and Pat and Hugh Armstrong, *The Working Majority* (Ottawa, 1983).

5. International Labour Organization, *Second Tripartite Technical Meeting for the Clothing Industry* Report II, (Geneva, 1980), p. 92.

6. *Ibid.*

7. *Ibid.* Report III, p. 8.

8. Carla Lipsig-Mummé, "Le travail à domicile: un retour à l'époque pré-syndicale," *Le Devoir*, 25 January 1982.

9. Lipsig-Mummé, "L'UIOVD et le travail phantôme," *Le Devoir*, 26 January 1982.

10. But what of the homeworkers themselves, today forming the majority of garment workers? We can, I think, make short shrift of the argument that homework represents the wave of the future, the healing of the artificial separation of home and work life created by the Industrial Revolution. For the non-professional homeworker, homework is economic exploitation, legal vulnerability, social isolation — far worse than she experiences even in the most alienated unionized production jobs. Homework always entails displacement of the locus of production from the garment shop, where workers are clustered, to individual residences, where they are isolated. This displacement always results in the decentralization of production. Decentralization of production, in turn, tends to recompense the division of labour

— without paying the worker for the additional tasks — and to shift a significant range of costs associated with the maintenance of factory operations back to the individual producers. Thus, for example, the sewing machine operator, paid for sewing shifts at home, is paid by the unit or by the dozen. She may also have to pick up the "bundles" at the factory, finish the garments, pack them for transport back to the contractor or factory, and have her husband or older child deliver them to the contractor or factory. None of these additional tasks is paid. The recomposition of the division of labour adds unpaid tasks to the ones for which the piece rate is calculated, while implicating unpaid family members in the production process, and sometimes making the homeworker dependent upon this unpaid help for the delivery of her work. Conventionally, the homeworker pays for her own machine and machine maintenance, electricity, thread, delivery costs and telephone bills. Work at home blurs the lines between work time and private time, and the workday can reach a chopped-up eighteen hours. Bulky material and dangerous machinery invade her home. There is little that is utopian or self-liberating in the homeworker's life.

11. For a longer discussion of homework, see Carla Lipsig-Mummé, "The Renaissance of Homeworking in Developed Economies," *Relations industrielles* 38/3 (1983).

12. *Dossier noir sur l'UIOVD* (Montreal, 1981).

13. Lipsig-Mummé, "Le travail à domicile..."

14. Harley Green, "Homework," *Labour Unity*, September 1980.

15. The Twin Plants Agreement between Mexico and the United States allows American companies to set up production facilities in a zone just inside Mexico, stretching from Texas to California. Goods produced there by Mexican workers (earning a fraction of their American counterparts' wages) will be sold in the United States without having to pay the import duties.

16. *ILGWU Report and Record*, various years, 1965-83.

17. See Paul Weiler, "Promises to Keep," *Harvard Law Review*.

18. Herbert Hill, "The ILGWU: Fact and Fiction," in Burton Hall (ed.), *Autocracy and Insurgency in Organized Labour* (New Jersey, 1982).

19. Sol C. Chaikin, *A Labour Viewpoint: Another Opinion* (New York, 1980), p. 108.

20. Hill, "The ILGWU," p. 176.

21. Joel Seidman, *The Needle Trades* (New York and Toronto, 1941), p. 157.

22. *Ibid.*, pp. 158-159.

23. *Ibid.*, pp. 159-185; and Jesse Thomas Carpenter, *Competition and Collective Bargaining in the Needle Trades, 1910-1967* (Ithaca, 1972), ch. 1.

24. Evelyn Dumas, *Dans le sommeil de nos os* (Montreal, 1971), pp. 43-75.

25. *Ibid.*, pp. 73-74. The Industrial Union of Needle Trades Workers, influenced by the Communist Party, had been successful in Montreal in the cloak industry in the 1920s, and the dress industry in the 1930s.

26. *Ibid.*, p. 74.

27. Herbert Hill, "The ILGWU...," pp. 147-160.

28. Nothing has been written beyond *23 Dossiers de Québec Presse* (Montreal, 1972).

29. Translated and adapted from *Dossier noir sur l'UIOVD*, pp. 25-27.

30. *Ibid.*, pp. 16-18.

31. *Ibid.*, p. 4; and Maurice Roy in *Chatelaine*, September 1981.

32. *Dossier noir sur l'UIOVD*, p. 21.

33. Debbie Field, "The Dilemma Facing Women's Committees," in Linda Briskin and Lynda Yanz (eds.), *Union Sisters* (Toronto, 1984).

34. *Ibid.*, pp. 301-302.

35. When the strike ended, the role of the Quebec Federation of Labour vis-à-vis the faltering ILG leadership, became an issue of bitter controversy within union circles. In fact, the strike broke the leadership as well as deflating the militant movement. Had the QFL deliberately fanned tensions between membership and leadership, seeking to push the leadership into a more militant stance? Had it feared the militancy of the membership? Were divisions among the counsellors the QFL placed with the ILG during the strike, crucial to its outcome? Nothing beyond the newspaper articles has been written on the QFL's role in the strike. It is an important question, but one for which very few concrete sources are available.

CHAPTER 7

IN THE PRIVACY OF OUR OWN HOME: FOREIGN DOMESTIC WORKERS AS SOLUTION TO THE CRISIS OF THE DOMESTIC SPHERE IN CANADA

SEDEF ARAT-KOC

Despite marked increases in the participation of women in the labour force, neither the availability and quality of socialized childcare arrangements nor the division of housework between men and women appear to have changed radically. The structure, demands and pressures of the labour market in Canada allow for less flexibility in the accommodation of family needs and responsibilities than is the case in several European countries. Under these circumstances, housework and childcare remain private burdens to be shouldered mainly by women, who must either work double and triple days or find substitutes.

In this context, employment of live-in domestic workers, a long-abandoned practice in North America, is once again being presented as a solution to the burdens of housework and childcare among high and middle income groups. Yet the organization of domestic service in capitalist society, and the specific conditions which most live-in domestic workers experience in Canada, make this type of work particularly oppressive. Not surprisingly, perhaps, 98 percent of these workers are women. As a collective ideal, this solution, therefore, presents a problem for the women's movement.

In discussing the implications of the domestic service solution to the housework and childcare problem, I will document and analyze the structural and historical conditions of live-in domestic workers in Canada. The primary focus is on foreign domestic workers with temporary work permits. The conditions of this group best demonstrate the complex articulation of gender issues with those of class and citizenship.

THE CRISIS OF THE DOMESTIC SPHERE

There has been a significant increase in women's participation in the labour force in Canada since the 1960s. With around 43 percent of the labour force comprising women,[1] the percentage of couples in the man-the-breadwinner/woman-the-homemaker category has been reduced to less than 16 percent from around 65 percent in 1961.[2] More dramatic, however, is the change in the participation rates of women with family responsibilities. According to the most recent statistics, 70 percent of married women between ages of 25 to 54 years are in the labour force.[3] Among women with children of pre-school age, 65.1 percent work outside their homes.[4]

The response of society and the state to these changes in women's employment has been negligible. First, the behaviour of men in the home has changed very little in terms of their contributions to housework and parenting responsibilities. Although attitudes among men have changed positively,[5] the actual number of men regularly doing some housework has changed very little. Moreover, even when men regularly contribute to domestic labour, the sex-typing of duties continues, with men performing only certain tasks and rarely doing any pre-task planning. Overall, the contributions of men to housework do not very often go beyond "helping out."[6]

Second, as the Report of the Task Force on childcare demonstrates, the childcare situation in Canada is in a state of crisis. Licensed daycare spaces only serve 9 percent of children whose parents work or study 20 or more hours each week. Over 80 percent of children receiving non-parental care are in unlicensed arrangements. The quality and dependability of such care is unknown.[7]

Parents also suffer the inflexibility of work arrangements. Canadian employers and the state have provided little accommodation for the family responsibilities of working people. Except for an inadequate maternity leave system, inegalitarian in gender terms, replacing only a relatively small portion of regular income, and covering a relatively short period of time — Canada has not officially recognized recent changes in the labour force. In stark contrast to most European countries, there are no systems of extended childcare leave, leave for care of sick children or other types of family responsibility leave. Without the right to refuse shiftwork and overtime and to work reduced hours or flexible work weeks (rights that are almost commonplace for their European counterparts) working parents in Canada find that even privatized solutions fail to meet their needs.[8]

As a result of the squeeze on working couples from pressures in the public and private spheres, there are signs that employment of domestic servants, a rare practice since the 1920s, is on the increase again. Several governmental and mass media sources have approvingly cited the employment of domestic workers as a solution.[9] Indeed, there is evidence to suggest that employers of live-in domestic workers are now overwhelmingly dual-career couples with small children. For 71.4 percent of the employers the major reason for hiring a domestic has been to "free both spouses for the labour market."[10] While the majority of employers are in upper-middle to upper income categories, the demand for live-in domestic servants among middle income families is likely to rise. An important reason for this is that user fees — as opposed to municipal, provincial or national government financing — constitute a high proportion of childcare costs and middle class families cannot get subsidies for such services in Canada. Calculations suggest that especially for parents with two or more pre-school children, employment of a live-in nanny would cost significantly less than sending children to a daycare centre or hiring live-out help.[11]

Though the demand for domestic workers rises, the conditions of domestic service in general, and live-in service in particular, are so undesirable that it is very difficult to find Canadians willing to do the job. As a result, the Canadian Department of Immigration has devised mechanisms to allow domestic workers, usually from the Third World, to enter Canada with temporary status. Since the mid-1970s between 10,000 to 16,000 foreign workers a year have been issued temporary work permits. Almost all (96 percent) of these workers are in live-in service.[12]

Esther Boserup, writing in 1970, predicted a constant decline in domestic service in advanced capitalist countries in the 20th century. She argued that widespread employment of domestic servants corresponds to an intermediate stage of development, and that the commercialization of services in later stages of development would make the need for domestic servants redundant.[13] Yet the relation of "development" to domestic labour is not necessarily an even, evolutionary process that is determined by the unhindered, inevitable expansion of the market. Rather it is one that is also determined politically. The survival of domestic service in Canada today is politically determined by the lack of adequate and good quality childcare services as well as the continuing availability, through immigration legislation and practices and discriminatory labour laws, of a cheap and vulnerable source of foreign domestic servants.

Although foreign domestic workers have certainly provided one solution to the pressures their employers face in meeting the demands of work and family, it is a questionable one considering the working and living conditions of the workers involved. Such a solution also has serious implications for the women's movement. Work in the domestic sphere becomes a source of division, rather than unity and 'sisterhood' among women.[14] For feminism, which has so far concentrated on relations in which men (as individuals and/or through the masculine role) and the structures of society, economy and the state oppress women, the analysis of the mistress-servant relationship, one in which women exploit women, poses an uncomfortable challenge. The complex articulation of class and citizenship status with gender inequality in the domestic worker's condition also poses a theoretical challenge to feminist theory which has only recently started to tackle such issues.

This discussion of the conditions of domestic workers is divided into three parts. The first part examines the labour process in domestic service and analyzes what the domestic worker shares with the housewife. The second part focuses on the ambiguous status of the domestic as a special type of worker who is neither a member of the family nor an employee in the public sphere enjoying the advantages of socialized work. Finally, the citizenship status of foreign domestic workers in Canada will be analyzed as a factor which contributes to, and perpetuates, the oppressiveness of their conditions.

THE MATERIAL CONDITIONS OF PRIVATIZED HOUSEHOLD WORK

The geographic, economic, social and ideological separation of a public work sphere from the home, which developed with socialized commodity production under capitalism, has led to a decline in the status of domestic labour — whether done by housewife or servant. One of the causes of this decline is the physical, economic, and ideological invisibility of domestic labour. Physically, what makes domestic labour invisible is the service or maintenance nature of the work whose products are either intangible or consumed very quickly. The domestic labourer is at a disadvantage compared to the factory worker in this regard:

> The appropriate symbol for housework (and for housework
> alone) is not the interminable conveyor belt but a compul-

sive circle like a pet mouse in its cage spinning round on its
exercise wheel unable to get off.[15]

Also domestic labour is performed in private, perhaps in greater isolation than ever in human history. As the production of goods as well as services such as education and health care moved out of the home, the husband and children left, and as the development of household technology made collaboration in certain tasks with other women less necessary, the household worker faced increased isolation, loneliness and invisibility.

Economically, domestic labour is invisible because it is not part of capitalist production which uses wage labour to produce commodities for the market. When performed by the housewife, domestic labour is unpaid, it produces use value without producing profit. In comparison to that of the housewife, the labour of the domestic servant is somewhat more visible because it is paid for. As one domestic servant stated, however, it still can remain invisible, even in the eyes of her female employer:

> You know how housework is; you could tidy up the house
> and wash the dishes twenty times a day. At the end of each
> day, especially with three growing boy child, the house
> look like a hurricane pass through it, so when she is in a
> bad mood she wants to know what I do all day.[16]

Domestic labour is physical as well as mental and psychological work which sustains the reproduction of labour power and the labour force. It is indispensable to the functioning of the economy. However, intertwined as it is with intimate, personal relations, domestic labour is considered a private matter, a 'labour of love'. As such, it is ideologically invisible as a form of real work, a status that is hard to change even when it is paid for.

Domestic labour generally does not appear on paychecks or in GNP figures; it is not considered real work, and is defined as non-productive. Yet it involves very long working hours.[17] Especially for care-givers of young children who have to be always on call, such work can be never ending — there is no clear boundary between work and leisure. For the housewife and the live-in domestic servant, the place of work is also the place of leisure. She does not go to work but wakes up to it. This makes her "leisure" vulnerable to interventions and her work hours stretchable to 24 hours a day, seven days a week.

Contrary to its safe, comfortable image, for the domestic labourer the home is often a hazardous and stressful place. Besides working with dangerous chemicals and in several activities that are accident prone, the domestic worker is also placed under stress. Stress is a typical facet of occupations that involve the worker in high demand and low control situations.[18] In domestic work, the need to adjust to the different schedules of family members and to juggle the conflicting demands of housework and childcare both create stressful conditions. The notion that the housewife is her own boss is largely a myth. The domestic worker, whose schedule and standards of work are controlled by others, does not even have the consolation of myth.

Unlike wage labour which is, at least theoretically, mobile, the labour of the housewife is a life-long, or at least marriage-long commitment. Compared to the housewife, the domestic servant should fare better in this respect. However, this is only the case when we consider the free labourer. Domestic servants in Canada, however, have very often been restricted in changing employers, and have not been free to change jobs, or to decide whether or not to sell their labour power.

While domestic labour under capitalism assumes several universal characteristics such as invisibility, isolation and low status, the way these are experienced by individuals performing such labour may vary significantly by class, race and citizenship. In the case of foreign domestic workers, isolation and the resulting loneliness, imposed by the privatized nature of housework and childcare, are perpetuated by racial, cultural and linguistic barriers. Likewise, the invisibility of domestic labour and the low status attached to it are further reinforced by the powerlessness of domestic labourers when they are visible minority women from the Third World on temporary work permits, who lack basic political rights.

NEITHER A WIFE NOR A WORKER: THE CONTRADICTIONS OF THE DOMESTIC WORKER'S STATUS

While sharing with the housewife many of the material conditions of privatized housework and childcare, the domestic worker also has an ambiguous status. She is neither a wife nor a full-fledged worker with corresponding rights and privileges. Squeezed between the private and public spheres, she belongs to neither one or the other and probably combines the worst aspects of both.

Historically, with the privatization of the family, the domestic worker has been excluded from membership in or close bonding with the employing family. Lost are the co-operation and companionship apparently characteristic of rural America.[19] The domestic worker today is like a stranger, "being in the family, but not of it."[20] She is involved in the work of a house, but not the pleasures and intimacies of a home. Positive aspects that are rightly or wrongly attributed to the private sphere — love, intimacy, nurturance, companionship — are not even part of her realistic expectations.

> I feel as if this is my home. It is my home, this is where I
> live. It's not like I come to work for them and then evening
> time I leave and go home. When you are living with them,
> they make you feel as if you really don't belong, and where
> the devil do you really belong? It's a funny thing to happen
> to us, because it make us feel like we don't know if we
> coming or going. This live-in thing really puts us in a funny
> situation.[21]

Potentially, lack of intimacy with the employing family is liberating. Since class differences turn close employer-employee relationships into paternalistic ones, many domestic workers actually prefer maintaining a business-like professionalism. Professionalism in relations, however, is not a matter of choice for the domestic worker but requires relative power in social, political and legal terms. Historically, the social construction of domestic work in Canada has deprived domestic workers of these forms of power.

In losing the close relationship of a family and becoming an employee, the domestic worker has not been compensated by the advantages other employees enjoy. The isolation of domestic service makes organization of workers as well as standardization and regulation of working conditions very difficult. This difficulty is greater for live-in workers for whom there is no separation between home and work. The result is generally a vulnerable and often exploited worker whose conditions are at the mercy of the employer:

> Wages are too often regulated by the employer's bank
> account, hours of service by his personal caprice, and
> moral questions by his personal convenience.[22]

Labour standards legislation, which is under provincial jurisdiction in Canada and therefore not uniform, either does not apply or only partially applies to domestic workers. Domestic employees in private homes are excluded from labour standards legislation in Alberta, New Brunswick, Nova

Scotia, the Northwest Territories, and the Yukon. In other provinces they are only partially covered; in many, only with provisions providing lower than the general minimum wage, longer than the 40 hour work week and rarely any overtime pay.[23]

In Ontario, which has about two-thirds of all domestic workers in Canada, the Employment Standards Act was finally extended to domestics in 1984. It set daily and weekly rates of pay based on a standard work week of 44 hours. This change, however, was almost meaningless for live-in domestic workers because they were not covered by the hours of work and overtime pay provisions of the Act. Since it is not uncommon to see live-in domestic workers working or on call 60-80 or more hours per week, the actual hourly wage can in many cases fall substantially below the minimum wage. Working very long hours and having little or no time off are, in fact, some of the most common complaints of live-in domestic workers:

> I want something where I can go home to my house at night, close my door and pray to my God in peace. I want to know that when I go to bed at night, I don't have to listen out for people shouting at me to come and look after their food or come and change diapers.[24]

After two years of negotiations and a Charter of Rights case filed by the International Coalition to End Domestic Exploitation (INTERCEDE) against the Ontario government, on the grounds that the existing legislation discriminated against domestic workers as women and as a group of workers different from other workers, the issue of live-in service was finally addressed in October 1987. New labour regulations gave live-in domestic workers the right to claim overtime pay after a 44 hour work week.[25] Whether or not the new provision is enforced will depend on how much de facto bargaining power domestics will have in relation to their employers. So far, even when protective legislation did exist, governments have generally failed to enforce it. In practice, especially when they are dealing with vulnerable workers who have no choice but to keep their jobs, employers are able to change work hours, duties and pay rates.

In Ontario, the government not only fails to enforce already existing legislation, but also prevents domestic workers from defending their rights in an organized, collective way. The Ontario Labour Relations Act denies the domestics employed in private homes the right to unionize. The same act also denies domestics access to the impartial tribunal for unfair practices.[26]

In some cases, existing regulations may even sanction abuse. One serious problem domestic workers face is the lack of clear job definitions. The Canadian Classification and Dictionary of Occupations (used by the immigration officials in connection with employment authorizations) may add to the problem. In this system "baby sitter" is defined as someone who, besides doing other work, "keeps children's quarters clean and tidy" and "cleans other parts of home." On the other hand, the "maid/domestic... may look after children" also.[27] The specific combination of the class status of the domestic worker and the fact that domestic service takes place in the private sphere creates the potential for a very peculiar relation of domination between the employer and the domestic worker, especially if there is a live-in arrangement. This latter is compulsory for foreign domestic workers on temporary work permits. There are social-psychological dimensions to the subordination of a domestic worker that make it different from the subordination of housewives (who also do domestic work) and workers (who also stand in an unequal class relation to their employers).

While a factory worker experiences subordination and control during work, once she leaves her job at the end of the day, she is a free person in relation to her employer. The live-in domestic worker, on the other hand, cannot leave her workplace and her employer's supervision. Sharing private space with the employers, and yet not part of their family, the domestic also finds it difficult to create her own private space and private life:

> Some domestics have to share a room with the children in
> the household or have their room used as a family room,
> TV room, sewing room, etc. One woman had to keep her
> door open at all times in case the children started to cry,
> others say their employers do not respect their privacy and
> walk in without knocking. In one case the piano was
> moved into the domestic's room for the children to practice
> on![28]

Living in the employer's home, makes it difficult to invite friends over. Other specific complaints about lack of privacy refer in certain cases to the scrutiny of mail and phone calls, the search of personal belongings and inquiries into activities on days off.[29]

With live-in domestic service creating the possibilities for full-time monitoring of the whole life of the domestic worker, it is probably not an exaggeration to call it a "total institution."[30] Clearly, during the development of the present historical form of domestic service, those performing such work lost only some of the elements of child-like status in the patriarchal household. Gone are the protection, security and bonding to the family that were typical of service in feudal society. Remaining are the supervision and the personal nature of the authority relationship which strip the domestic worker of full adult status. Linguistic practices are often reflective of this. For example, domestic workers are commonly referred to as "girls," regardless of their age, both by employers and by domestics themselves. It is also common for domestic workers to be addressed by their first names while they are expected to address employers as Mr. or Mrs.[31]

Besides heavy physical work, domestic service involves a personal relationship with the employer. Unlike factory work which requires completion of clearly defined tasks in clearly defined ways, domestic service is very unstructured. Especially in live-in arrangements, a domestic is not just hired for specific tasks, "but for general availability; above all, a servant ha(s) to take orders as well."[32] Consequently, the display of deference, obedience and submissiveness can sometimes be as important or more important than the actual physical work.[33] The domestic worker, therefore, is hired not for her labour alone but also for her personality traits.

Also unique to the employer-employee relationship in domestic service is that both the domestic and the mistress are designated, on the basis of gender, as responsible for domestic work. Many female employers indicate that they need domestic workers to help them because their husbands will not.[34] Employment of a domestic worker has enabled these women to avoid confrontations with their husbands about sharing domestic work. In this sense, the presence of the domestic worker "emphasizes the fact that women — all women — are responsible for cleaning the house, at the same time that it releases the housewife to become a lady of leisure or a career woman."[35] Given the gendered division of labour in the household, the labour of the housewife and the domestic worker are interchangeable: the domestic worker is employed to replace an absent full-time housewife; but when the domestic worker can't work, the housewife must. Given the social degradation of domestic work and the class inequality between the domestic worker and the mistress, however, their shared subordination does not often lead to solidarity.

> [T]he domestic represents the employer in the most devalued area of the employer's activities... Any identification the employer has with the domestic is a negative identification.[36]

Rather than solidarity, shared subordination can lead to "housewife power strategies" through which "many housewives seek to maintain class and race privileges vis-á-vis their domestics."[37] What characterizes servant-mistress relationships is deference from the worker and maternalism from the employer.

GOOD ENOUGH TO WORK, NOT GOOD ENOUGH TO STAY: IMPLICATIONS OF CITIZENSHIP STATUS FOR FOREIGN DOMESTIC WORKERS

From the nineteenth century on, the Canadian state has actively recruited and controlled domestic labour.[38] The amount of planning and energy involved tells us a great deal about the importance of domestic service for the Canadian economy and society. The low status and unfavourable conditions of the workers involved, however, stand in stark contrast to the attention given their recruitment and control. Working conditions have been so undesirable that, not only has it been difficult to find Canadians interested in the job, but sometimes the only way of keeping immigrant domestics in domestic work has been through indenturing them.

Active state involvement in recruitment and control of domestic workers started in the late nineteenth century when industrialization diverted women into other occupations and it became difficult to find enough Canadian-born women interested in domestic service. This involvement ranged from making the immigration of domestics easier through occasionally sending immigration employees to England and Scotland to select domestics, to encouraging and even enforcing the so-called "assisted passage" agreements that bonded servants to their employers for a certain period of time.[39] Bonding became such a necessary part of controlling the domestic labour force that the Department of Immigration sometimes evaded legislation in order to fulfil its policing function. For example, around the turn of the century, master and servant legislation was enacted in most provinces, which aimed to protect servants from an exploitive contract which they might have signed in order to immigrate. According to this legislation, contracts signed outside the province were not legally binding. The immigration department, however, aiming to enforce bonded status, avoided this legislation by having immigrant domestics re-sign their contracts upon arrival in Canada.[40]

Immigration of British and Scottish domestic workers in the late nineteenth and early twentieth century shared with later domestic immigration the practice of bonding. What made immigration practices in this period different from later periods, however, was that recruitment of domestics from abroad was closely linked to Canada's nation-building efforts. Until the 1920s, the middle class women and social reformers involved in female immigration work voiced racist, nationalist and moralistic concerns that went beyond a simple interest in meeting demands for the domestic labour force. Through their efforts in selecting, protecting and supervising domestics, the organizations involved in female immigration wanted to ensure that recruits would become more than servants: that these women of the "right" national and racial stock and character would, in the long run, constitute the "pure and virtuous mothers of the ideal Canadian home and the foundation of the moral Canadian nation."[41] While these expectations were certainly restrictive for domestic workers, they also conveyed the message that these women "belonged" in Canadian society, a message that would be missing in later immigration practices.

Although the demand for domestic servants has decreased since the early part of the twentieth century, it has still exceeded the supply. This has been especially true for live-in workers. As a result, the Department of Immigration has developed new schemes in the post-war period to bring domestic workers to Canada and to keep them doing domestic work. In 1955, for example, the Domestic Worker Program was started with the aim of importing domestic workers from the Caribbean region (primarily from Jamaica). Under this scheme single women of good health, between 18 and 40 years of age, with no dependents and with at least grade 8 education, were allowed into Canada as landed immigrants on the condition that they would spend at least one year as domestic servants before choosing other types of work.[42] Between 1955-1960, an average of 300 domestic workers per year were admitted through this program, and between 1960-1965 the numbers rose to 1,000 per year.[43]

According to the Department of Immigration the Domestic Worker Program did not help to solve the labour shortage in domestic service because most of the women who came found their working conditions unacceptable and left service for other work once they fulfilled their one year obligation. To solve this problem the government started issuing temporary work permits in 1973 which only allowed these workers to remain in the country for a specified period of time (usually a year), doing a specific type of work, for a specific employer. The new employment visa system is a version of indenture. Foreign domestic workers who come as "guest workers" —instead of immigrants—

have no rights to stay in Canada or claim social security benefits. Although foreign domestics may be allowed to change employers with special permission from immigration authorities, they cannot leave domestic service without also having to leave Canada. Extension of the employment visa beyond the first year is possible and common, but the foreign worker must inevitably leave. Under this new scheme increasing numbers of domestic workers are brought into Canada every year. The numbers of employment visas issued to domestics has risen consistently from around 1,800 in 1973 to more than 16,000 in 1982.[44]

The official purpose of the employment visa system is to meet the urgent and temporary needs of Canadian employers to fill jobs that cannot be filled domestically without ultimately threatening the employment opportunities of Canadian residents.[45] When we consider the case of domestic service, however, both the unwillingness of Canadians to take live-in work as well as the century-long efforts of the Canadian state to import domestic workers from abroad, suggest that neither the need nor the solution is temporary. Despite the persistence of a high demand/low supply situation, domestic workers are only accepted to Canada with temporary status. Except for foreign agricultural workers (who do seasonal work), domestic workers are the only occupational group to whom temporary work permits apply on a permanent basis.

In fact, when we look into Canada's immigration practices since the mid 1970s we see a tendency, to resort increasingly to temporary employment visas as opposed to permanent immigration to meet labour demands not only in domestic service but also in several other job categories. Since 1975 the annual number of people entering Canada on temporary employment visas has consistently exceeded the number of landed immigrants destined for the labour force.[46] Migration to Canada, therefore, has changed in part from a movement of people to a movement of labour power. The benefits of this to Canada as a labour-importing country are enormous. As the literature on migrant workers in Western Europe, South Africa and California has demonstrated, recipient countries benefit not only by avoiding the costs of developing a young and healthy labour-force, but also by avoiding a commitment to supporting them during old-age, sickness and unemployment.[47]

> Behind the term 'guestworker' (is) a belief that such workers (are) like replaceable parts. Like cogs in a machine, for every part that breaks down, there (is) a seemingly endless supply of replacements.[48]

There are also significant political advantages to employing workers without citizenship rights. Lacking electoral and political rights and freedoms, and dependent on their employers not only for wages but also for their continued stay in the country, workers on employment visas are expected to create a docile and acquiescent labour force. Historically, the presence of migrant workers has also been frequently associated with racist and xenophobic divisions in the working class.

> Canadians have the feeling that we are coming here to rob
> them, to take away their jobs, yet we are the ones who
> clean up their mess, pick up after them. We take the jobs
> they wouldn't take and yet they hate us so much.[49]

One significant ideological implication of temporary work permits is that the designation of a group of workers as temporary and foreign encourages a desensitized attitude towards their conditions. Hannah Arendt argues that with the development of nation-states and national sovereignty, basic human rights and freedoms became thoroughly bound up with the rights of citizenship.[50] In liberal democratic society where emphasis on formal equality has become a part of popular political discourse, separation of people into "citizen" and "non-citizen" categories, into "insiders" (to whom rights apply) and "outsiders," serves to legitimize inferior conditions and lesser rights for the latter group.[51]

The major effect of Canada's employment visa system on domestic workers has been the creation of a captive labour force which has guaranteed that the turnover in domestic service would remain low no matter how bad the working and living conditions. Unable to leave domestic service without losing their rights to stay in Canada, foreign domestics also find it difficult to change employers. A foreign worker's status in Canada changes to that of visitor if she leaves or loses her job. While workers are generally given a period of two weeks by immigration authorities to find a new employer, the decision to issue a new employment visa is at the discretion of the individual immigration officer who judges whether the working conditions with the previous employer have in fact been intolerable.[52] On top of the hassle they might receive from individual immigration officers, until 1986 there was a regulation which required workers on employment visa to have a release letter from the former employer before changing employers![53]

Unlike other workers who enjoy the basic freedom to leave a particular job or employer, the only freedom that the foreign worker on an employment visa has is to return to her country of origin. In the case of many Third World women who come to Canada out of conditions of economic desperation, there is no choice but to stay in Canada. As Nancy Hook reported, non-Canadian workers on employment visas were more likely to live in the homes of their employer, to work more days per week, more overtime without pay and receive a smaller hourly wage than Canadian workers.[54]

Even though their status in Canada is, by definition, temporary, domestic workers on employment visas are required to pay Canada Pension Plan, Unemployment Insurance premiums and income tax — about one month's earnings a year — without being able to claim benefits. The nature of the employment visa makes access to unemployment insurance benefits impossible because the worker must either find a new employer or leave the country if she loses a job. Benefits from Canada Pension Plan are also inaccessible because the "guest worker" is expected to retire in the country of origin.[55] Revenue Canada has calculated the total of revenues from CPP and UIC premiums collected from foreign domestics between 1973-1979 to be more than 11 million dollars.[56] Foreign domestics pay a very high price, for services that they do not expect to receive.

Since November 1981 changes in the Temporary Employment Authorization Program have enabled foreign domestics who have worked in Canada continuously for two years, to apply for landed immigrant status without leaving the country. While this is a progressive step, it fails to solve the problem of foreign domestic workers in Canada. First, there is still a two-year period of bonded service before domestics may apply. Second, there is no guarantee that landed immigrant status will be granted. Applicants need to meet Immigration Dept. assessment criteria and demonstrate a "potential for self-sufficiency."[57] Not surprisingly, given societal notions about domestic labour skills, these women get very low points for the Specific Vocational Preparation category.[58] Ironically, they also receive low points in the Occupational Demand category.[59] As a result, immigration officers require that domestic applicants (again without any guarantees to grant them landed status) take upgrading courses (with high foreign student fees) and do volunteer work in the community.[60] For live-in foreign domestics, it is difficult to find both the time and the money to fulfil these requirements.

Another problem is that domestics with children back in the home country, and older domestics face discrimination.

They say Immigration say any woman over 45 soon can't
clean house and will be just a burden on the government,

> and woman with over two children will bring them into the
> country and take away the opportunities other Canadian
> children have.[61]

So-called "rationalized" immigration policies, oriented towards the demands of the market, aim to import labour power rather than people. It is not, therefore, surprising to see dependents being treated as "superfluous appendages" (as they are called in South Africa) to the labour market.

The overall effect of the 1981 change in the Temporary Employment Authorization Program has been to create the possibility for individual upward mobility of (some) domestic workers while providing no structural solution to the problems of domestic service or foreign domestic workers in general. Indeed, it is ironic that a domestic must move out of domestic service altogether in order to accumulate enough points to get landed immigrant status. The implicit message that immigration policies and practices give is that domestic workers are "good enough to work, but not good enough to stay" in this country. This message says a great deal about the status of domestic labour in general.

It is also interesting to note the parallel between the modern attitude of the Canadian government and the historical treatment of domestic workers. Domestic servants did not receive legal equality and citizenship rights until the late nineteenth or early twentieth century. In France and England, for example, because they were considered to be too dependent on their masters to be recognized as civil persons, domestics (together with women) were the last groups to be enfranchised.[62] Many of the basic workers' rights and freedoms we take for granted and often associate with capitalist society are, in fact, connected to citizenship rights. With the alleged attempt to meet the temporary labour requirements of the Canadian economy without threatening the jobs of Canadians, the employment visa system has created a permanent temporary work force without citizenship rights.

By treating both the need and the presence of foreign workers as temporary the Canadian government may avoid doing anything permanent either to improve their conditions or to find other solutions to problems of housework and childcare. As long as it can maintain a captive labour force without citizenship rights to do live-in domestic service the government has little incentive to improve conditions of domestic work.

It is not simply the availability of a supply of foreign workers and the market implications of this supply that creates the conditions of their vulnerability. As Castells put it:

immigrant workers do not exist because there are "arduous
and badly paid" jobs to be done, but, rather, arduous and
badly paid jobs exist because immigrant workers are present or can be sent for to do them.[63]

The state plays an active role in structuring and controlling not only the volume but also the conditions of these workers. There is a striking contrast
between the laissez faire approach the liberal state has taken, which favours
private solutions to problems in the domestic sphere, and its rigid intervention
in the provision, organization and control of "help" for that sphere. Given the
specific combination of state policies in areas of childcare provision, labour
legislation and immigration, domestic service is not simply a private but a
politically constructed solution to the crisis of the domestic sphere.

Recently, the positions put forward by both the federal and provincial governments in policy debates on childcare indicate the persistence of a clear
preference for privatized solutions — with little concern about the quality and
conditions for either children or caregivers. The new federal childcare plan,
revealed in December 1987, emphasizes a tax-credit approach to childcare
with no commitments to providing universal access to dependable and affordable licensed care spaces. The plan proposes to double the number of daycare spaces available in seven years. Even with the number of children remaining constant this plan would meet less than 20 percent of the need. While the
government claims to have recognized the plurality of parental preferences for
childcare arrangements, the lack of socialized childcare spaces means that parents are left with no choice but to make private arrangements.

In Ontario, during the recent struggle for amendments in the Employment
Standards Act to provide set hours and overtime pay for domestic workers,
the government fought against these changes arguing that the potential
increase in costs would "upset the childcare arrangements of parents some of
whom may already be in financial squeeze."[64] Even the Labour Ministry
report, which itself proposed the amendment, expressed reservations about its
extension to all live-out domestic workers, including baby sitters, on the
grounds that it would jeopardize the inexpensive informal care arrangements
which included 400,000 children in Ontario.[65] While the financial squeeze
that many parents face in relation to childcare needs is a serious problem, the
assumption of these legislative debates and proposals is that domestic workers
should subsidize the childcare system by remaining underpaid and overworked.

Current domestic service arrangements bring the interests of employers
and employees into conflict. Given the pressures on budget and time that

some middle-class working couples face, a domestic service relationship may turn into a zero-sum game in which the improvements in the pay and working conditions of domestic workers will mean losses for the employers. As a relationship between female employers and workers, domestic service emphasizes, most clearly, the class, racial/ethnic and citizenship differences among women at the expense of their gender unity. Since gender is a social construct formed through relationships rather than a static biological category determined by sex, it would be interesting to see how domestic work as a power relationship between employer and employee shapes women's identities.

FEMINISM AND DOMESTIC SERVICE

The domestic service question is a feminist question not just because 98 percent of domestic workers are women, or because it potentially may create divisions among women that feminism needs to solve to make "sisterhood" a reality. It is also a feminist question because it is so closely linked with the privatized nature of domestic labour in our society. Domestic service, as it is organized in Canada, is not just a question of human and workers' rights. It is a question of women's oppression and liberation. Women's liberation has been defined by some as the upward mobility of individual women out of some subordinate positions and occupations. According to this definition, "women's liberation" can be compatible with general devaluation of the subordinate positions and occupations many women hold.[66] If we choose, however, to define women's liberation as a collective and transformative struggle — in addition to being one of individual liberation — that deals with class and racial inequalities and aims to re-structure society to eliminate subordinate positions, live-in domestic service is revealed as a very conservative solution for the crisis of the domestic sphere.

Domestic service leaves housework and childcare as women's work, still isolating and of low status and low value. Rather than solving the problem of gender inequality, it adds class and racial dimensions to it. Instead of housework and childcare being the responsibility of all women, it becomes the responsibility of some with subordinate class, racial and citizenship status, who are employed and supervised by those who are liberated from the direct physical burdens.[67] By reinforcing divisions of mental and manual labour, this helps perpetuate low status and low pay for domestic service.

The domestic service solution is also conservative because it does not solve the problems posed by the separation of spheres. Given the availability of a cheap source of vulnerable workers, it discourages a struggle for socialized services and more flexible work arrangements.[68] Rather than easing the public/private split in society, therefore, this solution polarizes and deepens it, with added class and racial dimensions.

The structural approach used in this paper has so far treated domestic workers as victims of unfavourable conditions that have shaped their work and living. The history of domestic service has shown, however, that domestic workers can and do act as subjects. Full of attempts to unionize and to standardize and improve working conditions, the history of domestic service and the political practice of domestic workers have a lot to offer to the women's movement. First, domestic workers help to "denaturalize" housework and childcare by doing domestic work for a wage rather than as a labour of love and doing it as an outsider to the family. Second, the struggles of domestic workers can help to decrease the invisibility of the domestic sphere and contribute to making the personal, political. While politicization of all domestic relations, including those between women, is not a comfortable task, it promises to enrich, deepen and extend the equality principle that feminism upholds.

While the issues raised and goals set by domestic workers' organizations can contribute to feminist theory and practice, these organizations and workers also need feminist support in their struggle. There are limits to how much can be achieved by domestic workers alone. Besides the obstacles domestic isolation places on organization and unionization, there are the legal restrictions imposed by provincial labour relations acts and the employment visa programs. In addition, the temporary, outsider status sustained by the employment visa system serves to increase the invisibility and marginality of foreign domestic workers and desensitize others to their conditions. Domestic workers need the wider women's movement to help overcome these obstacles and to liberate their struggle from its corporate boundaries.

The women's movement also has to address the larger domestic labour question. In the nineteenth and early twentieth century, during the first wave of feminism, there were some efforts to transform domestic labour through collectivizing it. Feminists like Charlotte Perkins Gilman, Melusina Fay Pierce and Mary Livermore developed radically creative and elaborate proposals for a changed architecture of the home, collective kitchens and cooperative housekeeping schemes. While the theory and practice of these feminists have been extremely useful in offering alternatives to privatized domestic labour, they did not deal adequately with the gender and class aspects of the issue. These feminists not only failed to demand increased male participation in domestic labour, but they also generally disregarded the interests of domestics as women and workers. They articulated their concerns as finding efficient and rational solutions to the "waste," "annoyance," "unreliability" and "laziness" of servants through rigid supervision and factory-like discipline imposed by collective housework schemes.[69] Domestic workers have been neither agents nor intended beneficiaries but rather the ground of change in these projects which seemed to prioritize extension of the principles of industrialization over concerns for equality.

The contributions of the new wave of feminism have been indispensable in terms of the critique that has been brought to sexual division of labour in society and in the family. The domestic labour debate of the 1970s and radical feminist analyses have, in different ways, also provided a critique of the privatized home. As Dolores Hayden has pointed out, however, the second wave of feminism still lacks a clear vision of positive alternatives to privatized and gendered home life.[70] In the absence of an honest, open debate around each solution and its gender, class and racial implications, and a vision of concrete, constructive alternatives that would emerge from these debates, individualized ad hoc solutions may bring more harm than good to both individual women and to the struggle for the emancipation of all women.

ENDNOTES

This is a revised version of a paper presented at the 22nd Annual Meeting of The Canadian Sociology and Anthropology Association in Hamilton, June 1987. I am grateful to Bonnie Fox, Meg Luxton, Charlene Gannage, Lynne Phillips, Esther Reiter, Michel Bodemann, Barry Wellman and Pramila Aggarwal for their constructive comments on an earlier version of the paper. The latest version has benefited from comments of SPE reviewers: Roberta Hamilton, Barbara Neis, Jane Ursel and an anonymous reviewer.

1. Statistics Canada, *The Labour Force*, July 1988 (Ottawa, 1987), p.26.

2. The Task Force on childcare, *Report of the Task Force on childcare* (Ottawa, 1986), p.7.

3. Statistics Canada, *The Labour Force*, p.27.

4. Statistics Canada, *The Labour Force*, pp.36-37.

5. 1981 Gallup poll cited in Meg Luxton, "Two Hands for the Clock: Changing Patterns in the Gendered Division of Labour in the Home" in Meg Luxton and Harriet Rosenberg, *Through the Kitchen Window. The Politics of Home and Family* (Toronto, 1986).

6. Luxton, "Two Hands"; and Joann Vanek, "Household Work, Wage Work, and Sexual Equality", in A.S. Skolnick and J.H. Skolnick (eds.), *Family in Transition* (Toronto and Boston, 1983).

7. The Task Force on childcare, *Report of the Task Force...*, pp. 45, 277.

8. The Task Force on childcare, *Report of the Task Force...*, Chapters 11 and 12.

9. See Nancy C. Hook, *Domestic Service Occupation Study: Final Report.* (Winnipeg, 1978); Royal Commission on the Status of Women, *Report of the Royal Commission on the Status of Women* (Ottawa, 1970); Ellen Vanstone, "The Heaven-Sent Nanny" *Toronto Life* April 1986.

10. The Task Force on Immigration Practices and Procedures, *Domestic Workers on Employment Authorizations* (Ottawa, 1981), pp. 35-45.

11. Vanstone, "The Heaven-Sent...," p. 51.

12. The Task Force on Immigration Practices and Procedures, *Domestic Workers,* p.53.

13. Esther Boserup, *Women's Role in Economic Development* (New York, 1970).

14. Christine Delphy suggests that the appropriation of women's labour power in housework by men in the "family mode of production" constitutes the major form of women's oppression and the material basis for "sisterhood". See "The Main Enemy" in *Close to Home* (Amherst, 1984).

15. Jan Williams, Hazel Twart, Ann Bachelli, "Women and the Family" in Ellen Malos (ed.), *The Politics of Housework* (London, 1980), p. 114.

16. Noreen in Makeda Silvera, *Silenced* (Toronto, 1983), p. 25.

17. According to one study, in Sweden, 2,340 million hours a year have been spent in housework, as compared to 1,290 million hours in industry. Cited in Sheila Rowbotham, *Women's Consciousness, Men's World* (Harmondsworth, 1973), p. 68.

18. Harriet Rosenberg, "The Home is the Workplace: Hazards, Stress and Pollutants in the Household" in Luxton and Rosenberg, *Through the Kitchen*...; and Harriet Rosenberg, "Motherwork, Stress and Depression: The Costs of Privatized Social Reproduction" in Heather J. Maroney and Meg Luxton (eds.), *Feminism and Political Economy* (Toronto, 1987).

19. In Canada and the northern US states, egalitarian relationships prevailed between "help" (as they were called, not "servants") and their small farmer and artisan employers. Participating in the hard work of the family economy, "help" shared the conditions and the table of the families they worked for, suffering no exclusion. These conditions contrasted sharply with relations in bourgeois households in the cities where the social distance between the employers and the employees had grown. *The Canadian Settlers' Handbook* advised immigrant domestics that they would enjoy "social amenities" in rural Canada and that "no lady should dream of going as a home-help in the cities, for there class distinctions (were) as rampant as in England." Cited in Helen Lenskyj, "A 'Servant Problem' or a 'Servant-Mistress Problem'? Domestic Service in Canada, 1890-1930" *Atlantis*, 7/1 (Fall 1981) p. 10.

20. Genevieve Leslie, "Domestic Service in Canada, 1880-1920" in *Women at Work*: Ontario, 1850-1930 (Toronto, 1974), p. 87. [Emphases added.]

21. Gail in Silvera, *Silenced*, p. 113.

22. Lucy M. Salmon, cited in Leslie, "Domestic Service...," p. 112.

23. See The Task Force on Immigration Practices and Procedures, *Domestic Workers*..., 74-78; and Alma Estable, *Immigrant Women in Canada: Current Issues* (Ottawa, 1986), pp. 51-53.

24. Noreen in Silvera, *Silenced,* p. 26.

25. While the new regulations may be a progressive step in recognizing the principle of overtime for domestic workers, they do not necessarily provide standard overtime protection since it is the employers who are given the option to negotiate with their employees to take the overtime in time off rather than in money for actual overtime worked. In this respect, regulations covering domestic workers still deviate from provisions of the provincial Employment Standards Act.

26. Estable, *Immigrant Women in Canada...,* p. 51. There is also the "Subversive Activities" provision in the 1977 federal Immigration Act which, through its vague wording, provides an intimidating message to all non-citizen residents in Canada that engaging in union activities may become grounds for deportation. See Sheila McLeod Arnopoulos, *Problems of Immigrant Women in the Canadian Labour Force* (Ottawa, 1979), pp. 41-45.

27. The Task Force on Immigration Practices and Procedures, *Domestic Workers...,* p. 76.

28. Rachel Epstein, "I Thought There Was No More Slavery in Canada: West Indian Domestic Workers on Employment Visas" in Linda Briskin and Lynda Yanz, *Union Sisters* (Toronto, 1983), p. 26.

29. Makeda Silvera, "Immigrant Domestic Workers. Whose Dirty Laundry?" *Fireweed* 9 (1981); and Silvera, *Silenced.*

30. Jacklyn Cock, *Maids and Madams* (Johannesburg, 1980), pp. 58-60; and Cissie Fairchilds, *Domestic Enemies: Domestics and Their Masters in Old Regime France* (Baltimore and London, 1984), pp. 102-104.

31. Hook, *Domestic Service Occupation...,* p. 63; Judith Rollins, *Between Women. Domestics and their Employers* (Philadelphia, 1985), p. 158.

32. Leslie, "*Domestic Service...,*" p. 83.

33. It is wrong, however, to confuse this appearance with the real thoughts and feelings of the worker. Responding to Lockwood who referred to the domestic worker as the "most socially acquiescent and conservative element" of the working class, Jacklyn Cock emphasizes the need to differentiate between deference and dependence. While the domestic recognizes her dependence on and powerlessness in relation to her employer, her deference is only "a mask which is deliberately cultivated to conform to employer expectations, and shield the workers' real feelings." Cook, *Maids and Madams,* pp. 104-106.

34. Elaine B. Kaplan, "'I Don't Do No Windows'" *Sojourner,* 10/10 (August 1985); Rollins, *Between Women....*

35. Kaplan, "'I Don't Do..,'" p. 17.

36. Rollins, *Between Women...*, p. 185

37. Kaplan, "'I Don't Do...'"

38. See Marilyn Barber, "Sunny Ontario for British Girls, 1900-30" in Jean Burnett (ed.), *Looking into My Sisters' Eyes: An Exploration in Women's History* (Toronto 1986); Varpu Lindstrom-Best, "'I Won't Be a Slave!' Finnish Domestics in Canada, 1911-30" in *Ibid.;* and Leslie, "Domestic Service..."

39. Leslie, "Domestic Service...," pp. 95-105.

40. Leslie, "Domestic Service...," pp. 122, ff.79.

41. Barbara Roberts, "'A Work of Empire': Canadian Reformers and British Female Immigration" in Linda Kealey (ed.), *A Not Unreasonable Claim. Women and reform in Canada, 1880s-1920s,* (Toronto, 1979), pp. 188-189.

42. Arnopoulos, *Problems of Immigrant...*, p. 26.

43. B. Singh Bolaria and Peter S. Li, *Racial Oppression in Canada* (Toronto, 1985), p. 178.

44. Bolaria and Li, *Racial Oppression...*, p. 178; Silvera, *Silenced,* p. 15.

45. Lloyd T. Wong, "Canada's Guestworkers: Some Comparisons of Temporary Workers in Europe and North America," *International Migration Review* 18/1 (1984), p. 86.

46. Epstein, "I Thought There Was No More...," p. 237; Wong, "Canada's Guestworkers...," p. 92.

47. See Michael Burawoy, "Migrant Labour in South Africa and the United States" in Theo Nichols (ed.), *Capital and Labour* (1980); Stephen Castles and Godula Kosack, *Immigrant Workers and Class Structure in Western Europe* (London, 1973); and Andre Gorz, "Immigrant labour," *New Left Review* 61 (1970).

48. Ray C. Rist, "Guestworkers and Post-World War II European Migrations," *Studies in Comparative International Development* 15/2 (1979), p. 51.

49. Primrose in Silvera, *Silenced,* p. 100.

50. Hannah Arendt, *The Origins of Totalitarianism* (New York, 1966), Chapter 9.

51. Here I have drawn on an argument made by Gerda Lerner in a different context. Commenting on the origins of slavery, Lerner has suggested that the process of marking a group of people as an out-group and "designating th(is) group to be dominated as entirely different from the group exerting dominance," has been essential to the mental constructs involved in institutionalization of slavery. See

Gerda Lerner, *The Creation of Patriarchy* (New York and Oxford, 1986), pp. 76-77.

52. The Task Force on Immigration Practices and Procedures, *Domestic Workers...*, pp. 26-27. The criteria for tolerability used by immigration officers can sometimes be very flexible. Silvera reports the case of a domestic from the Caribbean who wanted to leave her employer for reasons of sexual assault. Because the assault was less than sexual intercourse, her complaint was not found legitimate and she was deported from Canada. See Silvera, "Immigrant Domestic Workers...," p. 58.

53. Kelly Toughill, "Domestic Workers Praise Rule Change" *The Toronto Star* 22 September 1986, p. C2.

54. Hook, *Domestic Service Occupation...*, pp. 107-108.

55. The Task Force On Child Care, *Report of the Task Force...*, p. 121.

56. The Task Force on Immigration Practices and Procedures, *Domestic Workers...*, p. 70. In January 1986 the immigration department introduced a fee of $50 for issuing, extension and renewal of employment authorizations. In addition to being under-paid and over-taxed in a society that offers them none of the privileges and freedoms of citizenship, domestic workers are now being asked to "take the burden off the Canadian taxpayer" and pay the costs of their own processing and policing.

57. Many domestic workers who have had years of experience supporting themselves (and others) find it very offensive to have to prove such potential: "I supported five children before I came here, and I've supported five children since I came here, and they want to know if I can manage on my own?" Mary Dabreo, cited in Judith Ramirez, "Good Enough to Stay" *Currents*, 1/14 (1983-1984).

58. A point needs to be made about conceptions of the value of different occupations that immigration partly borrows from CCDO. CCDO has a rigid and static conception of skill as a "thing" that is largely determined "objectively" by the time spent in formal education. As Jane Gaskell has argued, however, "skill," far from being "a fixed attribute of a job or a worker which will explain higher wages or unemployment," is a result of a political process determined by the relative power (through supply/demand advantages, organizational capabilities, etc.) of different groups of workers. See "Conceptions of Skill and the Work of Women: Some Historical and Political Issues" in Roberta Hamilton and Michèle Barrett (eds.), *The Politics of Diversity* (Montreal, 1986).

59. The Task Force on Immigration Practices and Procedures, *Domestic Workers...*,

pp. 18-21.

60. Doris Anderson, "Ontario Should Heed Domestics' Plight" *The Toronto Star* 24 January 1987.

61. Noreen in Silvera, *Silenced*, p. 29.

62. Theresa McBride, *The Domestic Revolution. The Modernization of Household Service in England and France 1820-1920* (New York, 1976), p. 15.

63. Manuel Castells, "Immigrant Workers and Class Struggles in Advanced Capitalism: The Western European Experience" *Politics and Society* 15/1 (1975), p. 54.

64. Leslie Fruman, "Ontario's Domestics: The Fight for Basic Rights," *The Toronto Star* 30 March 1987, p. C1.

65. Ann Rauhala, "Amended Labour Law Would Give Domestics Overtime, Set Hours," *The Globe and Mail,* 27 January 1987.

66. This is Betty Friedan's position on housework. She approvingly cites others in *The Feminine Mystique* (New York, 1963), who think housework can be done by "anyone with a strong enough back (and a small enough brain)" and find it "peculiarly suited to the capacities of feeble-minded girls." See pp. 206 & 244.

67. With the emergence of surrogate motherhood, the same potential also applies to childbearing. The employment of surrogate mothers of working-class backgrounds may indeed become the solution upper class and career women opt for to avoid the time and inconvenience a pregnancy would cost.

68. During the 1920s, in the southern United States where there were more servants, the growth of commercial bakeries and laundries lagged behind such developments in the North and West. See David Katzman, *Seven Days a Week. Women and Domestic Service in Industrializing America* (New York, 1978), p. 275.

69. Dolores Hayden, *The Grand Domestic Revolution* (Cambridge, 1981).

70. *Ibid.*, p. 303.

CHAPTER 8

WORKERS, MOTHERS, REDS: TORONTO'S POSTWAR DAYCARE FIGHT

SUSAN PRENTICE

INTRODUCTION

The 'common-sense' history of organized feminism in Canada assumes a black hole of inactivity in the long stretch of decades between the early suffragettes and the recent 'second wave'. Yet a closer reading of history reveals a continuous struggle by and for Canadian women to improve their economic, political and social condition.

One example of such progressive and feminist organizing was the fight to ensure that postwar reconstruction addressed women's needs for childcare. There was a broadly-based daycare movement in Toronto between 1946 and 1951. For six years after World War II, the Day Nurseries and Day Care Parents Association (in which women from the Canadian Communist Party played a key role) led a high-profile and largely effective fight to save the wartime day nurseries from closure. In a remarkable coalition, supported by Communist aldermen, school trustees and their sympathizers, the Association organized to defend and expand childcare service through struggles in and against the municipal and provincial governments. In the period immediately after the war, daycare organizing had a mass base: hundreds attended public events, scores attended City Council and Board of Education meetings and deputations, and over one thousand attended a public rally and demonstration. Through this militant organizing, the Association made a successful front-line defence of many war-time childcare services.

Despite the federal government's 1944 commitment that the primary object of postwar domestic policy would be "social and human welfare,"[1] it used a traditional economic rationale, the need for fiscal restraint, to justify cutting daycare. By late 1951, Toronto City Council and the provincial Ministry of Public Welfare had closed over half the nurseries and daycare centres. The once strong Day Nurseries and Day Care Parents Association had dissolved. Childcare, which had been defended as support to the family and a measure of prevention against juvenile delinquency was re-fashioned as a communist threat and evidence of mothers' neglect. Daycare and daycare organizing effectively "dried up" in Toronto, and didn't reappear again in any equally significant form for over two decades.

How was this remarkable rise and fall possible? And what does it mean? What is its relevance to current feminist struggles? This paper discusses these questions, using French regulation economic theory and the social reproduction literature to analyze the complicated interactions of the state and the old 'new' social movement of women in the politics, history and organization of daycare.

CHILDCARE AND WORLD WAR II: THE EARLIEST DAYS

On May 8, 1945 at the end of the war, there were 13 day nurseries in operation in Toronto (part of Ontario's total of 28) and 22 daycare centres (part of the total of 42). Day nurseries cared for preschoolers under the age of 5 years, and daycare centres served children over the age of 5. Together Ontario's day nurseries and daycare centres served a total of nearly 2,500 children.[2] These childcare services were cost-shared between the provincial and federal governments under the 1942 Dominion-Provincial Day Nurseries Agreement, which was administered through the National Selective Services. Only Ontario and Quebec had taken advantage of available federal cost-sharing to establish wartime day nurseries to serve the needs of women employed in "essential war industry." Other provinces argued they were insufficiently industrialised and did not need childcare programs.[3]

The federal government moved to end its involvement with childcare at the end of the war. On November 9, 1945, Deputy Minister of Labour Robert MacNamara wrote the Ontario Minister of Public Welfare, William Goodfellow, to give notice of impending federal withdrawal from childcare funding:

> You understand that the financing of these and similar
> plans by the Dominion Government has been done as a

> war measure and our Treasury Board naturally takes the
> position "now that the war is over why do you need the
> money?"[4]

The federal government announced its intention to terminate cost-sharing on April 1, 1946. Despite the federal government's 1944 commitment that the primary object of postwar domestic policy would be "social security and human welfare," it invoked a traditional economic rationale — the need for fiscal restraint — to justify eliminating daycare expenditures.[5]

Beyond economic conservatism, state moves to revoke care were clearly based on sexist notions of the family and classist perceptions of why women worked. *The Globe and Mail* of July 11, 1946, reported that

> While the Provincial Government has expressed concern
> that any deserving cases should suffer from the cessation of
> the plan, welfare officials are agreed that whenever possi-
> ble mothers shouldn't shirk their responsibility in caring for
> their children at home in order to boost what is already an
> equitable income by working daily. "We believe that a child
> should be brought up in the proper environment in its own
> home, when possible" said one official.

In Quebec, Duplessis' closing of day nurseries generated protests from the Montreal Council of Social Agencies, the Welfare Federation, the Federation of Catholic Charities, the Montreal Association of Protestant Women Teachers, and mothers of children in care.[6] Despite their efforts, all war-time services in Quebec were closed. The qualified success of Ontario and the defeat of Quebec in defending childcare services, needs further attention.

Childcare protests began immediately, with a January 1st, 1946 deputation to City Council by the Toronto Welfare Council, the Women's Teachers Association, the Local Council of Women, the Toronto Trades and Labour Council, the YWCA and the YMCA, which argued for more day nurseries.[7] One month later, on January 30, sixty deputants to the Board of Control defended daycare services and demanded that civic government find a way to save them. They included representatives from welfare organizations, women's groups, cultural groups, teachers organizations and home and school associations.[8] On February 9, 1946 a large delegation, including Dr. Gordon Jackson, Medical Officer of Health for the City of Toronto, demanded City Council operate the nurseries "on a permanent basis."[9]

The Day Nurseries and Day Care Parents Association formed in Toronto on February 14, 1946 at a meeting sponsored by the United Welfare Chest.[10] It immediately took over the task of coordinating the broadly-based lobby for continued government funding of childcare. Five weeks later, the Association won its first, albeit double-edged, victory. On March 22, the Ontario government introduced the Day Nurseries Act. The Act, which received Royal Assent on April 5, 1946, and became effective June 30, 1946, provided for joint cost-sharing between municipal and provincial governments, with the municipality assuming 50 percent of costs and taking responsibility for administration.[11] Municipalities, with their smaller tax base and different revenue structure, were thus asked to take over the responsibility for childcare formerly assumed by the federal government. Given the national commitment to postwar reconstruction and welfare state expansion, it is a significant contradiction that no federal funds were forthcoming for childcare until the Canada Assistance Plan of 1966.

The provincial government's involvement in this transfer of childcare responsibilities to municipal government was also significant. The Communist Party, which had small but important electoral representation on Toronto City Council and the Toronto Board of Education, quickly hailed it as part of a "Drew plot" to "prevent fulfilment" of the Dominion Government's program of limited social reform, a program to which the CP had committed its support.[12] The CP railed against the "setting of the province against the nation, the part against the whole" which had "the primary object of paralysing all efforts to achieve social legislation, and a reorganization of taxation to compel the rich to pay their share to meet the costs of the crisis."[13]

The Day Nurseries Act established minimum regulations and standards, as well as funding arrangements. The Act's funding provisions had been essential to the continuation of war-time day nurseries. But the institution of relatively high standards of care, coupled with inadequate funds, resulted in the eventual closure of many centres. Schulz says that the standards and regulations of the

> Act proved to be a double-edged sword. Because the government was doing two contradictory things — setting good standards, but refusing to fund the service adequately — the net effect of the legislation was to close down a number of centres.[14]

This was an early example of a contradiction deeply embedded within the state: simultaneous support and undermining of childcare.

Despite the Day Nurseries Act, and the Province's apparent support for regulated childcare services, there was still strong resistance by and in the state to the idea of non-parental care. It was assumed that only those in "unfortunate circumstances" would need such services.[15] The Province argued that nursery schools (which were primarily used by full-time homemakers, not mothers in the paid labour force) offered "the maximum benefit for the children" when compared to the full-time care of day nurseries or daycare centres.[16] Even Dorothy Millichamp, a trained early childhood educator who held a senior position with the Day Nurseries Branch, commented that

> Professionally, we didn't want to see daycare bloom.... We never felt it was the right answer unless it was absolutely necessary...we felt daycare was for emergencies, not just for every child.[17]

THE DISCOURSE OF CHILDCARE

As important as the Act was the actual way childcare was talked about, organized around, defended, promoted and fought over. In the postwar period, childcare was repeatedly defended and promoted as a way of preventing juvenile delinquency. This language was widespread — Communists, welfare reformers, women's groups and religious leaders all seized on the issue of juvenile delinquency. The discourse of juvenile delinquency imbued childcare activists with a sense of urgency and moral righteousness. This moral righteousness deflected conservative criticism that childcare provoked the breakdown of the family and an abandonment by women of their proper role. Indeed, by arguing that childcare, as a measure of prevention against juvenile delinquency, actually *strengthened* 'the family', daycare activists manipulated a conservative idea without challenging it.

The media used the same discourse in its defence of childcare. *The Toronto Star*, in a June 24, 1946 editorial, entitled "Encouraging Juvenile Delinquency" asked

> What is the use of professing concern about juvenile delinquency and at the same time turning 3,000 [school-aged] children loose in the city streets with no parents, no teachers, nobody with authority or concern to look after them? ...It would cost less to run them [daycare centres] than to

> reform a few of the children who become criminals or to
> repair them in hospitals if they develop chronic ailments
> through neglect!

Conservatives were equally adamant about the preventive value of child-care. On May 30, 1946, at a protest meeting which attracted hundreds of daycare supporters, Rev. Tucker declared "Whatever day nurseries and day-care cost us, it is small potatoes compared with keeping a lad in our penal system."[18] On April 27, 1946, *The Star* reported that the Ontario Educational Association and the Federation of Home and School Associations had issued a terse declaration: "Day nurseries provide a relatively inexpensive means of preventing ill-health and delinquency among growing children."

An editorial in the Communist *Canadian Tribune*, "Why Mothers Grow Grey," used the same argument about juvenile delinquency, but turned it around, noting that,

> Certain woolly-minded people, more interested in dollars
> than children, are spreading the idea that parental respon-
> sibility — or lack of it — is the main cause of delinquency.
> Rubbish. The major causes of delinquency are: bad hous-
> ing, low pay, the lack of day nurseries and preschool care,
> poor recreational facilities and the medieval attitude that a
> mother must have no other interests in her life than
> minute-by-minute supervision of her children... Day nurs-
> eries, preschool care, plenty of playgrounds, better houses,
> higher pay, maternal care, and a modern attitude to a
> mother as a citizen of Canada and the world — these
> would cut delinquency to the bone and bring happiness to
> thousands of families.[19]

The language of juvenile delinquency permitted a broad coalition to work together for expanded childcare services. The notion of defence against juvenile delinquency allowed widely differing organizations to align, compelled by a sense of moral urgency. The political credibility which it lent the Day Nurseries and Day Care Parents Association, with its broad membership, meant that City Council and the Toronto Board of Education — the targets of their lobbying — had to pay attention.

'Juvenile delinquency' has a particular relationship to class. However, its obliqueness hides its class content. May Birchard, one-time school board trustee and alderman sympathetic to the Communist Party, was one of the chief promoters of the daycare and juvenile delinquency connection. She argued that "daycare expansion should be on the basis of need," in the "industrial districts of the city."[20] Her indirect reference was probably carefully determined: it was a non-class specific way to refer to a service most needed by working class mothers, without identifying them as such. This may explain why Communists used the juvenile delinquency argument to demand daycare for "working mothers" (another frequent, indirect reference to class) who were particularly disadvantaged through capitalist relations of work. Conservatives used the same terms, "juvenile delinquency" and "working mothers," in a very different and reactionary way.

DAY NURSERIES AND DAY CARE PARENTS ASSOCIATION

The Day Nurseries and Day Care Parents Association was founded on February 14, 1946.[21] The Association was an umbrella group organized for the purpose of political action. Its aim and function was "specifically to provide an organizational machinery for the parents themselves to make known to the public and to the elected representatives of the people the extreme importance of maintaining the services which do exist and extending these."[22] It was "composed of parents whose children are in nursery school or daycare centres, have been in such centres, or are on the waiting list for such service."[23]

The Day Nurseries and Day Care Parents Association was the major coordinating vehicle of childcare organizing in Toronto between 1946 and 1951. It played a leadership role in the childcare struggle, conducted with other community and women's groups. The Association undertook a wide and creative campaign to first defend, and later extend, childcare. The bulk of their organizing centred around lobbying, petitions, letter-writing, and deputations, although they also organized two mass rallies, and several public meetings. Many of their organizing efforts were particularly sensitive to the double-day of working mothers. For example, they held a protest meeting simultaneously in four different locations in the City of Toronto to minimize the distances women and children would have to travel. Their public demonstrations at City Hall and Queen's Park were particularly radical in an era when women's prescribed role, paid labour and domestic responsibilities strongly mitigated against participation in such activities.

A part of the Association's work was the establishment of parent study groups at different childcare centres. These parent study groups undoubtedly differed greatly in both orientation and activity, between centres. Study groups undertook to educate parents about the 'latest developments' in early childhood education. The University of Toronto's Institute for Child Study appears to have been involved in this educational work.[24] This 'expert' advice was undoubtedly welcomed by some mothers, particularly isolated and first-time mothers; however, it was also an important vehicle for complex and subtle, moral and gender regulation and was influential in the restructuring of 'mothering.' In addition to this conservative function, study groups also offered political education and an early form of 'consciousness-raising' to parents. It is more than likely that parents were recruited to political action — and possibly to the Communist Party — through the study groups.

Perhaps the most intriguing fact about the Day Nurseries and Day Care Parents Association was that many of its members were also members of the Canadian Communist Party. Communist activity in women's organizations had been steady ever since their 1938 Convention, at which the Party had set up a program of work among women that included forming neighbourhood groups, organizing women around the needs of their children, and forming and joining consumers' and housewives' associations.[25] The Party was also clear about the "necessity of joining those organizations where the masses of women are to be found: church groups, Home and School Clubs, Women's Institutes, Cooperative Guilds, fraternal organizations, etc."[26]

Many of the Day Nurseries and Day Care Parents Association's public spokespeople were members of the Communist Party. By 1948, the group itself was considered by many municipal politicians to be a Communist organization. Certainly the involvement of Party members in the Association was a factor in the close coordination of the Association with other militant women's groups, like the Congress of Canadian Women and the Housewives Consumers' Association. It is unclear whether these links between Communist women were organized formally through the Party, or informally through private and personal networks. Whichever was the case, their working relations and shared political analysis were important factors in the strength and organization of the Association.

Despite the strong presence of Communist women, women from the CCF also appear to have been members in, and supporters of, the Association. This alignment of CCF and CP women (whose parties were otherwise most hostile) in defense of childcare, appears to have been unique to Toronto.[27] It is unclear what leadership role parents of children in day nurseries and daycare centres played. Leadership seems to have been provided by women with more extended political connections than direct involvement in childcare alone.

Communist women played an important role in the Association in tying the issues of childcare, rising prices, housing, and the cost of living to a broader analysis. Their efforts to link these issues converged most dramatically on the issue of hot lunches and free milk for school children. Advocacy efforts around childcare and school feeding were coordinated, at the Board of Education and elsewhere, through their work. To a certain degree, childcare became linked with the issue of school feeding. This latter program linked the daycare fight to the "prices" campaign of the Communist Party, part of the Party's attempt to appeal to women on the basis of their domestic role. Paradoxically, stretching the "prices" fight into the childcare struggle meant that policies designed to appeal to women based on assumptions about their role in the 'private' realm, were being combined with those designed to appeal to women who were clearly engaged in the realm of 'public'.

The Committee for a School Lunch, and the Day Nurseries and Day Care Parents Association regularly made joint deputations to the Board of Education. There were subtle distinctions, however, in their positions. The more strongly Communist-influenced Association argued that families with "working mothers" (the standard reference to working class families) needed assistance, whereas the Committee for School Lunches (whose Communist membership was smaller) argued for charitable help to ensure the "success" (e.g. class transcendence) of the working class child.

By late June 1946, it was clear that the existing 13 day nurseries would continue to operate, but all 22 daycare centres were closed. Six daycare centres re-opened a few weeks later, on August 1st.[28] While the Association had not accomplished all it had set out to do, all of the vital preschool spaces, and over a quarter of the school-age spaces, were secure. The next step for childcare activists was to extend services.

Childcare advocates besieged municipal politicians throughout 1946 and into 1947. On November 12, 1946, City Council finally agreed to appoint a Special Advisory Committee to investigate the childcare situation.[29] The Special Advisory Committee, established as a response to urgent need, took over 18 months to report. Schulz says that although the committee "was ostensibly a response to the childcare community," the City's actions were characterized by "red tape, delay, and an unsympathetic attitude."[30]

Three months before the Committee's report was finally released, City

Council debated childcare for the 1948 budget year. During this meeting, Council heard deputations which supported 12 new daycare centres (estimated at $100,000) and a demonstration centre to integrate preschool and school-age children. In a debate over the cost of the new programs, Con. McKellar said, "the trouble is that the Daycare Association will not stop at 12, but will want more."[31] Con. Roelofson, Chair of the Special Advisory Committee, agreed saying, "these super socialists have it in their minds they are going to force this thing [daycare] down our throats," later warning that "the Communists will make an awful fight."[32] This heated exchange is evidence of both the rising identification of the childcare cause with communism, and a mounting red-baiting.

Despite the efforts of its right-wing Chair, the Special Committee did recommend twelve new daycare centres, as well as the integrated model childcare demonstration centre (later Jesse Ketchum Daycare Centre). However, at the same time, the report called for the doubling of daycare fees to "eliminate from care those children of mothers who work from choice rather than from economic necessity."[33] After a bureaucratic stalling of eighteen months, the final report of the Committee was adopted by City Council on June 23, 1947, amidst massive public protest over the proposed fee increases.[34] The state's support of daycare (the 12 new school-age programs and the demonstration centre) was contradicted by its simultaneous undermining of childcare through the fee hike.

During the 1946-47 period, a broad daycare advocacy coalition came together to defend childcare services. Their political analysis, while militant, was based on a limited understanding of the lives of working mothers, manifested in their argument about daycare as a measure of prevention against juvenile delinquency. The flexibility of their defence permitted a remarkable alliance of conservative and socialist women. Their successful struggle to preserve existing services against the very reluctant provincial government was based on this political strength and credibility. In municipal politics, the Day Nurseries and Day Care Parents Association's success at City Council and the Board of Education was due to collaboration with Communist (and sympathetic) aldermen and trustees and the Party organization that supported them.

1948-1949: THE MIDDLE YEARS

The major fight undertaken by the Association during the 1948-49 period was the expansion of twelve new daycare centres and the establishment of the

Jesse Ketchum Demonstration Project, an integrated day nursery and daycare centre for preschoolers and school-age children. Equally important was the work that the Association undertook to defend the rights of families with working mothers to government-funded services.

This middle period saw the rise of red-baiting, as well as a changing attitude towards working women. From a war-time acceptance of the legitimate right of working women to childcare, concern about "chiselers" and the "undeserving" family arose. Men like Alderman William Clifton, a Ward 6 conservative, argued against the right of two-parent families to care.[35] City Council reaffirmed its policy of "limiting Day Nursery care under Civic auspices to the children of mothers who must work in order to support their families and other special cases."[36]

> In November 1948, Mayor McCallum washed his hands of
> the daycare battle, and told the community to "go higher,"
> to the province, for assistance.[37]

This marked a turn away from a minimally supportive civic administration to one that began to overtly organize to erode childcare; it also, not coincidentally, reflected (and helps to explain) the electoral defeat of progressive politicians. In recognition of this conservative municipal turn, Isabel Bevis, Chair of the Day Nurseries and Day Care Parents Association gave the following dispirited summary:

> The result, after over two years, has been the stopping of
> parent study groups in the day nurseries, double and treble
> increases in the day nursery fees, and refusing to place chil-
> dren on the waiting lists of the day nurseries, very little
> improvement in the standards of daycare, no expansion of
> facilities, and finally the one concrete project passed and
> ordered at the beginning of this year, the alterations to the
> Jesse Ketchum Day Nursery building to provide a demon-
> stration centre, has not even been started.[38]

By late 1947, Board of Education trustees were increasingly hostile to childcare and, although to a lesser extent, school feeding which was linked to it. Trustee Borden, for example, argued that free milk would result in the "loss of initiative and entrepreneurship" on the part of children [39] Free milk, he said, was "going to do far more harm than good" because "we want to teach our children to get what they want by themselves."[40] The agitation for free milk (i.e. paid for by the Board) by the "labour women" trustees appears to have contradicted the Party's clear directives that social services should be centrally funded. Notwithstanding this, labour trustees (all women) carried out an effective milk fight. The strong opposition from right-wing trustees was insufficient to dissuade the Board from finally agreeing in late 1947 to CP trustee Elizabeth Morton's motion to distribute free milk to school children.[41]

The Board of Education, however, was stymied in the provision of milk because the provincial Education Act did not permit expenditures on non-education items. Communist school trustees actively organized for changes to the Act. However, their campaign was heavily criticized. One *Globe and Mail* editorial, "A Communist Ramp" railed that,

> The agitation for hot noon lunches has been one of the perennial policies of the communist trustee Mrs. Edna Ryerson and it was not surprising to find that a friend of hers, Mrs. May Birchard, was the chief spin in the delegation.... What is most surprising about the whole matter is the simple-minded manner in which leading women's groups will lend themselves to the malicious purposes of agitators.[42]

The Globe warned that attempts to change the Education Act were designed "to destroy the faith of democratic peoples in their government bodies." In stark contrast, *The Star's* editorial, "In Fairness to the Children," pointed out that,

> Judging from some of the pronouncements, it may be inferred...that many community leaders who have identified themselves with the school lunch movement are the dupes of Communists. In fairness, the school lunch is not a Communist invention. It was initiated in England after the 1914-18 war.... Credit for it has been claimed by conservative regimes.[43]

The Board of Education's policy with respect to childcare also shifted as a result of the identification of childcare with communism. For instance the Board argued for the institution of junior and senior kindergarten programs. By routing four year olds into the education system, the Board attended to the question of care for a large group of children of working mothers, yet did so by organizing their care out of the realm of 'red' day nurseries. This also marked a shift away from the earlier stress on the prevention of juvenile delinquency.

The shifting of the childcare issue out of the realm of contested politics, and into the discourse of education offered certain political advantages. One *Toronto Star* editorial, "Gratifying Progress," went so far as to comment approvingly on a report about British kindergartens, pointing out that "the good nursery school is the maker of young democrats."[44] A belief in education's potential for combating communism — a manifestation of Cold War anti-communism — underpinned this shift in discourse.

Yet even this conservative education strategy met with opposition. *The Globe and Mail* editorialized that the need for junior kindergartens was "limited." While they agreed that many "mothers favour the idea," they noted ominously that

> there is more at stake than freedom from the burdens of parenthood for a few hours. What is ultimately to be determined is the degree to which the state will be allowed to usurp the functions of the home.[45]

The 1948-49 period saw a sharp increase in red-baiting, and the linking of both childcare organizing and childcare service itself, with communism. Through this process, the broad alliances which had formed during the crisis of the immediate postwar period weakened. The City of Toronto moved away from its earlier reluctant support for childcare. The municipal government doubled fees and began to restrict access to the day nurseries, as part of an ideological campaign to eliminate 'undeserving' parents. At the Board of Education, anti-red campaigns played an important role in defeating Communist trustees in elections and in handicapping their work. As the numbers of elected Communist representatives decreased, the Day Nurseries and Day Care Parents Association had increasingly less influence on civic politics, contributing further to its internal demoralization and to public perception of it as a marginal left-wing group. As the anti-communist campaign heated up, the childcare movement suffered losses of both reduced membership, and decreased political legitimacy and strength in the eyes of the state and the media.

Simultaneously, and partly in response, the Communist Party retreated from the remnants of its Popular Front strategy to focus its energies on defending the Soviet Union through advocacy of the policy of mutual co-existence. In 1949, the Communist Party dramatically reorganized itself. Women's work was reoriented away from involvement in women's coalitions, a policy adopted in 1938, and towards an all-out Party effort to defeat the Mackenzie King government. This change was most dramatically seen in the Resolution on Women's Work passed at the February 1949 LPP Convention which read:

> Although our work among women is many-sided, including the real gains among the women engaged in gainful employment, concrete aids to housewives and mothers in care of children and services relating to the home; social services, etc., all our work from now on must be centred around the federal election programs.[46]

In response to Cold War anti-communism and as part of the Party's strategy for the federal election of 1949, women were directed into peace work. Communist women were organized away from childcare advocacy, leaving only a small core of committed activists to carry on the childcare struggle. This strategy deflected the energies of some of the most skilled and committed organizers.

1950-1951: THE END

By the end of 1950, Edna Ryerson was the only Communist to retain her seat on the Board of Education. Communist aldermen were entirely absent from City Council. A fiercely anti-communist climate prevailed.

On January 8, 1950, the Board of Education announced its plans to open eight more junior kindergartens, to bring its total up to 27 by September.[47] The Board had successfully taken childcare for four and five year-olds out of the day nurseries and placed it in the education system, as part of a political (although unarticulated) response to the 'threat' of communism. The Board of Education was increasingly reluctant to support childcare centres — the only exception was Trustee Ryerson.

In 1950, as City Council debated measures which might have prevented the imminent closure of three childcare centres, *The Star* wrote:

> It is known certain of the Board of Control's members,

> along with others on the City's Welfare Council, fear chil-
> dren's centres are the "camel's head" for what Alderman
> Belyea calls "statism." Since it is deemed politically unwise
> to attack progress with such a wide, logical and sentimental
> appeal, they fall back on the claim that care of the City's
> children is not the City's business.[48]

The Star's defense of "logical" childcare deflected rather than challenged the accusation of "statism."

The early 1950s saw the worst of Canadian Cold War anti-communism. Accusations flew thick and fast. One example of this hysteria is found in an article entitled "The Red's Pink Tea Circuit: This Communist Front Fools a Lot of Women," which ran in The Financial Post on June 9, 1951. It linked, by association, the Day Nursery and Day Care Parents Association to the Korean War, the Kremlin, and international communism, mainly by identifying the husbands of women active in the Association as communists. Its author concluded that,

> without the party liners and sympathizers there are enough
> outright party members of this organization to ensure that
> it stays on the rails to Moscow. All the evidence indicates
> that this organization's lines lead right to the Kremlin.

While many members of the Day Nursery and Day Care Parents Association were Communists, or Communist sympathizers, it is interesting to note how red-baiting functions to discredit and silence political opposition.[49]

At the level of municipal government, the Commissioner of Public Welfare for the City of Toronto, with the support of the Mayor and members of the Board of Control, was determined to undermine childcare services. Through close collaboration with the Ministry of Public Welfare at the Province, he developed a series of bureaucratic mechanisms designed to decimate childcare services in the City.

On January 15, 1951, the City of Toronto asked for "frank and confidential" advice from the Ministry of Public Welfare on how to restrict admission.[50] On February 8, 1951, an inter-office memo from the Ministry of Public Welfare to the City, cautioned that,

> mothers desiring to go to work should be very carefully
> investigated...thousands of families have debts to pay off

and eligibility for nursery care at public expense for this
reason alone was questionable.[51]

Senior bureaucrats emphasized the need for "careful screenings and meticu-
lous follow-ups to make sure continued care is justified under public
auspices."[52] In early February, representatives from the City and the Province
met to determine priorities for admission. As a result of a series of consultations with provincial bureaucrats in early 1951, the City Commissioner of
Public Welfare established a four-point priority scale for admission to care.
The new criteria could be put into effect with reasonable ease, because in May
1950 the City had instituted a Central Registry for admissions to ensure "uniformity in investigational procedures."[53]

Under the new scheme, families were means-tested to determine eligibility, and were admitted accordingly. The first priority for admission were children from homes "which were being kept together and maintained chiefly
through the personal efforts of the mothers, the fathers being out of the
homes for various reasons, viz. death, illness, separation, desertion, etc."
Second, were children having "individual and urgent needs for health or social
reasons." Third were "children from homes in which both mothers and fathers
were present, but where fathers' incomes were either insufficient or too inse-
cure" to meet living expenses without the mothers also working. Fourth were
children from homes in which both mothers and fathers worked, but in which
there were "special and urgent situations which could only be met by the
mothers employment in addition to that of the fathers and which in turn is
contingent upon the securing of Nursery or Day Care Centre care for their
children."[54] In his report to Council, Commissioner Rupert demurely noted
that the priority scale had been "discussed" with Mr. Heise, Deputy Minister of
Public Welfare who was "in agreement with the general principles
expressed."[55]

These astonishingly strict eligibility requirements were deemed necessary
by the province, based on the results of a January 1951 survey of family and
children's services in Toronto. This study had determined that "the emphasis
on care for children of working mothers has the effect of creating a large
demand for such care where this may not be the most appropriate solution to
the family problem."[56] In a press release discussing these findings, the provincial Minister of Public Welfare further pointed out that "the practice of waiving
the [daycare] fee or arbitrarily setting it at a low figure can discourage parental
responsibility." In a breathtaking display of class privilege, the Minister
breezed,

> It seems inequitable that, simply because the parents in the
> family *wished* to work for some purpose, public funds
> should provide a means of caring for their children if there
> is no real economic or social need for them both work-
> ing.[57]

This regulation had both a moral and an economic quality. Its economic functions were contradictory: productive labour that didn't challenge women's reproductive role was eligible for state support through provision of childcare. Yet at the same time, state protection of woman-as-mother, firmly domesticated, was the chief way women were organized through state policy. This gender regulation establishes and legitimates particular sex and sexuality roles. State policy on childcare is located at a contradictory intersection of class, gender, and 'family' issues. "Sex/gender systems" as Rubin reminds us, "are the products of historical human activity."[58] This state activity built on and intensified this historical regulation, paving the way for the 'feminine mystique' of the 1960s.

While state-funded childcare is often considered the 'gatekeeper' to women's labour force participation, it is clear that more than simple participation in productive labour was at stake for the City. Not just women's paid labour, but the *particular family form*, was the deciding factor. Two-parent families in which the mother worked for 'frivolous' reasons such as debt repayment or economic need, were the last category to be eligible for admission. If the state were only concerned about ensuring that economically productive mothers received publicly-funded care, then the four-point priority scale based on family form would be inexplicable. The reserve army of labour theory which posits a linear relationship between capital's need for (female/cheap) labour and state provision of service is incomplete. The City's admission policies are intelligible only when the regulatory and ideological function of childcare is theorized alongside an economic analysis.

The Day Nurseries and Day Care Parents Association responded to the new admission policy with fury, in part to the moral regulation implicit in the priority scale. On May 30, 1951, Mrs. Isabel Bevis, Association President, addressed the Committee on Public Welfare on behalf of a large deputation of working mothers and expressed strong opposition to the new regulations, fees, and administrative procedures. The Association demanded the City "withdraw all increases; dispense with the screening depot; discard the means test and the investigators; and re-establish the waiting list method of admission under the direction of the supervisors."[59] The demand that the waiting list be re-established under the direction of the supervisors was a tactic designed to limit the centralized power of the state to determine which families were 'most deserving'. The Association was adamant that all working mothers, by right, were equally deserving and should be considered equally eligible for care. The deputation of over one hundred people was composed of members of the Congress of Canadian Women, the Toronto Council of Women's International Union Auxiliaries AFL, the Housewives' Consumers' Association, the United Electrical Radio and Machine Workers Ladies Auxiliary, and "several mothers."[60]

The Commissioner of Welfare implacably defended the registry for the "centralized and overall control of placement of children" it offered, and explained the 200 percent fee increases, and admission scale, thus:

> It is a well known fact that in public welfare programs...
> economic need has been the governing factor in determin-
> ing eligibility. While many programs have broadened in
> scope during recent years in accordance with recognized
> standards in public welfare work, this basic principle has
> obtained.... There is a definite two-way responsibility which
> must be respected. It is therefore sound, both socially and
> economically that parents who are financially able to pay
> increased fees for Nursery and Day Care services should be
> expected to do so.[61]

Notwithstanding the strong protests of the Association, the new regulations were approved for September 1, 1951.

The flurry of organizing undertaken by the Association in the spring and summer of 1951 around the fee-increase proposals were its last activities. The Association never again addressed any of the Committees of Council or the Board of Education. One can only speculate that this last ditch effort, under-taken in the fiercely anti-communist and anti-daycare climate, completely demoralized the already disorganized Association. The weakened daycare movement could no longer sustain itself. The demise of the daycare move-ment had been accomplished, and the state's cutbacks proceeded apace with only minimal opposition.

In early 1951, 12 day nurseries and 3 daycare centres were directly oper-ated by the City of Toronto.[62] Childcare had dropped from a 1946 city-run high of 13 day nurseries and 6 daycare centres. Accelerating cutbacks were publicly attributed to low rates of enrolment, which were interpreted to indicate that parents were not interested in childcare. For example, the Commissioner of Public Welfare told the press in 1951, that falling attendance "proves that the actual need of the day nursery service was not as great as they [the Association] represented."[63]

Privately, the state told a different story. The City Commissioner acknowledged that his regressive fee and admission policy had the intended effect of eliminating service. On March 16, 1954, Commissioner Rupert wrote James Band, Deputy Minister of Public Welfare, to say "I am of the opinion that the prime political reason for the decline in the number of children requiring care in recent years has been due to our admission and fee policies." He further noted with satisfaction that

> in recognition of the decline in demand for care of children, there has been, as you know, a progressive closing of nurseries. We shall continue to watch the situation closely and will not hesitate to recommend the closing of additional nursery units if deemed necessary.[64]

In her evaluation of the role of the state after the War, Schulz says that while all three levels of government expressed their support for daycare during this period, their actions belied their words.

> The tactics used to limit the service included: passing responsibility for daycare to another level of government; allowing quality of care legislation to close centres rather than up-grade the service; implementing stated policy very slowly or not at all; making 'fraudulent use' rather than extent of need the focus of attention; and rendering the service so costly and demeaning that parents were reluctant to use it.[65]

By late 1951, the daycare movement was effectively demolished. Turner argues that the 1950s and 1960s were the "doldrum years" of childcare organizing.[66] Another history of the daycare movement sadly concludes that "by 1962, the gains of the Second World War had almost entirely disappeared."[67]

CONCLUSIONS

Denise Riley persuasively argues that one of the most pernicious effects of state and social emphasis on 'The Mother,' has been to create two "irreconcilable parties: the house-wife/mother and the woman worker."[68] The Day Nurseries and Day Care Parents Association (including its Communist members) did not challenge the contradictions between women-as-mothers and women-as-workers. Their attempts to work with the experiential reality of this split (even as it was untheorized in their politics) led them to defend childcare with the weak arguments of 'prevention of juvenile delinquency' and 'service to families'. These defenses, because of their partial and contingent nature, were vulnerable — especially so during a period of intense hostility to Communism, state cutbacks and a fiercely ideological imposition of a particular family form. When daycare was no longer seen as a measure which might prevent juvenile delinquency, and instead was equated with an anti-family communism, the daycare movement collapsed.

The Communist Party and the Day Nurseries and Day Care Parents Association argued that "mothers are workers too." Yet, as Riley also warns, this defense is prone to deeply conservative uses, "especially at points when pro-natalist alarm seeks to 'preserve the family' and 'protect motherhood' in a way which marks off 'the mother' as a separate species-being."[69] Despite this, "mothers are workers too" was the fundamental argument which sustained the Day Nurseries and Day Care Parents Association. Because the Association did not challenge the great division of women into 'public' or 'private' roles, its understanding of childcare was politically contradictory. The Association was unable to notice the policy schizophrenia that Riley identifies when she says

> The lot of working mothers in war time and after points up
> the incoherence built into social policy addresses to 'the
> family', which speak as if the interests and needs of
> women, men and children were always harmoniously uni-
> fied. Mothers who work strain these assumptions of
> unity[70]

To some degree, there was a division of labour: the Day Nurseries and Day Care Parents Association fought for "mothers," and the Party fought for "workers." Neither the Association, nor the Party could adequately advance a notion of social struggle that integrated the deeply complex intertwinings of class and gender, at the level of social policy, political practice, and personal lived experience. Nor could either organization address the real contradictions between women and men in their productive and reproductive roles, hence their appeals to a unified family. This highlights the need for socialist and feminist theory that can address both the complex intersections and alignments of class and gender, as well as their conflicts.

The demand made by the Association was for a reconstruction of the relations between family and work — public and private — that no longer relied on the privatized work of women. In their insistence that working families — and more particularly, "working mothers" — required assistance, the Association made a radical critique. This challenge was not always clear, and indeed (for tactical reasons) was occasionally inverted. Nonetheless, against a liberal notion of class transcendence, the daycare movement demanded service as a right, breaking a long association of childcare with charity and the 'deserving' poor. In a preliminary way, the Association's demand for the socialization of childcare was a demand for redistribution of the labour of social reproduction. It was a forerunner of contemporary feminist organizing with and against the state that forces us to question why social reproduction has been so undertheorized.

It also takes us to the strategy of using the state to redistribute women's work. This case study reveals that the state's decision to provide childcare services only to particular types of families had both an economic gatekeeping function (in terms of controlling women's labour force participation) and, equally importantly, an ideological and moral function — the regulation of mothering, and family. Welfare policies invariably (although with differing weights) address both these aspects of social reproduction. At the level of theoretical explanation, we must move beyond understanding the functions of the capitalist state as simple accumulation and legitimation, in order to account for the complexity of social and ideological regulation. This unravelling will be especially significant for contemporary feminist engagements with the state.

Perhaps most importantly, this case study has implications for Marxist social theory. Marxist economic theory (like the reserve army of labour theory) has a powerful explanatory value, yet it cannot address, for example, the gendered aspect of state policy. The long-standing and most basic assumptions of socialist theory are incomplete when they do not address the gendered nature of social organization. It is, of course, by now a truism to point out that this weakness in Marxist theory is crucially important and must be addressed by all political economists — not merely those who 'do women'. All adequate theory must address the mutual interdependencies, as well as the contradictions and outright conflicts, of gender, economics, class and politics without underestimating the full significance of each.

Despite the Day Nurseries and Day Care Parents Association's ultimate failure to prevent state closures of childcare centres, this moment in the history of childcare organizing is more than a story of defeat and political error. The childcare movement was, and is, more complex than that. In addition to their five year defence of childcare, the Day Nurseries and Day Care Parents Association put forward a transformative demand. In their insistence, however articulated, that all working mothers and children needed and deserved care, they undermined a conservative notion of family and increased the possibilities of choice in women's (as well as men's and children's) lives.

One of the clearest lessons to be gained from an historical analysis of childcare is that we need better theory before we can predict the results of political practice with any certainty. Sophisticated and conjuncturally perceptive theory about the enormous power of the state to blunt, incorporate and absorb political challenge is particularly necessary — but this must be complemented with theory which recognizes the existence of real moments of possibility and can shed light on strategy for those moments. This theorization can only be made with historically specific experiences. This history of daycare organizing is a small contribution to the long task of painstaking analysis and historical discovery. We need to recover, learn from and move beyond the history of women's organizing with and against the state.

ENDNOTES

In the preparation of this paper material from the following collections was consulted: Public Archives of Ontario, James Band Papers; City of Toronto Archives, City Council Minutes; Toronto Board of Education, Newspaper Clipping File, 1946-1951; the Kenney Collection, Thomas Fisher Rare Book Library, University of Toronto; and the Schulz Collection, Baldwin Room, Metro Toronto Library.

1. D. Wolfe, "The Rise and Demise of the Keynesian Era in Canada: Economic Policy 1930-1982," in G. Kealey and M. Cross (eds.), *Modern Canada: 1930-1980* (Toronto: McClelland and Stewart, 1984), pp. 54-55.

2. R. Pierson, "Women's emancipation and the recruitment of women into the labour force in World War II," in S. Mann Trofimenkoff and A. Prentice (eds.), *The Neglected Majority: Essays in Canadian Women's History* (Toronto: McClelland and Stewart, 1977), p. 138.

3. P. Schulz, "Daycare in Canada: 1860-1962," in K. Gallagher-Ross (ed.), *Good Daycare* (Toronto: Women's Educational Press, 1978), p. 150.

4. Pierson, "Women's Emancipation...," p. 142.

5. Wolfe, "The Rise and Demise...,"pp. 54-55.

6. Pierson, "Women's Emancipation...," p. 141; *Canadian Tribune*, October 6, 1945.

7. *Globe and Mail*, January 1, 1946.

8. *Toronto Star*, January 30, 1946.

9. *Toronto Telegram*, February 9, 1946

10. *Toronto Star*, February 14, 1946.

11. Turnbull, May 1949, p. 2, "Day Nurseries, Correspondence with the City of Toronto, 1944-1945," PAO RG 29-01-840, Series 74.

12. *Canadian Tribune*, January 19, 1946.

13. Communist Party of Canada, "Brief on Dominion-Provincial Relations," Introduction, p. 3, Kenney Collection, Box 7, Thomas Fisher Rare Book Library, University of Toronto.

14. Schulz, "Daycare in Canada...," pp. 153-4.

15. Letter, City of Toronto's Commissioner of Welfare to the Deputy Minister of Public Welfare, November 18, 1949, PAO RG 29-01-840.

16. Deputy Minister of Public Welfare, Supplementary Memorandum on Day Nurseries, July 3, 1948, PAO RG-29-01-840.

17. Taped interview with Dorothy Millichamp, conducted by Pat Schulz, April 20, 1977, Schulz Collection, Baldwin Room, Metro Toronto Library.

18. *Toronto Star*, May 30, 1946.

19. *Canadian Tribune*, June 7, 1947.

20. *Toronto Star*, November 22, 1946.

21. *Ibid.*, February 14, 1946.

22. Helen Muller, Letter to Editor, *Ibid.*, May, 1947.

23. *Ibid.*

24. Taped interview with Millichamp, 1977.

25. Resolution on Work Among Women, *Proceedings of the Second Ontario Convention of the Communist Party*, 1938, p. 45, Kenney Collection.

26. *Ibid.*, p. 55.

27. Interview with Joan Sangster, May 1988.

28. *Globe and Mail*, August 1, 1946; *Toronto Star*, July 31, 1946.

29. Toronto City Council, *Minutes*, November 12, 1946, p. 179.

30. Schulz, "Daycare in Canada...," p. 154.

31. *Toronto Star*, March 12, 1948.

32. *Ibid.*

33. Toronto City Council, *Minutes*, Committee on Public Welfare, Report No. 5, 1946.

34. *Toronto Star*, June 23, 1947.

35. *Ibid*, January, 1947.

36. Toronto City Council, *Minutes*, Committee on Public Welfare, Report No. 5, 1947.

37. *Toronto Star*, November 3, 1948.

38. *Ibid.*

39. *Globe and Mail*, March 3, 1947.

40. *Toronto Star*, March 3, 1947.

41. *Globe and Mail*, December 5, 1947.

42. *Ibid.*, March 3, 1950.

43. *Toronto Star*, March 7, 1950.

44. *Ibid.*, September 30, 1949.

45. *Globe and Mail*, March 1, 1949.

46. L.P.P. National Convention, Proceedings, February 1949, Kenney Collection, Box 3, Thomas Fisher Rare Book Library. Italics in the original.

47. *Globe and Mail*, January 8, 1950.

48. *Toronto Star*, June 8, 1950.

49. Of even more interest is the astonishing regularity with which collective childcare is equated with communism. Attitudes towards childcare have careened wildly. One American report argued that nurseries were designed "to begin proper education and to Americanize foreign children." See D. Kerr, in P. Roby (ed.), *Childcare: Who Cares?* (New York: Basic Books, 1973), p. 159. Later, critics argued that childcare would "sovietize" children. See E.T. Zeigler, in E.T. Zeigler and T.W. Gordon (eds.), *Daycare: Scientific and Social Policy Issues* (Boston: Auburn House, 1982). Childcare advocates have often tried to avoid the conflicts by avoiding the ideological debates and concentrating on simple service discourse.

50. Inter-Office Memo, January 14, 1951, PAO RG 29-01-840.

51. Ministry of Public Welfare, Inter-office Memo, PAO RG 29-01-841.

52. *Ibid.*

53. Toronto City Council *Minutes*, Committee on Public Welfare, Report No. 4, February 14, 1951, p. 619.

54. *Ibid.*, pp. 619-20.

55. *Ibid.*

56. Goodfellow, Ministry of Public Welfare, News Release, May 28, 1951, p. 2, PAO RG 29-01-841.

57. *Ibid.*

58. G. Rubin, "The traffic in women: Notes on the `political economy' of sex," in R. Reiter (ed.), *Towards an anthropology of women* (New York: Monthly Review

Press, 1975), p. 204.

59. Toronto City Council, *Minutes*. Committee on Public Welfare, Report No. 145, June 14, 1951, p. 1546.

60. Undated newspaper clipping, Shulz Collection.

61. Toronto City Council, *Minutes*, Committee on Public Welfare, Report No. 147, June 14, 1951, p. 1546; *Toronto Star*, May 30, 1951.

62. *Toronto Star*, May 30, 1951.

63. Toronto City Council, *Minutes*, Committee on Public Welfare, Report No. 11, June 14, 1951, p. 1551.

64. Box 21, File 876, PAO RG 29 Series 01.

65. Schulz, "Daycare in Canada...," p. 155.

66. J. Turner, "Daycare and Women's Labour Force Participation: An Historical Study," (M.A. thesis, University of Regina, 1981).

67. Schulz, "Daycare in Canada...," p. 157.

68. D. Riley, *War in the Nursery: Theories of the Child and the Mother* (London: Virago Press, 1983), p. 191.

69. *Ibid.*, p. 185.

70. *Ibid.*, p. 151.

CHAPTER 9

GENDER AND REPRODUCTION, OR BABIES AND THE STATE

JANE JENSON

INTRODUCTION

The capitalist state's contribution to the oppression of women has been relatively under analyzed in recent Marxist feminists' debates about the material bases of gender oppression.[1] Nevertheless, Marxist feminists can not escape a concern with the capitalist state which obviously continues to have a major effect on the structure of the family and gender relations. Everyday observation of the law, welfare programs, educational institutions, and family policy indicates that state actions affect the ways in which feminine and masculine lives are constructed. However, while from observation it is clear that the policies of the capitalist state contribute to gender-based oppression, observation of such effects does not constitute an explanation of *why* they exist.

Some feminists have tried to understand women's oppression within neo-Marxist theories of the state. While acknowledging that the sources of patriarchal relations lie outside the state, these feminists have tended to assume that the capitalist state has a necessary role to play in the reproduction of gender oppression. Too hasty acceptance of this assumption has, unfortunately, weakened analyses of women and the state. In addition, analyses which do examine this question have quickly moved from a statement — either theoretical or historical — of the needs of capital to the actions of the state. This is a variant of economism denying the state any meaningful autonomy from economic forces and confining it to the function of reproducing the labour force. Therefore, both because it is impossible to assume a priori that the capitalist state must play any particular role in the oppression of women, and because non-economic analyses of the capitalist state must proceed from the logic of the state itself rather than being reduced to a reflection of the needs of capital, new attention is warranted. It is necessary not only to theorize the reasons why any particular form of gender relations is present, but also why it is that the state involves itself in the reproduction of such relations. In other words, acknowledging that gender inequality exists does not automatically imply that every capitalist state is involved in the reproduction of that inequality in the same ways or to the same extent.

Mary McIntosh's article, "The State and the Oppression of Women," is a good starting point because it is one of the strongest efforts to date to examine women's oppression from within a neo-Marxist theory of the state. Moreover, it has been very influential not only on McIntosh's later work with Michèle Barrett, but also on the work of others. McIntosh builds on the arguments made by several authors, especially Veronica Beechey, that women's oppression is a consequence of both the labour process — more specifically, women's availability as part of an industrial reserve army of labour — and the family. According to McIntosh,

> the state plays a part in the oppression of women...through its support for a specific form of household: the family household dependent largely upon a male wage and upon female domestic servicing. This household system is in turn related to capitalist production in that it serves (though inadequately) for the reproduction of the working class and for the maintenance of women as a reserve army of labour, low-paid when they are in jobs and often unemployed.[2]

It is, then, the state's role in the reproduction of capitalism via its support for a particular family form (the wage-earning husband and dependent wife and children) which ensures that women perform unpaid domestic labour and creates them as an industrial reserve army.

There are three essential elements to McIntosh's argument. First, within advanced capitalism women serve as an industrial reserve army because of the sexual division of labour within the family. This division of labour involves women doing almost all the unpaid servicing work of reproduction, and men receiving a family wage to support dependent wives and children. Next, women can serve as an industrial reserve army because of the ideology of the family which defines women as dependent on a male wage-earner and assigns to them a servicing role; it is this ideology which allows them to be paid less and to move in and out of the labour force easily. Finally, the state sustains the family household because it is a capitalist state with a necessary role to play in the reproduction of the forces and relations of production. Examining each of these points critically raises four concerns.

Central to McIntosh's argument is the existence within capitalist society of a widely-shared assumption that the cost of reproducing women's labour power is in large part paid for by male wages. From where does this assumption come? How is it created? Why is there no socially-shared assumption that both men and women can be paid less because both contribute to the costs of reproducing the couple (and any children)? In other words, McIntosh's argument makes two prior assumptions: first that women do not usually do waged work; and second, that men are assumed to earn a family wage.

These are rather big assumptions. Moreover, they seem more appropriately classified as matters for empirical investigation than as theoretical statements. It is possible that they are not present in all capitalist social formations. What happens, for example, if we insert into the argument the existence of a socially-shared assumption that women do and will work, that female paid employment is inevitable? By replacing one set of assumptions (working man, dependent wife and children) with another assumption (working women), the argument about the state begins to unravel. For McIntosh, state policies are also made with the assumption of the family household, and it is in that way that the state encourages dependency of women on men. This shared assumption must be present in the state for her argument to be coherent.[3]

McIntosh's search for the roots of oppression in the ways that women labour raises another concern. This search has led to a focus on not only women's participation in the production process but also on the impact of their traditional role in domestic labour. This focus is based on the observation that capitalist society was quickly divided into separate public and private spheres and reproduction assigned to the private sphere, with women taking primary responsibility for reproduction. Once again, however, this division can be criticized for being no more than a description. Both the history of the nineteenth century and the very recent past, make it very clear that the extent to which reproduction is private and/or commodified varies across social formations; whether goods and services are provided by public or private means is variable across time and space. The division of labour within the family has also proved changeable in accordance with economic conditions and political struggle. Any analysis which is dependent upon assumptions about who does the housework, about family forms, and even about the characteristics of women's waged work, can be no more than historically contingent. Moreover, these analyses deny capital any interest in female labour except as an industrial reserve army. What happens to the argument if we insert a proposition that some capitalists may have strong reasons for needing a permanent and reliable female labour force? If capital has such a needs, there would be little reason, within McIntosh's argument, for the state to sustain a family household or a family myth which blocked or hindered access to female workers.

A third concern is that these discussions of the capitalist state's involvement in reproduction of the forces of production pay most attention to daily servicing of the labour force. While reference is, of course, made to intergenerational reproduction, the thrust of the analysis and the examples discussed are most frequently, if not exclusively, those of housework and childcare. However, it is impossible to see any reason why capital requires this kind of domestic labour be done exclusively or primarily by women. All that capital "needs" is a rested labourer. In other words, assuming that capital requires the reproduction of the forces of production does not lead to the conclusion that it requires daily servicing be done by women. All we know is that historically it most often has been done that way. Similar arguments can be made about childrearing.[4]

In general, McIntosh's analysis suffers from a problem with levels of analysis. Using the concept of "reproduction" to account for the relationship between the capitalist state and women, it moves immediately from the assumption that the capitalist state plays a role in the reproduction of capitalism, to a description of the contribution of the state to the oppression of women through reinforcement of the ideology of the family wage and specific policies.[5] This analytic slip is inappropriate. To say that the capitalist state is implicated in the reproduction of the capitalist mode of production is to make a statement at the highest level of theoretical abstraction. Reproduction occurs at the level of the mode of production until there is a transition to another mode of production. The mistake that McIntosh and the others who utilize similar categories make, is to generalize about reproduction out of the experience during a specific stage of capitalism of a specific state, one which has contributed to the oppression of women by reinforcing an ideology of familialism and the family wage. In turn, the roots of this ideology are located in the strategies of the British labour movement (both in and out of government), the British middle class reform movement, and the actions of the imperialist and post-imperialist British state. Such a description of the British experience can never constitute, however, a statement of theoretical generality.[6]

Ultimately, these analyses suffer most from being ahistorical. They slip from discussing the capitalist state in the abstract to a discussion of a specific capitalist state, and then generalize from that to the capitalist state *tout court*. This occurs despite the good intentions expressed of being historical, and despite the recognition that things could be different in other situations. While acknowledging that the assumption upon which so much of the argument is based is socially constructed, careful distinctions between the British state and the abstract capitalist state are not maintained.

GENDER, BABIES AND THE STATE

With these weaknesses identified in even the best arguments about women and the capitalist state, the issue is worth re-thinking. An understanding of the capitalist state's contribution to the oppression of women cannot be founded upon assumptions derived from the specifics of any national case at a particular stage of capitalism. Once the logic of the capitalist state's situation in any conjuncture has been identified, a detailed understanding of that state's contribution to the oppression of women follows from analysis of that social formation. In other words, there must be a clear distinction among levels of analysis so that, while abstractly designating the fact of the state's contribution to the reproduction of the mode of production, the description of *how* that role is organized is found in analyses of political struggle in concrete social formations.

It is in the nature of abstract formulations that they are necessarily very general. It is sufficient for our purposes here to say that because the capitalist state exists within a particular system of capital accumulation, its actions will be shaped by the social relations and structures which characterize that mode of production. We can assume the fundamental importance of class relations for the actions of the capitalist state. The implications of this assumption are that class struggle will cross the state, and that state policies will reflect the balance of class forces at that time. Moreover, we can assume that reproduction of the mode of production is fundamentally important to the dominant class within any capitalist system. At the same time, exploitation and the relations of unequal power which accompany it — which are defining characteristics of capitalism — will lead to resistance from subordinate classes. Class struggle, not only at the point of production but in all politics, will reflect the competing interests of the dominant class in the continuity of class relations, and of the subordinate classes (as well as some other social groups) in transforming those relations.

One common problem placed on the agenda of capitalist states since the nineteenth century has been the development of a healthy and disciplined labour force. Capitalist states, with the extension of industrial capitalism, began to take on some responsibility for the reproduction of a waged labour force. At times this intervention involved constraining individual capitalists who defined their interests more narrowly and in the short-term, and who worked their labour to death. At times intervention involved collectively organizing protection against the effects of industrial production (urban squalor, threats to health and safety, etc.), often after mobilization by workers against such conditions. Therefore, capitalist states frequently compelled capital to inhibit its tendencies toward unduly rapacious behaviour, in the interests of guaranteeing the continued existence of the current generation and the appearance of the next. Historically, both cross-generational and daily reproduction of the labour force have been concerns of capitalist states confronted with the effects of industrial capitalism in full flower. Nevertheless, it is not possible to predict a priori anything about the specific policies by which this is accomplished.

Earlier stages of capitalism have been characterized by a system of separate nation states within which much accumulation is organized, yet which also depend upon systems of international exchange of capital and goods for accumulation. These systems attribute great importance to national actors, and capitalist states have been concerned with maintaining the nation state's influence. The tools available for this task have included practices of diplomacy and warfare, and capitalist states seeking success in the international system supported military establishments to reflect and enhance their international standing. These armies and navies needed not only hardware but also troops. Capitalist states had another reason, then, to be concerned with the health and well-being of the national population.

For these two reasons at least, it is not surprising that states did try to organize the one activity which is inevitably gendered — childbirth. To the extent that the capitalist state was concerned with its national population, the social construction of maternity became a likely area of state activity. The question of infant and maternal protection arose in the context of widespread concern about declining birthrates, infant mortality and public health, and occupied policy makers in many countries from the last quarter of the nineteenth century. Discussions of babies are found deeply imbedded in all contemporary considerations of social policy (housing, health, schooling, etc.), labour policy, civil rights and foreign policy.

In both Britain and France, infant mortality and public health were major social problems connected not only to labour force needs and requirements for national defence but to the "social question" more generally. French demographers discovered that the rate of population growth was declining so dramatically that, in 1896, an absolute decline seemed possible.[7]

Depopulation was considered a threat to national wellbeing, particularly in the event of another war with Germany. The experience of mass mobilization for the Boer War taught British policy makers that national strength — in the form of healthy young men who could be conscripted into the army — was much less than it should be.[8]

By 1900, most European countries had enacted legislation to prohibit women from working in industry for limited periods before and/or after giving birth. In Britain, the 1895 Factory and Workshop Act prohibited women's return to work for a month after childbirth. At least one of the rationales of the Act was that such restrictions would minimize the threat to children's lives — and, thus, to the nation's population — coming from mothers' work.[9] Nevertheless, commentators saw the law as incomplete, only a preliminary step in the direction of infant protection:

> The law, as it stands, prohibits the employment of mothers in factories and workshops during the first month after childbirth. It is so worded that it is hard to enforce, but, at best, it is a law for the mother and not for the child. If the child is to be saved, we must extend the present period of prohibition until gradually this system of employment dies. Gradually, then, the proper balance would be restored; the mother would serve her children and her husband by her presence in the home, not by her presence in the factory. In that way she best serves the State...And the State should take charge: the children of the State are the business of the State; if it neglect that business there is nothing that will atone.[10]

The principal efforts for infant and maternal protection in Britain were not this Act but the efforts to teach housewives to nurture their babies better. This policy too emphasized the necessary presence of the mother in the home, not the factory.

France (along with Russia) was an exception to this international trend until 1913 legislation provided a possible prenatal, and a compulsory postnatal, leave for women working in "all industrial and commercial establishments."[11] Most importantly, a daily allowance to compensate for lost wages was made available for eight weeks before and after childbirth. This allowance would be paid to "all women of French nationality who habitually work for wages outside the home, whether as a worker, an employee, or a domestic," if their personal means were limited.[12] Dispute over this allowance held up the legislation until 1913, but it was finally passed after a debate which stressed the needs of the State.[13] Thus.

> in this second round of debates, proponents of leaves made fewer appeals to humanitarian sentiments and more arguments about 'the grave national peril' of depopulation. As Senator Strauss wrote, 'A utilitarian preoccupation has come to double and reinforce the humanitarian concern. Patriots and philanthropists must therefore cooperate....' Since the *patrie* needed babies 'for its defence and maintenance', maternity leave was presented as a way 'to save' infant lives 'for national advantage'.[14]

Paid maternity leaves represented the primary state effort to decrease infant mortality rates and improve the health of newborns.[15] Moreover, it remained the principal program until after 1945.

We can see from this brief description that there were some similarities in the response of Britain and France to what was defined as a grave national problem. In both countries, the concern was more with babies than with mothers, although the connection between the two was close. Moreover, both discussions were located in the pre-war environment of international competition, in which large and healthy armies were essential. In both cases, infant mortality rates were used as a measure of the problem. If mortality rates could be brought down, population would increase; better childcare (also reflected in lower mortality rates) would improve the quality of the national stock.[16] The same culprit was identified — poor infant feeding, which led to gastrointestinal problems and diarrhoea. In both countries, proposals to lower infant mortality rates focused on feeding and especially nursing — since cow's milk and the germs which would accumulate in it were a cause of mortality, illness and failure to thrive.

Yet, a more detailed examination of the responses of the British and French states indicates more divergence than agreement. In both countries, expert analysts sought a "single cause" for the problem, but the solutions promoted differed immensely. In France, the identified single cause was too hasty return to work of new mothers because of their poverty. By the 1890s, demographers had found that forty-five percent of infant deaths in the first year of life occurred within the first month, and they concluded that leaves of four to eight weeks would substantially alter mortality rates. They arrived at this conclusion by a process of ignoring other alternatives — alternatives seized upon by similar experts in other countries. French demographers did not link infant mortality to maternal occupation per se.[17] Moreover, as one historian of these policies writes with some incredulity:

> Strangely, researchers did not connect the incidence of infant diarrhoea to the feeding practices of working mothers. Instead, they analyzed maternity hospital records to show that most poor women left the hospital earlier than recommended to return to work and interviewed working mothers who had lost many babies to learn that most had stopped nursing early to resume work. Given this indirect evidence, and new information about the large proportion of women of childbearing age in the labour force, many policy makers inferred that postnatal leaves would significantly lower the infant mortality rate.[18]

It was these findings which led many policy makers to insist upon state benefits to compensate for lost wages.

While France did have organizations devoted to both infant health and programs promoting it (for example, well-baby clinics which made payments to mothers who nursed for an extended period, and voluntary associations to promote breast feeding) state initiative relied on the development of a program of maternity leaves. Experts and politicians expressed concern about women's failure to stop work for the last part of their pregnancies (thus provoking premature births, underweight newborns, difficult deliveries, maternal weakness, etc.), and about their insistence on returning to work immediately after delivery (thus leaving their newborns to be fed bottled milk, to be cared for by others less careful than the natural mother, and risking postpartum complications which threatened the health and long-term fertility of the mother). The proposed solution was compulsory leave, and mobilization around this proposal took place between 1886 and 1913.

The French state was therefore called upon to find a way of guaranteeing a workable balance between motherhood and French capitalism's employment of women. The emphasis on leave clearly reflected a widely-shared assumption that women's participation in the paid labour force, even after marriage and during childbearing years, was widespread, inevitable, and even desirable. Yet, something had to be done so that women could combine both their productive and reproductive activities. Representatives of capital, and both revolutionary and reformist workers' organizations mobilized alongside nationalists and social Catholics to demand — with different rationales — a state policy.

The alternatives debated ranged from the status quo of no protection (which was often justified in the ideological terms of laissez-faire liberalism) to the demand by some socialists that maternity be recognized as society's responsibility, and that working mothers be given adequate leave to give birth and nurse their children — adequate being defined in terms of both time and payment for lost wages. In between were advocates of compulsory leave without compensation, and proponents of various lengths of leave and benefits dependent upon need. The legislation eventually passed when political conditions broke up an impasse which had developed between those supporting compulsory leave without compensation, and those insisting that some form of benefit was necessary if the real needs of poor working women were to be met. Much controversy centred on whether maternity leaves were most properly considered labour legislation or social policy. Most interesting, however, is that little was heard from those who wanted to discourage or forbid women to engage in paid labour in order that they might bear more and healthier children.[19] In this way, state policy makers in France indicated their acceptance of women's employment as a fact of life, and selected policy from a range of alternatives delineated by that given. Moreover, none of the participants in the policy debate — the demographic and medical experts who collected the data on infant mortality, the women workers, the trade unionists who agitated for the payment, the capitalists who established private programs and promoted public ones, and the politicians who debated the specifics of the programs — thought that poor working women could count on a male wage to carry them through even a limited unpaid maternity leave.

Other policy initiatives of the state confirmed this focus on babies, rather than women's work. Efforts at establishing pronatalist policies were legion throughout the century, and they certainly contributed to the oppression of women — the infamous Law of 1920 forbidding contraception and abortion is only one example. Nevertheless, in France, all of these policies were directed towards a single goal — obtaining babies. In the inter-war period it was any babies, and then after 1945 attention shifted towards healthier and happier babies. Multiple efforts were made to reconcile work and childbearing, for example, with the promotion of maternity leaves, nursing stations in factories, state-provided childcare in the schools from the age of three, etc. In all of this, however, the state showed little interest in the women who were the mothers. It was not particularly interested in their morals — unmarried mothers were always supported on the same terms as married ones.[20] Nor did the state care about their health. Arguments that repeated pregnancies and abortions were unhealthy for women never carried any weight for the defenders of the ban on contraception. Discussing the late development of protective legislation in France, McDougall concludes, "the proponents of laws restricting women's work were more concerned about increasing the birth rate, lowering infant mortality, improving child care, and moralizing the working class than they were about women's health and welfare."[21]

It is only by cross-national comparison that we can really appreciate the extent to which the assumptions made and the range of alternatives considered were contingent on the specific national situation. I have already described the British state's concern with exactly the same problems of infant mortality and health at exactly the same time. The British experts also sought a "single cause" of the problem, but the identified source of the problem and the solution were quite different.[22] In consequence, the implications for the long-term character of state programs (even up until the present) and their effect on women were also quite different.

Even the use of experts reflects cross-national differences. The marshalling of statistical and medical evidence that marked the French debate was less visible in Britain, where attention focused on feeding patterns and cleanliness, often within a eugenic framework of analysis. While the French expert was the demographer and the obstetrician, the British expert was the Medical Officer of Health, a public health official concerned with local conditions, including housing, medical facilities, visiting nurses, etc. At this time in Britain, a comprehensive social policy (which would eventually culminate in the post-1945 "welfare state") was emerging; in France, maternity leaves were incorporated into the labour code.

As the 1913 report of the Chief Medical Officer to the Board of Education said: "The principal operating influence [in causing infant mortality] is the ignorance of the mother and the remedy is the education of the mother."[23] As a result of this interpretation of the problem, all efforts were made to educate mothers in proper "scientific" feeding and cleaning. Teaching mothercraft and housekeeping skills was stressed, as visiting-nurse schemes, clinics and educational programs were established to train both working and middle class women in domestic tasks. For example, home visitors, while inspecting the baby — weighing, examining, etc. — could also inspect the housekeeping and make helpful suggestions to mothers on managing, even when funds were short.[24]

The British state opposed paid maternity leaves and, even in the inter-war years, never ratified the International Labour Organization's Washington

Convention provision for six weeks paid leave before and after delivery for women in industrial and commercial work. As one policy maker argued then, such provisions would be wrong because they would usurp the father's responsibility for supporting the family and thus encourage family disintegration. Many policy makers made the further assumption that women's waged work was, in and of itself, detrimental to their infant's health. Campaigns against working mothers heated up in the 1890s and, according to Lewis, arguments were based more on the *belief* that the mother's place was at home than on any empirical evidence of the consequences of work.

Two general assumptions underpin these British policies for infant protection. The first was an expectation that women's place was exclusively in the home. A second was an often-expressed fear that any state interference in the form of income transfer would threaten the family, either by encouraging men to abandon their dependents and/or by hurting their pride. This was the rationale for the state not providing any direct payment and distributing only services and advice. Thus, not only were women not supposed to work, but the family's well-being in everyday terms was defined as their personal responsibility. If the family did poorly, it was because women were ignorant, unskilled or careless. For example, the British state attributed the nutritional weaknesses of poor people to women's lack of knowledge about housekeeping, rather than to the effects of poverty.[25] Teaching women to keep house better and feed their families more nutritiously — beginning with nursing babies — was part of a coherent analysis by social policy experts of the nature of the family and the gender division of labour within it.[26]

These two case studies demonstrate that, despite sharing a similarly timed and equivalent concern for cross-generational reproduction, the British and French states proceeded to develop programs which reflected quite different assumptions about women's status as potential workers and potential mothers. Absent from the French case is the assumption which informed the behaviour of the British state (and the present discussions of the state and women's oppression described above) that women do not and should not work for wages. Instead, in France the state's concern was to balance the two female roles, rather than to have one dominate or forbid the other.

DISCUSSION

From this concern with reproduction came a set of policies which were not, and could not, be gender-neutral. After all, women were the ones who produced all those babies, and they were always caught up in the actions of the capitalist state which shaped the conditions of maternity and the family. To the state, women were *both* workers and mothers, and the two roles had to be considered if potential workers and soldiers were to be born. Nevertheless, the remedies selected in each social formation resulted from its specific situation, as state policies reflected the conditions of capitalist production as well as the balance of political forces and the strategies pursued by political actors. The states may or may not have assumed that women provide free labour in the family. They may or may not have discouraged women's work outside the home. They may or may not have tried to establish equality between female and male workers. They may or may not have encouraged childbearing in a way that would subordinate women to men, to the state, or to both.

Despite such variation, it is evident that the capitalist state has participated in the reproduction of women's oppression. Its actions did permit, and even encourage, the maintenance of unequal power relationships between women and men. This participation can be seen not only in the social construction of maternity — the assumption of a gender-based division of labour in the family was made in both the British and French cases examined here — but in many other instances as well. It required organized struggle by feminists and their allies well into the twentieth century, for example, before women were granted equality in citizenship. Control over female sexuality also has been an area where the assumption of the difference and inferiority of women has been expressed by many capitalist states. In general, in the past, acknowledgement in state policy of the existence of gender difference has meant the effective subordination of women to the needs of men and/or of the state. The question to be posed now becomes how to explain the capitalist state's participation in the maintenance of relationships of oppression of women by men?

There are three ways that Marxist feminists might answer the question thus posed. The first is a "dual-system" argument, which posits the existence of two separate systems that contribute to the oppression of women. Patriarchy and capitalism are equally at fault in the subordination of women to men in capitalism. The state then becomes a crucial link across both systems. The second is one which posits the existence of a material basis to the oppression of women which makes the social inferiority of women inevitable under capitalism. A first wave of Marxist feminists looked to domestic labour for this material base; and a second wave, dissatisfied with the domestic labour argument, turned to discussions of biology, particularly the fact that only women bear children. The role of the state is relatively under analyzed in these discussions, with most attention focusing on the ways in which biological difference, inserted into the heart of the capitalist mode of production, is translated into gender relations in specific social formations. A third kind of answer locates the oppression of women in the ideological remnants of precapitalist patriarchy. In this version, the capitalist state is assigned a central role in the reproduction of this ideology, as well as the capitalist relations of production, because the subordination of women is helpful to capitalism.

None of these answers by themselves could satisfactorily account for the two stories which this paper tells. The dual system approach must be rejected here, as it has been by many Marxist feminists, because the notion of an autonomous patriarchal system which reproduces itself along side capitalism is impossible to sustain.[27] Moreover, theorizations of patriarchy as an abstract concept have tended to ignore the analytic necessity for historical specification, which this paper assumes any theorization of class or gender relations must include. For these reasons, this paper (as well as many recent debates among Marxist feminists) has circled around some version of the second and third answers.

They too are problematic. In observing the impact of a societal assumption of the inferiority of women, while rejecting the dual-systems argument, McIntosh turned to ideology and capital's need for a reserve army of labour for the explanation of women's inferiority in the workplace and confinement in the family. However, as has been argued above, despite McIntosh's assumption of its universality, this argument is historically contingent. Others concerned to locate women's oppression in something more material than the ideology of familialism, turned to biology — the simple fact that only one sex bears children.[28] In response to such argument, Barrett claims that the emphasis on biology is also ahistorical, because maternity can only be a socially-constructed relationship. The fact that a low social value has been placed on it, and/or that it meant women's lives have more often been lived in the privacy of the family, are both consequences of social relations, not childbirth per se. Therefore, she turns back to ideology to understand how that social construction occurs.

Reflecting on all rounds of this debate, everyone seems caught in an inappropriate fear of granting the principal point of the dual-system argument — that gender relations can not be reduced to material conditions — in order to avoid falling into the trap of that argument. To recognize that relations of power beyond class power exist is not immediately to assume an equality of those relations. To recognize that men oppress women, and that oppression is not reducible to the workings of capitalism, is not to require that the relationship of gender-unequal power be granted the same theoretical status as class power. In other words, a system of gendered power can be acknowledged and resisted without immediately requiring that it be articulated at the highest level of abstraction to the capitalist mode of production. A sense of that necessity follows *only* from the a priori assumption that sexual differences are as important as differences in the relationship to the means of production. Many feminists wish to begin from that assumption; but if it is made, then either a dual-system or a biological argument logically follows, because only with one or the other can sex be inserted into the heart of the capitalist system.[29] If the assumption is not made a priori, then there is no requirement that sexual difference have the same status as that of class.

Barrett's comment on Brenner and Ramas is telling here for both their article and for that of the Armstrongs. For Barrett, maternity — as are all gender relations — is socially constructed, and we now know that it can be constructed in a large number of ways — including, through technological possibilities, the exclusion of men altogether. Armstrong and Armstrong place sexual difference at the heart of the capitalist mode of production by arguing that the social division into public and private sphere is necessary for — in fact, almost a defining characteristic of — capitalism. However, by correctly identifying the interpretation of biology as a social construct, they are left with no argument for why biological difference will necessarily lead to inferiority for those who bear children. Inferiority can only be historically determined.[30] In other words, the argument is thrown back onto accounts of the social construction of power relationships. Such accounts, however, must — as the cases discussed here demonstrate — allow more space for variety than McIntosh, Barrett, et al. have as yet actually granted.

All social formations are divided by a multitude of relationships of difference — class, age, gender, race, and language are but a few. In many cases, the recognition of difference is accompanied by inequality of power. Thus, the recognition of childhood is usually accompanied by the subordination of children to adults. The recognition of racial difference has in the past led to all the familiar evils of racism. Nevertheless, it is also obvious that the mere existence of difference does not lead to its congealment as a system of unequal power. Such a system is socially constructed and can also be resisted. Progressive social forces have struggled against the divisive effects of racism and sexism in the name of equality, positing a universality of human dignity against the inequalities of power structured around some types of difference.

To clarify the ways in which unequal power is both constructed and resisted it is helpful to use the concept of the universe of political discourse. This concept is defined as the universe of socially constructed meaning resulting from political struggle. Within this universe, the parameters of political action are established by the process of limiting the set of actors accorded the status of legitimate participants; the range of issues considered within the realm of political debate; the policy alternatives considered feasible for implementation; and, finally, the alliance strategies available for achieving change. The multitude of possible relations of difference in any social formation are given social meaning within the universe of political discourse, and relations of unequal power are thus established. With this understanding of the social production of political meaning, attention is focused on the material, political and ideological parameters of discourse. In any capitalist society, the universe of political discourse will be unequally structured, as are the relations of production. Yet, the specific identities which emerge out of the social constitution of difference can not be known in advance. Only an examination of that social formation can make visible the struggles over the construction of difference.

This notion of the universe of political discourse leads to an analysis which concentrates less on the bases of difference than on the way that difference is constituted in any social formation. For example, just as it is obvious that working class movements can be mobilized only in industrial societies, it is also obvious that all industrial societies do not experience that mobilization in the same way, or to the same extent. Whether the organization of the working class, *qua* class, occurs is a profoundly *political* outcome, dependent on the activities of political parties and other institutions of the labour movement.[31] The "working class" is an identity which can take on popular resonance only *after* political struggle and *after* the hegemonic ideology has been breached by the worldviews propounded by organizations of workers and their allies.[32] Similarly, while there is obviously a biological basis to difference between genders, the relevant question here is how, in any particular social formation, this difference is given meaning. It is possible to constitute it as a maximal or a minimal difference. Sexual difference could be permitted to cross all other relationships, or, such a process of differentiation could be effaced through the political actions of resistance. Whether a minimalist or maximalist strategy is followed, however, can be understood only by examining the characteristics of political struggle in any time or place.

If, as this formulation would suggest, the constitution of difference occurs in struggles over a multiplicity of power relationships, the capitalist state must in some fashion reflect such struggle. Political struggle occurs among actors imbedded within a universe of political discourse, which includes not only a discourse about class but also one about other types of difference.[33] Each of these discourses is articulated to the discourse of class which every actor bears, and it is the universe of these discourses, combined in struggle, which provides the bases for strategic action. Thus, as the capitalist state is crossed by class relations, so it is crossed by other forms of domination represented in the complex discourses carried by all actors that is the universe of political discourse, with which actors of that social formation are imbedded. But, in turn, this universe is constituted by the strategic actions and struggle of the actors in that social formation, and it can be known only via historical analysis.

With these notions in mind, we can return to the case studies and look for the reasons for differences in responses to the problems of maternity which both the British and French states faced around 1900. The search for reasons is conducted by exploring both the balance of class relations in each of the two social formations, and the ways in which other power relations based on difference were articulated to those class relations.

A first step in describing relations in the two social formations delineates the participation of women in the paid labour force. In both France and Britain, industrialization introduced women to capital as a cheap source of labour. The first thrust of industrialization in Britain — which brought women and children into the textile mills and served as the symbol of the new era — occurred before the middle of the nineteenth century. By the latter part of the century, the most modern sectors were heavy industry — like iron and steel — which were employers of men, both because they required the greater strength of that sex, and because political mobilization against female labour produced protective legislation which hindered women from competing with men. Therefore, in the mid-nineteenth century, forty-five percent of British women who did waged work were found in manufacturing, but fully thirty percent of that group were employed in one sector — textiles and clothing. Almost all the rest of women workers (forty percent) were in domestic service.

Industrialization was slower to arrive in France, and concentration of production did not occur as quickly. Manufacturing was carried on in smaller, often family-based firms outside large factories. Moreover, agriculture remained a much more important part of the total economy and employed forty percent of women workers in 1866. Textiles never attracted as large a proportion of the labour force in France as it did in Britain, and took a smaller percentage of women (twenty-two percent in 1866).

By the beginning of the twentieth century, the patterns were changing in both countries, but the alterations affected working women differently. In Britain, textiles continued to decline in importance, as did domestic service. Opportunities for women were found increasingly in the expanding service sector. Since the rate of female employment in Britain remained remarkably stable throughout the period, it seems reasonable to conclude that there was a more or less straightforward transfer of workers from textiles and domestic service to jobs in the tertiary sector.[34]

In France, in contrast, around 1870 both the percentage of women in the total labour force and the proportion of all women who worked began to rise, so that France had the second highest rate of female employment of seventeen European and North American countries at the end of the nineteenth century.[35] In addition, at least up until the First World War, women's employment in the secondary sector increased as much as it did in the service sector. A result was that the labour-market segmentation characterizing the British case — men in manufacturing and women in services — was less visible in France.[36]

At the beginning of the twentieth century, several French industries were employing more women; and these industries were not only declining ones, like textiles (which was then being feminized) but also the most dynamic, like metals, chemicals, electrical, automobile, printing and food processing. Modernizing capital substituted semi-skilled and unskilled female workers for more expensive and more skilled male ones. In this way, new feminized sectors were emerging. By 1906, one in every three workers in industry was a woman. New forms of work organization, which divided jobs into parts performed by workers without traditional craft skills — later labelled Taylorized work — were increasingly established. Not only new factories but also offices — where clerks' jobs were sub-divided into filing, typing, etc. — were places where more and more women worked.[37]

What were the consequences of these different patterns of female employment in the two countries? First, a British worker was less likely to be a woman. Moreover, working women in Britain tended to be isolated in highly feminized sectors. Textiles, before World War I, was both more highly feminized and took more women than in France; and domestic service, which was almost totally feminized, took the other large group of women workers. Later, the service sector became the major location of women's employment. These two factors meant that male workers — the most visible as well as the most numerous — symbolized the status of "worker." In addition, British working women were less likely to be found in the same workplaces as men; and working men were less likely to have female relatives, especially wives, who earned their own living. At the level of everyday experience of working people, it was a lot easier in France — especially in Paris, which was a centre both for women's work and for trade union politics — to assume that working women were a common phenomenon.

Coming to the conclusion that women's work was not about to be eliminated is even more likely when the interests of capital are examined. Because of the slower rates of large-scale industrialization and the differing characteristics of the leading sectors, French capitalists were very likely to resort to female labour. Capitalists were introducing women into modern production, and it was difficult for the state or the labour movement to assume that this process could be halted.

The logic of the theoretical argument made above is that it is not sufficient to point to these differences in objective conditions and derive consequences. It is also necessary to examine the meaning given to these relations by the social forces engaged in political struggle. Only by examining the universe of political discourse within which meaning is constructed can we understand the ways that employment and sexual differences were given political meaning in Britain and France. While French capital had learned to rely on female labour, workers and other subordinate classes might have insisted on, and therefore struggled against that reliance. In fact, this is precisely what seems to have happened in the earlier part of the nineteenth century in Britain. A difference strategy was followed in pre-1914 France.

Discussions of women's employment and the sexual division of labour were part of the universe of political discourse of both Britain and France from the earliest years of industrialization. Working class and other reform movements all took positions on these issues, and defined their organizational strategies in light of these views. One important difference, however, is that it appears the space for a discourse based upon the legitimacy of women's work was closed down much earlier in Britain than in France. The reasons for the narrowing of the universe of discourse can be found in the differing organizational strengths of reform movements as well as capital's resort to female labour.

Mobilization against women's employment and for protective legislation was successful in Britain, beginning in the middle of the nineteenth century. After that time, political discourse was influenced by a labour movement which defined the family wage as one of its primary goals, and by middle-class reform movements for improved social conditions and women's emancipation which accepted the notion that each gender had a different role to play in society. Discussions of the British state's role in gender relations all place a great deal of explanatory weight on three factors: the effects of industrial capitalism on the demand for women workers; the middle-class reform movement's concern with protecting women and children from the effects of industrial employment; and the labour movement's concern with protecting male wages and working class families from capital's efforts to lower wages by employing women. While capitalists may have been interested in increasing the rate of female employment in certain industries and sectors, the goal of reformers and the labour movement was to reduce women's participation rates. These last two groups united around the demand for a family wage.[38]

In the early nineteenth century, parts of the labour movement did utilize a discourse of gender equality, and took practical steps to organize working women, as well as men, in struggle against industrial capitalism. Owenites, the major proponents of these positions, placed much emphasis on reform of the "marriage system," which they identified as the source of women's subordination. Nevertheless, while they did organize working women, conflict persisted within the movement over the threat to male wages that women's employment implied, particularly among the more skilled segments of the male working class (tailors for example), whose work was threatened by technological change and the women employed to operate the new technology.[39] Moreover, the Chartists and the Christian Socialists, who employed the discourse of separate spheres, had a much more lasting influence on the British labour movement than did the Owenites. In their campaigns against the Poor Law, and against employment practices, which they argued both provided free labour to capital and destroyed the working class family, the Chartists agitated for the family wage.[40] The puritanical revival of the early nineteenth century, which provided so much energy to the labour movement, emphasized the moral power of women and their importance in the home.[41] Resistance to pressures on wages and living standards involved not only the demand for restrictions on capital's use of labour (the ten-hour day) but also a family wage. In the class struggle of nineteenth century Britain, a discourse of gender emancipation was overwhelmed within the organizations of the working class by the discourse of the family wage, protection of women and children, and separate spheres.

This remained the discourse of the labour movement for decades afterwards, in part because it became an essential part of the strategy of a movement dominated by skilled craftsmen.[42] The fear of female competition never disappeared as the de-skilling effects of rapid industrialization and the anti-union efforts of employers threatened to block new rights, or rescind some which had been earlier acquired. By the end of the nineteenth century, along with the decision to engage in independent political action (in order to have leverage against judicial decisions which threatened traditional trade unions) came more protective actions against lowered wages resulting from employers' introduction of new technology and union-busting tactics. High on the list of threats to male wages was the competition from women who could be employed for less than men. Therefore, unions organized against women's work, and for the family wage, in order to protect themselves.

It is, of course, obvious that all women were not excluded from the paid labour force by the actions of trade unions and reformers.[43] Unmarried women often worked to support themselves and/or to contribute to the family income, and many married women worked because the family wage may have been the goal without ever being the reality.[44] However, the reality of the family wage is not really the issue; more relevant is the discourse which informed the union strategy. Behind the unions' actions was an imagined utopian future of an idyllic family household in which women would be spared the horrific working conditions of the factory, and where they could devote themselves (in health and with time) to their families. This imagined idyll obviously also benefitted men who would find a healthy, happy home after work, one which would be their "castle." Threatened by developing capitalism, and concerned not only about themselves but also their wives, daughters and mothers, male trade unionists allied with other reformers to seek protection.

There was no reason for them to imagine another solution. The British trade unions of the nineteenth century were protective associations, and were not motivated by a high level of class consciousness. Their goal was to do well by their members; and if the membership was threatened by women working for lower wages, and unhappy about the "unnaturalness" of this situation, the unions would struggle against women's employment. The assumption that there were separate spheres was shared by women active in the trade unions and the Labour Party, and influenced the universe of political discourse within which maternal and infant protection was discussed in the twentieth century: "Mary MacArthur, the most prominent woman trade-unionist, declared that women had no desire to go on working in factories while trying to nurse their children in creches that might be provided by the factory owner and that 'every encouragement' should be given to mothers to stay at home." Therefore, instead of creches, nursery schools were demanded to provide children of working class families with educational opportunities. In discussions of women's condition, debates did not include the option of women's right to work; it encompassed instead a debate about whether wives had a right to part of their husbands' wages, or whether family allowances would be more helpful.[45]

Of course, the strategy of the labour movement was successful in part because other actors similarly contributed notions of the appropriateness of a gendered division of labour to the universe of political discourse. Therefore, the labour movement found allies among those operating with bourgeois ideology.[46] Many feminists, for example, employed the same language. While agitating for the vote and equality of citizenship, the feminist movement was dominated by "maternal feminists" who subscribed to a notion of women's moral superiority and the civilizing effect of women's participation in politics; equal but separate was their basic position. An alliance of the workers' movement and middle class feminism was not an uncommon one in the late nineteenth century. For example, the campaign to repeal the Contagious Diseases Acts (regulating prostitution) brought together organized middle class women opposed to the sexual exploitation of poor women by a double standard of sexual behaviour, and workers' organizations like The Workingmen's National League and the Trades Union Council, which acted out of a desire to protect working girls from the need to resort to prostitution when no other job opportunities were available.[47]

In advocating programs of maternal protection, feminist organizations did not question the discourse of separate spheres assigning women responsibility for housekeeping and homemaking. What they did dispute was whether the filth and disease which plagued many workers' homes were the fault of the women, or of the conditions of urban life. Feminists insisted on municipal responsibility for dirt, claiming that no housewife, no matter how skilled, could be expected to overcome the lack of municipal services.[48]

The link between feminists and other social reformers was often more than one of discourse. The same people moved among several groups, advocating women's political rights and the reform of society so as to improve the lives of the poor and the working classes. In the late nineteenth and early twentieth century, social workers—often middle class women—went about among poor families, and pressured male politicians for reform. The discourse of social work emphasized strengthening the family in order to avoid the social costs that were associated with industrial and urban societies. In effect, social workers aided in establishing the Victorian family among the working class, and the instrument selected for this establishment was the working class mother. Critical of existing state practices dealing with poverty (like the Poor Law which segregated recipients by sex and age, thus breaking up families) the new professionals proposed programs for the "deserving poor" which would increase their self-reliance. Imbedded in this discourse of reform was an assumption that social cohesion required overcoming the alcoholism, poverty and ignorance of the working classes. The strategy was to promote "individual responsibility," which meant the responsibility of the working *man* for his dependent family.[49]

These reformers with middle class origins feared the "natural" tendencies of workers at the same time as they desired the improvement of workers' lives: without careful intervention workers would undermine their own life chances and the nation as a whole. Education to the standards of the middle class became the goal. The discussion of infant and maternal protection was part of a more general campaign by eugenists to improve the nation. Fearing working class weakness and debauchery, the reformers sought the improvement of the relations by both teaching working class mothers to be more like those of the middle class and encouraging middle class mothers to have more children, so that the British nation would not be swamped by supposedly inferior babies.[50] Thus, programs to decrease infant mortality and promote maternity were clearly part of a larger strategy to overcome the ignorance and irresponsibility of the working class. Social workers stressed the importance of teaching, of providing the means of self-help, and of interaction between middle class advisors and working class families. Thus, home visitors and baby clinics were obvious expressions of this philosophy of class relations.

All of these actors created a relatively narrow universe of political discourse about women at the beginning of the twentieth century in Britain. Organized workers, acting out of both self-protection and acceptance of a gender division of labour, demanded inhibitions on women's employment. At the same time, they supported state policies which provided real improvements in the living conditions of non-working mothers. Feminists, frequently in alliance with working men, also promoted a discourse which contained no assumption of the importance or desirability of women's participation in the paid labour force. The discourse about women's role in the family — which defined paid work as inimical to that role — also informed the first stirrings of welfarism as the makers of social policies began to lay the foundations for the British welfare state, which has subsequently been identified by so many observers as a fundamental factor sustaining women's dependency. Able only to imagine a family system in which women could perform domestic labour without the destructive impact of outside work, the universe of political discourse, dominated by a protectionist labour movement and middle class reformers, contained little notion of the costs of women's isolation from the world of paid labour.[51] Not surprisingly, when the British state developed policies for infant and maternal protection it did not act out of an assumption of the importance of women's work.

In France, the universe of political discourse within which policies of maternal protection developed was quite different. Neither the labour movement nor middle class reformers tried as hard to discourage women's paid work. By the beginning of the twentieth century, the French labour movement had moved beyond a simple protectionist position to one of revolutionary syndicalism; and by the first years of the twentieth century, a class struggle perspective had been established at the heart of the French labour movement. The dominance of revolutionary syndicalism brought with it the dominance of a broader and more egalitarian discourse on women's role than that of the traditional Proudhonist perspective (offering women a choice between housewifery or harlotry) which had captured the union movement of the nineteenth century.[52] Women gained representation rights in unions and collective institutions while they were still denied fundamental civil rights by the National Assembly.[53] Committed to a class revolutionary rather than a protectionist trade unionism stance, and confronted with rising rates of female employment and capital's frequent preference for women over men, the Confederation Générale du Travail (CGT) chose to organize rather than....block women from participation in the paid labour force.

These actions constitute a crucial turning point in the history of French social relations. Commentaries on French unions and women have never observed the same emphasis on the family wage as dominated the British labour movement, even in the nineteenth century.[54] The family wage was advocated by a few union activists, but the definition of the concept was quite different in France. The family wage meant a family income sufficient to support any size of family, *no matter the number of children*. In other words, it was a concept that made no reference to the activities or earning potential of women; it was directed towards the needs of children. Moreover, because it involved questions of redistribution, the state was implicated from the start. Thus, as a well-known liberal Leroy-Beaulieu said in 1896: "This theory of the family wage is nothing less than the socialist theory of wages related to requirements. It leads straight to collectivism, because it cannot be applied by private persons and can only be put into place by the State, distributing all the work and all the wages."[55] Despite Leroy-Beaulieu's fears, the family wage was *not* advocated by the labour movement in the pre-war years; it was instead more associated with various positions of the natalist movement. More common within the union movement was an argument that women ought to be segregated in work suitable to their physical characteristics and household responsibilities. By the second decade of the twentieth century, even the notion that women could be confined to a separate sector of the labour force and/or female employment reduced was overturned by events. As has been described above, female employment in France was substantially higher than in Britain, and technological change was putting women and men into the same workplaces.

The Couriau Affair was a crucial turning point for the labour movement. In this 1913 controversy, the upper levels of the CGT disciplined the Lyon Printers' Federation for denying union membership to a female printer, Emma Couriau, and for expelling her husband because he refused to forbid her to seek work and union membership. This historic and controversial dispute traced the same lines of cleavage within the union as did a long-standing difference among radical and conservative printers over the union's whole political strategy. The specific dispute was resolved only after the intervention of the feminist movement and the national labour movement in a local controversy. The resolution in the direction of equality and acceptance of working women's rights was tremendously influential for the whole union movement.[56]

The consequence of this strategic choice made in the Couriau Affair was far-reaching. The inclusion of women in unions became a political task of the first order so that women could be brought around to support the revolutionary goals of the union movement. Similarly, confronted with capital's resort to women workers in order to reduce wage bills, the French unions instituted a strategy of emphasizing increases in the salaries of the lowest paid, as well as introducing into political discourse the mobilizing demand of *travail égal, salaire égal* (equal pay for equal work).[57] If capital could no longer pay women less than men, women would not threaten men's jobs. Moreover, unions' mobilizing actions would solidify the commitment of women to the goals of societal transformation which the revolutionary union movement promoted. This strategy of solidarity had the same potential effect as one which would have been divisive: the male workers were protected. It did not divide the working class by gender, and the assumption of the "naturalness" of women's unemployment was not systematically promoted by the unions or their political allies.

This description of the French labour movement's position on women's work demonstrates both the contrasting effects of the labour movement in the two countries and the differing composition of the universe of political discourse. For French unions and the social reformers close to them, the world imagined was one in which women were not necessarily confined to the private sphere. Rather, the imagined ideal was one in which there was sufficient time, for both work and family, for leisure and for homelife. The campaign for the reduced work week, for example, emphasized the *semaine anglaise* (a half-day off on Saturday) arguing it would allow women to do their domestic work on Saturday and still give time for both women and men to enjoy a leisurely Sunday.

Also tremendously important in the social construction of gender in these years was the natalist movement, which publicized the problem of a low birthrate and thus the shortage of babies. This movement, motivated by the goal of sustaining a population and army sufficient to withstand any military challenge, very often defined men — not women — as the source of the problem. Seeing the low population figures as primarily a manpower or military issue, the natalists identified a lack of patriotism on the part of French *men*; the crisis was even defined as one of French virility. Individualism leading to a self-centred refusal to have children needed to be replaced by an understanding that the nation was at risk.[58] The Alliance Nationale, the most important pro-natalist organization, lobbied for a set of state rewards to the fathers of large families. Women, or their jobs, were not at issue.

This emphasis within the political discourse on the role of fathers resonated in a political system in which the social philosophy of Solidarism had a great deal of influence. The notion of a social Solidarity was predominant within the Radical Party, a major source of initiative for social reform in the first part of the Third Republic.[59] The philosophy provided middle class reformers with a rationale for social programs which also laid the foundation for the French welfare state. It was based on a notion that citizenship brought not only reciprocal rights but also duties. Citizens owed each other — and ultimately the state — certain things because they were inextricably bound in interdependency (solidarity). Society, composed of these links of rights *and* duties, resembled a contract.

The society envisaged in this social theory was very different from one of pure liberalism, or from a class society. Solidarism was a philosophy of the petite bourgeoisie, which was still economically and politically hegemonic in Third Republic France. For Solidarists, the state was the coordinating mechanism for the expression of solidarity; and so social programs reflected not individual rights to equality of opportunity or income, but solidarity — which was the duty of the rich to help the poor, the young to aid the old, adults to raise children, the well to care for the sick, etc.

With such a discourse, the Radicals could appreciate the natalist notions of family responsibility to the state. Raising children for the *patrie* was a duty. Men who refused this duty were selfish; that is, not solidaristic. Women were relatively absent from the discussion because, for Solidarists, the family was the fundamental unit of interdependency, not the individual (although the public representative of the family was the father). Women and men together had duties — family duties — to the state, to each other and to children. There was little questioning of women's employment in all of this. The family model was derived from the petite bourgeoisie, in which an enterprise was very often founded on the capital and work of the couple.

The Family Movement, which formed part of the natalist movement, did advocate the withdrawal of mothers from the paid labour force in the interests of family well-being. However, from the early years of the twentieth century until the present, this movement faced a fundamental dilemma. Its primary goal is to improve the nation's family life and increase the population, which has meant encouraging traditional values, especially stable marriage. If employers continue to offer women employment, any effort to formally ban work by married women would likely result in an increase in the concubinage rate. The Family Movement has always understood this dilemma.[60] Recognizing a contradiction, the Movement did make use of a discourse emphasizing the dangers of women's paid labour, but its primary goal over-rode any insistence on enforcing that position. Therefore, it was willing to compromise around a policy which would give working women the time to have their children and stay with them in the post-natal period.

The French feminist movement also supported an improvement in the conditions of child-bearing. Using a discourse influenced by Solidarism, the feminists emphasized women's duties to the nation. In contrast to other actors, however, they insisted that women's rights had to be improved if they were to perform their duties. Feminists therefore demanded the vote, as well as improvements in the conditions of maternity. All of this was presented by a feminist movement which insisted upon women's right to training and education equal to men's and encouraged women to work and, when working, to unionize.[61]

The universe of political discourse within which policies for maternal protection were discussed in France was hence quite different from that of Britain. The French state was crossed by class organizations and other groups struggling with quite different arguments. Capitalists sought the employment of more women in the face of labour shortages, and they could not imagine a maternal protection policy which assumed the absence of women from the labour force. The revolutionary syndicalist organization of the working class had defined for itself strong reasons to promote women's employment and equality. Parliamentarians close to the labour movement insisted that adequate allowances be paid because these politicians both assumed and advocated paid work by women. Other reformers—including the natalists, the Family Movement and bourgeois feminists—were either indifferent to women's partic-ipation in the paid labour force or willing to accept it, and some actually promoted it. For all these reformers the real emphasis was on a strong nation for which many babies were needed. With the exception of the feminists, women were not much discussed.

Of course what resulted from this universe of discourse was a policy that provided a way of combining maternity and waged work. Moreover, this solution — arising in a different universe of political discourse than that in Britain — was one which gave less space to policy makers to assume female dependency in the design of subsequent social policy. Its consequences were potentially far-reaching.

CONCLUSION

The two cases examined here demonstrate much variation across social formations in popular and policy expectations about the proper amount, location, and effect of women's participation in the paid labour force. It is, therefore, impossible to found a general theoretical statement of the capitalist state's contribution to gender relations on the presumed existence of shared assumptions that the family wage is "natural," that the basic family unit is the wage-earning husband and dependent wife and children, or, that the state will act to exclude women from the labour force. In France, there was clearly a different assumption about women's employment, as well as a high rate of participation of women in the paid workforce.

Moreover, as the description of the universe of political discourse in France has shown, despite the acceptance of working women, and despite the fact that so many women had jobs, emancipation of women in France was not greater and perhaps even less than in Britain. The focus on the family as the basic social unit — which so many reformers accepted — denied women independence of their own. They were encased within the family, and visible only as mothers. These assumptions about the family were powerful historical constructs, rooted in the French social formation of the nineteenth and twentieth century. It would take more than waged work and the social acceptance of working women to liberate them from the stifling effects of a universe of political discourse which continued to define them always as potential or actual mothers. In the universe of political discourse, and then politically, women still had to be disengaged from the family and motherhood before they acquired a real right to difference. This disengagement waited upon the struggles of the modern women's movement to alter the universe of political discourse and state policies.[62]

This paper has sketched a method for understanding such alterations over time. Beginning with the logic of the capitalist state's location in any conjuncture, and mapping the articulation of power relations such as those of class and gender in the politics of any social formation, it is possible to understand the ways in which any state contributes to the oppression of women. Moreover, it also points to the space for resistance. An important implication of this method is that the state's contribution is variable, not only across social formations but also across time. The need of capital for reproduction of the labour force, and the state's activities to create and maintain the nation, are dependent upon the stage of capitalism as well as particular patterns of social relations. In pre-1914 Europe, the character of finance capitalism, Taylorizing production, and British-dominated imperialism all had profound effects on the way that capitalist democracies like Britain and France confronted the agenda of expanding citizenship rights and social policy. In that conjuncture, the state's concern for healthy babies and a productive labour force motivated the policies which have been examined. Only detailed analysis of other conjunctures can determine whether the state's motives are the same. And only then will the space for resistance to the state became visible.

ENDNOTES

The support of the German Marshall Fund of the United States is gratefully acknowledged for the project of which this is a partial report. This paper is a revision of one presented at the Annual Meetings of the Canadian Political Science Association, June 1985. For detailed and very helpful comments on earlier versions of this paper, I want to thank Greg Albo, Tashin Corat, Richard Hamilton, Fuat Keyman, Eleanor MacDonald, Ted Magder, Rianne Mahon, Sonya Michel, Paul Nesbitt-Larking, Leo Panitch, George Ross and Donald Swartz.

1. A very interesting debate around Michèle Barrett's *Women's Oppression Today* (London, 1980) and Pat and Hugh Armstrong, "Beyond Sexless Class and Classless Sex: Toward Feminist Marxism," *SPE* 10 (Winter 1983), pp. 7-44, has addressed the theoretical relationship between capitalism and the oppression of women, without accepting the assumption of a dual system of capitalist exploitation and patriarchal oppression. See also Patricia Connelly, "On Marxism and Feminism" *SPE* 12 (Fall 1983), pp. 153-62; Johanna Brenner and Maria Ramas, "Rethinking Women's Oppression," *New Left Review* 144 (1984); M. Barrett, "A Reply to Brenner and Ramas," *New Left Review* 146 (1984), pp. 123-28; and, Jane Lewis, "The Debate on Class and Sex," *New Left Review* 149 (1985), pp. 108-20. However, it must be recognized that the same issues have been raised elsewhere. See, for example, *La condition feminine* (Paris, 1978), especially the article by Moynot.

2. Mary McIntosh, "The State and the Oppression of Women," in A. Kuhn and A. Wolpe (eds.), *Feminism and Materialism*, (London, 1978), p. 255.

3. For Michèle Barrett and Mary McIntosh, too, state policy makers operate within a myth which leads them to perceive women as dependent: "At first sight, then, there appears to be a neat fit between women's place in the labour market and their place at home. Their part-time or less permanent involvement in paid work frees them to run the home; men's full-time work enables them to earn a 'family-wage' to support a dependent wife and children... 'It is normal for a married woman in this country to be primarily supported by her husband, and she looks to him for support when not actually working,' was the way a minister in the Department of Health and Social Security put it. Yet when we realize that this

supposedly normal pattern of dependence is in fact a myth, it becomes clear that the supposedly appropriate pattern of women having less training, fewer job opportunities, and lower pay is nothing less than a con trick made possible by the power of the family myth." *The Anti-Social Family* (London, 1982), p. 79.

4. There is a tendency to assume—rather than question—the connection between childrearing and women, even in theoretical (as opposed to historical) statements. For example, Barrett in *Women's Oppression...*, p. 231, does this without comment.

5. McIntosh, "The State...," p. 202.

6. McIntosh, of course, does qualify her argument to say that historical variation can exist, and she does begin to address the issue of historical variability when she turns at the end of the article to the potential contradiction between maintaining women as a reserve army and the need for a reproduced labour force. She also raises the question throughout the article that the family household system may not be the most efficient for advanced capitalism, and the state may have to take on more and more responsibilities (see *ibid.*, p. 284, for example). Yet, raising such issues and making such caveats does not change the analytic form of her argument.

7. Karen Offen, "Depopulation, Nationalism and Feminism in Fin-de Siècle France," *American Historical Review* June 1984, pp. 648-76.

8. Jane Lewis, *The Politics of Motherhood: Child and Maternal Welfare in England 1900-1939* (Montreal, 1980), p. 15.

9. Louise Tilly and Joan Scott, *Women, Work and Family* (New York, 1978), pp. 15-6, quote the Government's "Report of the Interdepartmental Committee on Physical Deterioration" on this point. The Committee was established after the Boer War to find ways to improve the race and nation. Other proposals it made were that meals be provided in schools (legislated in 1906) and medical inspection of school children (instituted in 1907). That the focus was children's, not mothers', well-being is clear from these two programs. Also see Lewis, *Politics of Motherhood...*, pp. 15-16.

10. Quoted in Tilly and Scott, *Women, Work...*, p. 173.

11. France had passed little special protective legislation for women. The first appeared in the 1890s, 50 years after the British Factory Acts.

12. The prenatal allowance required a medical certificate that continued employment would endanger the mother or unborn child but no restrictions other than need applied to postnatal benefits. Thébaud estimates that in 1915, thirty-five percent

of the new mothers of Paris met the means tests for the allocation, despite the minuscule sum being paid. Françoise Thébaud, *Donner la vie: Histoire de la maternité en France entre les deux guerres* (Paris, 1982), p. 88.

13. Mary Lynn McDougall quotes an influential 1901 study by a doctor/statistician who, after studying infant mortality and disease, "claimed that France lost one army corps a year to preventable infant disease." See "Protecting Infants: The French Campaign for Maternity Leaves, 1890s-1913," *French Historical Studies* XIII/1 (1984), p. 92.

14. McDougall, "Protecting Infants...," p. 98.

15. There were other programs for maternal protection involving extended medical care for the needy, payments to nursing mothers, and guarantees of time off during the work day for nursing mothers. For details, see Thébaud, *Donner la vie...*, p. 87 and Communauté Economique Européenne (CEE), *La Protection de la maternité dans les six pays de la CEE: Situation en 1966* (Paris, 1966).

16. There was something of a difference here between the two countries. The French were most concerned with keeping babies, any babies, alive while the British exhibited more interest in the quality. This difference seems to be in large part due to the greater influence of the eugenist movement in Britain and the dominance of eugenists in the campaign for infant and maternal health. See Lewis, *Politics of Motherhood...*, pp. 30ff, 73.

17. André Martin lists the occupations considered dangerous to infant and maternal health. This law thesis also documents in detail the debates around proposed programs, both those made to and by the state, and those instituted privately by corporations. Prior to 1913 a number of companies—department stores, for example — were making a flat payment to their employees who gave birth. *La Protection de la maternité en France* (Dax, 1912).

18. McDougall, "Protecting Infants...," p. 82.

19. Offen, "Depopulation, Nationalism...," pp. 652-4.

20. During the Vichy regime, publicly most insistent upon confining women to the family, a conflict among branches of the state over paying family allowances to unmarried mothers was resolved in favour of the single mothers. Not even in Vichy were the familialists hegemonic. See Jane Jenson, "Liberation and New Rights for Women" in M. Higonnet, J. Jenson, S. Michel and M. Weitz, *Battlelines and Genderlines: Reconceptualizing World War I and II* (New Haven, 1987).

21. Mary Lynn McDougall, "Protecting Women or Preserving the Family: The French

Campaign for Protective Labour Legislation, 1974-1914" (Paper presented at Yale University, February 1981), p. 1.

22. Lewis, *Politics of Motherhood...*, Chapter 2.

23. *Ibid.*, p. 89.

24. There was also a system of French visitors, but their major task was to verify that the conditions for payments were being met. For example, they checked that women receiving the pre and post-natal allowances were not working and that babies whose mothers received nursing allowances were still feeding them. See A. Martin, *La Protection...* Lewis describes the continued rejection of any programs that would have given more than advice to English mothers. Lewis, *Politics of Motherhood...*, pp. 13-14.

25. Lewis, *Politics of Motherhood...*, pp. 80, 17, 168, 184.

26. Elizabeth Wilson describes the link between this solution for the problem of the falling birthrate and other aspects of Fabian Socialist policy prescriptions. As part of the mistrust of income transfer, Labour MPs and trade unionists in 1913 rejected a proposal that they support maternity payments. *Women and the Welfare State* (London, 1977), p. 101ff.

27. Veronica Beechey, "On Patriarchy," *Feminist Review* 3, (1979), pp. 66-82; Barrett, *Women's Oppression...*, Chapter 1.

28. Armstrong and Armstrong, "Beyond Sexless Class..."; Brenner and Ramas, "Rethinking..."

29. This is precisely the assumption that the Armstrongs make in setting up their argument for a material base to women's oppression: "marxism must recognize that sex differences are integral to all levels of theory and analysis. The issue is not 'women's questions' or 'the question of women' but the efficacy of an analytical framework which fails to recognize or explain how and why sex differences pervade *every* aspect of human activity." See "Beyond Sexless Class...," p. 7. While this analytic assumption is a perfectly reasonable one to make, it must be recognized that notions of "integral" and "pervasiveness" do *assume* that sexual difference must be elevated to a theoretical status similar to that of class relations. Of course, the Armstrongs differ from the dual-system theorists because they do not claim that a system of patriarchal power lies at the root of women's subordination.

30. It is worth noting the difference between the analyses about women's inferiority and about relationships of unequal class power. Marxism does not depend upon an analysis of capital's notion of the inferiority of workers; subordination follows

from the real differential in power, but a differential which also never leaves the workers without class power.

31. Janine Brodie and Jane Jenson, *Crisis, Challenge and Change: Party and Class in Canada* (Toronto, 1980), Chapter 1.

32. Adam Przeworski, "Social Democracy as an Historical Phenomenon," *New Left Review* 122 (1980), p. 42ff.

33. Nicos Poulantzas, *L'Etat, le pouvoir, le socialisme* (Paris, 1977), Part II.

34. Tilly and Scott, *Women, Work...*, pp. 69ff; 152.

35. George D. Sussman, "The End of the Wet-Nursing Business in France, 1874-1914," in Robert Wheaton and Tamara K. Harevan (eds.), *Family and Sexuality in French History*, (Philadelphia, 1981), p. 227.

36. If, at the same time, employment in the textile industry was declining, women must have been entering "non-traditional" areas of female employment. J. Daric, *L'Activité professionelle des femmes en France—étude statistique, evolution, comparisons internationales* (Paris, 1947) pp. 31-32.

37. Martine Martin, *Femmes et societé: le travail menager (1919-1939)* (Paris, 1984), p. 23; Marie-France Lamberioux-Chapet, *Les ouvrières pendant l'entre-deux-guerres (1920-1936)* (Paris, 1980), pp. 18-19. The service sector in France was also increasing in size and women filled new jobs created in commerce, banks, the post office and the educational system, which under the Third Republic, made state schooling compulsory for girls as well as boys.

38. Michèle Barrett and Mary McIntosh, "The 'Family Wage': Some Problems for Socialists and Feminists," *Capital and Class* 11 (Summer 1980), pp. 51-72.

39. Barbara Taylor, *Eve and the New Jerusalem: Socialism and Feminism in the Nineteenth Century* (New York, 1983), Chapter IV.

40. Jane Humphries, "Class Struggle and the Persistence of the Working-Class Family" in A. Giddens and D. Held (eds.), *Classes, Power and Conflict* (Berkeley, 1982), p. 482ff.

41. Taylor, *Eve and the New Jerusalem...*, pp. 126ff; 263.

42. Paul Adelman, *The Rise of the Labour Party 1880-1945* (London, 1972), pp. 15-19.

43. This is a major point of Brenner and Ramas' critique of Barrett. Brenner and Ramas, "Rethinking..."

44. Barrett and McIntosh, "The 'Family Wage'..."

45. Lewis, *Politics of Motherhood...* pp. 80, 167.

46. Humphries, "Class Struggle...," p. 484.

47. Judith R. Walkowitz, *Prostitution and Victorian Society: Women, Class and the State* (Cambridge, 1980), pp. 6-7; and Sheila Rowbotham, *Hidden from History: 300 Years of Women's Oppression and the Fight Against It* (London, 1977), p. 52.

48. Lewis, *Politics of Motherhood...,* p. 65.

49. Wilson, *Women and the Welfare State,* pp. 47, 51.

50. Lewis, *Politics of Motherhood...,* p. 30ff; Rowbotham, *Hidden from History...,* p. 106.

51. This goal was not necessarily based upon any notion of women's inferiority, nor was it intended to subordinate women. In fact, if the model were the older household economy, the expected autonomy of women was no doubt greater than the experience which the wage economy actually did bring. Tilly and Scott, *Women, Work...,* Part I.

52. Charles Sowerwine, "Workers and Women in France before 1914: The Debate over the Couriau Affair," *Journal of Modern History* 55/9 (1983), p. 412.

53. Michelle Perrot, "Le Syndicalisme français et les femmes: Histoire d'un malentendu," *CFTD Aujourd'hui* 66 (1984), p. 41.

54. Michelle Perrot, "L'Eloge de la ménagère dans le discours des ouvriers français au XIXe siecle," *Romantisme* 13-14 (1976), pp. 105-22.

55. Quoted in Nicole Questiaux et Jacques Fournier, "France," in Sheila B. Kamerman and Alfred J. Kahn (eds.), *Family Policy: Government and Families in Fourteen Countries* (New York, 1978), p. 122.

56. Sowerwine, "Workers and Women..."; and Marie-Helene Zylberberg-Hocquard, *Féminisme et syndicalisme en France* (Paris, 1978), Chapter III.

57. Perrot, "Le Syndicalisme...," p. 47.

58. Offen, "Depopulation, Nationalism...," pp. 669, 648-9.

59. J.E.S. Hayward, "Solidarity: The Social History of an Idea in Nineteenth-Century France," *International Review of Social History* 4 (1959), pp. 261-84; and J.E.S. Hayward, "The Official Social Philosophy of the French Third Republic: Léon Bourgeois and Solidarism," *International Review of Social History* 6 (1961), pp. 19-48. Also, Léon Bourgeois, *Solidarité* 3rd ed. (Paris, 1902).

60. Lamberioux-Chaptet, "Les ouvrières...," p. 75; M. Martin, *Femmes et société...,*

p. 49; Fernande Paris, *Le travail des Femmes et le retour de la mère au Foyer* (Paris, 1943), p. 300.

61. Offen, "Depopulation, Nationalism...," p. 652; Thébaud, *Donner la vie...*, p. 44; Perrot, "Le syndicalisme," pp. 46-47.

62. Jane Jenson, "Struggling for Identity: The Women's Movement and the State in Western Europe," *West European Politics* 8/4 (1985), pp. 5-18.

CHAPTER 10

"WHO HAS THE BABY?" NATIONALISM, PRONATALISM AND THE CONSTRUCTION OF A "DEMOGRAPHIC CRISIS" IN QUEBEC 1960-1988

HEATHER JON MARONEY

INTRODUCTION

In the aftermath of the failed 1980 sovereignty-association referendum, demographic politics have come to the fore in Quebec. Against the background of an unresolved national question, and with the intervention of journalists, demographers and politicians, data and predictions that were at least five years old were invoked to create a (renewed) sense of demographic crisis. Most dramatically, a 1988 television programme, *Disparaître* [To Disappear], hosted by former Parti quebecois (PQ) cabinet minister, feminist and *indépendantiste*, Lyse Payette, suggested both that too few babies were being born to francophones "de vieille souche" ["of the old stock"] for political and economic stability, and that new (black) immigration would lead to failures of assimilation and problems like those of England's inner cities. Such anxieties have in turn validated a pronatalist emphasis on "family policy" which poses problems for feminist organizing.

How then was a particular demographic evolution in Quebec constructed as a "crisis" of national importance? And what are its implications for feminist politics? Overall, two political issues have been, and continue to be, at stake. The first is discursive, and concerns control over, and the meaning given to, such terms as 'woman', 'nation', and 'birth' in the realm of the imaginary where Quebec is symbolically constituted as a nation. The second concerns the actual formation and direction of state policies. At issue, in effect, is: "Who has the baby?" Who possesses the baby as an element of discourse? Who has the right to speak in the name of birth? What bearing does that have on the actual conditions in which — in a trope that confounds a bodily act with social possession — it is women who "have" children, i.e., give birth to and care for them?

My aim in this paper is to analyze a first developmental stage of what I call demographic pronatalism (1980-1988), focusing particularly on its discursive moment.[1] In such an analysis several factors need to be taken into account: the relation of the demographic discussion to Quebec's unresolved national question on the one hand, and to gender, class and ethnic/race inequities on the other; actual population patterns; and the positioning of feminist, nationalist and political actors on the discursive field constituted by the demographic debate. In addition, it is important to consider the political role of demographers themselves, with particular regard to their long-standing efforts to institutionalize their own profession.

NATIONALISM, FEMINISM AND PRONATALISM BEFORE 1980

The pairing of pronatalism and nationalism as a solution to the national question is not a novelty on the Quebec political scene, but neither is it inevitable nor static. Contexts, contents and enunciators of each have changed, as has the relation between them. If nationalism fundamentally holds that a distinct "nation," a French-speaking population with specialized cultural institutions, is worth preserving in a sea of North American Englishness, the meanings attributed to that cultural distinctiveness have varied markedly, as have the strategies chosen for its preservation. Although linguistic and cultural vitality clearly depend upon the nation's living embodiment in its population, this paper treats them only insofar as they touch pronatalist demographic politics. Still we should note that by the late 1980s, Quebec faced diverse pressures from a post-referendum political impasse, from integration within a commercialized North American culture, and, increasingly, from demands for recognition on the part of its old and new ethnic/racial and national minorities.[2] It was in this context that the terms nation, birth, woman were in play.

Prior to this, clerical nationalist discourse, which endured into the 1960s, gave a central place to 'woman', but only as objectified in *la femme au foyer* [woman in the house] and not as a speaking subject. In this view, the survival of involuted Catholic cultural institutions — *survivance* — was divinely and naturally guaranteed by a gender order in which women were fertile, obedient and loving daughters of the Church, wives of men, and mothers of children. Women, as mothers of the nation, actually birthed and cared for the baby (or better, babies), but men were able to appropriate the baby symbolically. Patriarchally situated politicians and intellectuals — priests and those trained (until the partial secularization of the educational system in the 1960s) in their sex-segregated schools — controlled the enunciative positions of church, intellectual, or state authority, which allowed them to speak in the name of the baby by integrating it into nationalist and pronatalist discourse.[3]

Any theoretical inadequacies or gender inequities in this approach were veiled by its apparent efficacy. During the period of the *revanche des berceaux* [revenge of the cradle] from 1870 to 1940, Quebec women had extraordinarily high rates of fertility (the highest, according to demographers, in the western world), able to compensate for outmigration yet still allow the population to grow in absolute numbers. While Quebec birth rates were declining constantly from the early 1850s and cyclically in the 1930s, between 1881-1961 they nevertheless remained higher than those of *established* communities in the rest of Canada.[4] Thus even in the recent past, it still seemed as if natural increase would guarantee the two demographic indicators that are read as crucial measures of Quebec's capacity for survival as a cultural entity: the number of francophones as a proportion of Quebec's own population, and the population of Quebec as a proportion of the total Canadian population.[5]

In the 1960s and 1970s, however, birth rates continued to fall in such a way as to undermine that guarantee. The synthetic reproduction index (SRI), which calculates the lifetime average number of children for women in a given population, had dropped below the minimum necessary for a population to reproduce itself (considered to be 2.1, to compensate for early deaths and infertility). While the Quebec SRI for 1961 was 3.99, and Quebec women still had about thirty percent more children than the pan-Canadian average, in the second half of the 1960s it fell more rapidly than anyone had predicted. By 1971 it had reached 1.9. After a period of stability, the SRI began to decline once more and, with some slight variation, continued to do so until 1988.[6] Overall then, these figures indicate that the notion that national survival could be guaranteed by women's "super-fertility" had in fact been undermined. Yet while the links between 'woman/birth/nation' had been severed in practice, the decline in the birth rate received relatively little attention outside of the narrow realm of demographic research, in part because vibrant social move-ments were busy reworking the terms 'nation' and 'woman'.

First during the quiet revolution, expansive new definitions of national security and development (épanouissement) stressed political and material improvements made possible through industrialization and modernization, and seemingly reduced the centrality of 'birth' to 'nation'. The site of the nation's defense was relocated from the church and faith to a (partially) secularized state where social planning was promoted as a mechanism of development, and science enthroned over faith. The state takeover and subsequent reorgani-zation of educational, health and welfare institutions involved the growth of secular occupations on the feminine side of a gendered labour force, so changing the social locations open to women. Concurrently under the influ-ence of Vatican II reforms, important Quebec clerics rapidly accepted that women could be something other than subordinates and baby machines. For example, their chaplain general encouraged members of the Catholic women's organisation, Association féminine d'education et d'action sociale, to become active in the electoral processes of the pluralist state and increasingly to take over the leadership of their own parish-based and province-wide women's assemblies. By the early 1970s, the moral control of the formally disestablished Church was also sharply reduced so that the contraceptive prac-tices of even its parishioners became ultimately indistinguishable from those of other North Americans. Still, fecundity fell long before the use of new contra-ceptives was possible or widespread. Indeed, there was not only quiet, unoffi-cial acceptance of so-called "mechanical" forms of fertility control, but, as I have argued elsewhere, relative silence on the issue of abortion.[7]

Electorally, neither of the rival provincial parties associated with moderniz-ing nationalism, the Liberals (in power 1960-1966, 1970-1976) or the PQ (in power 1976-1985), put 'birth' at the centre of their strategies for national sur-vival in the 1970s. As a result, the clerical nationalist notion of preserving "the French-Canadian race" could be displaced by a politicized emphasis on the acquisition of state powers (some new, some wrested from the federal govern-ment) in defence of Quebec's interests. In election platforms of the 1960s, the Liberals took for granted the persistence of the famille nombreuse [large Quebec families], both as an economic resource (as the supplier of an abun-dant labour force) and as the natural benefactor of economic and educational reforms. For the PQ, at least during its 1976-80 "social democratic" moment, the nation was best defended by language regulation, by changing its relation to the state, and by opening up membership in the nation to all Quebecers. It sought to interpellate feminists, nationalists and immigrants alike with a project of "Québec" as the bearer of gender and economic equality and of a vibrant culture able to integrate all its citizens. In turn, political independence of the Quebec state, or at least "sovereignty-association" with Canada, was necessary to the attainment of these ends. The revelation that francophone fertility had fallen below the reproduction rate in 1971 was interpreted as yet another reason why independence was strategically necessary. Historically innovative in its response to growing feminist movements, the PQ in effect rearticulated the connection between women and the nation as terms of a new triad: 'nation/independence/feminism'.

There is evidence that, by the mid-1980s, modernizing strategies for strengthening the 'nation' economically, culturally and politically had met with moderate success, at least within Quebec's provincial borders. For example, the link between low income and French mother tongue, the dominance of English in the workplace (especially the higher levels of capitalist enterprise), the anglicization of French, and the assimilation of allophone (first language neither English nor French) immigrants into the anglophone community noted in the 1960s and 1970s were all slowed or reversed during the 1980s. The proportion of francophones in the population was no longer declining, in part as a result of exceptionally high rates of anglophone and allophone outmigration between 1976 and 1981, in part as a result of high rates (96-98 percent) of intergenerational retention of French mother tongue. Particularly following passage of the PQ's 1977 Bill 101, *Charte de la langue français*, there was a euphoric sense that the language had been saved.[8]

Secondly, at the much same time 'nation' was reworked, feminists were emerging as subjects to challenge biological-reductionist views that made motherhood women's fate and identity.[9] Clerical nationalist pronatalism and its legacy in contemporary political and scientific formulations came under scrutiny, initially in *Québécoises déboutte!* (1971-1974) and *Les Têtes de pioche* (1976-1979) and later in feminist academic writing.[10] There were two aspects to this critique. Like feminists elsewhere, they attacked views that defined maternity as women's first and foremost identity and that placed women essentially in the realm of nature, the hearth and reproduction. In Quebec, as writers in these journals noted, this maternalist essentialism took a particular form. Not only were women procreators of the nation, but also, in so-called "matriarchal ideologies," they were defined as *empowered* matriarchs, and men as correspondingly weak.[11]

In contrast, feminists argued that the strategy of *survivance* relied on the procreative and domestic *work* of women. The material practices through which ethnic or national cultural content (language, folkways or ethnically specific food tastes) were inculcated overwhelmingly rested on women's unpaid domestic labour.[12] Unlike demographers and clerics, they saw high fertility levels as determined by specific structural and political conditions, and not just women's passive response to religious or nationalist ideology.[13] In the absence of women's or labour rights, pronatalism, including legal and moral bans on contraception, helped ensure the availability of a pool of cheap labour. All this contributed not only to gender, but also to class inequities: women and men of non-dominant classes endured "private" economic hardship by bearing the costs of social — and national — reproduction and those of their own subordination. Thus, the ideological underpinnings of clerical nationalist deployment of the 'woman/birth/nation' relation were exposed and attacked.

In this period, sectors of the women's movement, ranging from autonomous groups to trade union and political party caucuses, went beyond a critique of the lack of social support for women's mothering and domestic work to a positive program for reproductive self-determination and for reformed maternity and childcare. Although many feminists and *péquistes* initially supported "wages for housework," a more complex program eventually emerged. Demands touched on several areas, including: conditions for pregnant and lactating women (maternity leave, workplace health, and control of the birthing process); fathering (perinatal leave to facilitate increased male participation); childcare (childcare centres, parental leave, and greater attention to the particular problems of aboriginal women); and sexuality and fertility control (sex education, lesbian rights, better access to contraception, abortion and fertility services, while ensuring that new reproductive technologies are not harmful to women).[14] The significance of this program was twofold. In practice, it offered a challenge which any pronatalist, or "family," policy initiative had to address to be equitable or, indeed, effective. Discursively, it proposed a new relationship of woman and baby, embedded in the public and social, requiring practical "father-work."

This repositioning was, however, double-edged. Replacing "love" and noble "sacrifice" in the motivational mythology of motherhood with "work" and claims for wages for (or the socialisation of) that work may demystify its conditions, but only at the cost of also calling into question the "nobility" — hollow to be sure — with which clerical-nationalism had hallowed its practitioner. From a psychoanalytic perspective, the shift into a demystified feminist discourse of mothering can also be read as undermining the psychic security provided by the good mother of infantile fantasy, the mother who is interested in, and there for, the baby at all times.[15] That loss may, in turn, have fed a sense that a crisis of birth and of the nation actually existed. Indeed already through the 1960s, the good mother of national myth had come under attack by male writers. For example, behind praise for woman as the mother of the nation, Jean LeMoyne implied that she was too powerful. Or later, in the interests of a non-colonized masculinity, revolutionary nationalists misogynistically attacked mothers — agents of those other wearers of skirts, priests — as the source of repressive socialization which created character structures unable to resist national sell-out.[16]

Indeed, a good mother/bad mother opposition played an important role in nationalist politics during the debate surrounding the 1980 referendum on independence. Lyse Payette, who was then a popular Ministre des consommateurs et des coopératives, Ministre d'Etat pour la Condition feminine and a member of the powerful inner cabinet priorities committee, attempted to translate the PQ's association of mutual feminist and nationalist liberation into support for the *indépendantist* project among the female electorate. However, several groups resisted the association: a current of women, portrayed by themselves and the mass media as a spontaneous mobilisation of "housewives" ("mères de famille"), but politically structured by the Liberals; certain members of the mass media themselves; and most *péquiste* cabinet members.

To recap briefly, Payette urged women to reject the timidity of "Yvette," the obediently domesticated little girl of school texts, for her brother's autonomy and independence by voting "Yes" in the referendum. She argued further that, by virtue of his opposition to provincial independence, the Liberal leader of the federalist forces opposed women's independence: he wanted women to be Yvettes, and was indeed married to one. As Renée Dandurand and Evelyne Tardy point out, a press-defined "backlash against feminism" resulted, managed by both journalists and the Liberals.[17] Politically and discursively, this threatened to split nationalists from mothers-and-housewives ("mères de famille") or the actual mothers of the nation, and hence from babies. At the same time it also threatened to divide feminists from nationalists, mothers and housewives, and similarly babies. While not recanting her critique of feminine timidity, Payette did apologise to the Liberal leader's wife, adding that, as a mother herself, she had defended the nation by having children but felt that it was now necessary to turn to politics. The whole incident, and particularly the terms of her apologia, shows the enduring power of the traditional coupling of birth and nation. The loss of the referendum was blamed on Payette's remarks and taken as evidence of the unreliablility of feminism as a support for national survival.[18] Thus, even in the PQ, the party that most clearly espoused feminism and the one which housed a radical, organized feminist pressure group, the articulation of feminism and optimistic nationalism was fragile.

The emergence of Quebec feminists had the effect not only of challenging clerical or conservative ideology, but of furthering the rupture of women's discursive relation to babies and the nation. If at the level of discourse, the baby was not exactly thrown out, then perhaps new nationalist groups, some religious authorities, and "feminists" left it sitting in the bath while they got on with other projects. The baby was not abandoned, but, we might say, that the baby as produced by pronatalist discourse was left in the care of traditional nationalist, anti-feminist and religious guardians. When the political "father" returned, it was to discover that the number of babies had shrunk, that physical reproduction could no longer be left to ideological exhortation, women's natures, and the private realm of the family and that *something* new had to be done to ensure national survival. Demographers were ready to oblige.

DEMOGRAPHERS

The disestablishment of traditional pronatalist authorities, on the one hand, and the appetite of the modernized state for knowledge as a tool of policy management and administrative control, on the other, created a space for the production of secular demographic knowledge. Demographers were ready to take advantage of this unoccupied site to establish and advance their own profession. If pronatalism no longer spoke with divine authority, through this convergence of interests it gradually became able to do so with that of science and increasingly the state.

It has been argued that Quebec social science students of the 1960s were an upwardly mobile, technocratic petty-bourgeoisie, who made use of university certification as a stepping stone to central social positions and legitimacy.[19] Whatever their social origins, there is evidence that the emerging demographic profession adopted, consciously or not, a similar strategy. Increased state funding, rapidly expanding social science student enrolment — from 151 in 1955 to 1,338 in 1965 — the recruitment of a new generation of formally trained professors, and a policy of hiving off specialized departments from sociology led to the founding, in 1964, of the Département de démographie at the Université de Montréal, itself long an important site of clerical nationalism. The department was then, and still remains, the only fully independent academic department of demographic research and teaching anywhere in Canada.[20] Its founders, notably Jacques Henripin who, with his colleagues, has been responsible for most Quebec research on contemporary fertility patterns, all received graduate training at the pronatalist Institut national d'études démographique (INED) in France.[21]

After some initial intra-departmental difficulties, demographers turned to building a professional apparatus for academic legitimacy and public visibility. At its 1972 founding conference, the Association des démographes du Québec (ADQ) adopted three aims: to provide links among demographers; to make demography known on the labour market; and to diffuse demographic knowledge.[22] It immediately founded a publication, the *Bulletin*, later the *Cahiers québécoises de démographie*, supported proposals for a specialized research institute, the Institut provincial de démographie, on the model of the French INED, and sought membership in the French-language learned societies', Association canadienne française pour l'avancement de science (ACFAS).[23] With a startup membership whose average age was 27.6 years, the ADQ had a numerically and hierarchically male-dominant sex structure, with all 5 of the professors, 1 of 2 departmental researchers, and 2/3 of the 12 identifiable graduates or graduate students all being men.[24] Although membership in the ADQ grew from 22 to 40 in its first year and then to over 100 in 1974, this imbalance between the sexes was maintained.

Demographers also sought state sponsorship, by claiming a special knowledge that could be useful in the construction of strategies of modernization and economic development. Writing in *Recherches Sociographiques* in 1962, Henripin claimed that demographic study directed attention to social parameters — population, fertility, health, death, language and migration — that were undergoing rapid change, and hence were important to policy formation. He particularly stressed two areas: linguistic transfers and the "phenomena of population," both defined as essential to the nation. Indeed, a new object of study, "demolinguistics," was introduced.[25] Demographers also took formal positions, or organized colloquia, on draft legislation on the language of education and work, as well as on policy concerning migration and international population.[26] The first ADQ executive sent demography to Quebec's rescue ["démographie au secours du Québec"] in a demolinguistic situation perceived as critical. Thus, a panic enunciative mode was initiated which, oscillating with a contrasting scientific grandeur, has marked its pronouncements ever since.[27]

State authorities apparently agreed about the centrality of population projections to decision making and welcomed its "operational research" capacity to "determine the most favourable results, methods to arrive at them, and the organization, program, means and methods for policy implementation."[28]

Indeed, the Commissions of Inquiry that are a particular feature of the Quebec policy planning process have regularly offered employment to, or funded studies by, ADQ members and so provided a site for the uncritical "diffusion" of demographic "knowledge." Of its founding members, 12 worked for state agencies, nine were academics, and two, both women, worked at population or family planning agencies. (Evelyne Lapierre for the Population Council in New York and Nicole Lamarche for the family planning association in Quebec, respectively.)[29] More widely, despite some attempt to sell their techniques to the private sector for market studies and personnel planning,[30] demographers have been primarily employed in the public sector, with graduates going to both federal and provincial statistical bureaus, to planning positions at all levels of government, and to teaching. Also, excluding direct contract research, funding for projects like Henripin's and his associates fertility studies has been steadily available from federal and provincial sources as well as agencies, like the Vanier Institute of the Family, that were themselves dependent upon public financing to a large degree.[31] As a result, between the academic years 1972-3 and 1981-2, demography's proportion of the *Université de Montréal* research budget increased from 1.9 percent ($78,248) to 14.7 percent ($1,025,650), because its research problems were uniquely capable of attracting attention from state political milieux.

Parallel to their consistent instrumental orientation to the state, demographers have had an equally consistent theoretical orientation. From their graduate training in France under the positivist and pronatalist demographer Albert Sauvy, they brought a notion of demography as a distinct, predictive, empirical science devoted to description. Seemingly value-neutral and armoured against critical reflection, this view has dominated the profession every since.[32]

In the ADQ publications, Henripin, arguably the central figure in Quebec demography, has only one article that explicitly discusses the politics of knowledge or theoretical issues of interpretation. Here, he dismisses exogenous (and marxist) theorizing as merely responding to an individual psychological need to make a global picture of society, and cites Popper in defence of "facts." To engage in science is "être esclave des faits. Un esclave intelligent, bien sur, qui sellectionne, qui définit, qui abord la réalité avec un model mentale."[33]

Although in this article he makes use of the concept of "discursive formations" to castigate ideology as a polemical, passionate attempt to exercise social power, he does not address the more fundamental epistemological issues about how "social appearance" acquires the status of facticity. Rather, he feels comfortable with an empiricist epistemology slightly leavened with an (unacknowledged) Weberian fact/value distinction that enthrones beliefs as a source of models of the world from which to generate testable hypotheses.

However, despite the professed value-neutrality of Quebec demography, the presuppositions underlying its analysis have led it to highlight some aspects of the demographic picture rather than others in a way that is consistent with the very kind of ideological thinking its "science" claims to despise. For example, the 1960s fall in the birth rate is seen as "alarming" or hardly reassuring, and the number of children women have as the determining factor in Quebec's linguistic composition.[34]

What ideological commitments, then, substructure the positioning of 'woman/birth/nation', the elements of concern here, on the map of Quebec demography? These emerge most clearly in the interventions that directly address state natalist policy. The most important include presentations by Henripin, Evelyne Lapierre-Adamcyk, and others at the 1984-5 Cultural Commission hearings (see below) and Henripin and Lapierre-Adamcyk's *La fin de la revanche des berceaux*. The research for the latter also provided the basis for Lapierre-Adamcyk's report on women's views of ideal family size and daycare to the 1975 Quebec Liberal party convention (subsequently printed in *Le Devoir*). From an examination of these politically framed instances of demographic speech, several problematic features clearly emerge.[35]

First, procreation itself is taken for granted as a universal and transhistorical drive. Whether biologically or psychologically determined, giving birth to (many?) children is the unfettered or natural state. Although this statement is not usually made directly, it is implicit insofar as social factors — like housing, women's work, rising aspirations for children's education — are seen as "barriers" to birth. Indeed, Henripin's normative bias was made especially clear when he more recently asserted that human birth rates below reproduction should be read through ethological theory as an index of social sickness.[36]

Secondly, this ahistorical and atheoretical approach extends to social life as a whole. On the surface, there is constant reference to the temporal categories of past, present, and future. Global terms like "consumer" or "traditional" society are used as if they have some explanatory power. Yet the terms themselves remain structurally undefined and hence have no capacity to specify the workings of social change. According to Victor Piché, who has been a rare critical voice in ADQ publications since 1975, Quebec demographers have adopted American functionalist models of demographic transition. In these models, childbearing "behaviour" is seen as a result of "attitudes," themselves affected by a range of socio-economic and technological factors, among which no causal hierarchy is established.[37] As Piché concludes:

> Pour la plupart des auteur-e-s d'ailleurs, l'allusion aux fac-
> teurs explicatifs demeure fort limitée, le plus souvent en fin
> de texte. Il n'en demeure pas moins que l'interpretation ad
> hoc, même si elle réfère rarement à des cadres conceptuels
> précis, baigne dans les cadres dominants du moment.[38]

Within this schema of disassociated variables, women's roles in procreation are moralistically problematized as a matter of good or bad will. Thus,
demographers have claimed that, prior to the 1960s, women responded to
clerical injunctions, and saved the nation through high levels of procreation.
More recently, because women have adopted "values" that emphasize the
need for objects (consumer durables), services (insurance), or pleasures (vaca-
tions), or have conceived ambitions for their children (tertiary CEGEP or university education for daughters and sons), they have entered the labour force
and *hence* had fewer children. Working to have a financially "easier life for my
family," is, according to demographers, to work for a "salaire d'appoint" ["pin
money"].[39]

This historiography is particularly problematic in its treatment of women
since it fails to see gender as a political relation. In his 1980 foray into
methodological reflection, Henripin may have warned against letting current
theory (by which he meant empirical generalizations) affect prediction; but he
did or could not go any further. Precisely because of its lack of reflexivity, its
failure to understand the ways in which facts are value-saturated, the dominant
tendency in Quebec demography has no way of untangling naturalized elements of hegemonic ideology from its own "science." This has two important
consequences.

First, by accepting a sexual division of labour in which childcare is more
the responsibility of women than men, and women's earning capacity is less
than men's, it ignores the male/female power differences which this supports.
While reflecting real gender inequalities, adopting power-blind role theory only
naturalizes women's status as procreators and care-givers in an asymmetrical
heterosexual couple.[40] To be sure, the assumptions have not always been
entirely coherent: the same text that uncritically uses the notion of secondary
wage and part-time work, suggests that the "liberation" some women are
seeking will only be found by adopting a Swedish model of ungendered part-
time work and childcare. However, this proviso's placement in one passing
line at the end of *La fin de la revanche des berceaux* makes it a radical limiting case. It is conceived only as a life-style choice at the imaginary extremes,
which individual Quebecers might adopt in pronatalist interests, and not as a

strategic policy alternative. Thus, at the same time as it testifies to the "modernity" of a book whose real policy proposals all reinforce the gender and child-raising status quo, it presents "women's liberation" as foreign, indeed Swedish (sexy but suicidal, in the North American popular imagination, and hence not just aberrant but morbid).

Second, as Marie Lavigne argues, official Quebec demography's reliance on averaging has led to problems in its empirical analysis. In particular, the numerical importance of "la famille nombreuse" [families of 5 or more children] vis-à-vis one, two or three child families has been exaggerated. First, many women had no children (nuns, the unmarried and the physiologically infertile). Secondly, other family patterns were diverse. But, because more people are produced in large families, superficial perceptions confirmed normative belief in their actual predominance. Here, the very methods, which demographers tell us are scientific, have distorted data presentation in ways that reflect pronatalist assumptions.[41]

In sum, although there was a secularizing rupture in the move from clerical nationalist pronatalism to demographic analysis, there are also certain continuities. Science may replace God, the demographer the priest, the survey the confessional; but men retain authoritative sites of speech, birth remains in the realm of nature, women are still interrogated as objects and still linked with falling birth rates, and a procreative strategy, which emphasizes population over political project, is accepted as the main way to ensure national survival.

THE POLITICS OF INTERVENTION INTO THE POLICY DEBATE

In the early 1980s, a new set of discursive practices regarding national survival began to emerge in the Quebec political arena. They did so in a context where net migration balances were negative, birth rates continued to fall, and where there had been, at best, weak success in integrating immigrants into the francophone community. In addition, the optimistic nationalist reform strategies of both the Liberals and the PQ were blocked, in part, by the mediation of gender politics.

While in office during the late 60s and 70s, the Liberals had not been able to stabilize the population through a policy of capital investment directed at sustaining high levels of employment, nor had it been able to contain militant feminist, nationalist and class mobilizations. As I have argued elsewhere, the defection of the liberal feminist Fédération des femmes du Québec from the electoral bloc headed by the Liberals after the War Measures Act of 1970, and its conjunctural support for the kind of feminism that looked to the PQ, was significant in Liberal party election losses in 1976.[42] As for the PQ's relation with feminism, it had cooled considerably after its 1980 sovereignty-association referendum loss.[43] After a 20 percent rollback in public sector wages in 1981, affecting unions in which women were numerically dominant (i.e. teachers, nurses and service and clerical workers), the PQ's base further crumbled, and it lost power in 1985.

Nationalist discourse now had to address demographic changes in a situation where faith in reformist and "pro-feminist" strategies for the social reproduction of the nation had been shaken. In so doing, it had both to construct a political meaning for projected population profiles, and to organize the short and medium term implementation of an appropriate policy. Not surprisingly, it sought solutions by turning once more to strategies of national survival through biological reproduction.

In this conjuncture, politicians and demographers, speaking from positions of state and scientific authority, began to introduce the new demographic pronatalist discourse through two sets of province-wide state consultations. The first was on family policy. The ADQ's chair, Maurice Champagne, was appointed by the PQ to the policy consultation in 1982, and again by the Liberals to run a revamped Conseil de la Famille in 1987. The second, the PQ government's 1984-85 Cultural Commission hearings, was chaired by Liberal anglophone Richard French. In effect, the two consultations divided their tasks: the former developed "family policy," which was implicitly pronatalist, while the latter provided material and symbolic resources crucial to updating demographic panic.[44]

The most optimistic of a series of population projections, carried out for the PQ and popularized by the 1984-85 Cultural Commission hearings, predicted fertility rates at about replacement, increases in life expectancy and a net migratory balance of about zero.[45] From this, dire economic and social implications were drawn: too few consumers and too much productive capacity to sustain investment leading to high unemployment and capital flight; an untenable "dependent" population balance, with high-cost social programs to support an aging or "super-aging" population; a loss of political clout in Canada; and political and cultural sclerosis in Quebec. Once more, the nation was primarily identified as its population and only secondarily as bearers of its language. The third constitutive national element, "culture," perhaps more properly the Commission's purview, was left as an unexamined residual, at most something which could be approached through the linguistic dimensions of population policy, or something which had to be defended against the tastes of teens for "American" popular music.[46] Once this basic alignment (nation = population) was in place, the "problem" could emerge as a demographic crisis occasioned by "dénatalité" [declining birthrates]. Happily, this problem had its own pre-given, inevitable solution: to raise the number of Quebec babies born by directly or indirectly intervening to remove barriers to birth or to improve family life. Thus two elements of the original triad, 'birth' and 'nation', which had been separated by modernization, were reconciled, while 'family' overtly displaced the third, 'woman,' as the valorized object of pronatalist intervention.

In the absence of a concerted national policy, this configuration provided politicians with a response to inescapable popular-democratic concerns with national survival. It also provided a way to maintain the ambiguity of their responses to feminism. In the past, both major parties had played both sides of the family/feminism fence. In reforming moments, each had claimed that a link between reform on gender and other issues was a mark of their respective forms of progressiveness. In periods of social crisis, they had turned to "family policy" as a symbol of their reliable stability.[47]

The Cultural Commission hearings make particularly clear the ascendency of demographers. They, in turn, actively provided academic legitimacy for revivified pronatalism. In 1981, for example, the ADQ held its academic colloquium on population policy, *Pour ou contre un politique natalist.* Publications like Henripin's 1981 report to the Liberal party, his report with colleagues *Les enfants qu'on n'a plus au Québec* or George Mathews's *Le choc démographique* served to focus attention on the debate.[48] Demographers most extreme projections, coded as science, were prominent in various mass media attempts to shape "public opinion," of which *Disparaître* was only one.

This latter was important since, as Richard French concluded, the big problem in policy formation was that "people" did not care about the "demographic crisis."[49] There was, in other words, a radical difference between the individual and the state focus, a gap that could be overcome either by cathecting the charged symbol of nation onto the scientific statistics of population, or by individualizing the impact of these projections. For both of these tactics demographers had the tools. All of this meant not only a chance to lobby for more funding for more studies, and greater access to government files,[50] but also an opportunity to publicize the importance of their field. No longer plagued by the image problems of the early 1970s — "The demographer? A strange little man." The demographer became a celebrity.

At the hearings themselves, demographers almost monopolized the right to speak. Demographers took up more time than any other category of inter-venor — family, regional, or ethnic — but, because they were introduced as representing different organizations, any co-incidence in their views was implicitly attributed to the adequacy of the formulations produced from various dispersed sites of scientific investigation. All but two of the demographers present, however, had been students or faculty at the Université de Montréal demography department and were ADQ members.[51]

All the demographers shared the empiricist, micro-analytic framework described above. However, there were differences in the conclusions they drew about their science's "operational" capacity to derive specific pronatalist measures from research findings or to guarantee their efficacy. Contrast for example the views of Henripin and Lapierre-Adamcyk.

Henripin was at pains to make his pronatalism clear. While not rejecting measures to promote greater social equality, he stressed that benefits, whether fiscal (tax allowances or family benefits) or service (preferred access to housing or childcare), should be distributed on the basis of the number of children in a family, whatever the financial status of the recipients. Although hedging on results — in the absence of any theory that would permit cross-national com-parisons of the impact of demographic policy in advanced capitalist states — he insisted that adopting measures on the French or Austrian model would be worthwhile to raise — or to halt the decline of — the birth rate.[52] Thus, pronatalist logic permitted, if not required, violating the empiricist badge, "a slave to facts," which he had defended so vigorously.

Lapierre-Adamcyk's positions were less confidently and persistently pronatalist and ostensibly more feminist. In the face of persistent questioning she (along with Jacques Legaré) maintained that legalized abortion had no overall effect on net population growth. For her, any pronatalist measures had to be non-coercive, universal, and adopted with the goal of improving family life. Less willing than Henripin to go beyond description, she was also less willing to sanction any pronatalist measures.[53]

Yet her influence on Liberal policy formation should not be underestimat-ed. In her 1975 report to the Liberal party, she had defined the population problem as the lack of the third child and identified the barriers to childbearing as financial. Most women wanted direct monetary support for in-house care; those who supported extra-familial childcare were disqualified as a "radical vanguard." Her conclusions, reinforcing the privatized family feminists had cri-tiqued, were exactly reflected in the fiscal provisions ultimately introduced as family policy by the Liberal government in May 1988. A bonus (in the form of an advance on income tax credits) was to be paid at the birth of each child: $500 for the first two and $3000 for the third and subsequent children. These were raised in 1989 to $1000 for the second and $4500 for the third child; and again in the 1991 budget to $7,000 for the third child.

Thus, the hearings themselves were the site for some, if not all, demographers to develop a pronatalism based not on religious exhortation but on the monetary incentives of the market-driven new family economics.[54] However, the substitution of 'family' or 'couple' for 'woman' was not entirely innocent. While this move seemed to absolve women of the blame for declining birthrates, it also laid the basis for their exclusion from the list of legitimate intervenors. Feminists had dared to speak for the objectified 'woman' in political debate; yet once 'women' were elided as objects of demographic policy, women (as feminists) had no enunciative position from which to enter the debate unless they were willing to retreat back under the cover of the family. Nor were the Liberal party's choices about the mediations that made women's speech audible without effect. They chose to hear not the amplified chants of women acting together as feminists, but the objectified, fragmented, privatized speech delivered by social scientific survey.[55]

Women, particulary feminists, were marginalized in the new pronatalism of the mid to late 1980s. If demographic discourse constructed them as the source of the problem, submerged them in the couple, or interpreted their voices only through the fragmentary individualizing discourse of the survey, their own discursive practices were also ambiguous. In the 1960s and 1970s feminists of all stripes had sought to co-opt nationalist birth anxieties for their own ends. Their tactic was to question the conditions of childrearing in a way which deliberately resonated with fears of disappearance: How can you expect the birth rate not to fall, they asked, as long as there is no daycare, no maternity leave, no this, no that? However, their demands with regard to sexuality, fertility control, birth and childcare were explicitly justified in terms of individual autonomy and social justice for women, terms at best tangential to pronatalist emphases on collectivity, nation and family. In addition, this discursive move left unchallenged the charge that feminism itself was responsible for falling birth rates. Thus, as demographic pronatalism increasingly became official state discourse, and as contestation of biologically determinist justifications for women's subordination achieved some measure of success, feminists lost discursive control of the 'baby'.

This is not to suggest that women were completely silent about the state's pronatalist turn. Several commentators argued that the 1988 payment provisions were too little, too late, since the major capital investment is for a first child. Moreover, if they did not present briefs to the Cultural Commission demography consultations, women's groups were well represented at hearings on family policy. Criticism, however, was muted and political attention directed elsewhere.[56]

Of course this abandonment of the baby was only symbolic. Women continued to have the actual babies in a whole range of difficult conditions, in a society that remained structurally hostile to their aspirations to be both mothers and workers, feminists and nationalists. As pregnant teenagers, working women, lone parents, sometimes subject to abuse, living on reserves, farms, or in immigrant ghettos, or scattered suburbs, in all these situations, women had the babies as they have them still. In all these situations too they still turned to the state for help. But with the exception of first term PQ legislation on maternity leave and health care provisions for pregnant and breast feeding women, Quebec women have received little of what they asked for. To this day, most childcare remains inadequate, expensive and inconvenient, women continue to bear the brunt of the double day, and one estimate suggests that 100,000 Montreal children live in poverty.[57]

CONCLUSIONS

This exploration of the politics of demography raises a number of issues for feminist theory and strategy, two of which will be highlighted here. The first is conjunctural: how to respond to the appropriation of militant feminist demands and discourse in the interests of other political agendas. Demographic pronatalism is able to propose apparently radical solutions, while deflecting attention from underlying structural barriers to feminist goals. Demographers may suggest that "work" be reshaped without considering sexual and class power inequalities in the family or labour force; or pro-family spokesmen may take up renewed *paternité* [fatherhood] as an all-in-one answer to falling birth rates, problems of family organization and the ecological crisis, without considering the mediations of capital.[58] Indeed, in a 1988 speech on "La dénatalite: un débat stérile?" the Liberal Ministre deleguée à la condition féminine succinctly summed up feminist desire: "exister en dehors de la maternité, mais egalement pour être en mesure de profiter pleinement de celle-ci."[59] Yet increases in childcare places promised (once more) in that speech evaporated (once more) in the face of budgetary cuts. A clarification of contemporary politics of the family is evidently needed. As 1994 is the International Year of the Family, this task seems particularly urgent.

The second issue which arises from this consideration of the politics of demography is theoretical: how to analyze (and advance) the contradictory politics of feminism, childbirth, ethnicity and nation. The disarticulation of apparently solid national formations by new forms of mobilized ethnicity (themselves a long term result of imperialism on an international scale) has generated contradictions in race/ethnic relations among feminists, a problem not unique to Quebec.[60] This, in turn, has made it difficult for the women's movement collectively to develop a position on the demographic debate, or on the national question more generally. Other factors have compounded the problem: a specialization of issues and functions among women's organizations, the demobilization of the radically critical current of the 1970s and early 1980s, and the normalization of liberal feminism in official state discourse. Still, for demographic pronatalism to be confronted by feminist solidarity distilled from diverse ethnic/national subject positions, minimally requires a cross-national and cross-cultural interrogation of the terms baby, woman, nation. As the controversy about *Disparaître* brought home, some babies, *"québécois-es pur laine"* ["pure wool," and hence white], might be considered more valuable by conservative nationalist forces. Such an awareness is central to the articulation and mobilization of an anti-racist and feminist policy of reproductive rights, one which would actually permit people to have the children they want, support parenting and women's autonomy through state redistribution of resources, and guarantee the rights of national and cultural communities in a francophone Quebec.

That the women's movements in Quebec and the rest of Canada were not able to chart such a course in the 1980s is not just a problem of will. It arises from the complexity and novelty of balancing collective and individual procreative interests in a contraceptive age, at a point in time when women are increasingly mobilized not only as feminists, but also as national, ethnic and class political actors.[61] Rosalind Petchesky and Lynda Lange have pointed out that procreation condenses irreducible, and irreducibly contradictory, dimensions of collectivism and individualism in women's embodied existence as members of real social communities.[62] Moreover, Lange argues, understanding the specificity of women as members of reproductive communities (particularly those of cultural and national minorities) can help transform the individual/collective dichotomy while retaining the strengths of each:

> Individualism and collectivism conflict with one another, but
> each is a foil for the inadequacies of the other, and each
> has important values to offer. The solution will not consist

> in opting exclusively for the one or the other, as we have
> known them.... It is their on-going interaction which will
> help to make a better politics.[63]

In this transformation, there is potential for developing non-oppressive political values where women's interests as individuals, as mothers and as members of national and ethnic communities can be fully developed.

ENDNOTES

This paper was prepared with the support of a SSHRC post-doctoral fellowship and of the Simone de Beauvoir Institute, Concordia University, where an earlier version was presented. Thanks to Sue Findlay, Meg Luxton, Alan Simmons, Robbie Swartzwald, Peta Tancred, Andrew Wernick, and the SPE readers for their comments.

1. Jane Jenson, "Gender and reproduction or babies and the state," *Studies in Political Economy* 20 (1986) takes a somewhat similar approach to analyzing the universes of political discourse shaping distinctive French and British strategies for organizing procreation, gender, and labour.

2. In addition to aboriginal peoples, these include English-speakers, southern Europeans and (sometimes French-speaking) people of colour, most visibly black and Asian immigrants from, for example, Haiti, Viet Nam and Cambodia.

3. On clerical nationalist ideology see Susan Mann Trofimenkoff, "Henri Bourassa and the woman question," in S.M. Trofimenkoff and A. Prentice (eds.), *The neglected majority: Essays in Canadian women's history* (Toronto: McClelland and Stewart, 1977) pp. 106-115; and Marie Lavigne, Yolande Pinard and Jennifer Stoddart, "The Fédération Nationale Saint-Jean-Baptiste," in L. Kealey (ed.), *A not unreasonable claim* (Toronto: Women's Press, 1979), pp. 71-88; on education see Roger Magnuson, *A brief history of education in Quebec: from New France to Parti Québécois* (Montreal: Harvest House, 1980).

4. Jacques Henripin, *Trends and factors of fertility in Canada* (Ottawa: Statistics Canada, 1972); Angus McLaren, "Birth control and abortion in Canada," in Prentice and Trofimenkoff (eds.), *The neglected majority...* 2nd ed., (Toronto: McClelland and Stewart, 1985), pp. 84-101; Yolande Lavoie, *L'émigration des québécois aux Etats Unis 1840-1930* (Quebec, Conseil de la langue française, 1974) estimates 2 million American descendants of Québécois emigrants.

5. Quebec, *Débats de l'Assemblée national* Commisson Culturelle, 1985, p. 491. (herafter referred to as *Débats... CC*). With respect to the population of Quebec as a percentage of the population of Canada, it declined from a high of 36.5 percent in 1851, to 26.9 percent in 1921, recovered to about 29.0 percent (1941-1951) and declined once more to 28.0 percent in 1971 and 26 percent in 1981. Quebec, Commission de la culture, *Etude de l'impact culturel, social et*

économique des tendances démographiques actuelles sur l'avenir du Québec comme société distincte 1985, 27ff [hereafter Etude de l'impact...]. Indeed, 25 percent has become so strongly fixed as the minimum to ensure the political weight of Quebec in the Canadian state, that Health and Welfare Canada's 1989 projection of 24.6 percent by 2011 was seen as catastrophic by Quebec journalists. Canada, Department of Health and Welfare, Charting Canada's future: A report of the demographic review (Ottawa, 1989); Le Devoir 13 décembre 1989.

6.   Jacques Henripin and Evelyne Lapierre-Adamcyk, La fin de la revanche des berceaux (Montreal: PUM, 1974), pp. 10, 130-1. Construed by Quebec, Commission de la culture, Etude de l'impact... as "the fastest fall of a peace time birth rate, by 1981 it reached 1.62, in 1987 1.4, to mount slightly to 1.47 in 1988." This rate is higher than that of such European capitalist states as Belgium, Denmark, Italy, the Netherlands, Norway, Spain, Sweden, Switzerland and the United Kingdom. Statistics Canada, Births and Deaths, 1986 (Ottawa, 1988) Cat 84-204, p. 71. But the rate was lower than Canada's 1.7. Débats... CC p. 162.

7.   See Colette Carisse, Planification des naissances en milieu canadienne-francaise (Montreal: PUM, 1964); Henripin and Lapierre-Adamcyk, La fin de la revanche... p. 108; J. Henripin, P-M Huot, E. Lapierre-Adamcyk, N. Marcil-Gratton, Les enfants qu'on n'a plus au Québec (Montreal: PUM, 1981); and Marie Lavigne, "Feminist reflections on the fertility of Quebecoises," in M. Barrett and R. Hamilton (eds.), The politics of diversity: feminism, marxism and nationalism (London: Verso, 1986), p. 316 for contraceptive practices. See Suzanne Messier, Réflexions sur les politiques de population. Incidences de la baisse de la fécondité québécoise sur la situation des Québécoises (Québec: Conseil du statut de la femme, 1985) for sterilization. I developed the argument about AFEAS and attitudes towards abortion in "'Were you overjoyed at your last pregnancy?' L'Afeas and the issue of abortion," Bulletin de l'Institut Simone de Beauvoir 9/1 (1988), pp. 24-26.

8.   See Quebec, Ministère du Conseil executif, Secrétariat au développement social, L'évolution de la population du Québec et ses consequences (Quebec, 1984) [herafter L'evolution de la population...], and Quebec, Commission de la culture, Etude de l'impact... for population figures and emigration; J-A. Boulet "L'évolution des disparités linguistiques de revenue du travail au Canada de 1970 a 1980" (Paper prepared for Economic Council of Canada, Ottawa, 1983) on wages. Jean A. Laponce, "Conseil au prince," Cahiers québécoises de démographie 17:1 (1988), pp. 35-47, argues that most demographers and politicians

(except federal proponents of bilingualism and those responsible for New Brunswick language policy) have accepted the anglicization of "Canada" outside of the Quebec region as inevitable. Lise Bissonette, "In search of a viable Canada: prophets wanted..." (Speech delivered at Carleton University, April 12, 1991), is one of many commentators on Bill 101.

9. Diane Lamoureux, "Feminism and nationalism, an impossible attraction" in H.J. Maroney and M. Luxton (eds.), *Feminism and political economy: women's work, women's struggles* (Toronto: Methuen, 1987); Heather Jon Maroney, "Contemporary Quebec feminism: the interrelation of political and ideological development in women's organisation, trade unions, political parties and state policy, 1960-1980" (Ph.D. thesis, McMaster University, 1988).

10. *Québécoises déboutte!*, with a revolutionary/marxist feminist orientation, focused on the hidden work of women, including domestic labour; *Les Têtes de pioche* identified itself as radical feminist, critiquing both nationalism and pronatalism.

11. See Jean Lemoyne's *Convergences* (Montreal: Hurtubuise, 1967) for an example and Mona Josée Gagnon, *Les femmes vues par les hommes: 300 ans d'histoire des idéologies* (Montreal: Editions du Jour, 1974); and Michèle Jean "Québécitude et femininitude," *Les Têtes de pioche* No. 9 (1977), pp. 5-7, for a critique.

12. Mary O'Brien, *The Politics of Reproduction* (London: Routledge and Kegan Paul, 1981); Danielle Juteau-Lee, "La production de l'ethnicité ou la part réelle de l'idéal," *Sociologie et sociétés* 15/2 (1983), pp. 39-54.

13. Lavigne, "Feminist reflections on the fertility of Quebecoises...". Under clerical guidance, settlement through low technology family-based agriculture, in which children's labour was a productive resource, continued through the 1930s. See Michel Verdon, *Anthrophologie de la colonisation au Québec: le dilemme d'un village du Lac-Saint-Jean* (Montreal: PUM, 1973). Angus McLaren & Arlene Tiger McLaren, *The bedroom and the state: The changing practices and politics of contraception and abortion in Canada, 1880-1980* (Toronto: McClelland and Stewart, 1986) show higher birth rates in such conditions across Canada.

14. See Maroney, "Contemporary Quebec feminism..."; and Denise Granger, "Réflexions sur les enjeux sociaux de la politique québécoise des garderies des années 1970 à 1982," *Sociologie et sociétés* 19/1 (avril 1987), pp. 73-81.

15. We cannot ignore this distinct level to the panic since unconscious processes have social effects. Roberta Hamilton, "The collusion with patriarchy: a psycho-

analytic account," in Barrett and Hamilton (eds.) *The politics of diversity*....
Disparaître can be death; but it can also be the ultimate here/gone (fort/da)
game whereby, Freud suggests, the infant deals with fear of abandonment by
(and the heady mastery of separation from) the mother.

16. Such claims, interpreting the writings of Frantz Fanon and Albert Memmi, were
made in articles in the left-wing journal, *Parti-pris* (1964), pp. 13-18, 34, and in
Pierre Vallieres's classic *White niggers of America* (1971/1967), pp. 61, 85,
104, 139 and *passim*. As well as anti-clericalism and misogyny, they carry a
homophobic freight.

17. Renée Dandurand & Evelyne Tardy, "Le phénomène des Yvettes à travers
quelques quotidiens," in Y Cohen (ed.), *Femmes et politiques* (Quebec: LeJour,
1981), pp. 21-56; Michelle Jean, *et al*, "Nationalism and feminism in Quebec:
the 'Yvettes' phenomenon," in Barrett and Hamilton (eds.), *The politics of diversity*...; *Le Devoir* 11 mars 1980, 13 mars 1980, 9 avril 1980.

18. Although supported by more than half of francophones, the referendum on
whether to seek political independence or sovereignty for Quebec was defeated
by the population as a whole. See Quebec, *Débats de l'Assemblée Nationale*
1980, pp. 5191-2; Lyse Payette *Le Pouvoir? Connais pas!* (Montreal:
Quebec/Amerique, 1982), p. 107.

19. Marcel Fournier & Louis Maheu, "Nationalismes et nationalisation du champ sci-
entifique Québécois," *Sociologie et sociétés* 7/2 (1975), pp. 89-114.

20. With respect to the creation of new social science disciplines at the Université de
Montréal, political science (1958), anthropology (1961), and criminology (1961)
were also established as departments in this period under the direction of social
sciences dean, Phillippe Garigue. For details about the establishment of demography see M. Fournier "Démographie comme discipline," *Sociologie et sociétés*
19/1 (1987), pp. 163-5.

21. Important academics, like Hubert Charbonneau and Jacques Legaré, and state
figures, like economist Yves Martin and PQ leader Jacques Parizeau and official
language commissioner, D'Iberville Fortier, received training at the Institut national d'études démographique in France. Some completed advanced degrees at the
University of Paris in cognate disciplines like geography or economics. The 1989
faculty numbered about 15, but it has no undergraduate majors. The following
section draws upon: the *Association des démographes du Québec - Bulletin*
(*ADQB*) and *Cahiers québécoises de démographie* (*CQD*) 1971-89; on demographer's presentations at the Commission Culturelle parliamentary hearings
(Quebec, *Débats... CC* 1984 and 1985); on Quebec, Commission de la culture,

Etude de l'impact...; as well as works cited.

22. *ADQB* No. 1 (1971).

23. *ADQB* No. 2 (1971) pp. 17, 3, 54.

24. *ADQB* No. 2 (1971) and No. 6 (1972) pp. 22-3.

25. J. Henripin, "Les études démographiques," *Recherches Sociographiques* 3/1-2 (1962); cf. M. Amyot, "L'utilisation de prévisions démographiques dans la prise des décisions," *CQD* 5/3 (1976) pp. 309-20.

26. *ADQB* 2/2 [no. special] (1973); 3/1 (1974); 3/2 (1974) p. 2. In "Commentaries sur le project de loi 22" the ADQ supported both the free choice of individuals as to language of education but overall restrictions on the number of places to be made available in English schools. *ADQB* 3/2 (1974) pp. 3-5.

27. *ADQB* 3 (1972).

28. *ADQB* 2/3 (1973) pp. 25-39.

29. *ADQB* 3/2 (1973) pp. 25-9.

30. Fournier, "Démographie comme discipline..." cited 24; Serge Sarazin, "La démographie au service de l'entreprise," *ADQB* 3/2 (1974) pp. 25-9 identifies one each at Bell Telephone and Hydro Quebec.

31. For sources of funding see *CQD* 5/3 (1976).

32. Carole Lalonde, in "La démographie au Quebec," *CQD* 9/1 (1980) pp. 7-26 confirms my interpretation that the sense of professional opportunity, mission and standards of the *dominant current* within the demographic profession (which did most of the historical work), were formed by the relation with the pronatalist INED. The pronatalist views attributed to "demographers" belong to this current. More critical, reflective views are held particularly by those working on population and development and, after 1988, on feminist critique.

33. "...to be a slave to facts. An intelligent slave to be sure, who selects, defines and approaches reality with a mental model." J. Henripin, "Démographie, théorie et idéologie," *CQD* 9/3 (1980), pp. 7-18.

34. Henripin & Lapierre-Adamcyk, *La fin de la revanche...* p. 10; George Mathews, *Le choc démographique: le déclin du Québec est-il inévitable* (Montréal: Boréal Express, 1984); Hubert Charbonneau & Robert Maheu, "Les aspects démographiques de la question linguistique," *Synthèse S3 (Rapport Gendron)* (1973), pp. 291-2.

35. Evelyne Lapierre-Adamcyk, "Adresse à la conférence du PLQ, Mont-Gabriel," reprinted in *Le Devoir* 23 août 1975. According to the preface, *La fin de la*

revanche des berceaux was "rushed" into publication — four years after the data was collected, but before it was completely analyzed. Henripin & Lapierre-Adamcyk *La fin de la revanche...* p. 10.

36. J. Henripin, "De la fécondite naturelle à le prévention des naissances: l'évolution démographique au Canada français depuis le XVII siècle," in M. Rioux and Y. Martin (eds.) *La Société Canadienne française* (Montreal: Hurtubise, 1971), pp. 215-226; Henripin & Lapierre-Adamcyk *La fin de la revanche...* p. 88. Henripin made this remark about the implications of birth rates below reproduction in an interview aired on the Montreal station of the public radio network, the CBC, in the context of a discussion of the state's introduction of pronatalist measures in 1988. cf. *Débats... CC* pp. 209-10.

37. In this functionalist funnel model, the dependent variable, fecundity, is seen as an outcome of a series of intermediate variables (spousal relation, family type) themselves influenced by variables at the macrosocial level (industrialisation, modernisation, religion, socioeconomic stratification).

38. "Besides, for most of the authors [i.e. demographers] reference to explanatory factors remains extremely limited, usually relegated to the end of the text. And these, nevertheless, are often ad hoc, steeped in the dominant framework of the moment, even when they occasionally refer to more precise conceptual frameworks." Victor Piché, "La démographie sociale au Québec: un premier bilan," *Sociologie et sociétés* 19/1 (1987), p. 13.

39. On women's response to clerical injunctions see J. Henripin & Yves Peron "L'Evolution démographique recente," *Annuaire du Quebec* 1972, pp. 201-18; and *idem* "La transition démographique" in H. Charbonneau (ed.), *La Population au Québec* (Montreal: PUM, 1973) p. 42; On women's adoption of new values see Henripin and Lapierre-Adamcyk, *La fin de la revanche...* p. 135; and Henripin, Huot, Lapierre-Adamcyk & Marcil-Gratton, *Les enfants qu'on n'a plus au Québec....* On women's wages as secondary income see *La fin de la revanche...* p. 75

40. Cf. Marianne Kempeneers critique of the asymmetrical use of the terms "life-cycle" and "career cycle" for men and women in "Quand la démographie s'interesse au travail des femmes...," *CQD* 14/2 (1985), pp. 147-165.

41. Lavigne, "Feminist reflections on the fertility of Quebecoises..."

42. Maroney, "Contemporary Quebec feminism..."

43. Payette, *Le Pouvoir? Connais pas!...*

44. This discursive positioning permitted reactionary and conservative forces to posi-

tion themselves close to family issues. See "Berets blancs," *La Presse* 5 octobre 1988; "Les solutions de la Société Saint-Jean-Baptiste" (i.e. to mobilize "families" against *"denatalité"*) *Le Soleil* 30 octobre 1988. Similarly, in a traditional clerical perspective, the Archbishop of Montreal saw low birth rates as a result of despair and resignation arising from materialism and individualism. See *Le Devoir* 7 octobre 1987.

45. Quebec, Commission de la culture, *Etude de l'impact...*

46. *Débats... CC* p. 155.

47. Contrast, for example, the Liberal Party's sponsorship of the first pro-feminist reform ending the legal incapacity of married women (Bill 16) with its profamily rhetoric in the elections of 1970, 1975, 1985; or the PQ's first and second terms.

48. A similar point is made in Marianne Kempeneers, "Questions sur les femmes et le travail: une lecture de la crise," *Sociologie et Société* 19/1 (1987), p. 288. See J. Henripin, "Textes référendaire: natalité, migrations et croissance démographique," (Report to the Parti liberal du Québec, Montreal, 1981); Henripin, Huot, Lapierre-Adamcyk & Marcil-Gratton, *Les enfants qu'on n'a plus au Quebec...*; Mathews, *Le choc démographique....*

49. *Débats... CC* p. 157.

50. *Ibid.*

51. For one of these two, I have no information, but the other, Gary Caldwell, was an active ADQ member.

52. *Débats... CC* pp. 210-16. Note here the impossibility of Popperian falsification, since we cannot know what the rate would have been without intervention. For a later critique of "blind" faith in pronatalist policy by a demographer working in France, see Hubert Gerard, "Possibilités et limites des politiques natalistes en Occident: Lieux d'action possibles et détermination de la fécondité," *CQD* 17/1 (1988), pp. 7-19.

53. *Débats... CC* pp. 142-4, 151, 159. Henripin had previously been criticized for overestimating abortions. *Le Jour* 11 août 1975.

54. *Débats... CC* pp. 145-6, 159.

55. *Débats... CC* pp. 136, 138, and *passim*. Commentators as diverse as M. Barrett & M. McIntosh, *The anti-social family* (London: NLB, 1982) and Margrit Eichler, *Non-sexist research methods: a practical guide* (Boston: Unwin Hyman, 1988), pp. 114-8, point to the sexism behind such familist eradications of women's existence. Contrast Maria Mies, "Towards a Methodology for

Feminist Research," in Gloria Bowles & Renate Duehli-Klein (eds.), *Theories of Women's Studies* (London: Routledge, 1983) on action research.

56. For criticism of the child tax credit scheme see *Le Devoir* 6 mars 1991. On the lack of women's participation cf. Jocelyne Richer, "Tant qu'il y'aura des enfants," *La Gazette des femmes* 12/6 (mars/avril 1991), pp. 11-18.

57. On childcare see Granger, "Réflexion sur les enjeux sociaux de la politique Québécoises...," pp. 73-81; and Damaris Rose, "Day care provision in Quebec," (Unpublished paper, Sociology Department, Carleton University, 1990). On the double day see Celine Le Bourdais, Pierre J. Hamel & Paul Bernard, "Le travail et l'ouvrage: charge et partage des tâches domestiques chez les couples québécois," *Sociologie et sociétés* 19/1 (1987); and *Le soleil* 2 octobre 1988.

58. Conseil de la famille president Maurice Champagne so argued in a speech to the Union international des organisations familiaux in Paris. Reprinted in *Le Devoir* 12 décembre 1987.

59. "...to exist outside of motherhood but also to be able to fully profit from it." From "'La Dénatalité' un débat stérile?," Notes pour l'allocution prononcée par la ministre déléguée à la condition féminine à l'occasion du forum régional organisé par la conférence des CLSC de l'Estrie, Sherbrooke, 8 octobre 1988.

60. Present from the beginning in the form of divisions between white and black women activists in the USA [Alice Echols, *Daring to be bad: feminism radical in America, 1967-1975* (Minneapolis: Univ. Minnesota Press, 1989)], this issue has become central to feminist politics in the last 10 years. See *Feminist Review* Nos. 17 (1984) & 20 (1985); bell hooks, *Feminist theory: from margin to centre* (Boston: South End, 1984); Daiva Stasiulis, "'Authentic Voice': Anti-racist Politics in Canadian Feminist Publishing and Literary Production," S. Gunew & A. Yeatsman (eds.), *Feminism and the politics of difference* (Sydney: Allen & Unwin, forthcoming, Jan. 1993); and conflicts at the annual general meetings of the (Canadian) National Action Committee on the Status of Women. See NAC, *AGM Minutes* 1989, 1990, 1991. According to a wide range of participants interviewed at Un Québec féminin pluriel, Forum National des Femmes, Montreal, 29-31 mai 1992 (organized by the Fédération des femmes du Québec, and representatives from women's groups, community organizations, and the unions) this conference marked, despite continuing political differences, real progress in developing a women's movement capable of representing Quebec's ethnic diversity.

61. Renée Dandurand, "Un politique familiale: enjeux et débats," *Recherches Sociographiques* 28/2&3 (1987).

62. Rosalind Pollack Petchesky, *Abortion and woman's choice: The state, sexuality and reproductive freedom* (Boston: Northeastern Univ. Press, 1985); and Lynda Lange "Feminism and political choice: reproductive labour and the tension between collectivism, cultural nationalism and individualism," *Resources for Feminist Research/Documentation sur la rechereche feministe* 16/3 (1987).

63. Lange, "Feminism and political choice...," p. 40.

CHAPTER 11

SOCIALIST FEMINISM: FROM THE STANDPOINT OF PRACTICE

LINDA BRISKIN

INTRODUCTION

Women's organizing in Canada in the last twenty years has netted some significant gains. Perhaps the 1988 Supreme Court decision declaring the abortion law unconstitutional is the most striking, but a balance sheet would also include other legislative gains in the areas of equal pay, affirmative action, sexual assault, family law and sexual harassment. Increases in women's union activism and the concomitant change in union ideology have begun to reshape the labour movement. Changes in state practices concerning spousal relations and police intervention in cases of wife abuse, in educational practices surrounding sex role stereotypes and career counselling, in cultural and media practices with respect to the images of women — all combine to highlight the reconstitution of the sex/gender reality.

Despite these successes, women continue to confront attacks on these gains from the new right, conservative economic policies, the feminization of poverty, inequality in wages and job opportunities, escalating family and street violence, expansion of the pornography industry, and resistance to change embedded in the structures of unions and political parties. This list is far from complete. Furthermore, continuing public discomfort with 'feminism', and, more importantly, the on-going invisibility of the more radical vision of women's liberation, calling for major social and economic transformation, reminds us of the distance yet to be travelled.

Lynne Segal in *Is the Future Female?* identifies a growing pessimism among British feminists about the possibilities of making change, a pessimism fuelled both by the limited gains of the last twenty years, and the fragmentation of the women's movement.[1] This pessimism has resulted in a tendency to seek a recreated sisterhood based on "the timeless truths of women's lives,"[2] and in a strategic orientation away from, economic and social change. The presence of a reconstituted radical or cultural feminism, although not as sharply felt in Canada given the hegemony of liberal feminism, is nonetheless part of what socialist feminists confront in our struggle to make change.

In this context, for the more radical vision of women's liberation to be strengthened, socialist feminism must emerge as a named politic in the public consciousness. As part of this process, we need a better understanding of the politics of socialist feminism, its unique strategic contribution and the organizational dilemmas it faces. This article makes a contribution to developing this clarity. The first part examines the categories through which the variety of feminisms have traditionally been explored — the political currents and the politics of identity — and both their contribution to, and limitations in, assessing and developing political strategy. The second part introduces a model of feminist practice situated within the activist map of the women's movement. Such a model uncovers the difficulties faced by feminists and identifies the potential resolution that is embedded in socialist feminism. The final section uses the model of feminist practice to highlight the organizational dilemmas that face socialist feminists in the Canadian context.

DIFFERENTIATING BETWEEN FEMINISMS

Feminism is not a unitary discourse or a unitary practice. Feminist theorists and activists generally distinguish between feminisms on the basis of long standing political traditions, out of which emerge what are often called the currents of feminism: liberal feminism, radical feminism and socialist feminism. Although internationally these particular terms are not used consistently, feminists have categorized feminisms in similar ways. Increasingly, feminists are also identifying themselves through what might be called the "politics of identity": for instance as a woman of colour, or a Jewish lesbian.[3] Both of these approaches have been significant to the development of feminism; each reflects, however, a weakness in our theorizing of feminist practice.

Organizing our understanding of feminisms through the political currents has been quite useful. Alison Jaggar's *Feminist Politics and Human Nature* has made an important contribution to this discussion in North America.[4] Jaggar systematically locates the roots of contemporary currents of feminism inside of the mainstream political traditions. In so doing, she reveals the underlying assumptions about human nature and about the possibilities for change that are embedded in different feminisms.

Understanding feminism through the categories of the currents, however, is not unproblematic. In the first place, such an approach reifies these categories, implying a rigid separation between them and suggesting an internal coherency to each, which, in fact, is only possible at fairly abstract levels of analysis. It also suggests that each current has a clear institutional base and a practice that can be clearly differentiated from the other.[5]

The sharp-edged clarity possible at an abstract level of analysis often becomes opaque when confronted by the complexities of daily political activity. Decisions to plan a demonstration, to build a certain alliance, to argue for a specific demand rarely emerge directly from theoretical constructs. In the 'real' world of politics, socialist feminists may disagree with each other as often as they agree, both in theory and in practice, though all feminists certainly agree more than they disagree (sometimes our rancorous interactions make this difficult to remember). Not only do all feminists agree about many basic demands for women, they also actively organize together and build alliances. Analyzing feminisms through the categories of the currents obscures this process of joint political struggle for women's liberation. In practice, then, the threads and currents of feminism blur, as it shifts and adapts to concrete political conditions. In practice, there are complex patterns of alliances and coalitions. It is not surprising that practice conforms to theoretical distinctions only to a degree. In contrast to a self-identification based on political currents, feminists have increasingly been defining themselves with reference to race, ethnicity and sexual orientation, and/or particular experiences such as being on family benefits, for example, as a black single mother. This practice must be examined in relation to a central dilemma of feminist practice: dealing with 'difference'.

The compelling notion of sisterhood — a key component of early feminist ideology — conceptualized woman as a unitary category of analysis around which a somewhat unitary practice could be organized. The inadequacy of this approach rapidly became apparent as the women's movement grew. Through struggle socialist feminists, in particular, have come to recognize the importance of building sisterhood on the basis of difference — in class, race, ethnicity and sexual orientation. Deconstructing the category of woman through the understanding of difference has inspired a more diverse, responsive and complex feminist practice and created the theoretical space for the articulation of a more differentiated feminist politics.

Despite the importance of the 'discovery' of difference, this approach intersects problematically with an over-emphasis on 'experience' inside the women's movement — an emphasis which has been mediated ideologically through the concept the 'personal is political'.[6] The 'personal is political' challenges the public/private split as well as the overvaluation of the rational and concomitant devaluation of the affective; it validates experience over expertise and, at the same time, de-personalizes/politicizes women's experience; and it provides the basis for a coherent analytical and strategic approach to women's oppression. However liberating, it has often been transformed into an overarching validation of personal experience which in turn has translated into both a competitive hierarchy of oppressions and an opposition to any kind of 'theory'.

An anti-theory emphasis on personal experience can individualize difference (each experience as unique) to such a degree that the deep rooted processes by which experience is socially constructed are concealed. As a result, the complex patterning of women's experiences of class, race, gender, and sexual orientation is masked; even the interconnectedness between different aspects of an individual woman's experience (for example, the links between household and workplace), can be made less accessible, thus exacerbating the fragmentation of everyday life within patriarchal capitalism. On the one hand, this tendency to anti-intellectualism and anti-theory in the women's movement, which accompanies the emphasis on experience, promotes individualism. On the other, it promotes the identification of women, not with reason, but with nature. Both of these are part of the ideology of patriarchal capitalism.

The overemphasis on the personal in the personal/political dialectic also intersects with the politics of identity to establish an exclusionary set of identifications which becomes a competitive hierarchy of oppressions. The strategic positions which flow from this are not unproblematic. For implicit in the operation of the politics of identity is the assumption that a political strategy and, indeed, often political 'correctness' flow directly from identity. In practice, this can conceal political differences, between lesbians, for example, and, at the same time, overemphasize differences, between lesbians and heterosexual women, for example. The politics of identity often interfere with open strategic debate, lead to moralism, and to the elaboration of a hierarchy of oppressions. The competitive identification of certain oppressions as more salient than others promotes bonding on the basis of shared victimization, and exclusion organized around guilt, both of which undermine the possibility of political alliance between feminists.[7]

Lynne Segal raises some similar concerns about the emphasis on experience inside the women's movement:

> Women's liberation has always stressed that women use their own feelings, experiences and perceptions to make their analyses.... It was necessary if we were to throw off the mythology of male 'expertise'.... It became a weakness when the emergence of differences and conflicts between women not only produced enormous distress but became immobilising. Either it silenced those who felt guilty for being articulate and privileged or it encouraged the defensive re-assertion of some common oppression, like the experience of male violence.... Within the women's movement the validation of personal experience and talk of 'common oppression' often hides straightforward ignorance of the lives of other women and of the factors beyond gender which determine women's lives.... So resentment and mistrust would seem to be eternal and inevitable features of feminism were we not able to move beyond individual experience.[8]

Both the movement from a unitary category of woman through the 'discovery' of difference and from a unitary category of feminism through the elaboration of political currents have been important in the development of the politics and practice of contemporary feminisms. However each, in itself, is inadequate in an exploration of the complexities of feminist practice.

This suggests the need for an additional framework for understanding feminisms that is situated more concretely within the activist map of the women's movement and which theorizes feminism from its practice. We need to analyze the complexities of feminism from the *standpoint of practice* as a counterpoint both to the *standpoint of theory* (generated by the model of political currents) and also to the *standpoint of experience* (within which the politics of identity can be situated). The concept of the 'standpoint of practice' which I develop in the remainder of this paper is not unproblematic since there can be many forms of practice: moral practices, sexual practices, personal practices etc. Perhaps it would be more accurate to refer to the 'standpoint of *strategic* practice' in order to highlight, in particular, its collective character and to distinguish it further from the standpoint of experience which is often understood in personal, individualistic ways.

Although this paper will focus on the standpoint of practice, it is worth emphasizing that an analysis of feminisms and the women's movement must weave together all three standpoints: theory, experience and practice. That the principles of socialist feminism, for example, do not provide a step-by-step blueprint for practical struggle, and in fact, often blur in the context of real political struggle does not mean that these principles are useless or only of concern to those who debate esoteric issues. On the contrary these principles establish a framework and a context from which to approach daily politics and within which to situate the myriad of issues, details and decisions which often threaten to overwhelm feminist activists. Nor am I suggesting that the understanding of difference, the validation of experience and the importance of shared identifications are unimportant — just that they are insufficient to understand the nature of feminist practice and to strategize about future directions.

To theorize from practice we begin not by distinguishing the currents or identities from one another but by recognizing feminist practice as an intersecting whole. This recognizes the impact that dispersed and diverse forms of feminist practice have on one another, and also highlights the fact that, despite local realities, Canadian feminist practice operates within a common socio-political, economic and ideological context.

A MODEL OF FEMINIST PRACTICE

A model of feminist practice which is more firmly situated within, and emerges from, activist feminist experience allows us to highlight a central dilemma of feminist practice, and is suggestive of a new strategic orientation. All feminist practice struggles with two poles of attraction — disengagement and mainstreaming. Disengagement which operates from a critique of the system and a standpoint outside of it, and from a desire, therefore, to create alternative structures and ideologies, can provide a vision of social transformation. Mainstreaming operates from a desire to reach out to the majority of the population with popular and practical feminist solutions to particular issues, and therefore relates directly to, and interacts with, major social institutions, such as the family, the work place, the educational system and the state.

To some extent these poles of attraction present a tension common to many political situations; however, each also contains certain uniquely feminist aspects.[9] The motivation for a standpoint of disengagement rests on the historically specific analysis of the patriarchal character of social institutions and the overwhelming evidence of women's exclusion from power in the public arena. It also draws on an alternative view of institutional mechanisms which is often referred to as 'feminist process'. Implicit in mainstreaming is the feminist commitment to transforming the everyday lives of women. This challenges the public/private split, and conventional notions of agents of change, and draws on the ideology of 'the personal is political'.

Both mainstreaming and disengagement are necessary to the feminist vision. The goal for feminist practice is the maintenance of an effective tension between the two; the dilemma is the tendency for feminist practice to be pulled towards one or other pole. This dilemma is complicated by the fact that each of these poles carries with it a strategic risk. Disengagement can easily lead to marginalization and invisibility; mainstreaming to co-optation and institutionalization. These strategic risks can be countered by an integrative politics which creates a bridge between disengagement and mainstreaming.

The building of alternatives is one of the concrete expressions of disengagement in the women's movement, one which too frequently suffers from marginalization. Charlotte Bunch makes the point that "alternative institutions should not be havens of retreat, but challenges that weaken male power over our lives."[10] Yet the socio-political and personal conditions of patriarchal capitalism, the lack of resources available to the women's movement, combined with an overemphasis on the 'personal' as a political strategy most often limit the possibilities of alternatives — in living arrangements, co-operatives and collectives, and in business ventures. In the best of circumstances, they provide safer personal spaces for a few women; rarely are they effective as political strategies.[11]

But even as personal havens, alternatives suffer from serious limitations. The difficulty of establishing any social/political/economic space outside of patriarchal capitalism means that feminist alternative organizations often are forced to reproduce the very norms they have set out to reject, just in order to survive. This has been well-documented in relation to feminist co-operatives, businesses and in particular in assessing the impact on feminist organizations of the funding practices of the state.[12] Feminist alternatives then are not able necessarily to provide a lived experience or a prefigurative vision of social transformation.

Further the distinctly 'feminist process' which emerges in part from an organizational elaboration of the 'personal is political' and which is seen to distinguish feminist alternatives from traditional organizations has, more often than not, been unsuccessful. Notwithstanding the accuracy of the feminist critique of the patriarchal and hierarchical functioning of institutions, nevertheless feminists have faced serious difficulties in developing alternatives.

Feminist process has suffered from a peculiar counterposition and defense of *personal* over political experience and a paradoxically *abstract* characterization (and rejection) of leadership, voting, organizational structures etc. as male and patriarchal by definition. Both lead to a depoliticization of feminist organizational strategies, one result of which is that process becomes separated from political analysis, particular strategies and an identifiable set of organizational norms; further process becomes a mechanism of exclusion. The internalized, personal, and often unarticulated character of the norms and practices of feminist alternatives make them inaccessible and uncomfortable to women on the outside. This process of exclusion reinforces a politics of isolation and exacerbates the potential for marginalization inherent in disengagement.

In this regard, it has been fascinating and perhaps discouraging to witness the use and misuse of 'feminist process' at the 1988 annual general meeting of the National Action Committee on the Status of Women (NAC). At this meeting political and strategic differences over the relative importance and nature of an organizational review provoked a divisive and highly charged debate during which feminist process as an ideology and as a practice were invoked. An analysis of the events suggests that feminist process was presented both as a reflection of a homogeneous 'woman experience' and as an alternative to politics, seen by definition as patriarchal. Miriam Jones and Jennifer Stephens in their assessment of that meeting said:

> In the discussions which circulated at NAC and since, this process is referred to as though it is apolitical in construction, an appeal to neutrality and homogeneity which is intricately linked to the notion of a unified 'sisterhood'.[13]

Despite the difficulty of developing a 'feminist process', the struggle to articulate alternatives to traditional practices needs to continue; yet at the same time we need to beware of a feminist process too deeply disengaged from concrete political practice.

Alternatives have not been an effective political strategy for making change largely because they have most often operated as a strategy of disengagement, unmediated by a degree of mainstreaming. Although this is often the result of conditions outside the control of feminists, an uncritical acceptance of the strategy of alternatives or an unelaborated political understanding of their role within the feminist community are also important contributing factors. The degree of disengagement embedded in alternatives means they are easily marginalized, creating a distance from the larger constituency of women and thereby increasing the inaccessibility and invisibility of the women's movement.

This is not to underestimate the importance to feminists of alternative ways of living our lives. For many of us these have provided support which is fundamental to our ability to sustain struggle as feminists in the work place, or within our relationships and even inside the women's movement itself. In this sense, such alternatives have contributed to building the women's movement. Yet however much they may improve the quality of our personal lives, this form of disengagement has not represented a viable political strategy. Space does not permit a detailed exploration of other forms of disengagement, but many exist. For example, the focus on theoretical development amongst socialist feminists in the United States and England is a form of disengagement which has exacted a high price given the degree to which it marginalizes and makes inaccessible socialist feminism. Of course the focus on theory may be the result rather than the cause of this marginalization.

Mainstreaming is also not unproblematic. Reaching out to the majority of women with popular and practical feminist solutions to concrete problems means engaging with mainstream institutions: the family, the work place, and in particular the state and government. Engagement with mainstream institutions often leads to co-optation and institutionalization.

The forms of organization inside patriarchal capitalist institutions such as the state and the school system are hierarchic and bureaucratic. They tend to be inflexible, reinforce patterns of uniformity, regulate and neutralize dissent and difference, and by definition, limit any substantive challenge to their goals and practices. It is difficult for feminists to confront these goals and practices from inside these institutions, in part because of their isolation, and in part because of the power of these practices to subvert the challenge.[14] The process of institutionalization often means that we lose sight of our larger goals of radical social transformation.[15]

Institutionalization does not, however, render an issue invisible. Once taken up — by the state, for example — the issue is reshaped and reconstituted, its continuing public presence creating a new, and sometimes more difficult, task for feminists. For example, in 1987 the Ontario government finally passed Bill 154, a watered-down form of equal value legislation. With the law on the books and the long term process of implementation underway, it seems almost overdetermined that feminist participation in the process will take a consultative and easily co-opted form. Maintaining a degree of disengagement is increasingly complicated as mainstreaming produces institutionalization. Yet participating in that implementation process as well as mounting a serious critique of, and mobilization around, the legislation will be significant in determining its long term impact on women workers. Institutionalization does not eliminate the possibilities of feminist agency (although feminists have often felt very disempowered by that process), but rather reconstitutes the task.

Understanding the tension between institutionalization and mainstreaming reveals, rather than conceals, our political task. For, despite the tendency toward institutionalization and co-optation, a central task, in particular for socialist feminists, is to engage with, indeed transform, mainstream institutions. An over-emphasis on the danger of institutionalization can lead to an over-valuation of strategies of disengagement.

The map of practice therefore is shaped by the pulls of disengagement and mainstreaming, and by the dilemmas posed by each: marginalization and invisibility on the one hand and co-optation and institutionalization on the other. The task for feminists is to maintain a complex strategic interplay between disengagement and mainstreaming.

This model of practice can illuminate the dynamic of particular feminist struggles. Carla Lipsig-Mummé assessed the contribution of feminist strategies to the Montreal garment workers strike in 1983.[16] In her description, she gives a striking example of the necessity to maintain a balance between disengagement and mainstreaming. In 1980 semi-skilled women operators set up the multi-ethnic Action Committee for Garment Workers (CATV). This committee was influenced by feminism and Quebec left wing socialism. In Lipsig-Mummé's words, it "crystallized a deep-seated rejection of the patriarchal aspirations of typical union elites" and was "profoundly anti-bureaucratic." It focused its energies largely on four tasks:

> first, informing and educating the members as widely as
> possible; second, using whatever formal protections existed
> in the contract as militantly as possible; third, exposing the
> collaboration and cynicism of the union leadership; and
> fourth, raising...the deeper, harder issues about homework
> and the future of the garment industry.[17]

It operated from a politics of disengagement in its critique and a politics of mainstreaming in its focus on the particular problems facing women workers on the shop floor. Lipsig-Mummé details many successes of the CATV which I would attribute in part to the delicate balance that was maintained between disengagement and mainstreaming.

During the strike, however, as a result of their fear of institutionalization, the informal feminist leaders of the garment workers (from the CATV) disengaged too deeply and were marginalized. They ran the strikes' daycare centre and "refused any formal responsibilities in organizing the strike."

> ...it was feared that even partial power would corrupt
> absolutely, would transform feminists into 'apparatchiks'
> and grind them up in the union machine.[18]

Lipsig-Mummé attributes the loss of the strike in large part to their refusal to continue to play a leadership role and points out that the contract was "the worst...signed in Quebec since the 1950s."

The 1917 cost of living protests in New York City, described in Dana Franks excellent piece "Housewives, Socialists and the Politics of Food," suggests that this model of political practice can be used to explore strategic dilemmas outside of explicitly feminist organizing situations.[19] Immigrant Jewish women organized violent street protests and food boycotts in response to spiralling food costs. Their purpose was very practical: to lower the cost of food. They acted from the context of the traditional sexual division of labour which gave them responsibility for the provision of food and for engagement with the market place. We could characterize their strategy as mainstreaming — the search for practical solutions. In fact, they explicitly rejected the political character of the struggle. Frank argues that the women's analysis was "neither abstract nor structural."[20] *The New York American* reported:

> But those speakers who talked plain potatoes, onions,
> milk, bread, eggs and butter were wildly applauded. It was
> for that they [the women demonstrators] had come, and
> not, as one woman screamed: 'To —— with politics; give us
> enough to eat.'[21]

In part this woman was reacting to the interventions of the Socialist Party in the boycott. In sharp contrast to the approach of the community women, the Socialist Party attempted to situate rising food prices in the larger context of war profiteering.

> [They] sought to define appropriate socialist solutions to
> the crisis. The party's primary demand... was that the city,
> state, and federal governments should reconstruct the
> country's food distribution centres, which would eliminate
> private intermediaries and thus profits on food.[22]

It was only in response to the militancy of the community women — on second thought, so to speak — that the socialists introduced a second demand: "immediate purchase and sale of food by the government at cost."[23] But as described by Frank, much of the work of the socialists centred on the larger propagandistic issues — a strategy of disengagement — and they were never able to make effective links with the community protest.

Although Frank indicates that it is not entirely clear why the boycott ended, the prices did drop somewhat, the women did resume buying and we assume that they returned to the more private world of family. Readers are impressed by the organization and collectivity of the Jewish women; in the final analysis, however, we are left with the question of how to harness the explosive energy of these women to the large-scale struggle for social and political transformation, that is, to combine their mainstreaming strategy with a greater degree of disengagement. The Socialist Party was ultimately unsuccessful in this task. Its strategy of disengagement unmediated by effective mainstreaming partially explains the inability to recruit the women to a larger struggle.

A third rather dramatic example of the tension around mainstreaming and disengagement can be found in the recent history of the Service Office and Retail Workers Union of Canada (SORWUC), an independent and explicitly feminist union, committed to organizing women workers in what have been seen as unorganizable sectors, like the banks.[24] In the first instance, SORWUC was extremely successful; it managed to organize 23 bank branches (although not all were certified) and win a Canadian Labour Relations Board (CLRB) decision that overturned a 1959 ruling against branch by branch organizing. In the language of this article, I would suggest that this success was rooted in the disengaged stance of SORWUC's organizing strategy and in its vision of more democratic unions based on feminist principles. But the degree of disengagement was too extensive; SORWUC failed to develop an effective negotiating relation with either the employers or the Canadian Labour Congress. Few of their organized locals were able to negotiate first contracts.

In the first place it is very important to recognize the powerful forces arrayed against their success — in the banks, in the unions and in the labour law itself. Rosemary Warskett documents, for example, the devastating impact of the legal certification framework of the Canada Labour Code.[25] Yet it is equally important to assess the role SORWUC's own decisions played in their marginalization and defeat. Maureen FitzGerald's conclusion that "an opportunity was lost when the decision was made to keep the UBW [United Bank Workers-SORWUC] out of the CLC [Canadian Labour Congress]," is significant.[26] Entering the CLC would certainly have threatened the degree of disengagement with which SORWUC was operating but it also might have afforded the protection available from a mainstream institution. The model of feminist practice helps make some sense of the tensions faced by SORWUC, in particular the difficulty of maintaining an effective balance between mainstreaming and disengagement.

These applications of the model of feminist practice demonstrate an alternative to using the construct of political currents to explore feminism and strategic possibilities. It is also the case, however, that each current of feminism relates to the poles of disengagement and mainstreaming somewhat differently — a relation mediated by the understanding of what kind of change is possible and necessary, and of how change occurs. Radical feminism's tendency to identify, in a transhistorical way, all social institutions with 'the patriarchy' pushes it toward a politics of disengagement unmediated by mainstreaming. This often leads to marginalization and isolation. Liberal feminism's tendency to enter into social institutions with the most limited degree of disengagement and to focus on remedial measures explains its susceptibility to institutionalization.

Socialist feminism is caught in a contradiction. Its politics pulls it simultaneously toward both poles of practice — mainstreaming and disengagement; this sets up, dialectically, both a recurring strategic dilemma, as well as a potential solution to the dilemma of feminist practice — maintaining a tension between these poles.

Socialist feminist politics is based on a radical critique of the entire society, in particular of existing institutions, ideological practices and the complex relations of power expressed through class, gender, race and sexual orientation. In its opposition to the dominant ideology and institutions, it stands apart from the consciousness of the majority. Socialist feminism is informed by a vision of fundamental transformation and by a desire to replace patriarchal capitalism. As such, socialist feminism is pulled toward the pole of disengagement.

At the same time, however, socialist feminism is pulled toward mainstreaming. For a presupposition of its politics is that such a reconstitution of the dominant ideology and social practices depends upon a *public* consensus about and commitment to a new social vision, and the active support and participation of a significant layer of the population in a mass political movement. Socialist feminists recognize that they cannot organize such a mass movement entirely through the politics of disengagement because of the risks of marginalization. The socialist feminist task, then, is to take its perspective, which fundamentally challenges mainstream institutions and ideology, into those very institutions and out to the public consciousness.

This tension between disengagement and mainstreaming poses a dilemma for socialist feminists, and in practice, often appears irreconcilable. Mainstreaming often leads to institutionalization which may cause socialist feminists to limit the vision of the change they seek, but disengagement may take the form of marginalization which results in an inability to mobilize the large numbers necessary to effect the kind of change desired. Socialist feminist practice must constantly struggle to combine and resolve the contradictions of mainstreaming and disengagement.

Each current of feminism situates itself in a different location on this map of feminist practice; in essence each evaluates the options for change differently. However, all feminist practice risks institutionalization by organizing for change, and involves a degree of disengagement by definition. The relation of the currents to the poles of attraction is more a matter of degree than a rigid separation.

It is worth emphasizing that what is most important about this model of feminist practice is not simply the additional insight it supplies into the nature of the feminist currents. This model facilitates the understanding of tactical decisions which may not conform to, or even arise from, abstract ideological principle. It allows us to see the flexibility, mobility and fluidity of feminist political practice; it recognizes that tactical political choices made on a daily basis reflect not only the set of abstract principles which inform feminist currents but also particular historical and conjunctural factors. The map of feminist practice is not shaped within the same parameters as the map of abstract theoretical principle.

The standpoint of practice not only enriches our understanding of the feminist currents but also suggests a way of avoiding a strategic and analytic dependence on them. It helps us to focus on the common feminist dilemma — the necessity to bridge these poles of attraction — and allows us to assess strategic choices in terms of their ability to build that bridge.

Despite what I see to be the usefulness of this framework, there is a danger inherent in this kind of 'model building'. What tends to get lost is the degree to which the choices of feminist practice are constrained and shaped by political, economic and social conditions: the nature of public consciousness, the level of development of the women's movement and other progressive movements, the degree of state repressiveness, the state of the economy etc. I am not suggesting that all strategic choices are available to feminists in any particular instance. The specific conditions we face greatly limit the options. Nevertheless this framework can help us to understand some of the tensions and contradictions of the choices we do make.

Having made this point I think it is equally important to stress the other side of the dialectic — agency. In emphasizing the degree to which the political and historical conjuncture shapes our choices, we often lose sight of the very premise of a feminist politics — a belief in our ability to make change. For socialist feminists, this agency is exercised through collective action. Increasing the level of self consciousness about socialist feminist practice should make strategic and tactical choices more effective in the long term.

SOCIALIST FEMINISM AND
ISSUES OF ORGANIZATION

The model of feminist practice outlined above can illuminate the difficulties and dilemmas of building socialist feminist organizations in Canada. Socialist feminism has been part of the autonomous women's movement as a named politic since the beginning of the second wave of the women's movement in Canada. In the Introduction to *Women Unite*, one of the first Canadian anthologies about women,[27] the editors state that

> Canadian women more uniformly developed an analysis of
> their oppression based on a class notion of society...the
> marxist perspective has since been central to the develop-
> ment of the Canadian women's liberation movement.[28]

In 1987 Mariana Valverde confirmed that assessment:

> In the unions, in the New Democratic Party (the social
> democrats), in the reproductive rights movement, in the
> area of culture and sexual politics, even in the mainstream
> of women's coalition (the National Action Committee), left
> feminism is a formidable force.[29]

Socialist feminism has always had a practice; it is not overly identified with the academy; it is not seen to be on the decline; and in fact socialist feminist politics have been influential in shaping the politics and practice of other currents of Canadian feminism.

Canadian socialist feminism has had an extensive and fertile ground on which to take root. Perhaps this explains the comparative importance and strength of socialist feminist theory and practice in Canada. In other countries socialist feminism has been connected to organized left or labour party formations, or to the academy to a far greater degree. In countries where there are large parliamentary communist, socialist or labour parties, socialist feminism has been forced to contend with clarifying its organizational, ideological and strategic relationship to them. These discussions and negotiations have often dominated the discourse of socialist feminism and contributed to its low profile inside the autonomous women's movement.[30] In contrast Lorna Weir, a Canadian socialist feminist, argues that

> sexual politics, the struggle for abortion access, and the day care movement are terrains of socialist feminist activism which extend far beyond an abstract notion of a minority of socialist feminists launching 'class intervention' in a pre-existing women's movement. In Canada today, socialist feminists are not simply 'intervening' but actually helping to define and create significant sectors of the women's movement.[31]

It is also the case that socialist feminism has often been overly identified with the academy, rather than the activist women's movement. For example, in a recent series of articles on American socialist feminism in *Socialist Review* which raised the question: 'Has socialist feminism died?', Barbara Epstein concludes pessimistically that

> socialist feminist theory has been narrowed and hobbled by academic environs; its been shaped to the demands of academia, and its been cut off from any kind of movement.[32]

Weir draws a similar conclusion:

> Travelling in England and the United States, Canadian socialist feminists have often been very surprised to discover the strongly academic and weakly activist formation of socialist feminism in these countries. The element of surprise arises from an assumption that the large quantities of English and American socialist feminist literature, which we in Canada consume, emanate (somehow) from vast sys-

tems of socialist feminist political mobilizing. Within
Canada, socialist feminists have an ongoing history of participation in popular movements, particularly the women's
movement, while comparatively few socialist feminists hold
academic positions.[33]

Despite the strong presence of Canadian socialist feminism in the women's
movement, it does not have a high profile, if any, in the public consciousness.
The reasons for this are complex but relate in part to the tendency of the
dominant ideology to picture feminism, particularly through the media, as a
unitary system; in fact, to equate feminism with liberal feminism. It is also due
to the strategic complexities of building socialist feminist organizations.[34] So
on the one hand, the Canadian context provides the opportunity for a variety
of socialist feminist organizational options to emerge; on the other hand,
socialist feminism lacks a public profile — a serious problem given the socialist
feminist political task.

Socialist feminism is pulled simultaneously in the direction of mainstreaming and disengagement and, therefore, socialist feminist practice can suffer
from both marginalization and institutionalization. It is this unique pattern that
helps explain the difficulties encountered building explicitly socialist feminist
organizations, which must accommodate both the 'inside' and the 'outside'
dimensions of the socialist feminist task. Socialist feminism faces three dilemmas in building organizations which emerge directly out of the politics and
practice of socialist feminism.

First, the concomitant pulls of disengagement and mainstreaming create a
dilemma about what kinds of organizations are appropriate. Disengagement
suggests the building of specifically socialist feminist organizations. This might
take the form of socialist feminist political organizations, such as the
International Women's Day Committee of Toronto, or Bread and Roses of
Vancouver, or a feminist trade union such as SORWUC. Mainstreaming suggests entering into, or creating parallel-style mainstream organizations. This
may take the form of organizing a women's caucus or committee inside a
mainstream institution like a trade union or in setting up organizations around
single issues such as daycare. Inside an organization like the Toronto-based
Action Daycare, for example, socialist feminists, often unnamed as such, fight
for better daycare.

Although these choices are not necessarily mutually exclusive, it is difficult
to sustain both strategies at once. And when the choice is to disengage and
build alternative organizations, it is often the case that such organizations are

marginalized. SORWUC provides a clear and somewhat painful example of this process. If the choice is to mainstream, co-optation and institutionalization often occur. The problems faced by trade union women's committees in sustaining their challenge to the goals and practices of unions demonstrate this process.[35] Despite the power of this dilemma, socialist feminists have had some successes in bridging the gap. For example, activists in the Ontario Coalition for Abortion Clinics (OCAC), who self identify as socialist feminists, explicitly attribute their success in establishing free-standing abortion clinics in Toronto to a strategy which combines what I have called mainstreaming and disengagement.[36]

> OCAC has tried to develop a strategy that works at two levels simultaneously: transforming immediate conditions, and building a consciousness and movement that could transcend the existing oppressive relations of reproduction. We have tried to pose the argument for clinics in this double way. The existing free-standing clinics have been indispensable in providing desperately needed services to thousands of women, in dramatizing daily how unfair and unworkable the existing law is, and in showing the solution in the most concrete and immediate fashion possible. At the same time, clinics can be posed as a model for the future: centres providing care for the full spectrum of women's reproductive lives.... Having a clear and attractive vision of ultimate goals is very important, not so much as a blueprint for the future, but as an understandable and realizable alternative that can seize peoples imagination and enthusiasm in the present.[37]

Second, the centrality of 'difference' to socialist feminist politics and practice creates some contradictions around the building of socialist feminist organizations. A politics of building sisterhood on the basis of difference is expressed organizationally in the women's movement, not through large homogeneous political organizations, but rather through alliances and coalitions.

Inside feminist coalitions, socialist feminists are torn between two political tasks: the need for a broadly-based mass movement (mainstream) and the need to win women to a socialist feminist vision (disengagement). The first goal lends itself to the building of alliances constructed on a limited basis of unity which would appeal to the widest audience but which would not offer much opportunity to highlight socialist feminism; the second suggests an explicit focus on building a socialist feminist organization or current — that is, attempting to win women to a socialist feminist perspective. The former functions in a politically heterogeneous environment; the latter aims toward a degree of homogeneity and is, by definition, threatening to the coalition process.[38] Perhaps one of the most interesting examples of the struggle to work out the tension between coalition building and the ideological and organizational propagation of socialist feminism lies in the history of IWDC and the March 8th Coalition in Toronto.[39]

Finally the socialist feminist belief in the necessity for a fundamental social transformation that challenges not only gender relations but also the relations of class, race and sexual orientation implies a commitment to the building of a mass heterogeneous political movement that reaches far beyond even the widest boundaries of the women's movement. This means alliances with organizations outside the women's movement, such as trade unions and progressive community groups who organize around peace, anti-intervention, environmental issues and if they exist, parliamentary and extra-parliamentary socialist and communist parties. In all these cases this means organizing with men and thereby raises complex questions about the relation between the building of such alliances and autonomous feminist organizing. In addition, in cases where socialist feminist groups have developed strategic links with institutionalized structures in the trade union movement or the NDP, problems of jurisdiction, of leadership, and of the range of legitimate issues continually surface.[40] This demonstrates the extent to which mainstreaming can limit the degree of disengagement. Yet despite these difficulties, it is interesting to note that in a recent overview of left organizing in Canada, the following assessment is made.

> The emergence and ongoing development by women of a socialist-feminist perspective has been central to this process. Some would see this perspective...as the single most important factor shaping the politics of the left in the last two decades. But at the same time, this new development has provided positive direction to processes that have shaped feminism and gay politics, the politics of social movements, and the political agenda and structure of the trade union movement.[41]

A recurring theme of these organizational issues speaks to whether it is more appropriate to build socialist feminist organizations (disengagement) or to enter into existing organizations and transform them (mainstreaming). A specific dilemma in this regard relates to the interior process of organizations. Feminists have developed an extensive critique of the process and practices of most social institutions (including the democratic centralism of far left organizations), and have attempted to develop, although not always successfully, an alternative feminist process. That feminist process is most easily explored in alternative organizations presents some difficulties for socialist feminists who reject alternatives as an adequate political strategy and yet who simultaneously reject the practices of mainstream institutions.

It is not so easy to juggle these various options and, as a result, building explicitly socialist feminist organizations has not been a priority. The exceptions to this are Saskatoon Women's Liberation, Bread and Roses of Vancouver and the International Women's Day Committee of Toronto (IWDC). Although IWDC has been the most long-lasting, its failure to sustain a membership beyond about thirty-five requires some analysis. Perhaps the tension between disengagement and mainstreaming helps to explain this: IWDC simultaneously attempts to play a role as an alternative and a haven at the same time that it operates as a political organization.

Heather Jon Maroney in her analysis of socialist feminist organizations says:

> Operating from a mainly ideological basis of unity, these organizations have lacked the focus of single-issue campaigns and the institutional cohesion of the self-help services that also evolved from the initial phases of the women's liberation movement. Externally, they have generally met with hostility from the mixed Leninist left, suspicion from the labour movement, and opposition from radical and bourgeois feminists.[42]

From the perspective on feminist practice presented in this article, the lack of single issue focus is the problem of inadequate mainstreaming; the hostility and suspicion, on the other hand, reflects one of the difficulties associated with disengagement.

Although the foregoing discussion looks at the complexities of building socialist feminist organizations, there is no consensus among socialist feminists about whether separate socialist feminist organizations *per se* are the best strategy. And, of course, at different historical and political conjunctures such organizations might be more or less viable. Notwithstanding this, assessments of existing socialist feminist organizations and discussions of establishing new ones must take account of the inherently contradictory nature and complexity of the task of building socialist feminism. Yet strategically, organizationally, and theoretically, socialist feminism has much potential. Certainly it is important to see how the on-going and creative struggle of socialist feminists has influenced the politics of feminism and of socialism in Canada, and contributed to improving the conditions of women's lives.

ENDNOTES

The first draft of this paper was presented at the Third International Interdisciplinary Congress on Women in Dublin in July 1987. It also draws on material from *Feminist Organizing for Change: the contemporary women's movement in Canada*, co-authored with Nancy Adamson and Margaret McPhail (Toronto: 1988). Isa Bakker, Mariana Valverde and Lorna Weir read an earlier draft of this paper and provided helpful comments and criticisms; thanks also to Roberta Hamilton for her skilful editing.

1. Lynne Segal, *Is the Future Female?* (London: 1987).

2. "The cultural politics of...the early seventies [were] extraordinarily, if naively, optimistic that as women we could change our lives and those of others once we saw through 'male lies.' Many feminists were eagerly attempting to change every aspect of their lives: how we lived with and related to other adults and children, how we worked and developed new skills, how we saw ourselves...Much of the cultural feminism of today, in contrast, is less concerned with change: it calls upon the timeless truths of women's lives, sufficient in themselves, but threatened by the perpetual and invasive danger of men. It suggests that women do not need to change their lives, other than to separate themselves from the lives of men, and that there is little hope of men themselves changing." Segal, *Is the Future Female?* pp. 68-9.

3. Mariana Valverde pointed out the importance of this kind of self-labelling in the women's movement and suggested the term the "politics of identity." Later I came across the following comment in an early statement from black feminists. "This focusing upon our own oppression is embodied in the concept of identity politics. We believe that the most profound and potentially the most radical politics come directly out of our own identity, as opposed to working to end somebody else's oppression." The Combahee River Collective, "A Black Feminist Statement," in Zillah Eisenstein (ed.), *Capitalist Patriarchy and the Case for Socialist Feminism* (New York: 1979), p. 364.

4. Alison Jaggar, *Feminist Politics and Human Nature* (Totowa, NJ: 1983).

5. It is interesting to note that only liberal feminists have even the glimmering of a clear institutional base. In both the USA and Canada liberal feminism operates through national umbrella structures: the National Organization of Women (NOW) in the US and National Action Committee on the Status of Women

(NAC) in Canada. Building and maintaining such an organizational base is easier for liberal feminism because of the practices of representative democracy in both these countries. It is also the case that socialist feminism faces a peculiar dilemma in attempting to build an organizational base. This will be addressed in the last section of this paper.

6.   For an extended discussion of the contradictory contribution of the 'personal is political', see "The Ideology of the Women's Movement," Chapter Six in Adamson, Briskin, & MacPhail, *Feminist Organizing for Change.*

7.   In her analysis of sisterhood, Bell Hooks makes the point that bonding based on shared victimization reflects male supremacist thinking since "sexist ideology teaches women that to be female is to be a victim." Further Hooks points out that by "identifying as 'victims', they [white women] could abdicate responsibility for their role in the maintenance and perpetuation of sexism, racism and classism, which they did by insisting that men were the only enemy." Hooks goes on to argue for bonding on the basis of "shared strengths and resources." See Bell Hooks, "Sisterhood: Political Solidarity Between Women," *Feminist Review* No. 23 (June 1986), p. 128. Although I agree with Hooks, my point is that the recognition of difference between women has not only challenged the notion of shared oppression for the category of woman as a whole but has, at the same time, reinforced bonding on the basis of 'shared victimization' for particular groups of women to the exclusion of building effective political alliances.

8.   Segal, *Is the Future Female?* pp. 59-61.

9.   Although beyond the scope of this article to develop it, it seems to me that this paradigm transcends some of the theoretical and strategic limitations of the perceived opposition between reform and revolution.

10.   Charlotte Bunch, "The Reform Tool Kit," in *Building Feminist Theory: Essays from Quest* (New York: 1981), quoted in Jaggar, *Feminist Politics and Human Nature*, p. 336.

11.   It is interesting to note that Jaggar uses the quote from Bunch cited in the text to distinguish between radical feminist and socialist feminist alternatives. "Radical feminists intend their alternative institutions should enable women to withdraw as far as possible from the dominant culture by facilitating women's independence from that culture....Socialist feminists, by contrast,...build alternative institutions as a way of partially satisfying existing needs and also as a way of experimenting with new forms of working together." She herself points out that these distinctions are not 'clear cut'. See Jaggar, *Feminist Politics and Human Nature*, p. 336.

12. For a recent rather damning discussion of feminist organizations, see Ruth Latta, "Working for Feminist Organizations," *Breaking the Silence* VI/4 (June 1988). For a discussion of the impact of government funding on the practice and organization of rape crisis centres, see Toronto Rape Crisis Centre, "Rape" in Connie Guberman and Marge Wolfe (eds.), *No Safe Place* (Toronto: 1985), pp.82-84. See also, Sally Hunter, "Government Strategies," *Priorities* V/9 (May 1977); Dorothy Smith, "Does Government Funding Co-opt?" *Kinesis* VI/11 (1977); Helen Maier, "We will Survive," *Kinesis* (June 1984) and Isabelle Bouvier, "Women's Groups and their Relations with the State," *Communiqu'elles* XII/1 (1986).

13. Miriam Jones and Jennifer Stephens, "Tempest in a Teapot: NAC Annual General Meeting 1988," *Rebel Girls Rag* II/4 (July/August 1988). For further discussion of feminist process in relation to this AGM, see Constance Backhouse, "If I Can't Dance..." *Broadside* IX/9 (July 1988); Eve Zaremba, "Collective Crisis," *Broadside* IX/10 (Aug/Sept 1988); and Nancy Adamson and Anne Molgat, "The Mystique of Feminist Process: A Report from the NAC AGM," *Cayenne: A Socialist Feminist Bulletin* (Fall 1988).

14. See Sue Findlay, "Facing the State: the Politics of the Women's Movement Reconsidered," in Heather Jon Maroney and Meg Luxton (eds.), *Feminism and Political Economy* (Toronto: 1987) for a description of the process of the Canadian state integrating the representation of women's issues into the policy making process, and a discussion of the difficulties faced by feminists working as civil servants in attempting to intervene in that process.

15. Dorothy Smith, in "Where there is oppression, there is resistance," *Branching Out* VI/1 (1979) discusses a process she calls 'institutional absorption,' which occurs as the women's movement interacts with the social institutions, a process not dissimilar to what I have called institutionalization. She says, "A major danger is the process of institutional absorption. I imagine it to be like a starfish eating a clam, sucking the living tissues from the shell. Institutional structures are set up to organize and control and they do it well. When critical positions and action emerge related to an institutional focus, processes are set in motion which bring things back in line, which absorb the anomaly, and keep things stabilized....Each new way of absorbing women's movement initiatives into the institutional structure isolates them from the movement and depoliticizes them...as the work is absorbed by the ruling apparatus it is withdrawn from the general struggle..." (pp.13-14) She goes on to argue that the problem is that much of feminist organizing has been "in relation to the institutional structure of the ruling apparatus. To do something about rape it seems that we should work in relation to the

police, the courts and the law." (p.14)

16. Carla Lipsig-Mummé, "Organizing Women in the Clothing Trades: Homework and the 1983 Garment Strike in Canada," *Studies in Political Economy* 22 (Spring 1987).

17. *Ibid.*, pp. 65-6.

18. *Ibid.*, p. 66.

19. Dana Frank, "Housewives, Socialists, and the Politics of Food: the 1917 New York Cost-of-Living Protests," *Feminist Studies* XI/2 (Summer 1985).

20. *Ibid.*, p. 265.

21. Quoted in *Ibid.*, p. 272.

22. *Ibid.*, p. 275.

23. *Ibid.*, p. 275.

24. For a detailed discussion of the attempts of SORWUC (Service, Office and Retail Workers Union of Canada) to organize the bank workers, see The Bank Book Collective, *An Account to Settle*, (Vancouver: 1979).

25. Rosemary Warskett, "Bank Worker Unionization and the Law," *Studies in Political Economy* 25 (Spring 1988).

26. Maureen FitzGerald, "Whither the Feminist Unions? SORWUC, AUCE and the CLC," *Resources for Feminist Research* X/2 (July 1981), p.20.

27. The other anthology published in 1972 was compiled by Margret Andersen and entitled *Mother was Not a Person* (Montreal: 1972).

28. "Introduction" in *Women Unite* (Toronto: 1972), p. 10.

29. Mariana Valverde, review of Roberta Hamilton and Michèle Barrett (eds.), *The Politics of Diversity* (London: 1986) in *New Statesman*, March 1987.

30. See, for example, Sheila Rowbotham, Lynne Segal and Hilary Wainwright, *Beyond the Fragments: feminism and the making of socialism* (Boston: 1981). See also Monica Threlfall, "The Women's Movement in Spain," *New Left Review* 151 (May/June 1985). She discusses the situation after the fall of the Franco regime in which the left attempted to hegemonize the newly emerging women's movement. "Within the women's movement ...opinions divided over the question of *doble militancia*, of whether women should spend their time being activists in a political party as well as in a women's group.." p. 46.

31. Lorna Weir, "Socialist Feminism and the Politics of Sexuality," in Maroney and Luxton (eds.), *Feminism and Political Economy* pp. 77-78.

32. In a conversation with Deirdre English, Barbara Epstein, Barbara Haber and Judy Maclean, "The Impasse of Socialist Feminism," *Socialist Review* 79 (Jan/Feb 1985), p. 101. Judy Maclean in the same article suggests pessimistically that socialist feminism "as a term and as a means of excluding other women... is dead." (p. 103.) This is number ten in a series of articles on socialist feminism in *Socialist Review*. Although many are quite pessimistic, this article generated a more optimistic view from Amy Bachrach and Carisa Cunningham, in "What do you mean the party's over? We just got here!" *Socialist Review* 81 (May/June 1985).

33. Lorna Weir, "Women and the State: A Conference for Feminist Activists," *Feminist Review* 26 (Summer 1987), p. 93.

34. The discussion which follows is one part of a larger discussion of feminist organizations and feminist process in Adams, Briskin & MacPhail, *Feminist Organizing for Change*. See chapter 7.

35. For a discussion of the difficulties building trade union women's committees and the conditions under which such committees get co-opted, see Debbie Field, "The Dilemma facing Women's Committees," in Linda Briskin and Lynda Yanz (eds.), *Union Sisters* (Toronto: 1983).

36. "But it was from socialist-feminist politics that we drew our guiding principles on how to build a campaign and movement in support of clinics and women's right to choose." Patricia Antonyshyn, B. Lee and Alex Merrill, "Marching for Women's Lives: The Campaign for Free-standing Abortion Clinics in Ontario," in Frank Cunningham *et al* (eds.), *Social Movements Social Change* (Toronto: 1988), p. 132.

37. *Ibid.*, p. 149. This article documents this process in detail. It is also interesting to note that Nancy Adamson and Susan Prentice, in "Toward a Broader Strategy for Choice," *Cayenne* 3 (May-June 1985) criticize OCAC for inadequate 'disengagement', in particular, for an underlying acceptance of the medical model.

38. It is also the case that the tendency of far left groups and the feminists aligned with them to enter other feminist formations with an already decided plan of action that is not openly presented has encouraged some feminists to be especially wary of socialist feminists and their organizations. Further, there still exists in Canada a few left front groups (for example the Congress of Canadian Women led and dominated by the Communist Party) who are not open about their political affiliation.

39. For some discussion of this, see Carolyn Egan, Linda Gardner and Judy Persad, "The Politics of Transformation: Struggles with Race, Class and Sexuality in the

March 8th Coalition," in Cunningham *et al* (eds.), *Social Movements Social Change.*

40. For a discussion of some of the tensions (and successes) faced by IWDC in working with the trade union movement, see Carolyn Egan and Lynda Yanz, "Building Links: Labour and the Women's Movement" in Briskin and Yanz (eds.), *Union Sisters.*

41. Sue Findlay, Frank Cunningham and Ed Silva, "Introduction," Cunningham *et al* (eds.), *Social Movements Social Change*, p. 12.

42. Heather Jon Maroney, "Feminism at Work," in Maroney and Luxton (eds.), *Feminism and Political Economy*, p.96.

CHAPTER 12

LESSONS FROM PAY EQUITY

PAT ARMSTRONG
HUGH ARMSTRONG

States have expanded enormously in modern times, and one consequence of that expansion has been an elaboration of the ways in which states affect the lives of women. While state initiatives have had sex-specific and often contradictory consequences, women have frequently looked to states for remedial action or protective legislation; at the same time, women resist state controls, especially over their bodies, and state restrictions on their access to jobs and education. For these reasons feminists throughout the world have become increasingly interested in theorizing the state.

While there is a general consensus that the state is not a neutral arbiter among competing interests, there is considerable disagreement about how the state is to be understood and about what action women should take in relation to the state. Some have argued that the state has served to maintain male power; indeed, may have replaced the father in ensuring women's subordination. Others have contended that the state has, on occasion, responded to demands from factions within the working class, with different consequences for women in different places, in different classes, in different racial or ethnic groups and in different times. Through their examinations of past experiences and through their debates with each other, these theorists have contributed to our understanding of the very complex and contradictory nature of state practices.[1]

Much of this work has been both enhanced and hampered by the need to interpret the past in light of the present. Current experiences around the struggle for equal pay and with the impact of equal pay legislation offer an opportunity to explore state initiatives as they occur, and from the perspective of those engaged in the process. The particular case of the development and consequences of pay equity legislation in the province of Ontario demonstrates the importance of theory as a guide to, and reflection on, action. It also illustrates the contradictory nature of state actions, even of those which seem to respond to women's demands. In addition, this case raises important questions about how women can organize to bring about the kind of change that will not serve to further divide women from each other.

The struggle over pay equity in Ontario demonstrates that the state is indeed a contested terrain; one in which there is no 'level playing field' but one in which women can win some significant, if contradictory, victories.[2] It reveals capital's resistance to the elimination of a cheap source of labour power and to the reduction of its control over wage determination, while it exposes state interest in maintaining the conditions for increasing profits based on low female wages. Small employers succeeded in obtaining exemption from the legislation; large employers engaged in continuing efforts to structure the technical details to limit the impact and to enhance their control over job content. At the same time, the Equal Pay Coalition's victories indicate that "common sense" can be transformed by struggles over legislation that make women's pay demands legitimate and that challenge the notion of a free market based on equity and choice. While such changes can benefit women in general, the particular consequences of the legislation are uneven and may serve to divide women from each other.

THE ONTARIO LEGISLATION

The Ontario Pay Equity Act[3] grew out of both the feminist struggles that began in the mid-1960s and the dramatic changes in women's labour force participation that have taken place over the last three decades. Although made possible by the particular conditions of the Ontario political economy in the 1980s, the Act illuminates the contradictory nature of state policies, of capitalist practices and of women's efforts to alter their conditions of employment. These have been contradictory not just in the obvious sense of having positive and negative consequences. They have also been contradictory in the Marxist sense, in that collective action may lead to transformations in conditions and consciousness, which in turn will give rise to fresh contradictions. Real gains, in other words, may result in new problems.

Although demands for equal pay between men and women have a long history, the story of the current legislation most clearly begins in the years following World War Two. The liberal political climate, the economic boom and the pressure from workers in the immediate postwar period all contributed to the Federal Government's 1948 ratification of a United Nations policy on equal pay for equal work. But policy makers were clearly aware of the limitations of legislation calling for equal pay for equal work. In the early 1950s, when there were few visible signs of a women's movement, the Canadian Government failed to ratify the International Labour Organization's Convention 100 which called for "equal remuneration for men and women workers for work of equal value."[4]

In most provincial jurisdictions, equal pay for equal work legislation became a reality only in the late 1960s. By this time, feminism was re-emerging as a political force, reflecting the dramatic increases in female labour force participation rates that began in the early 1960s and the related research that exposed large differences in female and male incomes. In the main, these provincial laws applied to identical or substantially identical work done for the same employer, and required an aggrieved employee to initiate a complaint. Maximum penalties were very low and many jurisdictions excluded a variety of employers from even these limited provisions. All legislation reflected a liberal interpretation of pay inequities. It was implied that pay inequality was a minor and individual problem for a few female employees who were discriminated against by a few misguided employers. Obvious inequities were blamed on ideas rather than structures; on values rather than profits. In general, the legislation suggested that the widespread practice of paying women low wages was justified and necessary, a matter of women's productivity or women's choices.

For a variety of reasons, provincial and federal legislation had a limited impact on women's wages. The primary reason was that inequality between women and men was mainly structural and collective rather than ideological and individual. Women's low wages were profitable for employers. Legislation based on other assumptions therefore touched few women. Most women and men worked in different jobs, or at least in jobs that were differently defined. And they often worked for different employers.[5] Consequently, it was difficult for women to find a male job in their work place that was identical, or to establish that male work was substantially identical. The complaint-based procedure meant that only the most secure unionized workers could take the risk of charging discrimination or could afford the time and expense of the proceedings. Given that in 1980 only a quarter of employed Canadian women were unionized,[6] and that many were in unions uninterested in devoting resources to this battle, few women had access to the process. Even when a case was won, the benefits from that decision were frequently restricted to that job in that work place. Moreover, the penalties for employers contravening the legislation were not severe.

The legislation indicated the state's willingness to defend individual rights while denying in practice women's collective access to decent pay. It provided some legitimacy for legislatures without fundamentally altering the sex differences in remuneration that were profitable for employers and that seemed to benefit many male workers.[7]

Employers, especially those in small enterprises where profits and unionization rates were relatively low and where the proportion of female employees was relatively high, did not support the equal pay for equal work legislation. They did not, however, launch a major campaign against it. Their resistance came mainly in the forms of new job descriptions designed to avoid female/male comparisons and legal battles against complaints.

Although the early legislation was based on a liberal and individual conception of the problem that limited its effectiveness in improving women's wages, women were able to make some not insignificant gains through the legal process. Unions used individual cases to establish the existence of a more pervasive inequality and to force a reinterpretation of the legislation. For example, in a case heard before the Grievance Settlement Board in Ontario,[8] lawyers for the union successfully argued that a particular female clerk was underpaid as a result of a classification scheme which significantly undervalued the work performed by all women at that level. When the Board agreed with this interpretation, the entire level was able to reap the benefits and the legislation was understood to apply more collectively and systematically than the legislators had intended. Legislation designed to have an impact on individual cases in the end provided a basis for broader demands, even though pay raises were mainly confined to unionized women in the public sector.

As women's labour force participation increased, so did their efforts to improve their wages and to reduce the wage gap. Work with the legislation and with unions had resulted in modest gains. As well, it had provided women with a range of experiences, had extended their skills in working with legislation and had indicated that more significant victories were possible. At the same time, however, it had also suggested that different strategies were required if very many women in the province were to receive more pay and if these improvements were to be realized in our time. The unions willing to devote resources to this struggle were mainly those that represented the female-dominated areas of the public sector. And legislative rulings, even when they applied to an entire classification of workers and to jobs that were not strictly identical, still were restricted to those working in the jobs and to the employer involved in the complaint.

Frustrated with the slow rate of progress, Ontario women from unions, from community groups, and from business and professional organizations joined together in what came to be called the Equal Pay Coalition.[9] Although it did not have a paid staff or a fixed organizational structure, the Coalition did, over time, develop a single voice representing a million women and men from widely divergent groups. It was thus able to help make stronger legislation a political issue, and to ensure that the issue then assumed public prominence. While it promoted change to make collective agreements as well as legislation more effective in equal pay terms, its location outside the structures of the union movement and the state reflected the limitations on working for significant change inside these structures. Meanwhile, the Coalition's very diversity encouraged it to focus on legislative change and to avoid discussion of more fundamental, theoretical issues. Constructed around a common concern with the fact that women are paid less than men, it was not in a position to set this concern in the broader context of a critique of the occupational structure or of wage labour. Capitalism and specifically the exploitation of workers were not on its agenda.

The Coalition had been at work for a decade when a particular set of circumstances created the conditions for major legislative change. In 1985, the New Democratic Party made equal pay legislation a condition of its support for a minority Liberal Government, enabling the Liberals rather than the Conservatives to form the Government. Moreover, the Ontario economy was rapidly recovering from the recession of the early 1980s, making it somewhat easier to make demands on private sector employers and on public coffers. At the same time strong feminists were employed in the Women's Directorate, the government bureau mandated to chair the steering committee of the Interministerial Task Force on Pay Equity. Such favourable conditions for intervention do not often occur.

In 1987 the Ontario Government introduced the Pay Equity Act. Based on the concept of equal pay for work of equal value, the Pay Equity Act represented a significant departure from earlier legislation and reflected some major victories for the Coalition. Primarily as a result of Coalition efforts, of feminist research and of rulings on the existing equal pay legislation, the Task Force recognized that pay differences were the product of "systemic discrimination." No longer could pay differences be dismissed as minor inequities resulting from a few employers underpaying women or from women's choices and inadequacies.

The legislation was based on the assumption that the problem was pay structures, not people. The solutions were to be collective, not individual. In other words, the legislation moved away from a focus on individual rights in a free market to an emphasis on collective rights in a segregated market. Moreover, the Coalition convinced the Task Force that only a proactive model, one which required employers to take positive action to rectify inequities and which assumed all employers guilty of discrimination, would be effective and acceptable to the groups represented by the Coalition. Furthermore, the Act was to apply to the private as well as the public sector, an important precedent in these deregulation times and an important victory, given the larger wage gap in the private sector. Perhaps equally important, the Act was to be administered by an independent Tribunal, implying that state bureaucracies had not always been on the side of women. Finally, the Coalition, with help from various unions, was successful in demanding that unions be involved in negotiating pay equity plans.

The Coalition also won some victories in terms of the Act's details. For example, the range of possible exclusions was significantly reduced from the original proposal. A time schedule was written into the Act and heavy penalties were included to deter delinquency.

But the Coalition was also hampered in a number of very important ways. Most significantly, and most obviously, employers objected to the plan. Small employers in particular claimed that they could not afford pay equity (in the process demonstrating that they did indeed discriminate against women and did profit from women's low pay). In the end, the Act did not apply to them. Employers with 10 or fewer employees do not fall under the Act. Private firms with 11 to 99 employees do not have to develop a Pay Equity Plan, although they are subject to a complaints procedure. Studies of its impact demonstrate that this means an enormous number of women are excluded from the provisions of the Act, just as the Coalition predicted.[10]

Large employers were also opposed but their resistance, after they became aware that some legislation was inevitable, mainly took the form of limiting the damage through adjustments to the Act. The technical details written into the Act reflected the concerns these employers expressed in public hearings. These details could be used to severely restrict the impact of the Act. For example, Pay Equity Plans are to be developed within establishments for employees working within a particular geographical area. Thus, most of the employees working for a chain operation such as McDonald's would be in establishments that had too few employees to require a posted Pay Equity Plan. Furthermore, the Plan applies only to the employees of individual employers, and not all employees working within a particular establishment have the same employer. Increasingly, many workers are employed by companies on contract or are hired from agencies and therefore would not be part of the Pay Equity Plan for that establishment. Rather, each of these employers is to develop a Plan. Many will not need to do so because they have too few employees. Furthermore, women must establish that they belong to a female job class (determined according to a complicated set of criteria). The female job class must then be compared with a male job class within the same establishment, working for the same employer. Moreover if there is a union, the female job class must first be compared with a male class within the bargaining unit; jobs outside the unit can only be examined if no appropriate counterparts are to be found within this group. If the male job class is paid more but is at least equal in terms of skill, effort, responsibilities and working conditions, the women in the female job class may benefit.

Although all large employers were required to develop a Pay Equity Plan based on equal pay for work of equal value, this was to be a one-shot program. It would appear that the problem of equity between the sexes was to be solved once and for all as a result of the legislation. As one employer explained, the Act says, "We're guilty until a certain day and after that we're innocent."[11] Furthermore, while the Act requires each employer to negotiate a Pay Equity Plan with a union, when there is a union in place, the employer does not need the union's agreement to establish a plan. According to one employer, this simply means that employers must demonstrate that they negotiated in good faith.

Finally, equal value legislation based on the comparison of male and female job classes seemed to imply the need for a detailed job evaluation scheme. Job evaluation schemes were of course not new, but the Pay Equity Act offered the opportunity to introduce new, detailed and systematically applied schemes to the entire work force. Although workers and their unions have sometimes seen job evaluation schemes as a means of regularizing their workloads and have frequently demanded changes in the schemes introduced, these job evaluations have been defined by both unions and employers as a management right and as a management tool.

JOB EVALUATION SCHEMES

The question of job evaluation is related to the most fundamental problem the Coalition faced. The Coalition for years had been demanding legislation that would be based on equal pay for work of equal value. It had supported equal value because it seemed to offer a way of applying equity rules to a segregated labour force. The Coalition had argued that women's work was often just as difficult as that done by men; that most women had as many years of formal education as men; that women's work was just as valuable and as skilled as that of men. Yet these factors were not reflected in women's wages.

What the Coalition had not done was work through the theoretical and strategic implications of equal value. The members had not agreed on what equity and value meant, on how equity and value were to be determined, or on how value should be measured. Value was understood to mean a vaguely defined worth and equity to mean paid like a man. Indeed, it is not clear that such a diverse group could have developed a more precise consensus on these fundamental questions. Although there was a long consultation period leading up to the drafting of the legislation, when an Act was introduced which offered a way of interpreting and applying the notion of equal value, the Coalition could do little but suggest modifications to the details. Presented with a complex piece of legislation, there was no time for the Coalition to go back to basics. Fearful of losing the gains already made, especially given the constraints imposed by a rapidly approaching election that was likely to see the Accord between the New Democratic and Liberal parties that gave birth to the legislation disappear, the Coalition could do little but agree to the methods proposed within the Act.

The Act called for a gender-neutral comparison system that would evaluate female and male job classes in terms of their skill, effort, responsibility and working conditions. Such an approach was based on two false assumptions: that men were paid on the basis of their worth, and that jobs can be objectively measured in a gender-neutral way.

Men are paid mainly on the basis of their power to demand wages, not primarily on the basis of some objective definition of the worth of the work they do. They are paid as the result of struggles or the potential for struggle and on the basis of their access to the means of production and of their control over techniques. What men do is more highly priced because worth is primarily negotiated, whether or not this is done through collective bargaining. Women, on the other hand, have, to a large extent, been excluded from these negotiations, regardless of whether they are part of a formal bargaining process.[12] Although there are great debates about why men became more powerful than women, it is clear that large numbers of men entered the labour force and remained in the labour market long before many women became relatively permanent members of the paid workforce. Men's lifelong dependency on their own wage labour and their prior access to the labour force helped establish their edge, an edge that encouraged and reinforced men's cultural dominance in all areas of society. Men's position was further buttressed by state legislation, by the dominant ideology that reflected and reinforced their power, by the exclusionary practices of various institutions and of men, in or out of unions, as well as by the failure of the state to provide support services for women who took wage work. The structural location of many men in the market served to strengthen men's position throughout all aspects of the political economy and to relegate women, structurally and culturally, to a secondary place. Value is not simply brought to the workforce from outside. Rather value is reinforced and even initiated by the very structure of work and authority patterns.

Value is not objectively determined on the basis of some pre-established set of criteria, on measurable job components. Rather it mainly reflects divisions of power. To call for equality on the basis of value is to ignore the negotiations through which value is defined, and to ignore the large differences in power between women and men. The worth of women's work is embedded in how work gets structured as well as in how work gets evaluated. Systems based on the assumption that men are paid on the basis of some objectively determined skill, effort, responsibility and conditions of work could primarily serve to reinforce the higher wages of men.

Thus, value-free and gender-neutral comparison systems are difficult to create because what are understood to constitute skill, effort, responsibility and working conditions are also a reflection of power relationships between women and men as well as between owners and workers and of judgements that are to a large extent under management direction. There are often objective components in what are defined as constituting skill, effort, responsibility and working conditions, but both the value attached to them and to the other related components included in evaluations are negotiated and renegotiated. Women often lose out more than men in two ways. First, women's skills, efforts and responsibilities frequently disappear in these negotiations; secondly their working conditions are often ignored. To the extent that there are objective components in the work, women's components get measured and valued in different ways than do men's.

Job evaluations of skill, effort, responsibility and working conditions combine three major components, each of which involves value-laden definitions and therefore should be matters of negotiation. Crucial value decisions are made in terms of what is recorded, how it is recorded, and how what is recorded is evaluated. Traditionally, all three processes have been collapsed into one process defined as a technical and managerial prerogative.

Yet what has been called gender bias pervades each of these three processes. In terms of what is counted, women's skills, efforts, responsibility and working conditions frequently disappear, or remain invisible. For example, the objectionable nature of garbage is used to justify higher wages for those collecting refuse. The objectionable nature of human waste or vomit is often not recorded, however, when the work of nursing aides is evaluated. Responsibility for subordinate workers is counted. Responsibility for children and patients usually is not. The effort involved in providing comfort, the patience involved in caring for the sick or the elderly, the stamina involved in working all day with sick, complaining, or dying patients, and the skill involved in lifting an injured patient usually go unrecorded when it is women doing the work. In the case of male orderlies, for instance, higher pay is justified on the grounds that they move heavy weights, not that they deal with patient concerns. The male task involving mainly strength is more highly valued than the female job involving more care. If those developing job evaluation schemes are aware of these factors, they all too often simply assume that women naturally possess the skills required, and that they easily adjust to certain difficult conditions or the imposition of certain types of responsibility.[13]

Moreover, many schemes capture only what is officially defined as responsibility, rather than what is, in practice, women's work. In health care, for example, doctors are officially responsible for the diagnosis and treatment of patients but in practice the day-to-day responsibility often falls on the women who provide the care. When patients die, for instance, the doctor is usually absent and it is a nurse or nurses' aide who is available to provide comfort and support to patients and relatives. These actual responsibilities are difficult to see, however, in official job descriptions. At the same time, many schemes also focus only on work that is performed regularly. Yet in nursing, for example, it is often the most irregular skills that are the most essential. A respirator may be required once a month but it is crucial that nurses know how to use the equipment effectively on these occasions.

Much more subtle, and difficult to correct, are the ways skill, effort, responsibilities and working conditions are recorded. Many job evaluation schemes hierarchically order factors, assuming some are much more valuable than others. Such schemes place responsibility for money and employees on the top; responsibility for other people such as clients, patients, students and customers on the bottom. It is, of course, women who are more likely to be responsible for these other people, and less likely to be responsible in a formal way for managing money or subordinate employees. Many schemes double or even triple count these typically male tasks, by asking about very similar factors in more than one way in several questions.

The hierarchical organization of skills also makes it extremely difficult to capture the multi-level and overlapping factors that characterize much of women's work. The skill involved in switching from one level to another or of doing many simultaneous tasks usually disappears. For example, a nurse may make beds, wash patients, administer medications and monitor patients' vital signs. She may have to communicate both in very simple terms with a child or a mentally handicapped person and in very sophisticated terms with health care professionals, adult patients and community leaders. In many job evaluations, only what is considered the highest level skill will be recorded and the others will not be factored into the overall evaluation. They falsely assume either that the person with the skills ranked highest has all the lower level skills or that only the most sophisticated skill level is regularly performed. Similarly, when a nurses' aide is bathing a patient, she may also be comforting the patient, taking into account the patient's illness and preferences and listening for other calls. This at least is what she has been taught to do, even if the structures increasingly make it difficult to provide this kind of care. If it is recorded at all, the job is simply defined as bathing and the other skills and effort disappear.

In addition, evaluations which ask women to rank their own work frequently fail to capture much of what is involved in the job at the same time as they place a low value on women's efforts and skills. Women have become accustomed to the undervaluation of their work and it is therefore not surprising that traditional questionnaires may merely serve to restate this low evaluation. Study after study has shown that women place less value on the work they perform that men do on theirs.[14] This is particularly the case if the evaluations are scrutinized by a supervisor. Women may be fully aware of the value superiors places on their work, or they may fear revealing that they do work which is formally assigned to supervisors. For example, a Public Health nurse appearing recently before the Pay Equity Tribunal Board explained that she would hesitate to indicate that her job required her to read and interpret complex material, even though she actually did this work, because it would mean that there would be no higher level skills left to be attributed to her nursing supervisor.[15]

Moreover, many schemes ask either supervisors or employees to estimate what proportion of their time is devoted to various tasks. The result is often a ludicrous distortion of reality, with nurses and childcare workers assigning 10 percent of their time to providing comfort and care. Such schemes do not reflect the overlapping nature of many women's jobs. They cannot measure those aspects of the job that are part of all day, every day. To the extent that schemes actually reflect what is done, they are much more successful at capturing task-oriented jobs than they are at capturing care-oriented jobs: at counting what men do rather than what women do.

These problems are most obvious in jobs such as nursing, teaching and childcare. But they are also present in many other areas of women's work. In sales jobs, for example, men who sell appliances and cars have their wages justified on the basis of their knowledge of the products while women who sell underwear or cosmetics are paid less, it is argued, because they need only do routine sales work related to customers. Similarly, although some clerical work is highly routinized and task-oriented, much of it still involves overlapping and multi-level factors that go unrecorded when women do the work. In Goobie vs The Ministry of Health (Ontario Labour Relations Board), for instance, the union demonstrated that the clerical workers who handle files for the Ontario Health Insurance Plan must constantly switch from typing to dealing with interpretations of complex legislation, must move from talking to customers with limited formal education and no literacy in English to civil servants or employers who speak in another language at another level, must translate complicated regulations into simple but accurate terms for clients who are often extremely distressed after an illness or death.[16] None of these skills or responsibilities were evident in their job evaluations or descriptions. Even in factory work, where tasks have been fragmented to a large degree, the women who sew garments together have to have a range of skills that enable them to work with different fabrics, different styles, and different parts of a garment, while they record their own piece work. On paper, however, their jobs do not compare to those of the male cutters.

Both what is counted and how it is counted are often inseparable from how these things are evaluated because such evaluations are frequently built into the methodology. These evaluations, camouflaged as objective measures, make it particularly difficult to sort out what must be negotiated and what constitutes gender bias. For example, few schemes place a high value on team work and the need to coordinate activities with other workers or with those for whom a service is provided. Indeed, such effort and responsibility may not be measured at all, but when it is, it usually is less valued than directing others to do the work. And it is women who are much more likely to be involved in work which requires them to take others into account.

Constructing and administering a job evaluation scheme is therefore critical to the entire process. All systems have value built in but the call for a job evaluation scheme free of gender bias implies that objective tests free of value are possible to develop through technical means.

Although job evaluation schemes have sometimes been promoted by unions, they are management tools. Management pays for them; they tend to reflect the concerns and needs of the employer. In his analysis of the labour process, Braverman[17] argued that managements have made widespread use of the principles developed by Frederick Winslow Taylor. Jobs were analyzed in detail and this detail meant that managers gained some of the knowledge that was formerly the property of the workers. This information allowed managers to separate conception from execution, to reorganize work in management-determined ways, to fragment work and to increase their control over workers as well as over the labour process. Job evaluation schemes can serve the same purpose that Taylor's time-motion studies did many years ago.

Many job evaluation schemes have measured only what the employer wanted measured; only those tasks and procedures the employer was willing to recognize as the basis for pay negotiations. So, for example, university secretaries who must constantly deal with distraught students do not have a place for counselling or public relations in their job evaluations because the employer says that it is not part of their job. But increasingly, especially with pay equity legislation, job evaluations are based on detailed job descriptions written by those doing the work and certified by supervisors. Indeed, many women's groups have argued for very detailed job descriptions prepared by the women who best understand the job. Detailed descriptions do demonstrate that the work women do is onerous, skilled and involves a high level of responsibility, but they also offer employers a great deal of information.

When job evaluations do reflect what is done on the job, the evaluations may serve to increase the power of the employer by documenting what workers can do. They thus may provide the basis for what Braverman called the separation of conception from execution. Employers can learn more of what workers know. What is done can be reorganized into management categories. And work reorganization done on this basis encourages workers to conceptualize their work along management lines. Furthermore, these job evaluations, and the job descriptions based on them, may become what the worker must do, the minimum requirements of the job.

Job evaluations can also serve to establish or confirm hierarchies among workers. These hierarchies are directly under management control and may serve to pit worker against worker as well as to reinforce pay differences. In addition, job evaluations can transform political issues into technical problems to be dealt with by consultants paid for by the employer. As one employer explained, job evaluation is a management prerogative. It allows managers to keep track of the employees and what they do as well as to make sure that they are doing their jobs.

IMPLICATIONS FOR ONTARIO WORKERS

In the end, Ontario has a Pay Equity Act that is unlikely to result in pay equity, however equity is defined. The very name of the Act, transformed from the Equal Pay theme of the Coalition, implies that justice will have been done; an aberration corrected once and for all. But many women will not see their pay increase significantly as a result of this legislation. As the Coalition made clear before the Act became law and as the Pay Equity Commission has since demonstrated, a very large number of women will not benefit under the Act because they will not be able to find a male group within their establishment for purposes of comparison or because they are employed in establishments that are too small to be covered by the Act.

Equally serious are the problems created in areas where the Act does apply. In those establishments where there are unions, a large proportion of union resources are being diverted into job evaluation schemes and comparisons which are assumed to determine the relative worth of the work done by their members. These job evaluation schemes may serve to increase managerial control, both by rigidifying job specifications and by dividing workers from each other. Meanwhile, the struggle for better pay may be removed from the hands of women and placed in the hands of the consultants with expertise in determining worth.

Moreover, because the nature of the Act means that it will apply unevenly, the very success of some comparisons may also serve to undermine unions and divide women from each other. Women doing the very same job in different establishments may find their job differently evaluated because different job evaluation schemes have been adopted. Even those with exactly the same evaluation may be awarded very different pay adjustments as a consequence of the male job classes available within their bargaining unit. For unions such as the Ontario Nurses Association that have negotiated a common provincial rate, the Act could undermine their hard-won rights and create inequalities among their members because each establishment may reach a different settlement based on different job evaluations and different male job classes. For those women without a union, there may be an imposed job evaluation and an imposed pay equity plan, neither of which will necessarily improve their remuneration. As is the case with some of the other efforts to improve women's position by legislating equality, those least likely to benefit are often those who have the greatest need. Many of those who will not win immediate pay gains under the Act will be immigrant and visible minority women who are concentrated in establishments that are too small to fall under the Act or in those that have no male groups with which female jobs may be compared.

The state gained legitimacy from the legislation while limiting its impact through the technical details. Although the legislators may have been committed to the principle of equity, they were restricted by their definition of the problem as well as by the pressures placed on them by employers. At the same time those who opposed the legislation and who tried to incorporate their concerns into the complex language of the legislation may find that the very details of the Act leave it open to interpretations that contradict their intent.

In spite of these significant problems, the legislation can provide the basis for more fundamental change and, itself, reflects changing consciousness. Women have demonstrated their collective strength, their ability to successfully demand state intervention to improve their conditions. They have made it clear that pay inequities reflect collective barriers women face, not women's individual worth. By demanding and getting a proactive component in the Act, they have also demonstrated that it is employers who are at fault. They have, in the process, made legitimate their demands for better pay and have challenged the notion of a free market based on productivity, equity and choice. A valuable, but largely unrecognized, consequence of the Act may well be access to information on pay, promotion, merit schemes, job descriptions, working conditions, qualifications and recruitment procedures. Employers have long kept such information secret and used it as a means of control. The information is essential to develop both job classes and appropriate means of comparison under the Act. Those with access to such information will have a powerful organizing tool. Employers' resistance to releasing this information for the purposes of the Act indicates that they fear how the information may be used.

Although the Act does much to transform a political process into a technical one, its very complexity may necessitate the involvement of large numbers of workers in collecting the information required to demonstrate compliance. In many cases, the development of a pay equity plan will also involve more than the traditional negotiating teams in formulating a proposal. The media coverage of the Act has meant that many women want to know just how they will benefit. Moreover, as women are struggling to complete detailed questionnaires that fail to capture their work, many are getting together to critique the schemes and to share a broad range of concerns. Participation in such a process is bound to have an impact on worker's consciousness. In the process "common sense" and "the discourse" have changed.

Finally, in spite of the assumptions that were built into the call for value comparisons based on an evaluation scheme that was free of gender bias, women's groups have again been able to use this legislation as a means of moving beyond it. The Pay Equity Tribunal is now hearing formal protests from unions that have objected both to employers' imposition of particular job evaluation schemes and to the bias inherent in the schemes. Employers are marshalling their resources to fight these union demands because they recognize the importance of the evaluation schemes to their power and to their pay systems. As the unions become embroiled in these battles, they too have increasingly recognized the power relations built into job evaluation schemes and have begun using the schemes as a means of challenging managerial control. The battle has, in many places, moved beyond a simple comparison of women's jobs with those of men, and has challenged aspects of capitalism itself.

IMPLICATIONS FOR COLLECTIVE ORGANIZING

The developments surrounding Ontario's Pay Equity Act raise other important questions related to our theories about and strategies for change. The Equal Pay Coalition was formed because even those women within unions did not feel their concerns were being met. That these women had to go beyond unions in order to achieve the kinds of changes they sought indicates some fundamental inadequacies in traditional union organizing and in their approach to collective change.

Much has been written about women and unions. It is clear that, by all traditional measures, women are better off with a union than without one. Women in a union have better pay, better working conditions and better job security than women without a union, although they often do not fare as well as men in or out of a union. Perhaps most importantly, with a union they have more right to say no. But as many have pointed out, unions are usually male-dominated. The executives and the bureaucracy are dominated by men; the meetings are often dominated by men and are structured to reflect male concerns as well as male ways of interacting and male time demands. Moreover, unions have been very slow, and often reluctant, to organize in many of the areas where women work.[18]

Various solutions have been offered to these problems; solutions that reflect the way the problems have been defined. Some have argued for affirmative action or quota systems to ensure that women have an equal representation on the executive. Some have called for a restructuring and rescheduling of meeting times; for daycare provisions and for an inclusion of what have been called women's concerns on the agenda. Some have organized women's caucuses within unions. Others have rejected the male-dominated union structures altogether and have tried to establish parallel female-dominated unions, especially in areas where unions have been unwilling or unable to organize.[19] All these strategies have helped improve women's position in the work place and in the unions.

What these strategies have demonstrated, however, is the limits of traditional union organizing. Current structures and strategies grew out of a labour process in male-dominated work places of the sort that are being transformed. The earlier shift from craft-based production to industrial production was accompanied by a fundamental shift in the nature of collective organizing; by a shift from trade unions to industrial unions. During the transition period, many old strategies that had been appropriate for workers who controlled their tools and techniques were no longer successful and had to be abandoned in favour of new structures and new methods of organizing that were based on the conditions and relations of the new labour process.

It was also during this transition period that women's groups organized outside the work place in order to improve women's conditions in the labour force. As is the case in Ontario today, some women were also struggling within trade union structures but many of the major changes in protective legislation, daycare centres and standards for female working conditions resulted primarily from pressure brought by these extra-work place coalitions. Much of our theoretical work on the early women's movement and on its more recent version has treated them as social movements that are not mainly understood in terms of their relationship to either the work place or to unions. In the process, the lessons they provide on the inadequacies of other organizations involved in work place change have been lost.

What is necessary is some radical thinking about the kinds of work place organizing that would be appropriate to a new kind of labour process and a new kind of worker. In 1986, 70 per cent of the Canadian women over 15 years of age were in the labour force at some time during the year; of women 15 and over, 68 per cent had some employment during the year. Women constituted 44 per cent of all workers and many women were employed in female-dominated work places.[20] Most unionized women work directly or indirectly for the state.[21] Women no longer drop out of the labour force to get married or to have children. Although their labour force participation is still interrupted by 'family responsibilities', no longer can we think of women's participation in paid work as transitory. When we speak today of a family wage, we are speaking of two people with paid employment. These changes are bound to have fundamental consequences for how people organize and what they organize about.

The flood of women into the labour market is related in turn to changes in the nature of the jobs available. Many of these jobs are in the state sector and involve caring for people, teaching people or providing people with other forms of assistance or information. More and more of the jobs in the private sector also involve service work. The control over these workers is much different than that on the shop floor. Perhaps most importantly in these terms, the structure of work may encourage workers to identify both with employer goals and with those they serve as clients, patients or students. Teachers and nurses, for example, are often prepared to think in terms of what their patients or students need as well as in terms of the reputations linked to their hospitals or schools. Traditional union strategies such as strikes and slow-downs tend to hurt clients and the long-term working climate of employees. When the employer is the state, strikes save the employer money. These developments suggest that old strategies which harmed the establishment may now be encouraged by the employer as a means of saving money or increasing control while delegitimating worker demands.

Many of the new jobs are in small work places or in large work places that are divided into smaller units. Jobs within large organizations are increasingly contracted out to small employers or relocated in dispersed shops. In these work places, those who would otherwise be called workers are often renamed managers. In some cases, they are made to buy part of the enterprise and may employ their friends and relatives. Increasingly, work is sent home and the old household shop is reborn, albeit under different conditions. More and more of the work is part-time or short-term. "Retraining" for new jobs is the new norm and the old, large shop is declining. Even where the huge enterprise remains, it is being internally structured into small establishments as management is broken down and work is contracted out to small firms. These restructuring processes are undermining traditional strategies.

Indeed, these processes have been encouraged by both old union methods of organizing and by the new technology. The very success of union strategies has been a factor in employers' efforts to decentralize, to divide up the work into small packages done by different workers and to contract out. The new technology makes it possible to coordinate and control these new structures more easily.

Many of the old union structures and old labour laws no longer fit this new reality. Although we can learn a great deal from what have become traditional techniques and although many are still crucial in work places organized along old lines, we need to go back to basics. We need to think in terms of new structures, new methods, new demands that reflect this new reality. We also need to recognize that women are the dominant labour force in many of these work places.

CONCLUSION

What then are we to conclude about the development and impact of state initiatives related to pay? In Ontario, women representing a wide variety of constituencies fought for, and won, legislation that is creating contradictory and uneven results. The political influence of the Equal Pay Coalition was dependent on the broad range of interests which it represented. But this diversity also limited the Coalition's ability to come to a shared understanding of the theoretical problems underlying equal value legislation. The demands of the Coalition were translated into an Act by legislators concerned with restricting the impact on employers, while retaining a stated commitment to equity. The legislation is now being used, mainly by unions representing women in the public sector, to transform the legislation itself and to challenge the assumptions on which it is based. The women who will most obviously and directly benefit will be those who work for large unionized employers. The effect may be to increase the wage gap among women, leaving some segregated at the bottom of the wage heap, because they will not fall under the Act. Nevertheless, the legislation and the struggles around its implementation are transforming what is legitimate and, in the process, altering the conditions and the consciousness of many women who work for pay. It seems clear that the state is indeed a contested terrain where women's demands must increasingly be responded to, but where the protection of the conditions under which profit is realized remains paramount. It also seems clear that even legislation that recognizes systemic discrimination and collective rights, that requires action and proof of innocence, is still unlikely to improve significantly the wages of all women in the short run, although in the long run it may alter "common sense" and enhance women's political strength as well as their consciousness. The impact is limited by the conception of how value is determined, by the state's efforts to take employees' concerns into account and by some unintended consequences of the legislation's details. As with the cases of legislation related to the family wage and to state protective practices, some women will benefit immediately while others may find their low wages even more firmly entrenched. At the same time, however, the limited impact of the legislation combined with the expectations it has engendered and with the struggles around its implementation are transforming both women's consciousness and what is considered legitimate. These changes may benefit all women as the free market is exposed as being not so free of bias after all.

The struggles around equal pay have also revealed the inadequacies in current union organization and practices when it comes to women's work. The first wave of feminism coincided with transformations in the labour process and with fundamental shifts in collective practices. What is necessary now is a radical rethinking of how women can achieve collective change in ways that reflect a new labour process and a new female worker. Such strategies must take into account not only new labour processes but also the importance of the state as direct or indirect employer and the reality that women predominate in the new kinds and locations of paid work.

ENDNOTES

1. See Feminist Perspectives on the Canadian State, *Resources For Feminist Research* 17/3 (September, 1988).

2. See Rianne Mahon, "Canadian Public Policy: The Unequal Structure of Representation," L. Panitch (ed.), *The Canadian State* (Toronto, 1977), pp. 165-198; and Rosemary Warskett "Valuing Women's Work — Dealing With the Limits of State Reform," *Resources For Feminist Research* 17/3 (September 1988), pp. 67-71.

3. *An Act to Provide For Pay Equity*, Bill 154, Statutes of Ontario, June 29, 1987.

4. See Pat Armstrong and Hugh Armstrong. *The Double Ghetto: Canadian Women and Their Segregated Work* [Revised Edition] (Toronto: 1984).

5. Statistics Canada, *Women in Canada: A Statistical Report* (Ottawa: 1985), p. 53.

6. Quoted in Debra Lewis, *Just Give Us the Money: A Discussion of Wage Discrimination and Pay Equity* (Vancouver: 1988), p. 24.

7. It was not until the early 1970s, after a Royal Commission on the Status of Women reported, the Women's movement had become more vocal, and women had flooded into the labour force, that the Federal Government ratified the International Labour Organization's Convention 100 designed to address the problem of comparing jobs in a segregated labour force. Lewis, *Just Give Us the Money*, p. 25.

8. Ontario Public Service Employees Union v Ministry of Health, Clerk 3 Reclassification Grievances.

9. The Equal Pay Coalition was formed in 1976. The Coalition has 27 constituent groups which represent over 1 million Ontario women and men from such organizations as The Law Union of Ontario, The Sudbury Women's Action Group, Elizabeth Fry Society, The Ontario Federation of Labour, Canadian Women's Educational Press, Ontario Federation of Students, Labour Council of Metropolitan Toronto.

10. The Pay Equity Commission was required by the Act to undertake a series of studies examining the impact of the legislation on predominantly female sectors.

These studies are available from the Pay Equity Commission

11. Research for Pat Armstrong (with Jacqueline Choiniere, Jan Kainer and Chris Gabriel), *Pay Equity in Predominately Female Establishments: Health Care Sector* (Toronto: 1988).

12. See, for example, Dorothy Smith, "Ideological Structures and How Women are Excluded," *The Canadian Review of Sociology and Anthropology* 12/4 (November 1975), pp. 353-369.

13. See Armstrong (with Choiniere, Kainer, and Gabriel), *Pay Equity....*

14. See, for example, Helen Remick (ed.), *Comparable Worth and Wage Discrimination: Technical Possibilities and Political Realities* (Philadelphia: 1984).

15. Transcripts from a Hearing before the Pay Equity Board, September 14, 1989, In the Matter of An Application under *The Pay Equity Act* Between Ontario Nurses' Association and The Regional Municipality of Haldimand-Norfolk. Volume 20, pp. 57-58.

16. See The Bank Book Collective *An Account to Settle: The Story of Bank Workers* [SORWUC] (Vancouver: 1979).

17. Ontario Public Service Employees Union v Ministry of Health, Clerk 3 Reclassification Grievances. 1984.

18. Harry Braverman, *Labor and Monopoly Capital: The Degradation of Work in the Twentieth Century* (New York: 1974).

19. For a discussion of these issues, see Maureen Fitzgerald, Connie Guberman and Margie Wolfe (eds.), *Still Ain't Satisfied* (Toronto: 1982); Julie White, *Women in Unions* (Ottawa: 1980); Linda Briskin and Linda Yanz, *Union Sisters* (Toronto: 1983); and Pat Armstrong and Hugh Armstrong, *A Working Majority: What Women Must Do For Pay* (Ottawa: 1983).

20. Statistics Canada, *Canada's Women. A Profile of their 1986 Labour Market Experience* (Ottawa: 1988).

21. Pat Armstrong, *Labour Pains. Women's Work in Crisis* (Toronto: 1984), p. 57; and Pat Armstrong and Hugh Armstrong, "Taking Women Into Account: Redefining and Intensifying Employment in Canada," in Jane Jenson, Elizabeth Hagen and Ceallaigh Reddy (eds.), *Feminization of the Labor Force* (Cambridge: 1988).

CHAPTER 13

THE CONCEPTUAL POLITICS OF STRUGGLE: WIFE BATTERING, THE WOMEN'S MOVEMENT AND THE STATE

GILLIAN WALKER

INTRODUCTION

This paper traces a crucial process whereby the efforts of feminist activists concerned with wife beating have been transformed and absorbed into existing institutional structures. The result of this process is that, although we have achieved much and are still working, struggling and angry, the sites of our struggles are dispersed, disconnected and depoliticized. The process of absorption is not magical or mysterious, but it is not an easy one to uncover, partly because of its complexity, and partly, as I will argue, because it involves ways of thinking and ways of using language that obscure important aspects of what we need to understand. The dilemmas we face as feminists are embedded in the conceptual practices which we must adopt when we take up our struggle in relation to the state. As we work to understand the relationship between women, the women's movement and state practices, it becomes increasingly evident that one-dimensional views of the state as a monolith, with either benign or hostile intentions toward women, are not adequate. The analysis developed in my study reveals a layered web of negotiated discursive relations in which ideological constructs play a coordinating role. In the face of pressures for social change, these provide a basis for developing government policies and the particular funding, reporting, and accounting procedures of different state institutions.

My work deals with a facet of the interaction between the state and the women's movement, and must be seen within the framework of the organization of social relations linking the local, everyday activities and practices of people with the general and abstracted procedures of ruling and administering an advanced capitalist society. In particular, this study examines part of a political process of control that shapes and develops "issues" and lodges them in the administrative procedures through which Canadian society is ordered, organized and ruled. Particularly, it explores how concepts, as ways of thinking, naming, and knowing, coordinate and make possible the process of institutional articulation and absorption. This approach allows the development of a framework that delineates the process in several stages which loosely correspond both to the temporal sequence of events and to the ideological aspects of how the struggle for control and action were played out.

The struggle can be characterized for analytic purposes as having three stages. The first involved the efforts of the women's movement to make the situation of women being beaten by their menfolk visible and actionable. At this stage, the women's movement struggled to define a "women's issue" in feminist terms, in the face of professional attempts to remove the issue from the political "movement" context and organization, and substitute a conception of the problem which revolved around the notion of "troubled families." The second stage saw the resulting struggle within the women's movement as the work of doing something about "the issue" was translated to and generalized within the relations of the state. Feminists strove to formulate an account of the problem, providing both an analysis of its roots and a basis for action in relation to increasing state involvement. In the third stage movement activists, service providers and others in various professional fields succeeded in getting particular sections of the ruling apparatus to respond properly to the needs of battered women. It marked a transformation and reorganization of the relations of the women's movement to the issue and to the agencies and institutions of the state. This study is part of a fourth stage in which dissatisfaction with outcomes provoked a number of theoretical and strategic re-examinations of this enterprise.[1] The temporal nature of these stages can be counterposed with a conceptual mapping of the process in question. This aspect of the process provides the focus for what follows.

THE LANGUAGE OF RULING

In the early years of recognizing and organizing around the plight of women beaten and brutalized by husbands and intimates, women did not have a term to define their situation. The process of making the experience of oppression in our own homes visible to ourselves and then getting it accepted as a matter of public concern involved defining it as a problem in our terms. The language available to us to do this kind of work presents us with a contradiction; it is the "oppressor's language," controlled by those who have the power to define its content and meaning.[2] We must use it however to express our concerns.

In detailing the conceptual processes underlying these developments, the use of language presents me with a problem. It is important to distinguish language used descriptively in relation to activities and experiences, from the conceptual forms produced by ideological practices which identify the relations of ruling. I am in no way denying the fact that men treat women in a variety of oppressive ways, some of which are brutal and coercive, in order to enforce their demands and desires. What I am addressing here is something different; I am mapping a discursive process, embedded in the work of intellectuals, professionals, and administrators, through which certain activities are selected and named as categories, intended to identify particular problems and particular solutions. To mark and clarify this distinction, I have used the device of placing certain terms in quotation marks when I address the technical nature of their ideological functioning as ruling concepts. Concepts, when they operate in this technical way, are not simply descriptive linguistic conventions, they organize the social construction of knowledge: ways of thinking about, defining and giving abstract and generalized meaning to our particular experience. Knowledge, thus produced, provides for particular courses of action. Understood in this way, concepts can be seen to do more than name a phenomenon. They are part of a social relation (used here to signify an ongoing, concerted course of action, involving more than one person) which brings into being and organizes particular phenomena in specific ways, and provides for a response to what has been thus identified.

In detailing this conceptual process I want to look first at the way particular aspects of women's experience — wife beating, battering and abuse — have been isolated and described so as to become accepted as discrete phenomena and taken up as "women's issues." Then, I shall explore the struggle over terms and definitions — "male violence," "domestic violence," and "family violence" — which took place both within the women's movement and in relation to institutional structures and professional practices. Finally I show that the common ground provided by the concept of "violence" has allowed for combined strategies among activists and professionals which led to the acceptance of wife battering as primarily a problem of assault under the crimi-nal code. While this has important short-term implications for the protection of individual women and the possibility of public sanctioning of men's violent behaviour, I argue that it is part of the process of absorption — a process which we need to understand if we are to develop strategies to avoid fragmen-tation and absorption in the future. While some of the data for this account and analysis are provided by documents or drawn from academic discourse, I also discuss some specific events in which I took part.

In Vancouver in the early 1970s I worked with a United Way task force, aimed at providing information and education, coordinating services and pres-suring government and agencies to recognize and respond to "the issue" of family violence. Here, as elsewhere, women's movement groups often found themselves in opposition to the approaches put forward by professionals from institutions and agencies. As "the issue" was made more visible through the work being done at the local level all over the country, feminists with connec-tions to the federal government sought to make an impact at that level by organizing, in 1980, a National Consultation of women's groups working in the area of wife battering. This consultation and later events such as federal and provincial (Ontario) public hearings before standing committees of both legislative bodies, which took place in 1981 and 1982, and the reports which resulted from both hearings, contributed key data to the analysis.

THE BATTERED WIFE

When women first spoke out about being hit and beaten by husbands or common law partners the terms "battered wife" and "wife abuse" were not available as ways to think about the experience. As women strove to make the situation public, in various local sites in which organization was taking place, these terms were extrapolated from the existing discourse on child abuse, already "discovered" and designated as a "syndrome" by medical practitioners in the 1960s.[4] "Battered babies" had already made media headlines, especial-ly in Britain. The use of the word "battering" in this connection was an adap-tation from legal terminology; "assault and battery" being a categorization of the degree of severity of an assault under the British *Criminal Code*. Though the terms may have arisen in the professional discourse in Europe and the United States, they were elaborated in the media and their use in reference to wife beating was in common parlance by the early 1970s. Women identify themselves as battered wives in some of the letters that Erin Pizzey published in her ground breaking 1974 book. She herself uses battering occasionally as an adjective to describe continued and severe beatings and refers to battered wives only once, qualified by quotation marks which imply some scepticism as to its professional implications:

> As far as I can see the reason why "battered wives" are get-
> ting a hearing is that for the first time a middle-class
> woman has said, "It's happened to me." That makes it
> respectable and all the more shocking. Now — just as "bat-
> tered babies" were once called "manslaughter" — wife
> beating has become the "battered wife syndrome." But it is
> not enough to call it a new name and then carry on as
> before.[4]

My memory of my own involvement with Vancouver Transition House and other related projects in those days is that we initially used the terms wife beating, battering and abuse in a loose and relatively interchangeable way. Any concern we may have had at the time about the implications of the terms related to whether using the term "wife" would act either to prevent women who were not legally married to their abusers from seeing themselves as welcome at the house, or to allow professional agencies to refuse them welfare and other services.

Del Martin's book, *Battered Wives*, published in 1976, contains an introduction by Diane Russel, an activist and academic doing research in the area of rape. Russel gives battering an actual definition as a more severe and extreme form of the phenomenon of wife beating, which she links with rape as a similar means of coercion and control of women. Martin took up the term wife battering, in the same way as we did in Vancouver, as problematic only in relation to the marital status of the victim; she opted to continue using the word "wife" because it conveyed the intimate nature of the relationship involved.[5] For Martin, battering was a specific descriptive term. Her book was a significant factor in the development of a discourse promoting the adoption of the term battered wife, which could counter neutralizing and degendering alternatives such as "spouse abuse" and "inter-spousal violent episodes." These were the terms employed by professionals responding to the issue, who tended to link it with child abuse under the rubric of family or domestic violence.

FAMILY VIOLENCE AND OUR DISCONTENTS

Activists in other places shared similar experiences as those of us working with the United Way in Vancouver. We found that linking wife battering and child abuse focused the issue in such a way that women's experience came to be subsumed by the professional emphasis on child abuse and services to men who battered their wives. We discovered that we had to be vigilant, vigorous and persistent to counteract the way that the framework of "family violence" obscured the actual actions of men, and the suffering of women, so that who did what to whom disappeared in an objectified professional language.

The designation of violence as occurring in the family or in the domestic realm also maintained it as a private matter concerned with the interpersonal relations of individuals. This framework arose out of and fed back into the work of professional agencies and institutions whose mandate was to maintain the organization and existing power relations of the family. In response, the political objective around which many of us focused our work was to force the professionals to recognize wife battering and abuse as an issue in its own right, and, indeed, as representing the overwhelming preponderance of instances of "family violence." This also involved us in a critique of "the family." The feminist analysis of the family as an institution embodying the political oppression of women at its most personal was not accepted readily by the professionals with whom we struggled. Their professional mandate of maintaining the traditional family form inclined them towards interventions designed to fix-up the family and help "it" deal with "its" violence.[6] We fought for the maintenance of the women's movement's control of its definition of the issue against attempts by professionals to remove the issue from its context in a political movement.

For some feminists, however, the use of the terms "family" and "domestic" violence served as conscious change strategy. In her 1981 update to the second edition of *Battered Wives*, for example, Martin notes that in the early stages the term "domestic violence" was used because it was necessary to cloak "the realities" in "diplomatic language...to get people to listen, or to keep from alienating those whose help we needed."[7] The coordinator of the Vancouver United Way Task Force reacted with anger to the suggestion that "family violence" as a term worked against women's interests. She insisted that, on the contrary, it allowed her to "slip women in" in circumstances where wife battering itself would have been "too contentious an issue."[8]

MALE VIOLENCE AGAINST WOMEN

This division over the uses of terms like "family" and "domestic" violence was not the only one amongst feminists working on the issue. At the National Consultation organized by the Canadian Advisory Council on the Status of Women in March 1980, the Council attempted to find a common position in relation to professional concerns for the proper management of the problem, and the conflicting accounts of the roots of the issue put forward by activists.[9] While we had no difficulty in agreeing that men's violence toward women must be addressed in the short term in any strategy for change, some of us concentrated on the structural features of women's dependence in relation to the family and the work force, emphasizing the trap that this creates for women, particularly women with children. Others saw the organization of the family as only a manifestation of the overriding issue of ultimate control of women by force or the threat of force in a patriarchal system. For them, male dominance and male violence thus became the primary target for action.

The proceedings published by the Council after the consultation show how our work was drawn together to emphasize this latter position. By taking up the theme of one presentation (that battering is something we all share), which extended the definition of wife battering to include almost every form of women's experience of oppression, especially rape, incest and sexual harassment, the document packaged the various positions into one which could be adopted to stand for all: "We women" stand opposed to "male violence" which must be countered; we women must maintain control of the issue. This was an attempt to link definitions that operate at a bureaucratic and professional level, such as family and domestic violence, to those with a political mobilizing intent such as wife battering, violence against women, and male violence. Slogans such as "Wife Battering is Everywoman's Issue" brought us together as women and dissolved differences in location between professionals, service providers, activists, and women who were beaten, all of whom became women vulnerable to male violence.[10] The term "wife battering" was taken up in a way that linked movement organization and impetus to bureaucratic and professional forms.

ASSAULT UNDER THE LAW

What was actually accomplished at this stage of the process was that, through focusing on violence itself, the male violence framework could be married to that of family violence. This gave women who occupied a range of positions a way to organize their work in opposition to violence as behaviour that should be brought under the rule of law. The issue of wife battering was reformulated in terms of the laws on assault which ostensibly protect everyone from violent attack by other members of society. The struggle concentrated on extending the application of the law to those women whose status as wives or intimates had hitherto left them unprotected within the private realm of the family, traditionally beyond legal intervention in any situation short of murder. In the process, the analysis of women's oppression in the broader structures of society became secondary to the strategy of invoking women's rights as individuals under the law. The emphasis on individual rights in the criminal justice system specifically obscured the different experiences and location in the social structure of black, minority, native, immigrant and white working class women and men. Class differences between the men who batter could only be accounted for in ideological terms, set up by a framework which designates family violence as crossing all cultures and classes.

The coalescence of this strategy and its consequences for lodging wife battering within particular institutional sites of the state's "social problem apparatus" provide the focus of my analysis of the events which took place before the Federal Parliament's standing committee on Health, Welfare and Social Affairs and the Ontario Legislature's Standing Committee on Social Development.[11] Representatives of a range of women's groups, social service organizations, government departments, and their researchers, appeared before both committees. In the transcripts of the hearings and in the reports produced by each committee it was possible to trace the development of a framework that allowed committee members to define the problem in ways that linked specific aspects to particular institutions and agencies within the government. Some of the conceptual underpinnings of that framework are detailed here.[12]

CONCEPTUAL PRACTICES

I have described the struggle over definition and control of the issue sequentially to illustrate that the process is one which has taken place over time and within activities and events, not as merely an abstract or linguistic concern. It could equally be presented schematically like this:

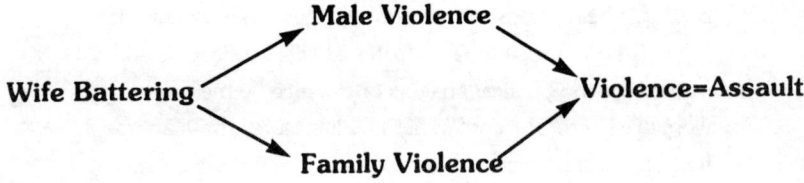

As a concept "family violence" organizes both a phenomenon and a course of action. How it is constructed, however, is in some ways invisible. It appears as the natural conjunction of two recognizable features of our society: "the family" and "violence." This conjunction is not a straightforward naming of related entities; it developed out of the work of professionals, researchers, theorists and information disseminators, as a discourse with distinctive properties. The conjunction of "family" and "violence" treats as naturalistic, and conflates, two concepts already developed for our understanding by sociological procedures, or as administrative products. These procedures construct as social facts the "ordinary forms in which the features of our society become observable to us as its features — mental illness, neighbours, crime, riots, leisure, work satisfaction, etc."[13] The processes by which these features are constructed is the making of ideology. Ideology understood in this way is a method of thinking and working that ruptures our ideas from the practical, everyday world of lived experience in which they arise, and enters them into theories within a discourse which represents the relevancies of those who order and rule. The practical actions, activities, and locations which make up social relations are stripped away and dropped out of the conceptual form and replaced by connectives which account for experiences in terms of theory and discourse.

Feminists have struggled against the concept of "family violence." But I suggest that there is a prior conceptual stage with regard to wife battering, as a category, which has seldom been addressed in our definitional debates. Although Pizzey acknowledged some ambivalence toward the naming of women who were beaten as "battered wives," it was Dorothy Smith who challenged the category itself.[14] As she pointed out, taking a particular aspect of women's experience of oppression out of context, and putting it through a process of abstraction which constructs a category — the "battered wife" — is also an ideological process, producing the conceptual forms through which professional intervention operates. Such a process is, she suggests, one of the ways that women's protest is absorbed into institutional structures:

The issue of men's violence against women in the family

> setting is being transformed into a professional psychiatric
> or counselling problem. The "battered wife" concept is sub-
> stituted for the political analysis of violence by men against
> women. There are conferences, a literature, the elabora-
> tion of a professional practice (often focusing more on men
> than on women).[15]

The significance of Smith's challenge was not fully appreciated at the time. The struggles to combat subsuming "wife battering" under the rubric of "fami-ly violence" obscured some of the implications of the term itself. Wife beating or battering might have some claim to the status of mere description but "the battered wife" is clearly a social construction. Its ideological properties, as a category ruptured from the social relations of women's lives, allows "the bat-tered wife" to be treated as an instance of "family violence," or as part of a theoretical framework which separates features of peoples' lives into pieces which can be managed and administered.

A subsequent development added a dimension not evident in 1979 when Smith first issued her warning. The political analysis of violence by men against women was elaborated into a framework which became a major orga-nizing focus for feminists in the early 1980s. In this process "the battered wife" was treated as an instance of the victimization of women by male vio-lence. I would argue that this is also an ideological feature of a discourse equal-ly ruptured from the social relations in which women's lives are embedded. The initial mobilizing efforts of the women's movement centred on oppression as part of the broad social structures of the division of labour in the work place and in the family. This was displaced by theories which emphasize men's vio-lent domination of women as the overreaching determinant of women's oppression throughout history. This shift in focus denotes a major rift in the contemporary women's movement.[16] Theories of male domination provided the basis for the conceptual co-ordination of the issue of wife beating as "vio-lence," defined as assault under the law. With this definition, the work of the women's movement could be aligned with that of the criminal justice system.

THE CONCEPT OF "VIOLENCE"

Feminists on many fronts drew attention to the ideological construction of "the family" as both normative and problematic for women.[17] "Violence," on the other hand, has been used extensively by feminists as if it were a purely descriptive term for behaviours or activities in which physical force is used to inflict injury, either randomly or to gain some specific end such as control. In the case of male violence against women its definition has been extended to include verbal threats and abuse, economic deprivation, sexual coercion or deprivation, and the creation of a general climate of fear which limits the full participation of women in society. Yet, "violence," as a term, also holds properties beyond the descriptive. Here I will simply sketch in some of the dimensions and implications of its current usage.

When a concept such as "violence" is constructed by the process of "making ideology," it is detached from its grounding in the social relations in which events and activities take place, and put through an abstract reorganization which conforms to the relevancies of a particular or a number of discourses.[18] In this process, it takes on a reified form as a single coherent phenomenon or force to which causal efficacy, as well as explanatory powers, can be ascribed. There is a shift in the concept; it ceases to describe what someone does — hitting, punching, kicking, stabbing, shooting someone else. The presence of people doing things disappears and is replaced by a term expressing the action in a general form but without the actor. "Violence breaks out" in families, in the streets, on the picket line; outbreaks of "violence" "occur." "Violence" can then be treated as a causal factor and motivator in a range of discourses which intersect and articulate several disciplines. Within the broad discourses of the social sciences, "violence" appears as integral in the psychosocial and socio-biological discourses concerning aggression, dominance, instinctual behaviour and sex roles. In sociology and criminology, it operates as a feature of the discourses of law and order and victimology. In legal discourse, "violence" is of particular significance in relation to the rule of law. "Violence" knits together these discourses and is given both a clinical and a criminal organization, each of which is salient to the analysis I am making here.

Already made available by the ideological practices of mainstream social scientists, building upon "the primary administrative work which constitutes murders, suicides, etc.,"[19] "violence" has taken its place as the unquestioned focus of two relatively new discourses: the professional discourse of "family violence" and a feminist discourse of "male violence." It provides a link both between these discourses and with the socio-legal discourse on "violence" in relation to the state.

"VIOLENCE" AND THE STATE

The sanctioned use of force in contemporary society is monopolized by the state as a feature of the practices of ruling. The state has developed myriad bureaucratic procedures to licence and control its use by the police, the military and other functionaries such as coast guards, prison guards and mental hospital attendants. It is in relation to the state's claim to the legitimate use of force in certain circumstances that "violence" as a concept can be seen to designate uncontrolled, unregulated and illegitimate use of force. "Violence," within this framework, has been worked up ideologically from a term in common usage, describing a wide range of activities used to enforce will, inflict injury or express discontent, into a technical category for the designation of non-sanctioned acts beyond the bounds of the law. This is part of a historical process in which the use of physical force to gain power and maintain order and control has been superseded by ideological procedures which regulate society through bureaucratic and professional operations.[20]

Brutal physical practices such as hanging, flogging, maiming and torture are no longer officially accepted in democratic societies as regularized features of the rule of law. Corporal punishment in schools is increasingly prohibited and, in countries such as Sweden, it is illegal to smack one's own children. This represents both a change in methods of law enforcement and a shift in the designation of the realm to which the rule of law applies. The internal governance of family matters was regarded until relatively recently as the domain of the male head of the household. The patriarchal organization of earlier family forms resulted from a hierarchical social structure whereby the chain of authority of the state was extended to the "pater familias." He was responsible for ensuring the law-abiding behaviour of the family members, servants, apprentices and employees within his household by such measures as he saw fit including physical correction. This responsibility, however, was not isolated from community, kin and state intervention. It is only in later forms of capitalist organization that the family takes on the restricted and relatively "private" nuclear grouping now taken as normative.

The juxtaposition within the professional discourse of the concepts "family" and "violence" has only taken place over the past decade and a half. At the same time, child abuse has also been subject to the processes of medicalization and legalization.[21] Feminist campaigns for child protection and the relief of women bound to brutal husbands in the last century and the early years of this century were not couched in terms of "family violence." They dealt with issues in terms of the husband's legal right of chastisement and his authority over his wife and children as property.[22] As late as 1969 wife beating had not yet been fully included in what prominent sociologist James Q. Wilson designated as "domestic violence":

> There are two kinds of domestic violence for which we would like to estimate future rates and thus two kinds of problems which make such estimates very difficult, if not impossible. The first kind is individual violence — murders, suicides, assaults, child-beatings — and the second is collective violence — riots, civil insurrections, internal wars and the like.[23]

Conceptualizing "violence" as a single coherent phenomenon spanning a range from individual pathology to large-scale social pathology opens the way for designating protest, dissent or resistance to the dominant class as riots, insurrections, terrorism or mob rule. That such definitions are operating unseen when "family violence" is considered can be seen in both the definitions of "domestic violence" offered by Wilson.

This conflated framework of individual and collective behaviour permits the kind of theory used by Dutton *et al*. They pull together a number of seemingly contradictory possibilities, theoretically reconciled into a causal hypothesis that suggests a form of personalized, "deindividuated" "violence" engaged in by men as individuals toward their mates. "Deindividuated violence" is a psycho-social construct which refers to theories of mass, uncontrolled, uninhibited and pleasurable rage expressed in vandalism, mob rampages and riots. "Violence" as a conceptual organizer enables the actions of people (here acknowledged as men) to be treated as if the acts are governed by a force independent of the will of the actors. Women are thought to remain with "violent" men because they, in turn, develop inappropriate but intense "trauma bonding" as a result of the erratic nature of their partners' behaviour. (This theory is based on studies of the hostage, or "Stockholm" syndrome.) Stress and "interpersonal aspects of the battering relationship" act as triggers of male rage.[24] A feature of the theory of individual yet "deindividuated " violence is that men, once past the rage threshold, have no control over and no memory of their actions, and thus presumably no responsibility for them; women, in turn, are helplessly unable to escape because of their own trauma. Theories such as these, often produced by state-funded research, provide the constructs necessary to direct the nature of state intervention into areas defined as social problems. "Violence" comes to be understood as a feature of social life, one which must be both deplored and managed, a pressing social problem in all its manifestations.

THE DILEMMA OF "VIOLENCE"

The feminist discourse of "male violence" did make visible the gender and power relations involved in "family" or "domestic" "violence." It helped advance the struggle for definitional control and action, and made the professional discourse accommodate women's experience. It has, however, produced a number of anomalies which mitigate its ultimate usefulness as a strategic base. At the simplest level it presents an explanation which suggests that every instance of the abuse and control of women is either an inevitable outcome of pathological models of masculinity, produced by society through socialization, or the result of innate, inherent and socio-biological characteristics that doom all men to dominate each other and all women by aggression and force.

These positions offer the option of a massive and immediate resocialization of the entire society or the setting up of a separatist society divided on gender lines. Neither position accounts for the anomalous situation of men who do not beat, rape, harass and abuse women, in spite of growing up in so-called "cradles of violence," or those who did not experience or witness physical abuse and do perpetuate it. Liddle points out that, despite the importance of the insights supplied by feminist theorists concerning both the pervasiveness and impact of violence against women, one-dimensional models of male agency and simplistic conceptions of male "interests" as the motivations for violence fail to adequately address the situation.[25] Nor do they give us any way to understand why some women abuse children or other dependents. These positions also open the way for clinical and legal initiatives which tie the most radical aspects of feminist mobilization into a conservative law and order framework for social control. In this process, men's actions toward their wives become instances of assault. The actors are again subsumed under the legal terms of perpetrator and victim and both gender and relational aspects are dissolved. This obscures any political understanding of society as structured through fundamental inequalities that render it disastrously out of tune with human need.

DISSECTING THE DILEMMA

The process I have examined can now be assembled schematically in a more complex and elaborate fashion:

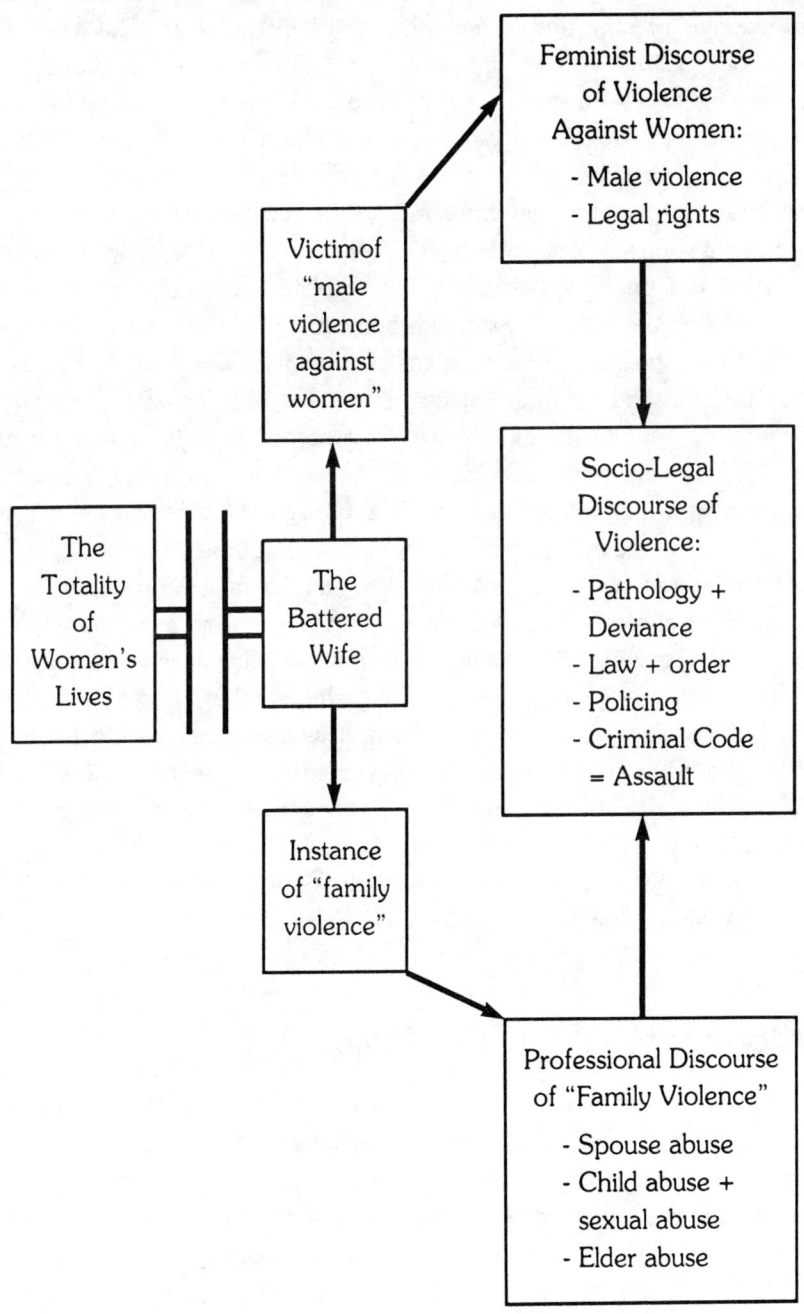

The dilemma of "violence" as a conceptual practice points to the larger dilemma for the women's movement which has been detailed in this paper. In order to act in ways which would alter the oppressive conditions that women experience in differing ways in the totality of their lives, experiences designated as belonging to the private realm had to be made public. The terms available in the public discourses, however, were more than a mere language of description. They were part of the conceptual coinage of ruling relations in contemporary society. When we took up such terms as the "battered wife" or "violence," we played a part in constructing the phenomenon and the terms in which it was to be made comprehensible. The language of abstraction is part of the making of ideology, which transforms our understanding of our daily experience, and implicates us in our own regulation, by shaping our concerns into "issues" organized on the grounds and within the relevancies and imperatives of the institutions and practices of ruling. Through this process the woman becomes the victim of "violence," constituted as an abstraction by procedures which rupture the experience being named from the general context of her life. The category thus constituted can then be assembled, with others, as an issue or social problem from which professional intervention extracts the political focus by providing social service or legal solutions.

The dilemma faced by feminists is contained in the practices through which ruling is accomplished. Naming the experience is a double-edged sword. It co-ordinates our mobilization and identifies our difficulties to ourselves and each other. Many women have spoken of the power that being able to identify themselves as "battered wives" gave them. It was a first step for some in recognizing that the experience was widely shared and that taking action was a legitimate response. At the same time, it directed such action into particular channels: seeking "help" in the form of social services, or legal redress. Neither of these mobilize women unless they are put in a feminist context; nor do they address the totality of women's lives.

CONCEPTS AS RULING PRACTICES

"Violence" can no longer be regarded as a straightforward term describing a pre-existing phenomenon. It is established by ideological practices as one of the concepts forming discourses which are the knowledge base for the exercise of power in contemporary society; it is a ruling concept, a ruling practice. As feminists we have taken the term into our own language to counter the ideology of "family violence" and to attempt to re-attribute the activities it names to the men who commit the acts of cruelty and coercion that it purports to describe. In the process, however, "violence" comes to be accepted as an independent force directing the activities of all men for all time.

This process, I suggest, has involved us in some strange alliances. Within the women's movement the position of "we women," battered or oppressed in other ways, mobilizing to change the actual conditions of our lives and the structures which enforce them, has been fragmented by strategies which align us with different aspects of the state's practices. Our organization becomes its organization. We take up "violence" within the family and use the linkages with the legal discourse to support the equation of certain forms of "violence" with assault. This allows feminists with differing political commitments to ally themselves with professionals, and within a civil rights framework, in seeking legal sanctions and protection for women under the law.

We become actors in a process which reflects shifts and tensions in the jurisdictional boundaries of state practices in relation to individual rights and family forms. As the organization of the family unit around the assumption of a single male wage deteriorates, men's authority in the family is challenged. At the same time, the individual rights model of participation and democracy permeates the ideology of the state. The relatively recently won right of women to be considered as persons, makes arguments against their right, as individuals, to freedom from assault harder to defend. "Family violence" seems to present a way of deflecting part of the focus from the criminal justice model and maintaining the power of intervention in the hands of those professionals more directly concerned with maintaining or implementing the family as represented in the ideology of the state. "Violence" as assault allows for either the treatment of men to "cure" them of their violence or the removal of men who "abuse their authority in the family," and the subsequent supporting of a new family form made up of women and children dependent upon the state. The clinical dimension of the concept of "violence" links together the two lines of development, "family violence" and "male violence," to give them a particular character. A framework for action is set up. The process of developing this framework gathers up local and particular threads, homogenizes and coordinates them, and then allows for the reapplication of the definition or diagnosis at the local level via appropriate divisions of the social problem apparatus. The particular dimensions of situations — that relate to gender, class location, racial or ethnic factors, the abuse of alcohol or any other way in which we might understand what is going on in a broader social context — are written out. At the same time, women's struggles against the many forms of coercion and abuse that arise in the context of oppression and inequality are subsumed within theories of a sick society in which individuals need treatment. The power relations inherent in the structure of "the family" are, at best, modified.

What is being modified, I would argue, is not men's authority in the family but their abuse of that authority. "Family violence" deflects the focus from the legal system towards health, welfare and social services institutions, but "male violence," reformulated in professional discourses in terms such as "spouse assault," paves the way for the entry of legal discourse. Patriarchal family relations are thus reduced to actions which support or defy the law and the hidden "law and order" frame that "violence" references.[26] Allying ourselves with aspects of the ruling apparatus, and particularly the state, by accepting the "male violence/family violence" conceptual frame risks substituting what Brown has called public patriarchy for private patriarchy.[27] It is ironic that the appropriation of "male violence" provides for short-term solutions which invoke the rule of law since feminists have often characterised the legal system as one which maintains male domination. Control of the issue is delivered over to those in the social problem apparatus who are charged with maintaining "the family" and who are encouraged to enforce further legal sanctions against individuals within the family unit.

WIFE BATTERING AND THE WOMEN'S MOVEMENT REVIEWED

I have identified a three stage process of generalization and appropriation in which issues which seemingly come out of "nowhere" are articulated to structures where there is a possibility of getting something done to address them. The paper is not an attempt to write a history of wife battering. Rather it describes some of the conceptual practices of the women's movement, as it struggled to make public this particular aspect of women's experience. My work stands beside that of other commentators in a fourth stage of reflection and assessment which seeks to account for some of the outcomes of the struggle so far. Writing in the early 1980s, both Tierney and Morgan concluded that, as far as the experience in the United States was concerned, the women's movement had lost any form of control over the disposition of the issue.[28] Susan Schechter's analytically perceptive and comprehensive review of the US shelter movement, published in 1982, ended on a more optimistic note, which called for feminists to continue to struggle against wife battering itself and against bureaucratic attempts to de-politicize it. Schechter, however, may have been overly optimistic. According to a recent report on the difficulties faced by the movement, in many states it is impossible to find government funding or services for battered women except through drug and alcohol treatment programs.[29]

Recent work in Canada has also explored the impact of government policies and practices on the women's movement's actions with regard to wife battering.[30] Much of this work confronts the limitations of reform as an effective social response. G. Geller documents examples of judicial indifference, prejudice and hostility which trivialize and undermine the strategy of laying assault charges by imposing inadequate or meaningless sentences on men convicted of rape, incest and wife beating.[31] In the same vein N.Z. Hinton argues that failure to address the role of patriarchy and the structural features of oppression by treating wife battering as a matter of individual rights leaves the justice system free to manage violence in ways which bolster and reassert the status quo.[32] She presses for a more effective justice system and resistance to any attempt to individualize and reprivatize the issue. Loseke and Cahill, on the other hand, suggest that the work of the women's movement has created a new class of experts who focus on battered women, and a new population of deviants, i.e. women who refuse to leave relationships in which they are abused. Ignoring the history of struggle over the form in which women's suffering could be made visible and the many different positions taken by feminists and professionals in that struggle, these authors recommend the re-privatization of personal relationships and respect for the right of adult women to choose their own fate. Though they fail to address power relations and structural oppression, Loseke and Cahill provide useful data which call into question the specificity of battered women's actions and experiences, showing that some of the features of the "battered woman syndrome" are present in most marriages and not necessarily contingent on a "violent" relationship.[33]

Using the experience of the Transition House movement in the Maritime provinces as an example, Andrea Currie suggests that the feminist analysis of wife battering as assault has been responsible for some of the dissatisfaction expressed by working class, aboriginal, ethnic and racial minority groups who feel excluded from services. Her persuasive discussion of what she describes as "one of the worst expressions of men's abusive power over women" leads her to the conclusion that only direct and adequate responses from the state in the form of fully-funded and far-ranging services can meet the immediate needs of individual women and their children.[34] Political action to change the circumstances that make women the targets of violence, she suggests, should be the responsibility of a broadly based social movement in which battered women from all class and racial backgrounds would work alongside feminist activists.

Currie acknowledges the fact that it was the work of the women's movement in founding transition houses that first brought wife battering to public awareness. If, however, shelters and other services continue to be run by professionals whose approach to the problem is guided by concepts such as "family violence," it is not clear, as Currie suggests, how women will be exposed to the political analysis required for membership in a broader battered women's movement. The experience of the Vancouver Transition House also indicates that full government funding is not necessarily a secure option. The only one in the country, at the time, to be entirely funded by the provincial government, the Vancouver house was a victim of the 1983 Social Credit policy of cutbacks and restraint. Despite a vigorous struggle, which included a sit-in and occupation by staff, activists and residents, the house was eventually closed. A Salvation Army Women's Shelter receives provincial funding as a transition house and there is a small shelter for women run independently of all government funding, but Vancouver is without a transition house as such to this day.

A number of questions raised in these studies support my argument that part of the problem with the outcome of the struggle so far stems from the ways in which we have come to conceptualize the experiences involved. I have been concerned with the ways in which our thinking came to be organized so that the state, through its social problem apparatus, could be induced, shamed or pressured to respond. Wife battering was first linked with "family violence" to provide an articulation to existing family policies and service agencies. The struggle to include wife assault introduced the possibility that sanctions already existing in the *Criminal Code* could be invoked. In the process of coordinating the work of government agencies and institutions, however, aspects of the mobilization of a movement for political change got lost. The work done with battered women has become, in many cases, the site for professional and voluntary service provision. This has taken the place of consciousness-raising within the context of a fully mobilized women's movement, which might allow the issue to be linked with others in the wider struggle against women's oppression. Working in women's shelters has become part of a career process in which women develop experience and expertise as social service workers or use their existing skills to provide services. This is not in itself negative or culpable, but it is assimilative. It is in this way that women's movement representatives come to be professionalized as experts speaking for and about battered women.

The contradiction embodied in this process of professionalization lies in the fact that its very success eliminates the possibility of a more radical critique. This is not a new problem, or one confined to the "battered women's movement" or the "shelter movement," or what is more commonly known in Canada as the "transition house movement." The professionalization and institutionalization of social movements have a long history. Social work, education (particularly adult education), labour and popular health movements and the initiatives of the previous wave of feminist organizing have all been subject to these processes. The extent to which this has class implications is revealed by the way in which the conceptually coordinated organization of state responses to wife battering creates divisions between volunteer and paid staff who work in shelters and makes the women using transition houses into welfare problem. Indeed, an informant suggested to me that shelters have become the new "poorhouses," with all the attendant poverty and stigma that the term implies. The implications of criminalization and its clinical correlates as a protective and "preventive" strategy for different segments of the population are eliminated from view, let alone discussion. Women who are beaten become a welfare problem; their batterers become a problem for the criminal justice system. Differences in the power relations of women and men are dissolved into individual difficulties and reformulated as a social problem affecting a mass of individuals — a new population to be managed. At the same time class relations and the operation of racism are also dissolved. Thus, linking "male violence" and "family violence," by defining wife battering as assault, shifts the attention of activists and governments alike to the global and undifferentiated problem of "violence" and "its" management, and away from the structural features of oppression.

CONCLUSION

Several commentators draw attention to the limitations of feminist use of "violence" as an untheorized and unproblematic concept, though the arguments they present are in a somewhat different context from mine.[35] I want to emphasize that this analysis is not intended as a moral judgement of the success or failure of strategies employed by the women's movement. It is a matter of seeing how social relations are socially constructed. In investigating this process I attempted not to proceed ideologically, by starting with concepts to be defined and discovered, but to discover instead their organization, as part of a social relation. In this context concepts are technical work processes which organize both phenomena and courses of action; thus their construction is integral to social relations. Categories and concepts of ideologies *substitute* the ideological expression of a textually mediated discourse for actual relations, that is, actual practices, work processes and the organization of practical knowledge of actual individuals. Thus an examination of the actual relations, practices and processes, and the discursive forms substituted for them, reveals the ideological features of social organization.

"Issue politics," formulated in relation to state practices, has provided for the creation of isolated organizations. Ideological constructs such as "the battered wife" lifted the experience of women who are beaten and abused out of the general experiences of women and made wife battering available as an issue to be absorbed into the social problem apparatus. The task of relocating it in the broader structures of the reproduction of relations of domination and control, which are the relations of ruling, confronts the women's movement with the necessity of renewing efforts to address the relations of knowledge and power and how we are incorporated into them.

This study attempts to move our efforts forward by uncovering for our understanding one feature of how our work comes to be organized against us by the process in which we engage. I agree with Currie that the battle, though complex, is not over. How to organize to change the oppressive conditions of women's lives, without being appropriated through our interactions with the ruling apparatus and participation in the relations of ruling, is the dilemma which confronts the women's movement as it moves into the nineties.

ENDNOTES

Parts of this paper are taken from my Ph.D. Thesis "Conceptual Practices and the Political Process: Family Violence as Ideology" (University of Toronto, 1988) published by the University of Toronto Press in fall 1990 under the title *Family Violence and the Women's Movement: The Conceptual Politics of Struggle*, and appear here with the permission of the publisher. My thanks go to Roberta Hamilton, Arlene McLaren, Barbara Neis and Jane Ursel for their helpful comments on an earlier draft and to Iris Taylor for her work in revising and adapting the manuscript.

1.   See, for example, P. Morgan, "From Battered Wife to Program Client: The State's Shaping of Social Problems," *Kapitaliste* 9 (1981); S. Schechter, *Women and Male Violence: The Visions and Struggles of the Battered Women's Movement* (Boston: South End Press, 1982): and K. Tierney, "The Battered Woman Movement and the Creation of the Wife Beating Problem," *Social Problems* 29/3 (1982). For more recent appraisals, in a specifically Canadian context, see N.Z. Hinton, "One in Ten: The Struggles and Disempowerment of the Battered Women's Movement," *Canadian Journal of Family Law* 7 (1989); and Andrea Currie, "A Roof Is Not Enough: Feminism, Transition Houses and the Battle Against Abuse," *New Maritimes* September/October, 1989.

2.   D.E. Smith, "Using the Oppressor's Language," *Resources for Feminist Research. Special Issue on Feminist Theory* Spring 1979.

3.   See E.H. Newberger and R. Bourne, "The Medicalization and Legalization of Child Abuse," in A. Skolnick and J. H. Skolnick (eds.), *Family in Transition*, 5th ed. (Boston: Little, Brown & Co., 1986), pp. 440-455 for a critical appraisal of the medicalization of child abuse.

4.   E. Pizzey, *Scream Quietly or the Neighbours Will Hear* (London: Penguin Books, 1974), p. 46.

5.   D. Martin, *Battered Wives* (San Francisco: New Glide Publications, 1976), p. ix.

6.   This battle has by no means been won. See, for example, R.L. Neely and G. Robinson-Simpson, "The Truth About Domestic Violence: A Falsely Framed Issue," *Social Work* Nov/Dec 1987, a paper which reviews major "family vio-

lence" studies to "prove" that women are *more* violent than men. Ignoring the many critiques of the data produced by these studies, the authors specifically refute every feminist tenet and all attempts to modify the "family violence" framework, developing an argument that is anti-feminist and punitively anti-women.

7. D. Martin, *Battered Wives*, 2nd ed. (San Francisco: Volcano Press, Inc., 1981), p. 279.

8. Flora MacCloud, personal communication with author, 1981.

9. For an expanded account of the consultation see G. Walker, *Family Violence and the Women's Movement: The Conceptual Politics of Struggle* (Toronto: University of Toronto Press, forthcoming 1990), Chapter 3.

10. L. MacLeod, *Wife Battering is Every Woman's Issue: A Summary Report of the CACSW Consultation on Wife Battering* (Ottawa: Canadian Advisory Council on the Status of Women, 1980).

11. Morgan, "From Battered Wife to Program Client...," p. 18, describes the mental health, welfare and the criminal justice systems as part of an apparatus designed to combat designated "social problems."

12. See: Canada, House of Commons, Standing Committee on Health, Welfare and Social Affairs, *Minutes of Proceedings - Hansard* Nos. 24-29, 1982; and *idem*, *Report on Violence in the Family: Wife Battering* (Ottawa, 1982); and Province of Ontario, Legislature, Standing Committee on Social Development, *Minutes - Hansard* 4, 10, 11, 12 May 1982; 19, 20, 21, 23, 26, 27, 28, 29, 30 July 1982; and *idem*, *First Report on Family Violence: Wife Battering* (Toronto, 1982).

13. D. E. Smith, "The Ideological Practice of Sociology," *Catalyst* 8 (1974), p. 53.

14. D. E. Smith, *Feminism and Marxism — A Place to Begin, A Way to Go* (Vancouver: New Star Books, 1977); D. E. Smith, "Women and the Politics of Professionalism" (Department of Sociology in Education, OISE, unpublished manuscript, 1979); D. E. Smith, "Where There is Oppression There is Resistance," *Branching Out* 6 (1979), pp. 10-15.

15. Smith, "Where There is Oppression..." p. 13.

16. See L. Segal, *Is the Future Female? Troubled Thoughts on Contemporary Feminism* (London: Virago Press, 1987).

17. See, for example D.E. Smith, "Women, the Family and Corporate Capitalism," in M. Stephenson (ed.), *Women in Canada* (Toronto: New Press, 1973), pp. 2-35; Smith, "Where There is Oppression..."; D. E. Smith, "Institutional

Ethnography: A Method of Sociology for Women" (Paper presented to the Political Economy of Gender Relations in Education Conference, University of Toronto, 1981); A. Griffith, "Ideology, Education and Single Parent Families: The Normative Ordering of Families Through Schooling" (Ph.D. diss., University of Toronto, 1984); M. Barrett and M. McIntosh, *The Anti-Social Family* (London: Verso Editions, 1982); B. Thorne and M. Yalom (eds.), *Rethinking the Family: Some Feminist Questions* (New York: Longman Inc., 1982); Segal, *Is the Future Female...* and many others.

18. Smith, "The Ideological Practice of Sociology."

19. Smith, "The Ideological Practice of Sociology," p. 53.

20. D.E. Smith, "Women and Violence" (Lecture given at Faculty of Social Work, University of Toronto, Fall, 1986); and *idem* "Feminist Reflections on Political Economy," *Studies in Political Economy* 30 (Autumn 1989), p. 42.

21. Newberger and Bourne, "The Medicalization and Legalization of Child Abuse."

22. L. Gordon, *Heroes of Their Own Lives: The Politics and History of Family Violence, Boston 1880-1960* (New York: Viking Press, 1988); E. Pleck, "Feminist Response to 'Crimes Against Women', 1868-1896," *Signs* 8/3 (1983), pp. 451-470; and *Domestic Tyranny: The Making of American Social Policy Against Family Violence From Colonial Times to the Present* (New York: Oxford University Press, 1987); C. Bauer and L. Ritt, "'A Husband is a Beating Animal', Frances Power Cobbe Confronts the Wife Abuse Problem in Victorian England," *International Journal on Women's Studies* 6/2 (1983), pp. 88-118; and "Wife Abuse, Late Victorian English Feminists, and the Legacy of Frances Power Cobbe," *International Journal of Women's Studies* 6/3 (1983), pp. 195-207.

23. J. Q. Wilson, "Violence," in D. Bell (ed.), *Toward the Year 2000* (Boston: Beacon Press, 1969), p. 53; cited in D. E. Smith, "The Ideological Practice of Sociology."

24. D. Dutton and S. L. Painter, with D. Patterson and C. Taylor, "Male Domestic Violence and its Effects on the Victim," Report to the Health Promotions Directorate, Health and Welfare Canada, 1980; S. L. Painter and D. Dutton, "Patterns of Emotional Bonding in Battered Women: Traumatic Bonding," *International Journal of Women's Studies* 8/4 (1985).

25. A.M. Liddle, "Feminist Contributions to an Understanding of Violence Against Women - Three Steps Forward, Two Steps Back," *Canadian Review of Sociology and Anthropology* 26/5 (1989).

26. I am grateful to Ian Taylor for making this point in comments on an earlier paper, and for drawing my attention to the news release from the Department of Justice, Ottawa, Dec. 21, 1983.

27. C. Brown, "Mothers, Fathers and Children: From Private to Public Patriarchy," in L. Sargent (ed.), *Women and Revolution: A Discussion of the Unhappy Marriage of Marxism and Feminism* (Montreal: Black Rose Books, 1981), pp. 239-267.

28. Tierney, "The Battered Women's Movement..."; and Morgan, "From Battered Wife..."

29. Schechter, *Women and Male Violence*; and Adele Mueller, personal communication with author, 1989.

30. See, for example M. Beaudry, *Battered Women*, trans. L. Houston and M. Heap (Montreal: Black Rose Books, 1985); L. MacLeod, *Battered But Not Beaten* (Ottawa: Canadian Advisory Council on the Status of Women, 1987); and J. Barnsley, *Feminist Action, Institutional Reaction: Responses to Wife Assault* (Vancouver: Women's Research Centre, 1985).

31. G. Geller, "A Feminist Case Against Patriarchal 'Justice' for Women Victims of Abuse," (Paper presented at the Canadian Sociology and Anthropology Association Sessions, Learned Societies Meetings, Quebec City, 1989.)

32. Hinton, "One in Ten..." p. 334.

33. I. Loseke and K. Cahill, "The Social Construction of Deviance: Experts on Battered Women," *Social Problems* 31/3 (1984).

34. Currie, "A Roof is Not Enough..." p. 17.

35. See Liddle "Feminist Contributions to an understanding of Violence Against Women..."; and M. Poster's review of Pleck's *Domestic Tyranny* in *Signs* 14/1 (1988), pp. 216-19.